22,50

Books are to be returned on or before
the last date below.

2 2 DEC 1995

1 8 DEC 2003

LIBREX—

NEW SOCIOLOGY LIBRARY
No. 3

General Editor: Professor NORBERT ELIAS
Department of Sociology, University of Leicester

The Sociology of Suicide

The Sociology of Suicide

A Selection of Readings

Edited by
Anthony Giddens

Fellow of King's College, Cambridge

 FRANK CASS & CO. LTD.

Published in Great Britain by
FRANK CASS AND COMPANY LIMITED
Gainsborough House, 11 Gainsborough Road, London E11 1RS

and in the United States of America by
FRANK CASS AND COMPANY LIMITED
c/o Biblio Distribution Centre
81 Adams Drive, P.O. Box 327, Totowa, N.J. 07511

First edition 1971
Second impression 1983

This selection copyright © 1971 Anthony Giddens

ISBN 0 7146 2591 4

Printed in Great Britain by
A. Wheaton & Co. Ltd, Exeter and London

CONTENTS

PART IV

PART V

APPENDIX

Preface

This book is intended for anyone wishing to gain an understanding of the contributions which sociologists have made to the explanation of suicide. While a few of the papers, unavoidably, are slightly technical in nature, most of the articles included in the book should be readily comprehensible to the doctor, psychiatrist or social worker who has an interest in the sociology of suicide.

The ideas of Emile Durkheim (1858–1917) have influenced the majority of the papers which comprise this volume. Durkheim's *Suicide*, first published in 1897,[1] has exerted an influence in sociology which goes far beyond the immediate subject-matter of suicide. *Suicide* represents Durkheim's most cogent demonstration of the fruitfulness of his views on the distinctive character of sociological explanation. Suicide, as Durkheim pointed out, may appear at first sight to be a wholly personal and private act, to which the relevance of sociology, the study of society, is by no means obvious. In fact, as he showed brilliantly, the involvement of man in society is of decisive importance to the explanation of suicide.

In selecting the contributions, I have not limited myself to works which have appeared only recently, but have tried to give some indication of the development of research into suicide over the course of the years since the appearance of Durkheim's work. The reader may judge for himself how much, or how little progress has been made during that time.

Part I includes selections from Morselli, Durkheim and Halbwachs, together with a paper by the editor which discusses the relationship of their views to the "psychiatric" tradition. In Part II, selections from the books of Henry and Short, and Gibbs and Martin, together with papers by Atkinson, the editor, and Douglas, indicate some of the lines of theoretical development which have been explored since the Second World War. Part III offers a number of studies of suicide in societies outside the West, including the Eskimos of Alaska, the Gisu of East Africa, Tikopia in the Western Pacific, and Japan, together with a more general paper on suicide in Africa. Part IV includes a cross-section of papers relating suicide to a number of different factors: the "ecological" structure of London, community growth and the incidence of depressive disorders in Massachusetts, the economic cycle, occupational mobility, climate, and finally, the influence of the press. In Part V is grouped a set of papers dealing with the more immediate social and psychological antecedents of suicide. These include studies of the "psychodynamics" of suicide, of the notes left by suicides, and of suicide pacts; a paper dealing with warnings of suicidal intent; and, in conclusion, three papers which take up the problem of the relationship between completed and attempted suicide. As an Appendix I have tabulated some general statistics of suicide. I have not included in this volume any papers dealing directly with medical or legal aspects of suicide, nor with its prophylaxis. These aspects of suicide have been adequately covered, within the limits of existing knowledge, in previous *symposia*.[2] Apart from the selection from Halbwachs, I have confined myself to selecting papers written originally in English. As in so many spheres of social science, much of the important sociological literature on suicide over the past forty years has appeared in the United States. While French and German authors have published various interesting studies on the subject, to my knowledge most of this material adds little of general significance to that contained in the English language sources.

1970   A.G.

NOTES

1 Émile Durkheim, *Le Suicide,* Paris, 1897; English ed., trans. John A. Spaulding and George Simpson, London, 1952.
2 For example, M. L. P. Resnick, *Suicidal Behaviours,* New York, 1968.

Introduction

Classical writings contain numerous references to suicide, and some of the leading schools of Greek and Roman philosophy—in particular the Roman Stoics—expressed the view that an individual, under certain specific circumstances, should have the right to take his own life if he so desired.[1] But in mediaeval Christianity, suicide was condemned absolutely. St Augustine set forth the doctrine that suicide was a murder of the self and therefore as reprehensible as any other kind of murder.[2] In 452, suicide was officially pronounced by the Church to be an act inspired by the Devil, and a range of ecclesiastical penalties against suicide came to be established which were maintained for hundreds of years. Most historians agree that suicide was infrequent throughout the Middle Ages, although, of course, there is no precise statistical evidence on the matter.

The modern literature on suicide dates from the seventeenth century. The earliest tracts on suicide from this period were largely directed against the mediaeval prohibitions condemning suicide. Thus John Donne's *Biathanatos*, published posthumously in 1648, proposed that some sorts of suicide should be regarded as legitimate.[3] Works such as Donne's prepared the ground for a debate on the morality of suicide which still goes on today.[4]

Concern with suicide as a moral issue, however, soon led to a more factual interest in the phenomenon of suicide. There are two streams of empirical writing on suicide which originated in the latter part of the eighteenth century. One consists of studies of individual cases of suicide, written for the most part by doctors and psychiatrists; the other developed as part of the studies of the "moral statisticians".[5] The publication of official statistics of rates of suicide, as well as those of other "moral phenomena" such as alcoholism, prostitution, homicide, and crime, dates from the late eighteenth century in the Western European countries. The moral statisticians considered that these figures provided a quantitative index which could be used to analyse the moral life of society. In the works of these authors, suicide rates were analysed in relation to variations in climate and temperature, race and inheritance, and to social phenomena such as religion, family structure, and economic conditions.

Durkheim's *Suicide* certainly drew heavily upon the works of the moral statisticians; but it was distinctively different from the majority of previous statistical writings in two main respects. Firstly, Durkheim set out an analysis of suicide which was wholly sociological. While most previous writers had recognized the influence of social factors, these were usually simply regarded as one among other sets of factors—climate, race, etc.—which were equally important in the aetiology of suicide. Durkheim rejected all these non-social factors as having no significance in determining variations in rates of suicide. Secondly, he attempted to establish a coherent sociological *theory* of suicide. Durkheim's theoretical standpoint was certainly partly derived from the previous literature on suicide—particularly his view that suicide in modern societies is connected with a decline in moral controls consequent upon the dissolution of traditional institutions.[6] But no one before Durkheim had successfully welded such ideas into a consistent theory of suicide.

The whole of Durkheim's thesis in *Suicide* is based upon the conception that there is an essential distinction between the explanation of variations in suicide *rates,* and the aetiology of any given individual case of suicide. Suicide, of course, is always an individual act; but if we examine the statistics of suicide—as the moral statisticians showed —we find that each society has its own characteristic suicide rate which remains very similar from year to year. Even where changes do take place in the suicide rate, they do not take the form of random fluctuations up and down, but rather of definite patterned movements. Moreover, during such periods of movement, the suicide rates of different countries retain the same *relative* distribution. Suicide rates were higher in both Italy and in France in 1886 than they were in 1878; but the relative discrepancy between the rates of suicide for the two countries remained the same. (Italy: 3.0 [per 100,000] in 1866, 3.8 in 1878; France: 13.5 in 1866, 16.0 in 1878.)

The study of individual cases of suicide, while necessary to the examination of the causes which lead particular individuals to kill themselves, cannot allow us to explain these patterns in the statistical *distribution* of suicide. The stable character of suicide rates must be analysed in relation to factors which act upon the social community in such a way as to produce a definite "collective tendency" towards suicide. These factors must consequently be of a very general kind. It could be argued, for instance, that the differing geographical position of the countries of Europe, which exposes them to different types of climate, provides the key. Other plausible possibilities among the kinds of explanation offered by previous authors include race and inherited insanity.[7] Through careful statistical analysis, Durkheim tried to show that none of these factors could adequately explain the distribution of suicide rates. The explanation must therefore be sought, Durkheim concluded, in the differing social characteristics of the various European countries.

Those countries which are predominantly Catholic have lower rates of suicide, in general, than those which are chiefly Protestant. This relationship holds good even in countries which have a mixed population of Protestants and Catholics: the greater the proportion of Protestants, the higher the suicide rate. The differential influence of the two religions on suicide cannot be explained in terms of a disparity in their attitudes to suicide, since both condemn suicide with equal severity. The main difference between the two is that the Catholic Church involves a traditionally established and closely woven set of beliefs and ritual practices, into which the life of the individual believer is closely bound. Protestanism is, by comparison, much more highly individualized: it is more committed to the principle of free enquiry, and the believer is forced to be "alone before God". The Catholic is thus more "protected" than the Protestant from the vicissitudes of life; the lower suicide rate of Catholics derives from the fact that the Catholic Church is more highly "integrated" than the Protestant Church.

Durkheim considered that the relationship which exists between marital status and suicide could be interpreted in much the same way. Unmarried people show higher rates of suicide than married people of the same age-group; and suicide rates decrease in proportion to increasing family size—the greater the number of children in the family, the lower the rate of suicide for the adult members. The degree of integration of a group depends upon the number of social ties which bind individuals to each other. Again, therefore, we see that suicide is related to social integration. The unmarried individual is not part of a family at all, and is consequently the highest suicide risk; the married person without children is less at risk than the unmarried person, but more likely to commit suicide than the individual who is a member of a larger family group.

We thus reach the conclusion that "suicide varies inversely with the degree of integration of the social groups of which the individual forms a part".[8] Durkheim called this type of suicide "egoistic" suicide: it derives from "excessive individualism", whereby the individual becomes detached from closely-knit contacts with others. This type of suicide is characteristic of modern societies in general, although it is more marked in some societies than others.

There is, however, a second type of suicide which Durkheim also distinguished as particularly characteristic of the advanced societies. This is "anomic suicide". Suicide rates tend to rise in times of economic crisis. This cannot be simply and direcly due to the poverty incurred in such circumstances, because suicide rates rise to an equivalent level in periods of unusual prosperity. Consequently, the increase in suicide must stem from the effects of rapid economic change itself, in whichever direction it takes place. Both directions of rapid economic fluctuation have the effect of placing numbers of individuals in circumstances in which the norms of behaviour which previously regulated their conduct are no longer appropriate to their changed conditions of life. The man who suddenly becomes wealthy, as much as the man who is forced to live in reduced circumstances, is left in a situation of moral de-regulation, or *anomie*.

Suicide in the more primitive societies is, Durkheim believed, quite different in character from egoistic or anomic suicide. Using the limited range of anthropological material at his disposal, Durkheim concluded that there are three main kinds of social situation involving suicide in traditional societies: suicides of old men and the infirm; suicides of women following the death of a husband; and suicides of servants on the death of a chief. In each of these instances, it is a duty for the individual to kill himself. Since the individual here commits suicide in response to the demands of the group, in furtherance of the values of the collectivity, Durkheim called this type "altruistic suicide". Altruistic suicide does not always rest upon a definite obligation as in the cases detailed above: there are forms of "optional" altruistic suicide where individuals choose to kill themselves in order to bring honour or prestige to their name.[9]

The ideas developed by Durkheim in his *Suicide* are closely bound up with the views expressed in his more general writings. Perhaps the most obvious connections are with the canons of research procedures given in *The Rules of Sociological Method* (1895).[10] In this work Durkheim set out his view of sociology as an autonomous discipline with its own theories and concepts which are not reducible to those of the neighbouring sciences. The subject-matter of sociology is the study of society. Society, of course, consists of individuals, but this does not mean that the existence of a science of the individual (psychology) makes sociology redundant. On the contrary, social phenomena cannot be understood simply in terms of the motives or actions of individuals. This can easily be shown: every individual is born into a society which is already organised, and and which influences him quite independently of his own volition. Society is "external" to the individual—that is, to any single, particular individual—in that it consists of an ordered system of norms and relationships to which that individual's own thoughts and actions form only one minute contributing element.

The suicide rate of any given society, then, must be explained in terms of the degree to which its institutions produce states of egoism, *anomie* or altruism. Each of these three types of suicide expresses a definite condition of society. No single individual creates the society in which he lives: whether or not a state of anomie exists, for example, is "given" independently of the wishes of any particular individual. This is why it is a matter for the sociologist to explain variations in rates of suicide: "At any given moment the moral constitution of society establishes the contingent of voluntary deaths. There is, therefore, for each people a collective force of a definite amount of energy, impelling men to self-destruction. The victim's acts which at first seem to express only his personal temperament are really the supplement and prolongation of a social condition which they express externally."[11] This does not mean that psychology is irrelevant to the explanation of suicide; the proper contribution of the psychologist is to study the particular motives and circumstances which drive specific individuals to commit suicide when exposed, for example, to a situation of *anomie*.

The theory contained in *Suicide*, besides being a particularly forceful testimony to the validity of Durkheim's conception of sociological method, also connects with other prime themes in his work. The smaller, traditional kinds of society, as Durkheim made clear in *The Division of Labour in Society* (1893),[12] are characterized by the dominance of a strongly held set of beliefs (the *conscience collective*), which are shared by all members of the society. Altruistic suicide is the typical form of self-destruction in these societies. In the course of social development, as society becomes more complex, the *conscience collective* becomes weaker: diversity of belief and opinion becomes more common, and the influence of the traditional forms of religion declines. The main moral beliefs underlying contemporary society are those which stress the dignity and worth of the human individual: beliefs which found their initial expression in the writings of the *philosophes* of the eighteenth century and in the moral ideals which inspired the French Revolution. Egoistic and anomic suicide are both products of this trend.

Egoistic suicide, Durkheim considered, is largely an unavoidable offshoot of this growth of moral individualism in modern societies. Where individual freedom and self-fulfilment are the primary values, it is inevitable that an increase in egoism takes place. Anomic suicide, however, in part reflects a pathological condition of modern society, a lack of moral regulation which is particularly evident in the economic sphere. Class conflicts, and other kinds of more specific industrial conflict, are manifestations of this. Anomic suicide would diminish, (not disappear altogether), Durkheim believed, if this moral deficiency were remedied.[13]

During Durkheim's life-time, and for some considerable period afterwards, his *Suicide* was not widely known outside France. In

Germany, for a combination of intellectual and political reasons, Durkheim's writings as a whole went practically unread. In the English-speaking world, Durkheim's ideas were in the main dismissed as a latter-day example of Continental collectivist metaphysics. *The Elementary Forms of the Religious Life*, the only one of Durkheim's major writings to be translated into English during his lifetime, was also for some years the only one which was widely known.

By the 1920's, however, particularly through the agency of Radcliffe-Brown,[14] Durkheim's influence was spreading through anthropology, and from there to sociology. In 1933, an English translation of *The Division of Labour in Society* appeared in America, closely followed by two important sympathetic discussions of Durkheim's sociology: Parsons' *Structure of Social Action* (1937), and Alpert's *Emile Durkheim and his Sociology* (1939). From this time onwards, Durkheim's work has exerted a great influence over the development of sociology in both the United States and Britain. But *Suicide*, which was still not translated into English at that date, had rather little effect upon research into suicide as much in the United States. The various studies of suicide which were published in the 1920s and the 1930s were mainly derived from the "ecological" theories of the Chicago sociologists.[15]

The real influence of Durkheim's *Suicide* on research in the field appropriate to its title dates from the appearance of its English translation in 1951. Since that time many sociological studies of suicide have been published in the United States, virtually all of them drawing inspiration from Durkheim. Among these may be ranked Henry and Short's *Suicide and Homicide* (1954); Bohannan's *African Homicide and Suicide* (1960); Gribbs' and Martin's *Status Integration and Suicide* (1964); and, more recently, Douglas's *The Social Meanings of Suicide* (1967).[16]

Very few significant sociological studies of suicide have appeared in Britain since the turn of the century—a fact which partly reflects the retarded spread of sociology in this country as a recognized academic subject. In Britain, most work on suicide has come from medical or psychiatric researchers. Research on suicide of this kind stretches back at least as far as the rest of the empirical literature on suicide. Indeed, in the eighteenth-century literature it is already possible to discover marked differences of opinion between those who stressed the overriding importance of the "individual"—i.e. biological and psychological causes, as opposed to the social causes of suicide.[17] Much of this literature until quite recent times has been dominated by the view that suicide is either itself a special form of mental illness, or to be explained as an outcome of the main types of mental illness. This sort of research has been based mainly on case-study material, and of course is very much concerned not only with the analytic study of suicide, but with its prophylaxis and with the therapy of suicidal patients.

Most British research on suicide has fallen squarely in this tradition, at least until recently. But there have been important exceptions. Thus Sainsbury's *Suicide in London* is a study influenced both by Durkheim and by work of the American "ecologists". Stengel and his co-workers have played a prominent role in recent developments in the study of social factors relating to attempted suicide.[18] Finally, British anthropologists have maintained an interest in suicide since before the turn of the century, although only one has published a book on the subject.[19]

It is obvious enough that the study of suicide involves difficulties over and above those encountered in other areas of sociology. There is, by definition, no earthly means of interviewing a suicide. The vast majority of sociological investigations of suicide have depended upon the use of official suicide statistics, with all the uncertainties which these entail. These statistics have been used in research on suicide for over one hundred and fifty years; but very few systematic attempts have been made to determine their reliability. To do so is by no means a simple matter. Research has suggested that many people who are contemplating suicide give prior indications to others of their intention. Thus whether or not a suicidal act occurs does not depend purely upon the actions of the individual concerned, but in part upon the reactions of *others*. Moreover, once a suicidal act has taken place, whether or not it leads to death may also in part depend upon circumstances outside the control of the person who commits the act. These contingencies include not only technical failures in the chosen method of suicide, but again the response of others to the act. Indeed, a certain proportion of suicides involve a definite element of "risk-taking", in which an individual quite literally stakes his life upon the intervention of others before death claims him.[20] Once a death has occurred, whether or not "suicide" is suspected depends upon the interpretations of the manner of, and motives for, the death made by the officials who investigate it. The final registration of the death as a suicide is in turn dependent upon the deliberations of other officials. Given the uncertain outcome of each of these stages intervening between a person's initial resolution to kill himself, and the actual official recording of a "suicide", it is evident that a suicide "rate", which seems on the face of it to be a simple quantitative measure, may in fact be the outcome of a complicated social process.[21]

It should be clear from some of the more recent papers in this book, such as the concluding three in Part II, and those in Part V, that significant redirection of research is today taking place in the sociology of suicide. That is to say, the statistical approach, correlating variations in suicide rates with very general social phenomena such as religion or social class, is giving way to an interest in the more microcosmic aspects of the *milieu* in which an individual commits the act of suicide.

It is only fairly recently that it has become apparent how problematic is the relationship between suicide and attempted suicide. As Stengel has pointed out, those who attempt to kill themselves, but do not die, used to be regarded either as mere *poseurs*, or as having not succeeded in consummating their action because of some unaccountable failure in the means of its execution. But many suicidal actions have what Stengel had termed an "ordeal character": the individual submits himself to an ordeal, the outcome of which is to some degree open. The act is at the same time an "appeal for help" to others. If the individual survives, and others respond through their timely intervention, this is regarded by the person concerned as a vindication of his worth. The result of such an "unsuccessful" attempt is often to produce some real change in his circumstances. Even hospitalization temporarily removes a man from the social isolation which is so often a prior condition influencing suicide. The effects of a suicide attempt upon relatives or friends may be various, but may include changes in their attitudes which are regarded as desirable by the individual involved, or which in some way remedy the situation which gave rise to his action.

Suicide is thus in some respects even more a directly social action than Durkheim recognized. The suicidal act often has immediate reference to others: not only as a form of appeal, but in various complex combinations of social motivations. There is no doubt that heavy reliance in subsequent research upon the methods and theory established by Durkheim has meant that these aspects of suicide have not received the attention which they deserve.

The generalizing disciplines have very definite limitations in the sort of knowledge they can provide. By their very nature they deal in abstractions, and discard the particular. No theory of suicide can capture the tragic desperation of a man who puts an end to himself in order to escape from his feelings of solitude; or the stoic calm of a man who deliberately allows himself to be burnt alive as a gesture of protest. (Although what a theory of suicide can do is to show that these apparently diverse acts may share certain important similarities.) Nor can a sociological theory directly supply any answers to moral-philosophical questions about suicide. It can, however, shed light upon the true nature of some of these problems. Thus

* *

the moral issue, at least, as it is often posed, of whether the individual should have the right to kill himself, involves the assumption that a man on the point of suicide has a clear and conscious wish to die which overrides all desire for life. But research shows that in many cases the intent to die is *not* clear-cut; the act of suicide is in reality an appeal for life. Thus suicide, if it is an escape from the world as it exists, is also at the same time an indictment of it. This must be understood by anyone attempting to resolve what Camus has called in a famous phrase "the only truly important problem of philosophy".

NOTES

1 For the views of the Roman Stoics on suicide, see W. E. H. Lecky, *History of European Morals*, London, 1869, Vol. I, pp. 223–39; on the views of Plato and Aristotle, cf. K. A. Geiger, *Der Selbstmord im Klassischen Altertum*, Augsburg, 1888, es. pp. 7–9.

2 cf. A. Michel: 'Suicide' in A. Vacant et al., *Dictionnaire de Théologie Catholique*, Paris, 1939, pp. 2739–49.

3 1648 is the most probable year of the appearance of the work, but its date of publication cannot be fixed with complete certainty.

4 The most famous of modern writings on the morality of suicide is Albert Camus's *The Myth of Sisyphus*, New York, 1955; originally published in French in 1942.

5 Perhaps the most influential of these authors was Quetelet; cf. particularly M. A. Quetelet, *Du système social et des lois qui le régissent*, Paris, 1848. On Quetelet and the moral statisticians see the papers by Giddens ('The suicide problem in French sociology'), and Douglas in this volume.

6 This is a view expressed at some length in T. G. Masaryk, *Der Selbstmord als sociale Massenerscheinung*, Vienna, 1881. Masaryk's work does not, however, have the same theoretical coherence and precision of Durkheim's.

7 The view that mental disorder offers a *passe-partout* to the understanding of suicide received an influential formulation in the work of the French psychiatrist Esquirol. (See Giddens, 'The suicide problem in French sociology', in this volume.)

8 *Suicide*, p. 209.

9 Altruistic suicide, according to Durkheim, survives in modern societies in those institutional spheres where there are still strong moral codes which subordinate the individual to the collectivity—as in the army. See *Suicide*, pp. 228 ff. Durkheim also distinguished a fourth type of suicide, "fatalistic" suicide, but his sole reference to it in the book is in the form of a short footnote. (For this brief note, see the selections from *Suicide* reprinted below.)

10 *The Rules of Sociological Method*, trans. Sarah A. Solovay and John H. Mueller, London, 1964.

11 *Suicide*, p. 229.

12 *The Division of Labour in Society*, trans. George Simpson, New York, 1964.

13 Durkheim advocated the setting up of occupational associations which, he believed, could help to introduce moral regulation and thereby

ameliorate the anomic division of labour. See his Preface to the Second Edition of *The Division of Labour,* pp. 1–31.

14 A. R. Radcliffe-Brown (1881–1955), the British anthropologist, played an important part, while at Chicago from 1931–7, in generating an interest in Durkheim in the United States.

15 The leader of the "ecological" school at Chicago, which flourished during the twenties and thirties, was Robert E. Park (1864–1944).

16 Selections from each of these works, or articles describing their main themes, are reprinted in this volume.

17 cf. Giddens, 'The suicide problem in French sociology', below.

18 A selection from Sainsbury's book, and a paper by Stengel on attempted suicide, are included in this volume.

19 Verrier Elwin, *Maria Murder and Suicide,* Bombay, 1943. (Elwin actually spent most of his life in India.)

20 cf. the papers by Stengel, Weiss, and Firth in this volume.

21 On these issues, see the paper by Atkinson, below.

PART 1

CHAPTER 1

Durkheim and his Contemporaries

Morselli's *Il suicidio*, published in 1879, was one of the outstanding statistical treatments of suicide produced in the nineteenth century. In the selection reprinted here taken from the introductory chapter of his work, Morselli discusses studies of suicide which preceded his own. He points out that, while suicide is a prominent feature of Classical history, its scientific study is relatively recent, dating from the post-Renaissance flowering of empirical science. Morselli recognizes the moral statisticians as the founders of the scientific study of suicide; but he shows that he is well aware of the pitfalls involved in the use of official statistics.

Durkheim made extensive use of Morselli's work, and devoted part of his own book to a critique of Morselli's claim that there is a close relationship between suicide and race. The main significance of Durkheim's work, however, lies not in the statistics which it contains, but in the use of those statistics to support a sociological theory of suicide. Accordingly, the sections from Durkheim's book reproduced here are those which convey the substance of his theoretical position.

Maurice Halbwachs' *Les causes du suicide*, which appeared in 1930, contains a general reappraisal of Durkheim's work in the light of more recent statistical evidence than was available to Durkheim. Halbwachs proffered a number of criticisms of Durkheim. Durkheim had set out statistical correlations linking, for instance, religious affiliation and suicide, and family size and suicide, as if these were separate generalizations each of which supplies independent evidence for the existence of egoistic suicide. But it may be that religion and family size are themselves closely related: in most countries of Europe, Catholicism is stronger in the rural areas, where families tend to be larger than in urban regions. The religious factor cannot actually be separated from other influences in the broader context of different types of community. This is true in both a methodological and a theoretical sense; in explaining variations in suicide rates, we must deal with the integrative effects of social communities as a whole. According to Halbwachs, the most important variations in rates of suicide can be traced to a cluster of differences in social life between rural communities on the one hand, and urban communities on the other.

Halbwachs further rejected Durkheim's emphasis that a sociological theory of suicide must eschew all reference to motivation. The motives which drive individuals to suicide are themselves at least to some degree determined by the very social phenomena which Durkheim saw as basic to the explanation of suicide.

The problem of the relevance of psychology to the explanation of suicide is one which entered into debates between psychiatrists and statisticians early on in the nineteenth century. Many of the psychiatrists, following Esquirol, considered that suicide is to be explained in terms of mental illness. Since, so they believed, the tendency to mental illness is largely a biological matter, it follows that social factors are of only marginal importance in the aetiology of suicide. Durkheim argued exactly the reverse: that, whatever significance hereditary temperament has in causing suicide, it is secondary to the influence of social factors. The precise nature of the relationship between suicide and mental illness has continued to be a subject of considerable dispute. The concluding paper in Part I places Durkheim's work in the context of previous and subsequent studies of this issue.

CHAPTER 2

Problems in the Study of Suicide*

Henry Morselli

Suicide is one of the voluntary human acts on which statistical works have dwelt with special predilection, and is one of the chief subjects of social physics. The psychological meaning of this moral fact has always been enveloped in great metaphysical obscurity, because suicide appears less susceptible of positive appreciation than all other expressions of the human will. The social significance of voluntary death began to be evident when a comparison was made between *homicide* and *suicide*,[1] and therefore the true literature of suicide did not arise before the time of the philosophic movement which distinguished the second half of last century. Nevertheless, mention was made of it amongst the ancients; Greek and Latin civilization had often seen their best representative men lost to them by means of suicide. But it is certain that the subject of self-destruction did not enter into its positive phase until after statistical researches.

If ancient history is rich in facts such as those of Zeno, Lucretius, and Cato, and if ancient literature is of philosophical and moral value, such as the often quoted words of Plato, Pliny, Cicero, and Seneca, yet the character which classical paganism attributed to suicide was simply individual. The famous phrase of the Stoics, *"Mori licet cui vivere non placet"*, is nothing more than the concrete formula of this individualism of the ancient philosophical opinions. Religion and laws have since declared suicide to be criminal, but they have never risen to the consideration of this crime under the more generic aspect of a tendency certainly hurtful, but one connected with the natural development of society.

This new aspect of suicide could not become clear where metaphysical systems prevailed; it was necessary to collect all the facts, to unite them together, to consider their analogy and differences, to do, in short, precisely the reverse of what philosophy had done up to that time. That is not to start from a preconceived system, but to base arguments on facts supplied by observation and, when possible,

* From the Introduction in *Suicide* by Henry Morselli, New York, 1903, pp. 1–9.

by experiment. In the natural sciences the experimental method was already introduced, and in the exact sciences the calculation of probabilities; thus the conviction came to be formed that to obtain knowledge of the true natural characters of phenomena, thought must remodel itself in its own way and recommence patient but productive analysis; that is to say, it must return to the natural process by which practical knowledge has been built up from generation to generation. For the phenomena of social life this aim can only be attained by statistics. The great reforms in habits and ideas which marked the second half of the eighteenth century prepared the ground, and the initiation of the people to a more direct participation in political events especially helped it. And since nations are constituted, by developing, and transforming themselves through millions of individuals, it was natural that the science of order and numbers should be applied in a uniform way to the progression of living and operating numbers. From this was brought to light that perpetual element of force and development, the principle of organic and functional transformation, or the *dynamics of population*.

The old philosophy of individualism had given to suicide the character of liberty and spontaneity, but now it became necessary to study it no longer as the expression of individual and independent faculties, but certainly as a social phenomenon allied with all the other racial forces. The real statistics of suicide began only in our century, and even late in it. It is true that from the end of the eighteenth century data were being collected in Switzerland and Paris (Mercier, 1783), but they were isolated figures, and perhaps on account of little exactitude not serviceable for analysis; later they were of value, however, in establishing the important statistical law of the progressive growth of suicide in civilized countries. To Switzerland belongs the credit of having been the first to gather its facts from the entire population; while France has the honour of having undertaken the regular and uniform publication of them in the registers of the Minister of Grace and Justice (1817–27). At the same time official statistics were begun in some other European States—Mecklenburg (1811), Prussia (1816), Norway (1816), and Austria (1819); which examples, on account of the impulse given to statistical works by the courage of the first sociologists, were followed by Hanover, the Canton of Geneva, Belgium, Saxony, Denmark, Bavaria, England, and so on by all the European States, from the most powerful to the smallest. The Southern States were the last to follow.

On the first statistical data of suicide Quetelet and Guerry[2] were able to found the bases of that part of moral statistics, finding therein, indeed, the laws making known new grounds of comparison between

State and State, between race and race, whence a marvellous reformation of ideas relative to voluntary death arose, recognized immediately as a most important element of social dynamics. This reform was aided by the simultaneous foundation and identification with the objective sciences of a new science which took for study the normal and morbid functions of the human mind. We find similarity of origin neither small nor indifferent between sociology and psychological physical pathology, both the progeny of our times, both arisen out of the ruins of the metaphysics of the schools, and united in the intention to get rid of the everlasting question of the relations between man and the rest of nature. It would be worth while, as far as it deserves, to investigate the historical and scientific relations between madness and suicide, and to show how often philosophical, religious, and judicial opinions relative to the morality and criminality of suicide clash with its obvious connection with the morbid perturbation of the mind; but ours is not a work intended to collect and explain the reason for suicide from the psychiatric side, which elsewhere has been fully treated by Esquirol, Falret, Lisle, Brierre de Boismont, Cazauvieilh, Petit, Des Etangs, Stark, Schürmayer, and a hundred other alienists, medical jurists, and moralists. It is true that statisticians and alienists have heretofore derived advantage from eath other's works in studying the psychological and racial laws of self-destruction, arriving at synthetical results previously unforeseen and unexpected. The knowledge of suicide, or rather of suicidal tendency, was only then received among the positive results of social psychology, and ceased to depend *exclusively* on the systems of philosophers and jurists.

At the same time, however, the objections with regard to the insufficiency of the method of observation apply more to the statistics of suicide than to those of other things. The difficulties of gathering exact data of various times and various places are great. Not only is it sometimes impossible to assign the true cause of death, not only is the medico-forensic question of the distinction between suicide or homicide or accidental death (especially in the case of drowning) difficult of solution, but with respect to violent death statistics encounter obstacles in the prejudices, habits, indifference, or bad faith of the public. It is more than ever apt to excite hostility and deceit; a feeling of shame and the remembrance of the infamy attached for a long course of years to this act, impel families, relations, and friends to hide or to falsify the true cause, the manner, and particulars of death. There are usages which are opposed to the examination of the circumstances of the case from which alone certainty can be obtained; usages which, as a relic of the middle ages, survive in central Europe, in Saxony, in some of the Swiss

Cantons, and are not wanting even to highly civilized Great Britain. All these inaccuracies were certainly greater in the early days of statistics than at the present time; nor do we wish to deny that, starting from figures not devoid of errors, certain additions and comparisons with different periods and countries may be set forth without sufficient prudence; but what we say of moral statistics in general may also be said of suicide. Demography—that is, the science of races—does not give its results as absolute; if, as is probable, it is granted that the technical process, the origin of obtaining data, was uniformly erroneous, these results may at least be taken at their relative value, and anyhow the homogeneity and the powers of comparison of figures may consist as much in approaching precision as in being removed from it at a uniform distance. The fear of important inexactitude would be exaggerated, especially in the statistics of suicide in those States which possess a long series of observations; therefore it is to be conjectured that statistics may by degrees approach a condition of greater exactness, as well by the lessened unwillingness of citizens to give information about themselves and their affairs, as by practical experience and the education of those chosen for the office of registrars and controllers. Such a result has been helped by the general increase of culture and the disappearance of many foolish popular prejudices, the reforms and uniformity of registered statistics, international congresses, societies, periodical publications, and all the copious literature of the new science; the greater decentralization in the administrative offices, the increased respect for laws and liberty, and perhaps, more than all the rest, the feeling in the public officials of serving the interests of their country and not those only of the Government. And if statistics are not yet without faults, it is to be hoped that with such improvements in the social and moral conditions of the people, they will become continually more exact and useful by true answers, that is to say, of absolute worth and of intrinsic homegeneity.

In the meantime it is certain that as long as facts are collected in their, so to speak, objective aspect, and, with regard to suicide, the sex, age, social condition, the race and religion of the individual, the time, place, and mode of death are registered, statistics can answer triumphantly to all these objections. Tangible and numerical facts are in question, and up to this point the subject matter lends itself to the measurement and elaboration of demography. But there is one defect in the statistics of suicide which can be easily pointed out, and on which it is well to say something; we refer to the limits and classification of *individual motives*. It is true that dealing here with the inward phenomena of conscience, statistics cannot presume to learn the true mental state or psychical movement which has preceded the act of suicide; it is necessary to limit ourselves to an approximation, which often errs by deceit, sometimes changes and sometimes forces the meaning of the facts. In the part of our work relating to causes it will however be seen that statistics do not assume undue powers and merits; the deductions on the psychological side are much more modest than its adversaries find it convenient to confess. If statistics speak of motives and seek their cause in sex, age, and race, it is because in the cases considered the determining causes of the act are evident, whether treating of physical causes or whether there remains unsuspected proofs of them by the act of the suicide himself. Brierre de Boismont[3] in 4,595 cases of suicide has found that 1,328 of them (1,052 men and 276 women) left their last thoughts written, to which must be added those who expressed them by word of mouth, and the life and habits of most of whom were so well known as to leave no doubt to those who wished to deduce a reason from them to explain the moving cause of their last act; for instance, those suicides who had always led dissolute lives, who had strong passions or domestic dissensions, or who had suffered financial catastrophes. The motives then which may lead a man to take away his life are nearly the same which lead him to crime; his passions, his overpowering needs, and his inclinations are too well known to us. There is also an abundant number of predisposing causes which give no support to the usual scepticism, and are dependent upon a morbid organization, either congenital or acquired— heredity, mental alienation, pellagra, delirium, drunkenness, hypochondria, physical disease. But also among the causes which touch rather upon the psychological aspects of cerebral activity (*moral causes*), not a few have been made plain by an exaggerated display, and are all the impulsive passions—love, jealousy, ambition, shame religious or political fanaticism, the fear of punishment, etc. Nevertheless the motive of every suicide is not alone that which is apparent; there are other more secret causes whose existence and influence elude even the suicide himself, because they act upon him almost unconsciously (such as education, moral contact, imitation, physical and moral atmosphere), and which statistics have had no means hitherto of investigating. Experimental psychology also meets nearly the same difficulties when the objective method is applied to the study of the passions, of the instincts, of human or animal habits; but neither psychology nor moral statistics claim to discover the nature of psychical activity, knowing well that such a metaphysical enquiry is beyond their aim and the powers of reason. Both arrive at positive knowledge by considering the protean prism of the human conscience through all its phases, but they stop short at phenomena, that is, at sensible phases; and it is unquestionable that even when the numerical element should happen to fail, or should appear inadequate for psychological deductions, we should draw the same results from the moral analysis of men and nations as those that the rough numbers of statistics would have furnished.

NOTES

1 According to most people the word *suicidium* was used for the first time by Desfontaines, in the last century. At the same time were also formed the words *propriicidium* (Latin) and αὐτοχειρία (from the Greek).
2 See A. Quetelet, *Sur l'homme et le développement de ses facultés* (2 vols.) Paris, 1835; A. M. Guerry, *Essai sur la statistique morale de la France*, Paris, 1833 [Ed. Note].
3 A. Brierre de Boismont, *Du suicide et de la folie-suicide*, Paris 1856 [Ed. Note].

CHAPTER 3

From Durkheim's *Suicide**

Since suicide is an individual action affecting the individual only, it must seemingly depend exclusively on individual factors, thus belonging to psychology alone. Is not the suicide's resolve usually explained by his temperament, character, antecendents and private history?

The degree and conditions under which suicides may be legitimately studied in this way need not now be considered, but that they may be viewed in an entirely different light is certain. If, instead of seeing in them only separate occurrences, unrelated and to be separately studied, the suicides committed in a given society during a given period of time are taken as a whole, it appears that this total is not simply a sum of independent units, a collective total, but is itself a new fact *sui generis*, with its own unity, individuality and consequently its own nature—a nature, furthermore, dominantly social. Indeed, provided too long a period is not considered, the statistics for one and the same society are almost invariable. This is because the environmental circumstances attending the life of peoples remain relatively unchanged from year to year. To be sure, more considerable variations occasionally occur; but they are quite exceptional. They are also clearly always contemporaneous with some passing crisis affecting the social state. Thus, in 1848 there occurred an abrupt decline in all European states.

If a longer period of time is considered, more serious changes are observed. Then, however, they become chronic; they only prove that the structural characteristics of society have simultaneously suffered profound changes. It is interesting to note that they do not take place with the extreme slowness that quite a large number of observers has attributed to them, but are both abrupt and progressive. After a series of years, during which these figures have varied within very narrow limits, a rise suddenly appears which, after repeated vacillation, is confirmed, grows and is at last fixed. This is because every breach of social equilibrum, though sudden in its appearance, takes time to produce all its consequences. Thus, the evolution of suicide is composed of undulating movements, distinct

* Reprinted by permission of Routledge & Kegan Paul Ltd. and the Macmillan Company from Emile Durkheim's *Suicide*, London, 1952, pp. 46–52; 217; 219–21; 246–8; 252–3; 254–6; 258; and 276.

and successive, which occur spasmodically, develop for a time, and then stop only to begin again . . .

. . . The suicide-rate is therefore a factual order, unified and definite, as is shown by both its permanence and its variability. For this permanence would be inexplicable if it were not the result of a group of distinct characteristics, solidary one with another, and simultaneously effective in spite of different attendant circumstances; and this variability proves the concrete and individual quality of these same characteristics, since they vary with the individual character of society itself. In short, these statistical data express the suicidal tendency with which each society is collectively afflicted. We need not state the actual nature of this tendency, whether it is a state *sui generis* of the collective mind,[1] with its own reality, or represents merely a sum of individual states. Although the preceding considerations are hard to reconcile with the second hypothesis, we reserve this problem for treatment in the course of this work.[2] Whatever one's opinion on this subject, such a tendency certainly exists under one heading or another. Each society is predisposed to contribute a definite quota of voluntary deaths. This predisposition may therefore be the subject of a special study belonging to sociology. This is the study we are going to undertake.

We do not accordingly intend to make as nearly complete an inventory as possible of all the conditions affecting the origin of individual suicides, but merely to examine those on which the definite fact that we have called the social suicide-rate depends. The two questions are obviously quite distinct, whatever relation may nevertheless exist between them. Certainly many of the individual conditions are not general enough to affect the relation between the total number of voluntary deaths and the population. They may perhaps cause this or that separate individual to kill himself, but not give society as a whole a greater or lesser tendency to suicide. As they do not depend on a certain state of social organization, they have no social repercussions. Thus they concern the psychologist, not the sociologist. The latter studies the causes capable of affecting not separate individuals but the group. Therefore among the factors of suicide the only one which concern him are those whose action is felt by society as a whole. The suicide-rate is the product of these factors . . .

Egoistic Suicide

[Durkheim has demonstrated that suicide rates vary according to religious denomination; and according to marital status and family size; and that suicide rates decline in times of political crisis and

in war-time. In each of these cases, he states, we see a relationship between suicide and social "integration".]

We have thus successively set up the three following propositions:

> Suicide varies inversely with the degree of integration of religious society.
> Suicide varies inversely with the degree of integration of domestic society.
> Suicide varies inversely with the degree of integration of political society.

This grouping shows that whereas these different societies have a moderating influence upon suicide, this is due not to special characteristics of each but to a characteristic common to all. Religion does not owe its efficacy to the special nature of religious sentiments, since domestic and political societies both produce the same effects when strongly integrated. This, moreover, we have already proved when studying directly the manner of action of different religions upon suicide. Inversely, it is not the specific nature of the domestic or political tie which can explain the immunity they confer, since religious society has the same advantage. The cause can only be found in a single quality possessed by all these social groups, though perhaps to varying degrees. The only quality satisfying this condition is that they are all strongly integrated social groups. So we reach the general conclusion: suicide varies inversely with the degree of integration of the social groups of which the individual forms a part.

But society cannot disintegrate without the individual simultaneously detaching himself from social life, without his own goals becoming preponderant over those of the community, in a word without his personality tending to surmount the collective personality. The more weakened the groups to which he belongs, the less he depends on them, the more he consequently depends only on himself and recognizes no other rules of conduct than what are founded on his private interests. If we agree to call this state egoism, in which the individual ego asserts itself to excess in the face of the social ego and at its expense, we may call egoistic the special type of suicide springing from excessive individualism.

But how can suicide have such an origin?

First of all, it can be said that, as collective force is one of the obstacles best calculated to restrain suicide, its weakening involves a development of suicide. When society is strongly integrated, it holds individuals under its control, considers them at its service and thus forbids them to dispose wilfully of themselves. Accordingly it opposes their evading their duties to it through death. But how could society impose its supremacy upon them when they refuse to accept this subordination as legitimate? It no longer then possesses the requisite authority to retain them in their duty if they wish to desert; and conscious of its own weakness, it even recognizes their right to do freely what it can no longer prevent. So far as they are the admitted masters of their destinies, it is their privilege to end their lives. They, on their part, have no reason to endure life's sufferings patiently. For they cling to life more resolutely when belonging to a group they love, so as not to betray interests they put before their own. The bond that unites them with the common cause attaches them to life and the lofty goal they envisage prevents their feeling personal troubles so deeply. There is, in short, in a cohesive and animated society a constant interchange of ideas and feelings from all to each and each to all, something like a mutual moral support, which instead of throwing the individual on his own resources, leads him to share in the collective energy and supports his own when exhausted.

But these reasons are purely secondary. Excessive individualism not only results in favouring the action of suicidogenic causes, but it is itself such a cause. It not only frees man's inclination to do away with himself from a protective obstacle, but creates this inclination out of whole cloth and thus gives birth to special suicide which bears its mark. This must be clearly understood for this is what constitutes the special character of the type of suicide just distinguished and justifies the name we have given it. What is there then in individualism that explains this result?

It has been sometimes said that because of his psychological constitution, man cannot live without attachment to some object which transcends and survives him, and that the reason for this necessity is a need we must have not to perish entirely. Life is said to be intolerable unless some reason for existing is involved, some purpose justifying life's trials. The individual alone is not a sufficient end for his activity. He is too little. He is not only hemmed in spatially; he is also strictly limited temporally. When, therefore, we have no other object than ourselves we cannot avoid the thought that our efforts will finally end in nothingness, since we ourselves disappear. But annihilation terrifies us. Under these conditions one would lose courage to live, that is, to act and struggle, since nothing will remain of our exertions. The state of egoism, in other words, is supposed to be contradictory to human nature and, consequently, too uncertain to have chances of permanence.

In this absolute formulation the proposition is vulnerable. If the thought of the end of our personality were really so hateful, we could consent to live only by blinding ourselves voluntarily as to life's value. For if we may in a measure avoid the prospect of annihilation we cannot extirpate it; it is inevitable, whatever we do. We may push back the frontier for some generations, force our name to endure for some years or centuries longer than our body; a moment, too soon for most men, always comes when it will be nothing. For the groups we join in order to prolong our existence by their means are themselves mortal; they too must dissolve, carrying with them all our deposit of ourselves. Those are few whose memories are closely enough bound to the very history of humanity to be assured of living until its death. So, if we really thus thirsted after immortality, no such brief perspectives could ever appease us. Besides, what of us is it that lives? A word, a sound, an imperceptible trace, most often anonymous,[3] therefore nothing comparable to the violence of our efforts or able to justify them to us. In actuality, though a child is naturally an egoist who feels not the slightest craving to survive himself, and the old man is very often a child in this and so many other respects, neither ceases to cling to life as much or more than the adult; indeed we have seen that suicide is very rare for the first fifteen years and tends to decrease at the other extreme of life. Such too is the case with animals, whose psychological constitution differs from that of men only in degree. It is therefore untrue that life is only possible by its possessing its rationale outside of itself.

Indeed, a whole range of functions concern only the individual; these are the ones indispensable for physical life. Since they are made for this purpose only, they are perfected by its attainment. In everything concerning them, therefore, man can act reasonably without thought of transcendental purposes. These functions serve by merely serving him. In so far as he has no other needs, he is therefore self-sufficient and can live happily with no other objective than living. This is not the case, however, with the cilivized adult. He has many ideas, feelings and practices unrelated to organic needs. The roles of art, morality, religion, political faith, science itself are not to repair organic exhaustion nor to provide some functioning of the organs. All this supra-physical life is built and expanded not because of the demands of the cosmic environment but because of the demands of the social environment. The influence of society is what has aroused in us the sentiments of sympathy and solidarity drawing us toward others; it is society which, fashioning us in its image, fills us with religious, political and moral beliefs that control our actions. To play our social role we have striven to extend our intelligence and it is still society that has supplied us with tools for this development by transmitting to us its vast fund of knowledge.

Through the very fact that these superior forms of human activity have a collective origin, they have a collective purpose. As they derive from society they have reference to it; rather they are society itself incarnated and individualized in each one of us. But for them to have a *raison d'être* in our eyes, the purpose they envisage must be one not indifferent to us. We can cling to these forms of human activity only to the degree that we cling to society itself. Contrariwise, in the same measure as we feel detached from society we become detached from that life whose source and aim is society. For what purpose do these rules of morality, these precepts of law binding us to all sorts of sacrifices, these restrictive dogmas exist, if there is no being outside us whom they serve and in whom we participate? What is the purpose of science itself? If its only use is to increase our chances for survival, it does not deserve the trouble it entails. Instinct acquits itself better of this role; animals prove this. Why substitute for it a more hesitant and uncertain reflection? What is the end of suffering, above all? If the value of things can only be estimated by their relation to this positive evil for the individual, it is without reward and incomprehensible. This problem does not exist for the believer firm in his faith or the man strongly bound by ties of domestic or political society. Instinctively and unreflectively they ascribe all that they are and do, the one to his Church or his God, the living symbol of the Church, the other to his family, the third to his country or party. Even in their sufferings they see only a means of glorifying the group to which they belong and thus do homage to it. So, the Christian ultimately desires and seeks suffering to testify more fully to his contempt for the flesh and more fully resemble his divine model. But the more the believer doubts, that is, the less he feels himself a real participant in the religious faith to which he belongs, and from which he is freeing himself; the more the family and community become foreign to the individual, so much the more does he become a mystery to himself, unable to escape the exasperating and agonizing question: to what purpose?

If, in other words, as has often been said, man is double, that is because social man superimposes himself upon physical man. Social man necessarily presupposes a society which he expresses and serves. If this dissolves, if we no longer feel it in existence and action about and above us, whatever is social in us is deprived of all objective foundation. All that remains is an artificial combination of illusory images, a phantasmagoria vanishing at the least reflection; that is, nothing which can be a goal for our action. Yet this social man is the essence of civilized man; he is the masterpiece of existence. Thus we are bereft of reasons for existence; for the only life to which we could cling no longer corresponds to anything actual; the only existence still based upon reality no longer meets our needs. Because we have been initiated into higher existence, the one which satisfies an animal or a child can satisfy us no more and the other itself fades and leaves us helpless. So there is nothing more for our efforts to lay hold of, and we feel them lose themselves in emptiness. In this sense it is true to say that our activity needs an object transcending it. We do not need it to maintain ourselves in the illusion of an impossible immortality; it is implicit in our moral constitution and cannot be even partially lost without this losing its *raison d'être* in the same degree. No proof is needed that in such a state of confusion the least cause of discouragement may easily give birth to desperate resolutions. If life is not worth the trouble of being lived, everything becomes a pretext to rid ourselves of it.

But this is not all. This detachment occurs not only in single individuals. One of the constitutive elements of every national temperament consists of a certain way of estimating the value of existence. There is a collective as well as an individual humour inclining peoples to sadness or cheerfulness, making them see things in bright or sombre lights. In fact, only society can pass a collective opinion on the value of human life; for this the individual is incompetent. The latter knows nothing but himself and his own little horizon; thus his experience is too limited to serve as a basis for a general appraisal. He may indeed consider his own life to be aimless; he can say nothing applicable to others. On the contrary, without sophistry, society my generalize its own feeling as to itself, its state of health or lack of health. For individuals share too deeply in the life of society for it to be diseased without their suffering infection. What it suffers they necessarily suffer. Because it is the whole, its ills are communicated to its parts. Hence it cannot disintegrate without awareness that the regular conditions of general existence are equally disturbed. Because society is the end on which our better selves depend, it cannot feel us escaping it without a simultaneous realization that our activity is purposeless. Since we are its handiwork, society cannot be conscious of its own decadence without the feeling that henceforth this work is of no value. Thence are formed currents of depression and disillusionment emanating from no particular individual but expressing society's state of disintegration. They reflect the relaxation of social bonds, a sort of collective asthenia, or social malaise, just as individual sadness, when chronic, in its way reflects the poor organic state of the individual. Then metaphysical and religious systems spring up which, by reducing these obscure sentiments to formulae, attempt to prove to men the senselessness of life and that it is self-deception to believe that it has purpose. Then new moralities originate which, by elevating facts to ethics, commend suicide or at least tend in that direction by suggesting a minimal existence. On their appearance they seem to have been created out of whole cloth by their makers who are sometimes blamed for the pessimism of their doctrines. In reality they are an effect rather than a cause; they merely symbolize in abstract language and systematic form the physiological distress of the body social.[4] As these currents are collective, they have, by virtue of their origin, an authority which they impose upon the individual and they drive him more vigorously on the way to which he is already inclined by the state of moral distress directly aroused in him by the disintegration of society. Thus, at the very moment that, with excessive zeal, he frees himself from the social environment, he still submits to its influence. However individualized a man may be, there is always something collective remaining—the very depression and melancholy resulting from this same exaggerated individualism. He effects communion through sadness when he no longer has anything else with which to achieve it.

Hence this type of suicide well deserves the name we have given it. Egoism is not merely a contributing factor in it; it is its generating cause. In this case the bond attaching man to life relaxes because that attaching him to society is itself slack. The incidents of private life which seem to direct inspiration of suicide and are considered its determining causes are in reality only incidental causes. The individual yields to the slightest shock of circumstance because the state of society has made him a ready prey to suicide . . .

Altruistic Suicide

If, as we have just seen, excessive individuation leads to suicide, insufficient individuation has the same effects. When man has become detached from society, he encounters less resistance to suicide in himself, and he does so likewise when social integration is too strong . . .

. . . Now, when a person kills himself, in all these cases, it is not because he assumes the right to do so but, on the contrary, because it is his duty. If he fails in this obligation, he is dishonoured and also punished, usually, by religious sanctions. Of course, when we hear of aged men killing themselves we are tempted at first to believe that the cause is weariness or the sufferings common to age. But if these suicides really had no other source, if the individual made away with himself merely to be rid of an unendurable existence, he would not be required to do so; one is never obliged to take advantage of a privilege. Now, we have seen that if such a person insists on living he loses public respect; in one case the usual funeral honours are denied, in another a life of horror is supposed to await him beyond the grave. The weight of society is thus brought to bear on him to lead him to destroy himself. To be sure, society intervention differs in the two cases. In one case, it speaks the sentence of death; in the other it forbids the choice of death. In the case of egoistic suicide it suggests or counsels at most; in the other case it compels and is the author of conditions and circumstances making this obligation coercive.

This sacrifice then is imposed by society for social ends. If the follower must not survive his chief or the servant his prince, this is because so strict an interdependence between followers and chiefs, officers and king, is involved in the constitution of the society that any thought of separation is out of the question. The destiny of one must be that of the others. Subjects as well as clothing and armour must follow their master wherever he goes, even beyond the tomb; if another possibility were to be admitted social subordination would be inadequate.[5] Such is the relation of the woman to her husband. As for the aged, if they are not allowed to await death, it is probably, at least in many instances, for religious reasons. The protecting spirit of a family is supposed to reside in its chief. It is further thought that a god inhabiting the body of another shares in his life, enduring the same phases of health and sickness and ageing with him. Age cannot therefore reduce the strength of one without the other being similarly weakened and consequently without the group existence being threatened, since a strengthless divinity would be its only remaining protector. For this reason, in the common interest, a father is required not to await the furthest limit of life before transferring to his successors the precious trust that is in his keeping.[6]

This description sufficiently defines the cause of these suicides. For society to be able thus to compel some of its members to kill themselves, the individual personality can have little value. For as soon as the latter begins to form, the right to existence is the first conceded it; or is at least suspended only in such unusual circumstances as war. But there can be only one cause for this feeble individuation itself. For the individual to occupy to little place in collective life he must be almost completely absorbed in the group and the latter, accordingly, very highly integrated. For the parts to have so little life of their own, the whole must indeed be a compact, continuous mass. And we have shown elsewhere that such massive cohesion is indeed that of societies where the above practices obtain. As they consist of few elements, everyone leads the same life; everything is common to all, ideas, feelings, occupations. Also, because of the small size of the group it is close to everyone and loses no one from sight; consequently collective supervision is constant, extending to everything, and thus more readily prevents divergences. The individual thus has no way to set up an environment of his own in the shelter of which he may develop his own nature and form a physiognomy that is his exclusively. To all intents and purposes indistinct from his companions, he is only an inseparable part of the whole without personal value. His person has so little value that attacks upon it by individuals receive only relatively weak restraint. It is thus natural for him to be yet less protected against collective necessities and that society should not hesitate, for the very slightest reason, to bid him end a life it values so little.

We thus confront a type of suicide differing by incisive qualities from the preceding one. Whereas the latter is due to excessive individuation, the former is caused by too rudimentary individuation. One occurs because society allows the individual to escape it, being insufficiently aggregated in some parts or even in the whole; the other, because society holds him in too strict tutelage. Having given the name of egoism to the state of the ego living its own life and obeying itself alone, that of altruism adequately expresses the opposite state, where the ego is not its own property, where it is blended with something not itself, where the goal of conduct is exterior to itself, that is, in one of the groups in which it participates. So we call the suicide caused by intense altruism altruistic suicide . . .

Anomic Suicide

No living being can be happy or even exist unless his needs are sufficiently proportioned to his means. In other words, if his needs require more than can be granted, or even merely something of a different sort, they will be under continual friction and can only function painfully. Movements incapable of production without pain tend not to be reproduced. Unsatisfied tendencies atrophy, and as the impulse to live is merely the result of all the rest, it is bound to weaken as the others relax.

In the animal, at least in a normal condition, this equilibrium is established with automatic spontaneity because the animal depends on purely material conditions. All the organism needs is that the supplies of substance and energy constantly employed in the vital process should be periodically renewed by equivalent quantities; that replacement be equivalent to use. When the void created by existence in its own resources is filled, the animal, satisfied, asks nothing further. Its power of reflection is not sufficiently developed to imagine other ends than those implicit in its physical nature. On the other hand, as the work demanded of each organ itself depends on the general state of vital energy and the needs of organic equilibrium, use is regulated in turn by replacement and the balance is automatic. The limits of one are those of the other; both are fundamental to the constitution of the existence in question, which cannot exceed them.

This is not the case with man, because most of his needs are not dependent on his body or not to the same degree. Strictly speaking, we may consider that the quantity of material supplies necessary to the physical maintenance of a human life is subject to computation, though this be less exact than in the preceding case and a wider margin left for the free combinations of the will; for beyond the indispensible minimum which satisfies nature when instinctive, a more awakened reflection suggests better conditions, seemingly desirable ends craving fulfilment. Such appetites, however, admittedly sooner or later reach a limit which they cannot pass. But how determine the quantity of well-being, comfort or luxury legitimately to be craved by a human being? Nothing appears in man's organic nor in his psychological constitution which sets a limit to such tendencies. The functioning of individual life does not require them to cease at one point rather than at another; the proof being that they have constantly increased since the beginnings of history, receiving more and more complete satisfaction, yet with no weakening of average health. Above all, how establish their proper variation with different conditions of life, occupations, relative importance of services, etc.? In no society are they equally satisfied in the different stages of the social hierarchy. Yet human nature is substantially the same among all men, in its essential qualities. It is not human nature which can assign the variable limits necessary to our needs. They are thus unlimited so far as they depend on the individual alone. Irrespective of any external regulatory force, our capacity for feeling is in itself an insatiable and bottomless abyss.

But if nothing external can restrain this capacity, it can only be a source of torment to itself. Unlimited desires are insatiable by definition and insatiability is rightly considered a sign of morbidity. Being unlimited, they constantly and infinitely surpass the means at their command; they cannot be quenched. Inextinguishable thirst is constantly renewed torture. It has been claimed, indeed, that human activity naturally aspires beyond assignable limits and sets itself unattainable goals. But how can such an undetermined state be any more reconciled with the conditions of mental life than with the demands of physical life? All man's pleasure in acting, moving and exerting himself implies the sense that his efforts are not in vain and that by walking he has advanced. However, one does not advance when one walks towards no goal, or—which is the same thing—when his goal is infinity. Since the distance between us and it is always the same, whatever road we take, we might as well have made the motions without progress from the spot. Even our glances behind and our feeling of pride at the distance covered can cause only deceptive satisfaction, since the remaining distance is not proportionately reduced. To pursue a goal which is by definition unattainable is to condemn oneself to a state of perpetual unhappiness. Of course, man may hope contrary to all reason, and hope has its pleasures even when unreasonable. It may sustain him for a time; but it cannot survive the repeated disappointments of experience indefinitely. What more can the future offer him than the past, since he can never reach a tenable condition nor even approach the glimpsed ideal? Thus, the more one has, the more one wants, since satisfactions received only stimulate instead of filling needs. Shall action as such be considered agreeable? First, only on condition of blindness to its uselessness. Secondly, for this pleasure to be felt and to temper and half veil the accompanying painful unrest, such unending motion must at least always be easy and unhampered. If it is interfered with only restlesseness is left, with the lack of ease which it, itself, entails. But it would be a miracle if no insurmountable obstacle were ever encountered. Our thread of life on these conditions is pretty thin, breakable at any instant.

To achieve any other result, the passions first must be limited. Only then can they be harmonized with the faculties and satisfied. But since the individual has no way of limiting them, this must be done by some force exterior to him. A regulative force must play the same role for moral needs which the organism plays for physical needs. This means that the force can only be moral . . .

. . . It is not true, then, that human activity can be released from all restraint. Nothing in the world can enjoy such a privilege. All existence being a part of the universe is relative to the remainder; its nature and method of manifestation according depend not only on itself but on other beings, who consequently restrain and regulate it. Here there are only differences of degree and form between the mineral realm and the thinking person. Man's characteristic privilege is that the bond he accepts is not physical but moral; that is, social. He is governed not by a material environment brutally imposed on him, but by a conscience superior to his own, the superiority of which he feels. Because the greater, better part of his existence transcends the body, he escapes the body's yoke, but is subject to that of society.

But when society is disturbed by some painful crisis or by beneficent but abrupt transitions, it is momentarily incapable of exercising this influence; thence come the sudden rises in the curve of suicides which we have pointed out above.

In the case of economic disasters, indeed, something like a de-classification occurs which suddenly casts certain individuals into a lower state than their previous one. Then they must reduce their requirements, restrain their needs, learn greater self-control. All the advantages of social influence are lost so far as they are concerned; their moral education has to be recommenced. But society cannot adjust them instantaneously to this new life and teach them to practice the increased self-repression to which they are unaccustomed. So they are not adjusted to the condition forced on them, and its very prospect is intolerable; hence the suffering which detaches them from a reduced existence even before they have made trial of it.

It is the same if the source of the crisis is an abrupt growth of power and wealth. Then, truly, as the conditions of life are changed, the standard according to which needs were regulated can no longer remain the same; for it varies with social resources, since it largely determines the share of each class of producers. The scale is upset; but a new scale cannot be immediately improvised. Time is required for the public conscience to reclassify men and things. So long as the social forces thus freed have not regained equilibrium, their respective values are unknown and so all regulation is lacking for a time. The limits are unknown between the possible and the impossible, what is just and what is unjust, legitimate claims and hopes and those which are immoderate. Consequently, there is no restraint upon aspirations. If the disturbance is profound, it affects even the principles controlling the distribution of men among various occupations. Since the relations between various parts of society are necessarily modified, the ideas expressing these relations must change. Some particular class especially favoured by the crisis is no longer resigned to its former lot, and, on the other hand, the example of its greater good fortune arouses all sorts of jealousy below and about it. Appetites, not being controlled by a public opinion become disorientated, no longer recognize the limits proper to them. Besides, they are at the same time seized by a sort of natural erethism simply by the greater intensity of public life. With increased prosperity desires increase. At the very moment when traditional rules have lost their authority, the richer prize offered these appetites stimulates them and makes them more exigent and impatient of control. The state of deregulation or *anomie* is thus further heightened by passions being less disciplined, precisely when they need more disciplining . . .

. . . If *anomie* never appeared except, as in the above instances, in intermittent spurts and acute crisis, it might cause the social suicide-rate to vary from time to time, but it would not be a regular, constant factor. In one sphere of social life, however—the sphere of trade and industry—it is actually in a chronic state.

For a whole century, economic progress has mainly consisted in freeing industrial relations from all regulation. Until very recently, it was the function of a whole system of moral forces to exert this discipline. First, the influence of religion was felt alike by workers and masters, the poor and the rich. It consoled the former and taught them contentment with their lot by informing them of the providential nature of the social order, that the share of each class was assigned by God himself, and by holding out the hope for just compensation in a world to come in return for the inequalities of this world. It governed the latter, recalling that wordly interests are not man's entire lot, that they must be subordinate to other and higher interests, and that they should therefore not be pursued without rule or measure. Temporal power, in turn, restrained the scope of economic functions by its supremacy over them and by the relatively subordinate role it assigned them. Finally, with the business world proper, the occupational groups by regulating salaries, the price of products and production itself, indirectly fixed the average level of income on which needs are partially based by the very force of circumstances. However, we do not mean to propose this organization as a model. Clearly it would be inadequate to existing societies without great changes. What we stress is its existence, the fact of its useful influence, and that nothing today has come to take its place.

Actually, religion has lost most of its power. And government, instead of regulating economic life, has become its tool and servant. The most opposite schools, orthodox economists and extreme socialists, unite to reduce government to the role of a more or less passive intermediary amng the various social functions. The former wish to make it simply the guardian of individual contracts; the latter leave it the task of doing the collective bookkeeping, that is, of recording the demands of consumers, transmitting them to producers, inventorying the total revenue and distributing it according to a fixed formula. But both refuse it any power to subordinate other social organs to itself and to make them converge towards one dominant aim. On both sides nations are declared to have the single or chief purpose of achieving industrial prosperity; such is the implication of the dogma of economic materialism, the basis of both apparently opposed systems. And as these theories merely express the state of opinion, industry, instead of being still regarded as a means to an end transcending itself, has become the supreme end of individuals and societies alike. Thereupon the appetites thus excited have become freed of any limiting authority. By sanctifying them, so to speak, this apotheosis of well-being has placed them above all human law. Their restraint seems, like a sort of sacrilege. For this reason, even the purely utilitarian regulation of them exercised by the industrial world itself through the medium of occupational groups has been unable to persist. Utimately, this liberation of desires has been made worse by the very development of industry and the almost infinite extension of the market. So long as the producer could gain his profits only in his immediate neighbourhood, the restricted amount of possible gain could not much overexcite ambition. Now that he may assume to have almost the entire world as his customer, how could passions accept their former confinement in the face of such limitless prospects?

Such is the source of the excitement predominating in this part of society, and which has thence extended to the other parts. There, the state of crisis and *anomie* is constant and, so to speak, normal. From top to bottom of the ladder, greed is aroused without knowing where to find ultimate foothold. Nothing can calm it, since its goal is far beyond all it can attain. Reality seems valueless by comparison with the dreams of fevered imaginations; reality is therefore abandoned, but so too is possibility abandoned when it in turn becomes reality. A thirst arises for novelties, unfamiliar pleasures, nameless sensations, all of which lose their savour once known. Henceforth one has no strength to endure the least reverse. The whole fever subsides and the sterility of all the tumult is apparent, and it is seen that all these new sensations in their infinite quantity cannot form a solid foundation of happiness to support one during days of trial. The wise man, knowing how to enjoy achieved results without having constantly to replace them with others, finds in them an attachment to life in the hour of difficulty. But the man who has always pinned all his hopes on the future and lived with his eyes fixed upon it, has nothing in the past as a comfort against the present's afflictions, for the past was nothing to him but a series of hastily experienced stages. What blinded him to himself was his expectation always to find further on the happiness he had so far missed. Now he is stopped in his tracks; from now on nothing remains behind or ahead of them to fix his gaze upon. Weariness alone, moreover, is enough to bring disillusionment, for he cannot in the end escape the futility of an endless pursuit . . .

. . . *Anomie*, therefore, is a regular and specific factor in suicide in our modern societies; one of the springs from which the annual contingent feeds. So we have here a new type to distinguish from the others. It differs from them in its dependence, not on the way in which individuals are attached to society, but on how it regulates them. Egoistic suicide results from man's no longer finding a basis

for existence in life; altruistic suicide, because this basis for existence appears to man situated beyond life itself. The third sort of
suicide, the existence of which has just been shown, results from
man's activity's lacking regulation and his consequent sufferings.
By virtue of its origin we shall assign this last variety the name of
anomic suicide.

Certainly, this and egoistic suicide have kindred ties. Both spring
from society's insufficient presence in individuals. But the sphere
of its absence is not the same in both cases. In egoistic suicide it
is deficient in truly collective activity, thus depriving the latter of
object and meaning. In anomic suicide, society's influence is lacking in the basically individual passions, thus leaving them without
a check-rein. In spite of their relationship, therefore, the two types
are independent of each other. We may offer society everything
social in us, and still be unable to control our desires; one may live
in an anomic state without being egoistic, and vice versa ...

Fatalistic Suicide

... there is a type of suicide the opposite of anomic suicide, just
as egoistic and altruistic suicides are opposites. It is the suicide deriving from excessive regulation, that of persons with futures pitilessly
blocked and passions violently choked by oppressive discipline. It
is the suicide of very young husbands, of the married woman who is
childless. So, for completeness' sake, we should set up a fourth
suicidal type. But it has so little contemporary importance and examples are so hard to find aside from the cases just mentioned that
it seems useless to dwell upon it. However it might be said to have
historical interest. Do not the suicides of slaves, said to be frequent
under certain conditions, belong to this type, or all suicides attributable to excessive physical or moral despotism? To bring out the
ineluctible and inflexible nature of a rule against which there is no
appeal, and in contrast with the expression "anomie" which has just
been used, we might call it fatalistic suicide.

NOTES

1 By the use of this expression we of course do not at all intend to hypo-
stasize the collective conscience. We do not recognize any more substantial a soul in society than in the individual. But we shall revert to
this point.

2 Bk. III, Chap. I, pp. 297–325 in the English edition [Ed. note].

3 We say nothing of the ideal protraction of life involved in the belief in
immortality of the soul, for (1) this cannot explain why the family or
attachment to political society preserves us from suicide; and (2) it is
not even this belief which forms religion's prophylactic influence, as we
have shown above.

4 This is why it is unjust to accuse these theorists of sadness of generalizing personal impressions. They are the echo of a general condition.

5 At the foundation of these practices there is probably also the desire to prevent the spirit of the dead man from returning to earth to revisit the objects and persons closely associated with him. But this very desire implies that servants and followers are strictly subordinated to their master, inseparable from him, and, furthermore, that to avoid the disaster of the spirit's remaining on earth they must sacrifice themselves in the common interest.

6 See Frazer, *Golden Bough* and *passim*.

CHAPTER 4

The Causes of Suicide*

Maurice Halbwachs

More than one reader, particularly the reader with a philosophical turn of mind, has no doubt had the feeling on closing this book[1] that suicide is no longer a problem, and that the answer is now known. Is it the argument, or is it the statistics, which bring this conviction? It is both, without it always being possible to distinguish one from the other. Sometimes—not however of any failing of Durkheim's— it is the argument rather than the facts. But this has made for more than one drawback: it has not been noticed that the structure of the work rested upon foundations which were not everywhere equally firm. How could it have been otherwise? There is no scientific work which does not have to be revised and completed in the light of new tests.

There was therefore some point in taking up this study where Durkheim left off, in the first place to compare his results with statistics which have since been published. Durkheim relied upon figures which only exceptionally go back before 1840, and which never go beyond 1890–1. These data are of very uneven value. In one of the most important countries in this regard, Prussia, suicide statistics have been virtually complete only since 1883. In England they begin in 1856, and in Italy only in 1864. For the German Empire as a whole, we only have figures from 1881 onwards. There is reason to suppose that in the more recent period in a number of countries the data have been improved and made more complete from decade to decade. It is not too much to say that, in terms of their number and validity, the data which we have available on suicide since 1890 are at least as significant as the figures from which Durkheim worked. We were able therefore to check the tests which he carried out, and make them more precise by using more detailed statistics. What these data of the last thirty or forty years have to teach us can be seen by referring to Chapters 8 to 10 of our book.[2] There we study, within the framework selected by Morselli and Durkheim, the problems which they dealt with, and if perhaps we have furthered the

* Translated by the Editor and reprinted by permission of Presses Universitaires de France from *Les Causes du Suicide,* Paris, 1930, pp. 3–15.

solution, it is because we have the advantage of coming after them and of having at our disposal a field of observation which is broader both in space and in time.

But, above all, methods of statistical analysis have been more advanced for some time. One can no longer be content with calculating averages, proportions or percentages. An American sociologist, John Rice Miner, has recently expressed surprise that no one has yet applied modern statistical methods to the study of suicides, such as measures of deviation, correlation coefficients, measures of dispersion, etc.[3] We have moved in this direction. We have employed procedures which are sufficiently empirical for us not to be charged with treating these imperfect statistical data like the rigorous observations of physics; but which draw sufficient inspiration from mathematical methods to be able to perform more or less the same services.

It is thus that we were led at once to direct our attention to an aspect of suicide which has been neglected hitherto, but which seems to us to be very important. Up to now, what has been done most often is to record the growth or decline in the number or proportion of suicides, in the same way as one follows variations in the temperature of a man with fever. Is suicide on the increase? Can one predict that it will increase still further? On this matter we shall see that observations made over a longer period have allowed us to modify significantly the conclusions and predictions of Durkheim. But that does not exhaust our research; it is not even perhaps the most essential thing about it. The number of suicides in a region is a purely relative datum which becomes clarified and acquires full significance only when one compares regions which are fairly close to each other. Are suicide rates becoming more alike in the major European countries, and in the different regions or provinces in large, medium and small towns within the same country? How quickly, and exactly to what degree? This is what we have been able to establish, by means of relatively simple calculations.

The interest of such research stems first of all from the fact that the number of suicides can be considered as a sort of thermometrical index which informs us about the moral condition, the moral temperature, of a group. It is not sufficient to portray the customs, beliefs, modes of being and acting which we can observe in a region. A description of this kind which is not accompanied by quantitative data remains imprecise, and leads only to uncertain conclusions. If, on the other hand, it appears that the distribution of suicides is or is tending to become, more homogeneous in a country, or within a country in one group of provinces than another, one can correctly assume that, in such and such a context, province, country or continent, a certain moral uniformity is coming about. From this point of view, however, the theory of suicide proper appears somewhat in a new light. The different environments comprised within regions are complex. Quite simple characteristics can however be derived from them, and which also lend themselves to measurement, such as the density and mode of distribution of the population, and the predominance of an urban or of a rural way of life. When one studies suicides within the framework of a region, one must relate them to this kind of factor. Neither Morselli nor Durkheim gave prominence to the influence of the town or of the country upon the number and distribution of voluntary deaths, perhaps because this was not easy for them to study. If the reader consults the first, and most extended part of our study, he will see that variations in suicide can be explained most clearly in terms of changes in way of life thus defined.[4] Family sentiments and religious practices—of which we are far from failing to appreciate or from underestimating the importance—are part of a totality of customs and of a whole type of social organization from which in part they draw their strength, and from which they cannot be separated. This is what we call a way of life (*genre de vie*), and our position is different from Durkheim's only in that we put the family and the religious group in the more embracing social environments of which they are only one aspect.

But the consequence of this difference of method is that, on several important points, we have been led to results which differ from his.

Durkheim summed up his explanation of suicide in this way: "Suicide varies inversely with the degree of integration of religious society, of domestic society or the family, and of political society or the nation." Morselli had in fact suggested, but Durkheim was the first to demonstrate, that unquestionably fewer married people kill themselves than single people: the family, particularly where it includes children, protects against suicide. He added further that the continued increase in suicide during the nineteenth century is explicable in terms of the weakening of ties of all kinds which hold together the members of a family group. However he was not able to demonstrate that given a similar composition, the family, protects less today than in the past: and no doubt he could not have done so, for simultaneously with the family, the social environment of which it was a part has changed, so that one cannot study in isolation the influence which the family, and the environment, exerts on suicide. The fact which Durkheim put beyond dispute is not thereby made less crucial, and we have shown that it can today be confirmed by other statistics which bear particularly upon the number of children

of those who commit suicide. But this has not as yet the full significance which he attributed to it.

The early researches of statisticians drew attention to the relatively
low number of suicides among Catholic groups. Catholics kill themselves much less than Protestants. This is a fact which Durkheim
lays great stress upon. We know how he accounted for this: "the
inclination of Protestanism towards suicide is connected with the
spirit of free enquiry". But free enquiry results from the disintegration of traditional beliefs. "The greater concessions a confessional
group makes to individual judgement, the less it dominates lives, the
less its cohesion and vitality . . . the superiority of Protestanism with
respect to suicide results from its being a less strongly integrated
church than the Catholic church." The author who has published the
best study of suicide since Durkheim, Father Krose, believes that, if
Catholicism turns men away from suicide, it is because it inspires
fear of punishment in the world to come.[5] He also attributes to the
Catholic religion as such a powerful preservative value. For our
part, we do not dispute that, in many cases, religious beliefs and
practices turn Catholics away from committing the mortal sin of
self-murder. But what do the statistics tell us about this? In effect,
very little. From a comparison between two countries, Italy and
Germany, one can infer nothing, because they differ from each other
in many other respects besides religion. There are, on the other hand,
very few states which record the religious confession of their suicides.
Prussia and Switzerland are virtually the only ones. Now in Prussia
there is most often a difference in national origins between Catholics
and Protestants, the Protestants being Prussians and the Catholics
Polish; or a difference in way of life, Catholics being more numerous
in rural areas, Protestants in the towns or in those regions most
subject to urban influences. Is this because the Poles, or peasants, or
because the non-Protestants, i.e. the Catholics, in Prussia commit
less suicide? We shall see that the analysis of more detailed Swiss
statistics leads us to the same conclusion. It has not been possible,
up to the present, to isolate the religious factor and to measure its
influence. This is a problem which remains, and it is not even possible to see how it could be resolved.

As for national sentiments, there is reason to suppose that they
do become stronger at moments when the country is in danger. The
experience of the last war confirms observations which have been
made previously, since in most of the country, and in the civil population of both sexes and all ages as well as in the armed forces, suicide
claimed far fewer victims during this period than in peace-time. It
is the same with revolutions and political crises: we have been able
to establish that, in France from 1872 to 1913, each of the events

which produced clashes between parties was reflected in the suicide curve. From this point of view we studied, month by month, the period 1899–1904 in particular, because there is no other in France over the whole century which shows this kind of effect so clearly. Is it true, however, that, as Durkheim says: "these facts are therefore susceptible of only one interpretation; namely, that great social disturbances and great popular wars rouse collective sentiments, stimulate partisan spirit and patriotism, and concentrating activity towards a single end, at least temporarily cause a stronger integration of society"? But a war does not merely heighten national feeling; it profoundly transforms society, slows down or paralyses some of its functions while creating or developing others. In particular, it simplifies the structure of the social body, and greatly reduces, as Spencer would say, the differentiation of its parts. If suicides are less numerous, is this not because, in part at least, there are fewer clashes and less friction between individuals living a more unified daily life within a more uniform social environment—that is to say, because there are fewer occasions for dissatisfaction and despair? But this is also the case in revolutions, and perhaps even in those periods of political disturbance in which, externally, nothing has changed in the structure of the social body. No doubt functions remain the same, and continue to operate: tradesmen, workers, officials, peasants, remain at their post. But their thoughts are elsewhere. Their life in the family and at work and their social relations, goes on, but in a much more automatic fashion, and their whole person is less involved in all this. All of this activity which is not political in character is thus correspondingly reduced. We may conclude that, if suicides decrease in such periods, this can be explained in several ways, for while as national or party feeling is more widespread and more intense, the social life comes to be simplified and offers fewer occasions for conflict and disequilibrium.

Durkheim certainly saw that suicide was the result of social causes. Is it not true that every group formed by men tends to produce annually the same number or the same proportion of voluntary deaths? But he considered within society only the mainsprings of collective life. When these are weakened, he argued, man loses all reason he had to keep alive. If the individual becomes discouraged and neglects himself or if he becomes desperate and turns his anger against himself, it is because he has not wife and children to whom the double bond of affection and duty unite him; it is because he finds neither support nor guidance from the group of men who accept the same dogma and practise the same religion; or, finally, it is because he is not taken out of his selfish preoccupations and raised above himself by great political or national interests. This theory is paradoxical both at first sight and even on further inspection, for the causes of suicide are ordinarily sought in quite another direction. "Suicides stemming from desire to atone, to avoid the disgrace of punishment, to escape from illness, suffering, old age, not to outlive a dear one: husband, wife, child, friend, leader; to prevent or to wipe out an insult, to avoid disgrace, not to fall into the hands of the enemy, suicides stemming from disgust with life, suicides carried out by command"; to these may be added: "desire to shock, desire to make others talk about oneself, a fit of madness or idiocy".[6] The two lists of motives from which these are drawn are very old, referring as they do to the Roman age, but nevertheless one could still today enumerate the reasons for suicide in much the same way.

According to Durkheim these particular individual motives are pretexts or opportunities, but not causes. The individual whom nothing holds to life will find, in any case, a reason to end it: but this is not the reason which explains his suicide. In the same way, when one comes out of a building which has several exits, the door one passes through is not the cause of one's departure. There must first be some sort of desire, however vague, to leave. A door has opened in front of us, but had it remained closed we could always have opened another.

Should we say, therefore, that the unhappy beings who kill themselves are impelled towards death by forces whose nature they do not understand, and that the motives which they furnish for themselves to explain their act do not enter into their decision at all? If Durkheim seemed to go this far it is because in his eyes there exists a gulf between the great collective forces, and motives or circumstances. He attributed causal power only to social factors. No doubt in order for this power to become translated into the deed it is necessary that it moves down into the world of individual actions, and it cannot manifest itself except given circumstances of anxiety, suffering or discouragement. But, in the same way, in order to kill oneself, one must of course employ some means. The causes which explain the choice of means are not the same as the causes of the suicide. Likewise, according to Durkheim, the causes which explain the number and distribution of motives are not the same as the true causes of suicide: in this, chance and whim play a much more important part.

We would advance two arguments against such a clear-cut distinction between motives and causes. Durkheim's thesis would be credible if there existed no connection between the influence of such motives and that which results from dislocation of collective sentiments. But this is by no means the case. When one reviews the various specific motives for suicide one perceives that, if men kill themselves, this is always as a consequence of an event, or under the influence of a condition arising either from outside, or from inside (in their body or mind), which separates or excludes them from their social environment and which imposes on them an unbearable feeling of solitude. But this is also the effect which a man experiences when, as Durkheim puts it, he has ceased to be "integrated" in one of the groups which are the backbone of society. There is thus no essential difference between what he calls motives and causes. When the emotional deprivation of an unmarried man is combined with *déclassement*, with the ignominy of ruin, with moral isolation arising from sickness or despair, then we have two conditions of the same kind which are superimposed, forces of the same sort which act in combination. There is thus no reason, in explaining suicide, to exclude some and to retain others.

On the other hand, however, Durkheim believed that the circumstances which are invoked as motives of suicide are individual, not only in that each of them affects one individual, but because their number and distribution do not depend upon the particular structure of the group within which they occur. Certainly, if they were merely the result of differences of temperament, since human nature conceived from the point of view of its organic traits is virtually always the same and varies in roughly the same way in different groups, it would then be understandable for them to be the same everywhere, and it would not be necessary to take account of them in explaining variations in the number of suicides. But even if the different human physical types were distributed in the same proportion in all groups—which is itself questionable—the circumstances and motives are certainly related to the organization of society. *A priori* one may assume that events such as reversals of fortune, career worries and disappointments, and even those conditions which can be grouped under the rubric of boredom with or distaste for life, are produced more frequently in a more complex society where individual circumstances change more often and more rapidly, where the rhythm of life is faster, and where there is more chance for people to find themselves maladapted to their environment. No doubt one does not perceive this at the outset, when one considers each particular case in isolation. But taken as a whole, those phenomena which we call the circumstances or the motives of suicide are simply one aspect and one effect of the structure and way of life of a group.

Thus suicides are always to be explained in terms of social causes. But sometimes these manifest themselves as collective forces proper—such as family and religious practices or great political and national movements—and sometimes in the form of individual motives, more or less numerous and distributed in varying fashion according to the degree of complexity of the society itself. Moreover it is not up to us to isolate the familial or religious customs from other ways of life with which they are interwoven with differing degrees of closeness within a single fabric in a given group. What would be warp without woof, and how could one distinguish whether the strength of the cloth came from one rather than the other? But we can no more observe separately all the circumstances and specific motives of suicide, which are like so many ambushes set along the road of the living: for they lurk hidden. What, therefore, is the reason for this surprising increase in suicide which took place for more than half a century? Is it the disintegration of traditional groups? Is it, in an increasingly complex society, the inevitable multiplication of chances of unhappiness and of individual suffering? We cannot know what role has to be attributed to each of these two sorts of causes. Durkheim limited himself to considering the weakening of traditional bonds which in prior times both imprisoned but also sustained men. According to him, this is the sole cause of the increase in suicide, in which we should therefore recognize not merely an evil, but an absolute evil. For if those traditions disappear, nothing replaces them: society gains nothing in exchange. Suicide is not a ransom paid for some benefit. This is why one must express alarm. However if, on the contrary, suicide increases primarily because social life is becoming more complex, and because particular events which expose a man to despair become multiplied, it is still an evil, but perhaps a relative one. In fact there is a necessary complexity which is a condition of a richer and more intense social life.

Durkheim's achievement was to provide a fully comprehensive treatment of the phenomenon of suicide, and to offer an explanation which could be modified and added to, but which in principle seems unassailable. Having been able to use new sources, we have naturally been able to advance further along the paths which he marked out and, perhaps, to open up some new ones.

NOTES

1 Durkheim's *Suicide*.
2 Chapters 8 to 10 of Halbwachs' book deal with suicide and the family, suicide and religion, and suicide and homicide [Ed. Note].
3 J. R. Minor, 'Suicide and its Relation to Other Factors', *American Journal of Hygiene Monographs*, No. 2, 1922, pp. 72–112 [Ed. Note].
4 See especially pp. 169–293 in Halbwachs' book [Ed. Note].
5 H. A. Krose (S. J.), *Der Selbstmord im 19 Jahrhundert*, Freiburg, 1906; and *Die Ursachen der Selbstmordhäufigkeit*, Freiburg, 1906 [Ed. Note].
6 A. Bayet, *Le Suicide et la Morale*, Paris, 1922, pp. 275 and 278.

CHAPTER 5

The Suicide Problem in French Sociology*

Anthony Giddens

My purposes in this paper are to describe the origins and the course of a controversy in French sociology revolving around the question: what contributions can sociology make to the analysis of suicide?; and to examine critically certain of the issues arising out of the controversy. The suicide controversy in French sociology, which reached its peak in the period between the two world wars, centred particularly around the thesis advanced by Durkheim in *Suicide*, but its beginnings can be traced much further back.[1] It is not generally realized today, in fact, how far Durkheim's work itself was grounded in previous studies of suicide produced by earlier nineteenth-century writers.

I

Suicide was the subject of extended debate even in the eighteenth century.[2] Most eighteenth-century works on suicide were concerned with the moral implications of the suicidal act, but towards the end of the century writers began to turn their attention to discussing the significance of the apparently rapidly rising suicide rates in Europe,[3] and out of this a more objective concern with the determinants of suicide began to develop.

One of the earliest comprehensive investigations of suicide was made by Falret in his *De l'hypochondrie et du suicide* (1822).[4] Falret examined at some length both "internal causes" of suicidal tendencies in the individual, which he attributed principally to certain forms of inherited mental disorder, and "external causes" producing variations in suicide rates between different groups.[5] *De l'hypochondrie et du suicide* was followed by a proliferation of works on suicide by French, German and Italian writers. Perhaps the most influential of these were those by Guerry (1933), Lisle (1856), Legoyt (1881), and, Quetelet (1835) in French, Wagner (1864) and Masaryk (1881)

* Reprinted by permission of Routledge & Kegan Paul Ltd., from *The British Journal of Sociology*, Vol. 16, No. 1, March 1965, pp. 3–15.

in German, and Morselli (1879) and Ferri (1883) in Italian.[6] There
were many others. In terms of sheer bulk of material, suicide was
probably one of the most discussed social problems of the nineteenth
century.[7] By the time at which Durkheim wrote, a substantial number
of empirical correlations had been established linking suicide rates
with a range of social factors. Later writers confirmed Falret's contention that suicide rates tend to rise during periods of rapid social
change and in times of economic depression;[8] and that rates vary
positively with socio-economic position, being highest in professional
and liberal occupations, and lowest among the chronically poor.[9] The
fact that suicide rates are higher in urban localities than in rural areas
was extensively documented.[10] Some writers claimed to have shown
that suicide rates co-vary with crime rates, but are inversely related
to rates of homicide.[11] Wagner was perhaps the first to identify clearly
a direct relationship between rates of suicide and the religious de-
nominations of Protestanism and Catholicism, but this was quickly
substantiated by later investigation.[12] It was widely shown that
suicide rates vary by sex, age and marital status; as well as by time
of the year, day of the week, and hour of the day.[13]

Some writers gave prominence to racial and climatic factors in
accounting for differential suicide rates. Most, however, questioned
this type of explanation, and looked instead to social causes. Quetelet
placed great emphasis, as Durkheim later did, on the relative stability
of suicide rates from year to year in comparison with other demographic data,[14] attempting to interpret differences between suicide
rates in terms of variations in the "moral density" of society. Many
writers attributed the general rise in suicide rates to the dissolution
of the traditional social order and the transition to industrial civilization, with its concomitants of increasing "rationality" and individualism—an explanation close to that later elaborated by Durkheim.[15]

Most of the early nineteenth-century investigations of suicide took
for granted a close relationship between suicide and mental disorder.
The notion that suicide derived from "miserable insanity"[16] was
clearly in part a survival of the belief that suicide is of diabolical
inspiration, a view which, under the impress of the Church, held
sway until some way through the seventeenth century. The theory
that suicide is always associated with some form of mental disorder
was, however, given its most definitive formulation in Esquirol's
classic *Maladies mentales* (1838).[17] "Suicide", asserted Esquirol,
"shows all the characteristics of mental disorders of which it is in
fact only a symptom."[18] In this view, since suicide is always symptomatic of mental illness, it is to the causes of the latter that the
student of suicide must turn in order to explain the phenomenon.

The nature and distribution of mental disorder in any population determine the distribution of suicide in that population.

The question of how far, and in what ways, suicide is related to mental disorder became a major problem occupying writers on suicide during the latter half of the nineteenth century, and was discussed at some length by Durkheim.

II

The originality and vitality of Durkheim's work did not lie in the empirical correlations contained in *Le Suicide*: virtually all of these had been previously documented by other writers. Durkheim took material directly from the works of Legoyt, Morselli and Wagner, and used Öttingen's *Die Moralstatistik* extensively as a source of data.[19] Where Durkheim's work marked a decisive advance was in the attempt to explain previous findings in terms of a coherent sociological theory. Previous writers had used a crude statistical methodolgy to show relationships between suicide rates and a variety of factors: Durkheim developed this technique in order to support a systematic sociological explanation of differential suicide rates. Durkheim was by no means the first to recognize that suicide rates could be explained sociologically;[20] but no writer before Durkheim had presented a consistent framework of sociological theory which could bring together the major empirical correlations which had already been established.

A basic contention made by Durkheim in *Le Suicide* is that problems relating to the analysis of suicide rates can be separated in a clear-cut fashion from those relating to the psychology of the individual suicide. The suicide rate of a society or community "is not simply a sum of independent units, a collective total, but is itself a new fact *sui generis*, with its own unity, individuality and consequently its own nature..."[21] The factors governing the distribution of suicide are "obviously quite distinct" from those determining which *particular* individuals in a group kill themselves.[22] Having rejected inherited insanity, psychological imitation, race and various "cosmic" factors as possible determinants of the distribution of suicide, Durkheim located these determinants in aspects of social structure, distinguishing three main types of suicide: egoistic, anomic and altruistic. Strictly speaking, these are not types of suicide, but types of social structure producing high rates of suicide. "Egoism" refers to a low level of "integration" in social structure; anomie to a dearth of regulative norms in society. Egoistic and anomic suicide are the predominant types in modern society.

Durkheim used the analysis of suicide explicitly as a platform for the vindication of his sociological method. He did not limit himself, moreover, to delineating a sociological analysis of suicide rates, but tended to argue as if the role of psychology in the explanation of suicide would be a subordinate one.[23] In a general way Durkheim's polemic was directed at Tarde and other "reductionist" schools of social thought.[24] More specifically, however, Durkheim's argument was also directed at Esquirol and other representatives of the view that suicide rates could be explained directly in terms of the distribution of mental disorder.

The publication of *Le Suicide* stimulated divergent reactions in France. Durkheim's immediate disciples were prepared to adopt the text as a model of sociological method. Others, particularly in the field of psychology, were equally ready to reject entirely the claims for sociology advanced in the book. Most psychologists and psychiatrists continued to be heavily influenced by the "psychiatric thesis", stemming from the position established by Esquirol, in relation to suicide. This thesis entailed the following four propositions: (1) suicide is always the product of some psychopathological condition;[25] (2) the causes of suicide must thus be sought in the causes of the relevant types of mental disorder; (3) these causes are biological rather than social;[26] (4) sociology can therefore make little if any contribution to the analysis of suicide.

III

The foundations were thus laid for a controversy which, although part of a broader conflict between Durkheim's advocacy of sociology as an autonomous discipline and the resistance of its detractors, did not become fully-developed until the period following the First World War, after the death of Durkheim himself.

The first major assault on Durkheim's position was launched in 1924 by de Fleury, a psychiatrist, in his *L'Angoisse humaine*.[27] Following broadly the theoretical standpoint established by Esquirol, and supporting his argument with case-history material, de Fleury reiterated that suicide is always derivative of mental disorder, the causes of which are biopsychological rather than social. Suicidal tendencies, he concluded, are found mainly in persons suffering from cyclical depressive disorder (cyclothymia). This type of affective disorder, stated de Fleury, depends upon inherited characteristics of temperament: the disposition to suicide is biologically "built into" such individuals. The tendency to states of morbid depression, moreover, according to de Fleury, develops largely independently of the objective circumstances of the individual. It is of little consequence, therefore, whether the individual is integrated into a group or not. While fluctuations in suicide rates can possibly be linked in a very crude way to social or economic changes, their role in the aetiology of suicide is even then only a secondary one: such changes may only serve to partially "cluster" the suicides of individuals who would in any case kill themselves at a later date. The state of morbid anxiety into which depressive individuals periodically lapse, wrote de Fleury, "is, in the immense majority of cases, the only cause of suicide".[28]

In 1930 Halbwachs published *Les Causes de suicide*, a work intended to review, in the light of later statistics, the conclusions reached by Durkheim thirty years earlier.[29] Halbwachs provided confirmation in detail of Durkheim's generalizations relating suicide rates to family structure[30] and religious denomination.[31] However, Halbwachs emphasized that it is illegitimate to use, as Durkheim did, statistical relationships of this sort independently as if each had a separate significance. The influence of family structure, for instance, cannot, argued Halbwachs, be detached from "a much broader social milieu".[32] The same is true of the religious factor. In France, for example, the more strongly Catholic groups tend to be also the most conservative and "traditional", and have a strongly integrated family structure. It is not possible to separate the specifically religious practices from a broader community structure of which they are one part. According to Halbwachs, several of the factors which Durkheim isolated as producing a high suicide rate combine in the characteristics of modern urban life. Halbwachs provided an extensive comparative analysis of suicide rates in urban and rural areas showing that, in general, rates are highest in large towns.[33] Reviewing Durkheim's propositions regarding suicide and social change, through an examination of the relationship between fluctuations in the business index and suicide in Germany during the period 1880–1914, Halbwachs confirmed that suicide rates do tend to rise during economic crisis. The increment in the rate does not, however, take place only at the lowest point of a trough, but is spread over the whole phase of the depression. Durkheim's thesis that rates of suicide rise during periods of marked economic prosperity was not substantiated: on the contrary, during such periods suicide rates tend to decline.[34]

Although his statistical analysis is generally supportive of Durkheim's, Halbwachs did not develop the typology of egoistic, anomic and altruistic suicide proposed by Durkheim.[35] In Halbwachs' own theory, suicide is attributed directly to the "social isolation" of the suicidal individual. Suicide rates are high in social structures promoting the detachment of individuals from stable relationships with others—as is the case, according to Halbwachs, in urban communities.[36] Halbwachs discussed in some detail the psychiatric thesis advanced by de Fleury. According to Halbwachs, only a minority of suicides are associated with a recognizable form of mental disorder;[37] and these, he claimed, are not incompatible with his theory. "Normal" suicides in Halbwachs' theory may become detached from relationships with others as a consequence of many factors, which include many of the "motives" popularly offered for suicide—such as failure in business, unrequited love, chronic illness, etc. But "pathological" suicides also derive from the social isolation of the suicidal individual: it is precisely those mental disorders producing "a failure of adaptation between the individual and his *milieu*"[38] which culminate in suicide. In both "normal" and "pathological" suicides, Halbwachs concluded, the "true" cause of the suicide is a social *hiatus* which surrounds the individual suicide. In reaching this conclusion, although questioning Durkheim's analysis in several respects, Halbwachs reaffirmed the validity of the sociological approach to suicide: suicide is primarily a social phenomenon.[39]

Those who were favourable to the psychiatric thesis found Halbwachs' arguments unconvincing. Courbon, for example, reviewing Halbwachs' book, accused the latter of an incompetent assessment of the relevance of psychopathology to suicide. Courbon repeated that suicide derives universally from pathological anxiety and depression and that these are "through their purely biological nature" as completely independent of social factors as are colour of eyes or reaction time.[40] In his *Psychologie pathologique du suicide* (1932), Delmas summed up the views of the psychiatric school on the question of suicide, and made an explicit attempt to destroy the sociological standpoint of Durkheim and Halbwachs.[41] Social factors cannot possibly play a significant role in the aetiology of suicide, argued Delmas, since suicide takes place in such small proportion to any population. It sounds impressive to say that one country A has a suicide rate of 450 (per million) per year, while another country B has a rate of only 50. But invert these proportions, and we have a comparison of the following order: 999,550 (per million) per year *do not* commit suicide in country A, while 999,950 do not commit suicide in country B. The proportional difference between those who do *not* commit suicide is very small indeed. How could we say that there exist general social factors which "protect" 999,950 in every million in country B, whereas only 999,550 are "protected" in country A?[42]

Using the same psychiatric classification as de Fleury, Delmas repeated that the "fundamental cause" of suicide[43] is pathological depression; and that the tendency to depressive states develops largely independently of the external situation of the individual. Endogenous changes, according to Delmas, produce with advancing age more profound and protracted states of melancholic anxiety: this, he claimed, rather than any changes in the social position of the ageing individual, is the major factor behind the common observation that suicide rates tend to rise with increasing age. The same can be said, he concluded, of other apparent direct causal relationships between suicide and social phenomena. If suicide rates are higher among unmarried than among married people, it is because depressives tend not to marry. It is nevertheless the endogenous process of depression which is aetiologically crucial; the vast majority of suicides "are exclusively the result of a biopsychological mechanism into which nothing social enters . . ."[44]

In *Le Suicide* (1933) Blondel finally attempted to reconcile the *thèse psychiatrique* with the *thèse sociologique*.[45] According to Blondel, in "normal" suicides the social situation of the suicidal individual is a crucial determinant; the depressive personality, however, is born with a constitutional tendency towards pathological depression, and this is the "deep-lying cause" of his suicide. Although the role of social factors in the aetiology of cyclothymic suicides is less central than in "normal" suicides, in both cases there is nevertheless an interaction between the social and the non-social.[46] This view was endorsed by several other writers.[47] Dombrowski, for example, in his *Les Conditions psychologiques du suicide* (1929) had stressed that the controversy could only be resolved by examining the interplay between psychological and social factors.[48] Psychopathological states, he suggested, produce in certain individuals a *Minderwertigkeit* which promotes a "disharmony" in social relationships, thus leading to the social isolation of the individual emphasized by Halbwachs as the "true" cause of suicide.[49]

IV

Little further progress in the resolution of the controversy was made before the intervention of the Second World War, and since the war suicide has not received the same amount of attention as a test problem in French sociology.[50] This is partly due to a pronounced shift in the predominant character of French sociology. Until the period immediately preceding the Second World War, sociology in France remained firmly set in the theoretical cast moulded by Durkheim. Although some of Durkheim's most able followers were killed in the First World War, several of the prominent figures (such as Halbwachs) survived and dominated the sociological scene up to 1940.

In the late nineteen-thirties, and following the Second World War, however, sociology in France began to come increasingly under the influence of other theoretical traditions.[51] In his *Essais de sociologie* (1939) Gurvitch propounded a detailed series of criticisms of the fundamental tenets of Durkheim's sociology, attempting to expose certain of the major theoretical questions with which Durkheim had concerned himself as "pseudo-problems"—problems falsely posed.[52] One such "pseudo-problem" involves the debate over "society" and "the individual". Both Durkheim and Tarde, Gurvitch emphasized, while engaging in a protracted polemic with each other, made a false opposition between society and the individual; there is, in fact, a constant "reciprocity" between the "individual" and the "social." In an article published in 1952, Bastide took up again the suicide controversy within the framework laid down by Gurvitch, arguing that the controversy hinged upon the same mistaken conception of the relationship between society and the individual.[53] The psychiatric thesis states that suicide is an "individual" matter, since it depends mainly upon "internal" biopsychological mechanisms, and that consequently the study of suicide is a psychological rather than a sociological matter. But this argument only has any weight if we accept the ontological realism of a dichotomy between society and the individual. To admit that psychology can properly contribute to the analysis of suicide does not mean that suicide, in certain aspects— particularly as a demographic phenomenon—cannot be studied sociologically; conversely, to accept that social factors play a role in the aetiology of suicide does not entail the exclusion of other factors as having causative force.[54]

Conclusion: suicide and sociological analysis

The suicide controversy in French sociology is of interest not only because of the direct content of the argument. Tracing the origins of the dispute allows an illuminating insight into the historical "depth" which an intellectual controversy may have: the issues involved in the debate were already set out, and not in a radically different guise, in the early nineteenth-century literature on suicide. Through the agency of Durkheim, however, the analysis of suicide became a critical issue in the struggle to establish sociology as a recognized academic discipline in France. This was, of course, largely due to Durkheim's own stage-management; as Lévi-Strauss remarks, "the class occurred on the ground Durkheim had himself chosen: the problem of suicide".[55]

Durkheim's interest in suicide as a research problem was a direct development from his concerns in *De la division du travail social*.[56] But two other factors lay behind his selection of suicide as a topic for a comprehensive investigation. Firstly: the very volume of work which had already been carried out by previous writers provided an abundant source of data which could be used to develop a systematic sociological analysis of suicide. Secondly: suicide appears to be wholly "an individual action affecting the individual only...."[57] The demonstration of the relevance of Durkheim's sociological method to the analysis of an apparently purely "individual" phenomenon had a particular significance in the context of the dispute with Tarde over the nature of social reality. *Le Suicide* represents a brilliant vindication of Durkheim's fundamental thesis that social facts can be studied as "realities external to the individual"[58] as against Tarde's position that the subject-matter of sociology consists in "the sum of consciousness in individuals".[59] The character of the subsequent suicide controversy cannot be fully understood apart from the broader dispute between Durkheim and Tarde. As Gurvitch has shown, the Durkheim–Tarde debate depended in part upon a fruitless argument about the primacy of the "social" over the "individual". The degree of interdisciplinary rivalry which became manifest in the suicide controversy was largely contingent upon the acceptance of the same misconceived ontological dichotomy.

The major substantive issue separating the *thèse sociologique* from the *thèse psychiatrique* concerns the "pathological" nature of suicide. In one sense this question is easily resolved; since suicide is in all societies statistically a rare phenomenon, considered in terms of deviation from the majority suicide is necessarily an "abnormal" act. But the real problems are the extent to which suicide must be explained in terms of factors producing recognized forms of mental disorder, and the relationship of *these* factors to variables of social structure. There is no systematic evidence to support the contention that suicide is universally associated with identifiable forms of mental illness.[60] It is probable that most suicides are preceded by some form of depression: but only in a minority of cases is this part of a recurrent pathological depressive disorder.[61] Moreover, only a small proportion of individuals suffering from depressive disorder actually attempt or commit suicide.[62] Empirically, therefore, the *thèse psychiatrique* has not been borne out by later research.

The question of the relationship between suicide and mental disorder served, however, as a cloak for the real theoretical problem in the French suicide controversy: the relevance of sociology to the explanation of suicide. As has been indicated, the dispute depended at least partly upon a misconception shared by both sides and integral to the Durkheim–Tarde debate: that suicide is "fundamentally" either a "social" or an "individual" phenomenon.[63] It It would be facile, however, to dismiss the core of the dispute as a "pseudo-problem". The relationship between social and psychological factors in the aetiology of suicide is a focal problem in suicide theory, and one which bears directly upon the analysis of other phenomena which can be construed in terms of rates (e.g. homicide, crime and delinquency, or divorce).

It was Delmas' contention that, since suicide is statistically infrequent in relation to the total population of a society, social factors cannot play a significant role in its aetiology. The only necessary implication of this argument, in fact, is that sociology cannot furnish a *complete* explanation of suicide since only a small proportion of those in, for example, a loosely integrated community actually kill themselves. But to pose the question: why are suicide rates *so small*? does allow a clearer insight into the error of Durkheim's supposition that the explanation of incidence,[64] as a psychological problem, can be conceptually and methodologically separated from the sociological analysis of suicide rates. In Durkheim's conception, optimally integrated social structures "protect" their component individuals against suicide; in loosely integrated structures, or in states of anomie, the members of the group are less "protected". In the former conditions, suicide rates will be low; in the latter, rates will correspondingly increase. The question of why individual A commits suicide—why A is a suicidal personality—while B, in an identical social situation, does not, is, according to Durkheim, a psychological matter, and not relevant to the explanation of rates: in an economic depression, for example, it will be A, rather than B, who commits suicide. However, to ask: why are rates so small?, which is clearly a central question in the aetiology of any rate, is to ask: *why are most of the population "B"s rather than "A"s*? Such a question, the answer to which depends upon an understanding of the factors producing suicidal propensities in the individual, is directly relevant to an explanatory assessment of suicide rates. The factors governing the distribution of suicide in a community cannot therefore be usefully considered in isolation from those determining why individual A commits suicide while individual B does not, i.e. apart from the study of suicidal personality. Durkheim's position is given a spurious plausibility by the assimilation of an ideographic question (why did this *particular* individual A commit suicide?) to the more important general psychological problem (why does a particular *type* of individual commit suicide?). The answer to the first question depends partly upon the investigation of strictly "individual" factors in the particular suicide's life-history; the answer to the second question entails a generalized psychological theory of suicidal personality.

This has important implications. Advance in theory since Durkheim published *Le Suicide* has been limited indeed: writers have offered substitute terms to embody, often in less precise formulation, Durkheim's major concepts; but little has been added in extension of his theory.[65] A major reason for this is that, although the same degree of interdisciplinary rivalry has not developed as among their French counterparts, writers outside of France have tended to follow Durkheim in maintaining a strict conceptual and methodological separation between statistical analyses of suicide rates and case-history studies of individual suicides. It is symptomatic of this separation that in one of the most influential psychological studies of suicide, Menninger's *Man Against Himself*, Durkheim is not even mentioned.[66] While the theoretical literature on the psychology of suicide is fragmentary and tentative in character, there are certain ideas, based mainly upon the psycho-analytic theory of depression, which emerge from it.[67] The major proposition of this theory is that suicidal tendencies in the individual can be interpreted as aggression stimulated by external objects, but displaced against the self, a process governed basically by the nature of super-ego formation. Further advance in theory might be obtained by the establishment of connections linking "suicidogenic" social structure (e.g. egoism/anomie) with the determinants of suicidal personality as conceived in psychoanalytic theory.[68] That fruitful lines of relationship are potentially open to development has already been demonstrated by Henry and Short in their *Suicide and Homicide*, which examines correlation between suicide rates and certain social variables in terms of such a framework.[69]

There are also important empirical lines of convergence between sociological and psychological studies of suicide which offer as yet unexplored research possibilities. Egoistic suicide in Durkheim's conception derives from a low level of integration in social structure. If "low integration" is considered in terms of the individual member of the group it can be said that it entails the relative detachment of the individual from defined relationships with others. A social structure which is loosely integrated tends to promote the isolation of individuals from closely structured relationships. It was this aspect of Durkheim's theory which was taken up by Halbwachs. Now one finding which emerges from studies of case-histories of individual suicides is that many suicidal individuals from childhood either (1) show an incapacity to form lasting affective relationships with others, or (2) depend excessively upon one single relationship with another, usually a parent. Here we are evidently approaching the same net result—the social isolation of the individual—from the standpoint of the suicidal personality. The essential question here is: under what conditions does social isolation become psychologically "translated" into a phenomenal situation which the individual defines as "suicidal"?

In conclusion, it should be emphasized that in this paper I have limited myself to the consideration of certain important problems relevant to the sociology of suicide raised in the French suicide controversy. I have not attempted a thorough analysis of Durkheim's *Le Suicide*, nor have I tried to provide an overall discussion of the present state of research into suicide. Both of these tasks would have to be tackled in a more comprehensive survey of problems involved in the sociological analysis of suicide.

NOTES

1 E. Durkheim, *Le Suicide,* Paris, Alcan, 1897. All further references are to the English translation: *Suicide* (trans. J. A. Spaulding and G. Simpson), London, Routledge and Kegan Paul, 1952.

2 A description of some of these works can be found in L. G. Crocker, 'The discussion of suicide in the eighteenth century', *Journal of the History of Ideas,* 13 January 1952, pp. 47–52.

3 See, for example, J. Dumas, *Traité du suicide*, Amsterdam, 1773, p. 2.

4 J. P. Falret, *De l'hypochondrie et du suicide,* Paris, 1822.

5 Ibid., pp. 5–6.

6 A-M. Guerry, *Essai sur la statistique morale de la France,* Paris, 1833; E. Lisle, *Du suicide,* Paris, 1956; A. Legoyt, *Le suicide ancien et moderne,* Paris, 1881; A. Quetelet, *Sur l'homme et le développement de ses facultés* (2 vols.), Paris, 1835; *Du système social et des lois qui le régissent,* Paris, 1848; A. Wagner, *Die Gesetzmässigkeit in den scheinbar willkürlichen menschlichen Handlungen,* Hamburg, 1864; T. G. Massaryk, *Der Selbstmord, Vienna,* 1881; E. Morselli, *Il suicidio,* Milan, 1879; E. Ferri, *L'omicidio-suicidio,* Turin, 1883. Studies of suicide published in English borrowed extensively from the French and German writers: F. Winslow *The Anatomy of Suicide,* London, 1840; J. J. O'Dea, *Suicide,* London, 1885.

7 A partial bibliography of works up to 1889 can be found in E. Motta, *Bibliografia del suicidio,* Bellinzona, 1890; a fuller bibliography is included in H. Rost, *Bibliographie des Selbstmords,* Augsburg, 1927.

8 See, for example, Lisle, op. cit.

9 In his statistical analysis of suicide in London, for example, Jopling echoed the conclusions of other writers in finding rates to be highest among the 'upper and middle classes'. R. T. Jopling, *Statistics of suicide,* London, 1852, p. 9.

10 As early as 1840, in cognizance of the differential distribution of suicide between urban and rural areas, Cazauvieilh made a specific study of suicide in rural area in France, showing some exceptions to the general

rule that suicide rates are highest in urban areas. See J. B. Cazauvieilh, *Du suicide,* Paris, 1840, pp. 2–3 and ff.

11 See, for example, A Corre, *Crime et suicide,* Paris, 1891; Ferri, op. cit.

12 cf. Masaryk, op. cit., pp. 141–241.

13 The most thorough statistical analysis of these factors is given in Morselli, op. cit.

14 'Not only are suicides, each year, of almost the same quantity; but, separating rates for groups in terms of the instruments used, we find the same constancy.' Quetelet, *Du système social et des lois qui le régissent,* p. 88.

15 Cf. esp. Masaryk, op. cit. The very earliest objective studies of suicide at the turn of the nineteenth century linked rising suicide rates to weakening religious beliefs and customs. A typical discussion is given in A. Brierre de Boismont, *Du suicide et de la folie-suicide,* Paris, 1856, ch. 4, pp. 352–89.

16 The phrase is taken from S. Miller, *The Guilt, Folly and Sources of Suicide,* New York, 1805, p. 14.

17 E. Esquirol, *Des maladies mentales* (2 vols.), Paris, 1838.

18 Ibid., Vol. I, p. 639.

19 A. von Öttingen: *Die Moralstatistik,* Erlangen, 1882.

20 Most writers recognized a division of the causes of suicide into two types; 'the external or social, and the internal or personal'. O'Dea, op. cit., Preface, pp. v–vi.

21 Durkheim, op. cit., p. 46.

22 Ibid., p. 51.

23 Ibid., esp. bk 3, ch. I.

24 Tarde's characteristic point of view is clearly enunciated in his *Études de psychologie sociale,* Paris: Giard and Brière, 1898.

25 Many psychologists took a less extreme view than this. Viallon, for example, after a survey of the problem, concluded that 'insanity is the most important, but not the exclusive, cause of suicide'. Viallon, 'Suicide et folie', *Annales médico-psychologiques,* 25, July–August 1901 (pt. I), p. 22.

26 Esquirol himself did allow that social factors play a certain role in the aetiology of mental disorder and, consequently, suicide. Cf. Esquirol, op. cit., p. 526 ff.

27 M. de Fluery, *L'Angoisse humaine,* Paris; ;Editions de France, 1924. Prior to de Fleury's book, Bayet's important historical survey of suicide appeared, written from a broadly sociological standpoint, and explicitly indebted to Durkheim. A. Bayet, *Le suicide et la morale,* Paris: Alcan, 1922.

28 De Fleury, op. cit., p. 79.

29 M. Halbwachs, *Les Causes du suicide,* Paris: Alcan, 1930.

30 Ibid., pp. 197–239. Halbwachs made an important survey of variations in modes of suicide registration in different countries in Europe, concluding that international comparisons of suicide rates can only be made with great caution. See pp. 19–39.

31 Ibid., pp. 241–86.

32 Ibid., p. 238.

33 Ibid., p. 266 ff.

34 Ibid., pp. 362–74.

35 Halbwachs distinguished between suicide and self-sacrifice. The latter category of self-destruction (which takes in most of Durkheim's type of altruistic suicide), according to Halbwachs, is so different from 'individ-

ualized' suicide, that it is impossible to fit the two usefully within the same explanatory framework. Ibid., pp. 451–80.

36 Halbwachs' theory, however, is a logical development of Durkheim's. Durkheim was more concerned to outline types of social structure producing high rates of suicide. Halbwachs said little about the broad structural conditions promoting the detachment of individuals from stable social relationships.

37 Serin carried out an intensive study of 450 cases of suicide in Paris, identifying about two thirds of them as associated with some form of psychopathological condition. S. Serin, 'Une enquête médico-sociale sur le suicide à Paris', *Annales médico-psychologiques,* 2 November 1926, pp. 536–62. Halbwachs, however, questioned her results, claiming that only a minority of her cases could be properly identified as 'pathological' in character. Halbwachs, op. cit., p. 381 ff.

38 Ibid., p. 426.

39 Ibid., p. 448. In other publications Halbwachs tried to show the relevance of sociology to the explanation of psychological functions. *Les Cadres sociaux de la mémoire,* Paris: Presses Universitaires, 1952, developed the thesis that memory has been only treated by psychologists as a function of the 'isolated individual' whereas in fact memory is essentially a social phenomenon. An ambitious survey of social motivation was attempted in B. Raynaud, M. Halbwachs *et al.: Analyse des mobiles dominants qui orientent l'activité des individus dons la vie sociale,* Paris: Librairie du Recueil Sirey, 1938 (2 vols.).

40 P. Courbon; review of Halbwachs' *Les Causes du suicide. Annales médico-psychologiques,* new series 1, March 1931, p. 322.

41 F. Achille-Delmas, *Psychologie pathologique du suicide,* Paris: Alcan, 1932.

42 Ibid., p. 49 ff.

43 Delmas separated off 'true' suicide from other kinds of self-destruction. Suicide of a sacrificial nature; suicide prior to the termination of a fatal illness; and the suicide of psychotics are all examples of 'pseudo-suicide'. 'True' suicide, according to Delmas, involves the possibility of choice of life or death on the part of the individual. Ibid., p. 87 ff. This closely echoes a distinction made almost a century before by Falret. Falret, op. cit., pp. 3–5.

44 Ibid., p. 234.

45 Ch. Blondel, *Le Suicide,* Strasbourg: Librairie University d'Alsace, 1933. Immediately prior to the publication of Blondel's book, Bonnafous made a spirited defence of the *thèse sociologique* in a review article of Delmas' work. M. Bonnafous, 'Le suicide: thèse psychiatrique et thèse sociologique', *Revue philosophique,* 115, May–June 1933, pp. 456–475.

46 Blondel, op. cit., p. 119 ff. See also Blondel's discussion in his *Introduction à la psychologie collective.* Paris: Colin, 1927, ch. 4, pp. 90–104.

47 For example, B. Abderrahman, *Du suicide émotif et suicide non pathologique* (M.D. thesis), Paris: Rodstein, 1933; P. Friedman, 'Sur le suicide', *Revue française de psychanalyse,* 8, 1935, pp. 106–48.

48 C. Drombrowski, *Les conditions psychologiques du suicide* (M.D. thesis), Geneva: Imprimerie du Commerce, 1929.

49 Ibid., p. 32.

50 The only important objective study of suicide to be published in France since the war is G. Deshaies: *La psychologie du suicide,* Paris: Presses Universities, 1947. The suicide controversy was also discussed by Deshaies in 'Les doctrines du suicide', *L'Évolution psychiatrique,* January–March

1952, pp. 41–54. A number of philosophical works concerned with suicide have been published in France in recent years. Probably the most well-known is A. Camus's *Le Mythe de Sispyhe*, Paris: Gallimard, 1942. Among the latest discussions of this type are L. Meynard, *Le suicide*, Paris: Presses Universitaires, 1958; and Touraine, *Le suicide ascetique*, Paris: Nouvelles Éditions Debresse, 1960.

51 A useful overall survey of the development of sociology in France is given in C. Lévi-Strauss, 'French sociology', in G. Gurvitch and W. E. Moore (eds.), *Twentieth Century Sociology*, New York: Philosophical Library, 1945, pp. 503–37. A more recent survey is J. Stoetzel, 'Sociology in France: an empiricist view', in H. Becker and A. Boskoff (eds.), *Modern Sociological Theory*, New York: Holt, Rinehart and Winston, 1957, pp. 623–57.

52 G. Gurvitch, *Essais de sociologie*, Paris: Librairie du Recueil Sirey, 1939, pp. 141–2. The same essay is reprinted, with minor alterations, in G. Gurvitch, *La vocation actuelle de la sociologie*, Paris: Presses Universitaries, 1950. Gurvitch's work is not without its critics. Cuvillier has been perhaps the most outspoken critic. See particularly A. Cuvillier, *Introduction à la sociologie*, Paris: Colin (5th ed.) 1954, ch. 4, pp. 84–124; and *Où va la sociologie française?*, Paris: Rivière, 1953.

53 R. Bastide, 'Le suicide du nègre brésilien', *Cahiers internationaux de sociologie*, 12, 1952, pp. 72–90. See also his 'Sociologie et psychologie', in G. Gurvitch (ed.), *Traité de sociologie*, Paris: Presses Universitaires, 1962, p. 71 ff.

54 Ibid., p. 89.

55 C. Lévi-Strauss, op. cit., p. 509.

56 The continuity is evident in an article Durkheim wrote on the demography of suicide, published eleven years before his major study: 'Suicide et natalité: étude de statistique morale', *Revue philosophique*, 26 November 1888, pp. 446–63.

57 Durkheim, *Suicide*, p. 46.

58 Ibid., pp. 37–8.

59 Quoted by Durkheim, ibid., p. 311.

60 Cf. E. Stengel and N. G. Cook, *Attempted Suicide*, London: Chapman and Hall, 1958, p. 14.

61 There is considerable division between psychiatrists over the role of somatic factors in depressive disorders. A good discussion of this problem is given in R. W. White, *The Abnormal Personality*, New York: Ronald Press, 1956, pp. 523–43. Psychiatry in England and America has generally tended to allow a lesser role to heredity and constitution in mental disorder than in France. As Pichot remarks: 'The French psychiatric tradition has always been strongly constitutionalist...' P. Pichot, 'Fance', in L. Bellak, *Contemporary European Psychiatry*, New York: Grove Press, 1961, p. 15.

62 See H. J. Walton, 'Suicidal behaviour in depressive illness', *British Journal of Mental Science* 104, July 1958, pp. 884–91.

63 See also R. Duchac, *Sociologie et psychologie*, Paris: Presses Universitaires de France, 1963, p. 17 ff.

64 See T. Parsons, *The Structure of Social Action*, Glencoe: Free Press, 1937, p. 324.

65 Cf. A. Inkeles, 'Personality and social structure', in R. K. Merton *et al.*, *Sociology Today*, New York: Basic Books, 1959, pp. 249–56.

66 K. Meninger, *Man Against Himself*, New York: Harcourt Brace, 1938.

67 The psychoanalytic theory of suicide is based particularly on Freud's

paper 'Mourning and melancholia', *Standard Edition*, London: Hogarth Press, 1955, vol. 18.
68 Simpson suggested this, in fact, in his Introduction to the translation of *Suicide*, pp. 17–25.
69 A. F. Henry and J. F. Short, *Suicide and Homicide*, Glencoe: Free Press, 1954.

PART II

CHAPTER 6

Theories of Suicide

The dominance of a field of research by one particular work, however brilliant it may be, has consequences which are not wholly desirable. While Durkheim's work has given focus and consistency to later sociological research on suicide, it has also had the effect of confining it within the same sort of approach which he employed. Thus, at least until quite recently, most sociological investigations of suicide have added virtually nothing of significance to Durkheim's theory. Two exceptions to this are the works of Henry and Short, and Gibbs and Martin, both of which, whatever their shortcomings,[1] attempt to go beyond Durkheim. Henry and Short develop a theory which connects social and psychological factors in such a way as to offer an explanation of both suicide and homicide; Gibbs and Martin offer a conception of "status integration" which, they believe, provides a more precise way of validating certain of Durkheim's ideas than was open to the originator himself.

The work of both pairs of authors, however, rests upon the use of correlations involving official statistics of suicide. As both Atkinson and Douglas show, the precision which the use of these statistics appears to offer may in fact be a spurious one. Douglas's book, *The Social Meanings of Suicide*, the main themes of which are summarised in his article reproduced here, attempts a radical critique of the sociological literature on suicide since Durkheim. Most subsequent authors (including both Henry and Short, and Gibbs and Martin), in Douglas's view, have followed Durkheim in holding two assumptions which Douglas believes to be erroneous. Firstly, in examining the differential distribution of suicide among social groups, they have assumed that different cultural values which might relate to suicide can effectively be ignored. But in fact, Douglas emphasizes, the *content* of such cultural values needs to be carefully studied in order to determine what meanings they lend to "suicide". The most comprehensive work in the literature on suicide which takes a similar standpoint to that now called for by Douglas is Albert Bayet's *Le suicide et la morale* (1922). Having surveyed at great length the *mores* relating to suicide in differing periods of European history, Bayet made a distinction between what he called *la morale simple,* and *la morale nuancée.* The first is characteristic of small, simple communities; suicide is regarded unequivocally as a crime, and prohibited in almost all circumstances. The second develops only with the formation of a fairly complex level of urban civilization (as in Greece and Rome, or in modern Europe); here, there are more differentiated values with reference to suicide which regard suicide as permissible in a given range of circumstances.

The second assumption made by most sociologists writing on the subject, which Douglas criticizes, is the view that the particular motives and circumstances which give rise to suicide are irrelevant to a sociological theory of suicide. In Douglas's view, it is precisely one of the most urgent priorities for sociologists to study these in a systematic way: "What is called for is a whole new sociological method for determining and analysing the communicative actions which can be observed and replicated in real-world cases of suicide." This entails examining the various "meanings" with which "suicide" and the notions, actions and events connected with it, are invested in specific cultural settings. It is of particular importance to study the "situated" meanings of suicide: that is, the meanings which a suicidal act has within the immediate situation in which it takes place.

No doubt we must recognize, as Douglas urges, that the man who attempts a suicidal act is not simply "pushed by society" into doing so: he (and any others who may be involved) seeks actively to secure objectives, and defines his act and the situation in which it occurs in relation to these. The conceptions of "self" and "others", of "suicide" and "death" which the individual holds, govern his phenomenal world and are clearly of critical importance in influencing the nature of his act. But the real theoretical problems which Douglas does not discuss, are how far (1) the cultural meanings of suicide (both general and "situated"), and (2) the social circumstances which lead an individual to consider his situation as a potentially "suicidal" one, *are random to the rest of the social structure* of a given community or society. There is actually a major division between social theorists upon the first of these issues on a general level: that is, concerning the degree to which cultural values or ideologies are "emergent" or "autonomous". But all sociologists agree that idea-systems are to some degree contingent upon, and determined by, other parts of society. Durkheim's position on this matter may be not wholly unambiguous; nevertheless it is the most essential implication of his theory that idea-systems are grounded in the basic structures of society. Thus, for example, the development of the moral "cult of the individual", which is associated with egoistic suicide, is an integral part of the growth in the complexity of the division of labour.

In relation to (2), the substance of Durkheim's position is very clear. The social circumstances which are "suicidogenic" are not, or are only to a minimal degree, within the control of the single individual. If *anomie* is prevalent in a certain sector of society, this is a social fact which is true independently of the volition of the individual actor. The social circumstances which lead to suicide are thus to a large extent determined by the organization of society. As Halbwachs pointed out, Durkheim's theory here can in fact be extended to cover most of the more *specific* circumstances leading to suicide.

The main difficulty in establishing a more satisfactory theory of suicide than the one offered by Durkheim is, therefore, that of bringing together Durkheim's emphasis that the actions of the individual who kills himself are determined by factors outside his control (and of which he has no knowledge, or at most is only vaguely conscious of), and the contrary (and equally valid) thesis that the individual is an active creator of social reality. This dialectic between the individual and society can only be adequately grasped through the formulation of conceptual links between motivation and meaning on the one hand, and norms and social relationships on the other. One way in which this might be attempted, is through relating Durkheim's basic theory to the most significant psychological theory of suicide, which stems from the psychoanalytic theory of depression. Some possible lines of thought to this end are suggested in the paper "A typology of suicide".

NOTES

1 For a critique of Henry and Short's theory, see Martin Gold, 'Suicide, homicide and socialisation of aggression', *American Journal of Sociology*, Vol. 63, 1958, pp. 651–61; for a recent assessment of the theory of 'status integration', see William J. Chambliss and Marion F. Steele, 'Status integration and suicide: an assessment', *American Sociological Review*, Vol. 31, 1966, pp. 524–5; and Gibbs's and Martin's reply, ibid., pp. 533–41.

CHAPTER 7

Suicide and External Restraint*

Andrew F. Henry and James Short

Durkheim and others[8] have suggested that suicide varies with the strength of the relational system in which the person is enmeshed. Persons deeply and intimately involved with others should be low suicide risks, while those isolated from meaningful relationships with their fellow men should be high risks. There are four possible tests of this hypothesis using data available for the United States population.

The central transitional sectors of cities are characterized by high residential mobility and extremes of personal and social disorganization. Anonymity, loneliness, and isolation from meaningful interpersonal relationships reach their extremes. On the streets in these areas are found the "homeless men" and cheap apartment-hotel dwellings with a very high rate of turnover. Inhabitants of these "disorganized" areas are not deeply enmeshed in meaningful interaction with other persons. The relational system typically is very weak. Suicide rates in these areas are higher than is outlying residential areas of the city. Studies of the distribution of suicide in Chicago,[1] Seattle and Minneapolis,[14] and London[13] all reveal extreme concentrations of suicide in the central, disorganized sectors of the city.

There is a direct relation between degree of urbanization and suicide rates. The suicide rate in the United States falls steadily from its high point in cities of over 100,000 population to its low point in rural areas. One of the critical differences between rural and urban living is in the stability and continuity of family and neighbourhood life. The strong control exercised by the neighbours on the farm or in the small town contrasts sharply with the anonymity and impersonality of life in the city. These characteristics of the city arc magnified in the central, disorganized sectors. The steady rise in suicide from the tightly knit rural community to the anonymity of the city may reflect the strong relational systems of the rural small-town dweller the relative isolation from meaningful relationships of many of the inhabitants of large cities.[8]

A third measure of the relation between suicide and strength of the relational system can be derived from statistics on suicide by marital status. The degree of involvement in meaningful relationships with other persons is greater, on the average, for the married than for the single, widowed, or divorced. The married are by definition involved in at least one more meaningful relationship than the nonmarried. When the effects of age and sex are held constant, the suicide rate of the married is lower than the suicide rate of the single, the widowed, or the divorced.[8] Suicide is highest for the divorced. When the factor of age is held constant, suicide is higher for the widowed than it is for the single, up to the age of thirty-five. From age thirty-five on, however, the suicide rate of the single is higher than that of the widowed. Strength of the relational system is related to the widowed and single categories in an extremely complex manner. It is probably weaker for the widowed than for the single at the younger ages, when widowhood comes as a greater shock and young family responsibilities are most likely to be disrupted. On the other hand, it is probably stronger for the widowed during the older age periods, when they are more likely to have the benefit of relations with their children grown to adulthood and when the single find their relationships curtailed by increasing mortality of their age group. These are all complex relationships, and our marital status classifications are only relative measures, or indexes, of strength of the relational system,[5, 10] The findings, however, are congruent with the hypothesis that susceptibility to suicide will be lowest for those immersed in a meaningful network of interaction with other persons.

The relation between suicide and age provides a final test of the effect on suicide of involvement in meaningful relationships with other persons. Gerontologists point out that one of the chief problems of the aged is that of finding meaningful groups with which to associate. Our culture, with its emphasis on conjugal relationships, makes it more difficult for family bonds to remain intact and strong with the ageing process. Further, the degree of involvement in relationships within the "family of orientation" varies with age simply as a function of parental mortality. By age fifty-five to sixty-four, the probability that at least one of the two parents will be dead is virtually 1.0.[8] Death of the parents certainly weakens the strength of the relational system of those persons who maintain contact with their parents through the years. The suicide rates rises sharply with age from a low of 4.5 per 100,000 for those aged fifteen to twenty-four, to 27.0 per 100,000 aged fifty-five to sixty-four, and maintains its high level up to age eighty-five and over.[17] Part of the increase may be due to departure of children from the home; yet this fact does not explain the rise adequately, since the increase occurs for the single as well as for the married. The direct relation between suicide and age is also to some extent a function of sex. Schmid and Van Arsdol find that the suicide of males in Seattle increases with age, but suicide of females rises to middle age and decreases thereafter.[15] It seems probable that our cultural pattern of female dependency is reflected in the lowered suicide rates of aged females. That is, while aged males may be allowed to drift, thus weakening the strength of their relational bonds, the aged mother is more likely to be taken care of by one of her children. Much further research on this question is needed before this interpretation can be given more than very tentative standing.

In summary, the suicide rate is higher in the central, disorganized sectors of cities than in the outlying residential areas; it is higher in cities than in rural areas; it is higher for the single, widowed, and divorced than for the married; and, finally, it is higher for the old than the young. These relationships may reflect differences in the degree of isolation from meaningful relationships of those in the categories we have examined.

Since the suicide rate is related both to status position and to strength of the relational system, it becomes reasonable to ask whether these two variables include some common element which might explain their association with suicide. What is common to high status position and isolation from social relationships which might account for the very high suicide rates accompany these conditions? And conversely what is common to low status position and intense involvement in relationships with others which might account for the relative immunity these two conditions provide against suicide? Henry and Short suggest a common element in their concept of "external restraint".

> Weber has defined the term "social relationship" to denote "the behaviour of a plurality of actors insofar as, in its meaningful content, the action of each takes account of that of the others and is oriented in these terms." If the action of each "takes account of that of the others", the behaviour of one party to a "social" relationship must, by definition, suffer some degree of restraint to make it conform to the wishes and expectations of the other party to the relationship.
>
> Let us assume: (a) that present in every "social" or "cathectic" relationship is an element of restraint which acts to curb action or behaviour of parties to the relationship; (b) that this element arises directly out of the relationship and is

external to the personalities of the individuals who are a party to the relationship; (c) that acceptance of the element of restraint by each party to the relationship is a condition of the continuation of the relationship. [Ref. 8, page 74.]

With these assumptions, it follows that behaviour of a person involved in a "social" relationship as defined will be subject to a greater degree of "horizontal external restraint" than behaviour of a person not involved in a social relationship. Further, as the number of social relationships in which the person is involved increases, the amount of horizontal external restraint over his behaviour will increase. The degree to which the persons's behaviour is required to conform with the demands and expectations of others increases with the number of social relationships in which the person is involved. We have shown that the risk of suicide decreases as the number of social relationships increases. Since the degree of horizontal external restraint over behaviour increases with the number of relationships, let us suggest tentatively that the risk of suicide decreases as the degree to which behaviour is required to conform to the demands and expectations of others increases. Behaviour of the isolated person is freed from the requirement that it conform to the expectations of others. And the risk of suicide for the isolated is very high.

We have argued that behaviour of a person who is more involved in social relationships is subject to greater horizontal external restraint than is behaviour of a person not so involved in social relationships. Let us suggest further that behaviour of a person playing the subordinate role in a social relationship is subject to greater "vertical" external restraint than behaviour of the person playing the superordinate role. Negroes, women, enlisted men, and low income persons, in their relationships with whites, men, officers and high income persons on the average play the subordinate roles in the relationships. Members of the high status categories tend to play the superordinate role in their relationships with others.

The risk of suicide increases as position in the status hierarchy rises. Since the degree of "vertical" external restraint over behaviour is greater, on the average, for the low status than for the high status category, we may suggest that the risk of suicide decreases as the degree of "vertical" external restraint over behaviour increases. Behaviour of the high status person playing many superordinate roles—like behaviour of the isolated person—is freed from the requirement that it conform to the demands and expectations of others. External restraints over behaviour are minimal and the suicide risk is high. Behaviour of the low status person playing many subordinate roles

—like behaviour of the person immersed in social relationships with others—is subject to heavy requirements that it conform to the demands and expectations of others. External restraints over behaviour are maximal and the risk of suicide is low. This formulation has been summarized elsewhere as follows:

> We have grouped the correlates of suicide in two variables, position in a status hierarchy and degree of relational involvement with other persons. We have further deduced a common element of these two variables which we have labelled external restraint.
>
> Behaviour of subordinate status groups is restrained by the weight of the demands and expectations imposed by other groups higher in the status hierarchy. Behaviour of the Negro is subject to the demands of white persons to a greater extent than behaviour of the white person is subject to the demands of Negroes. The behaviour of an employee is subject to greater restraint than behaviour of his superior. Power is associated with status position and this is recognized by both parties to the relationship, subordinate and superordinate. But it is the behaviour of the subordinate which must conform to the expectations of his superior. The superior is not similarly limited. The vertical restraint demanded by subordinate status is of a different order from the restraint demanded as a condition of collective living. Whether a person is of the highest or the lowest status, as long as he is operating in a network of interpersonal relationships, his behaviour must also conform to the demands and expectations of other parties to the relationship. And this conformity requires that he restrain his behaviour. He must control and modify his impulsives behaviour to meet the definitions operating in the relationship.
>
> *But whether the restraint derives from subordinate status or from interpersonal relations with other persons, it seems to provide immunity from suicide.* [Ref. 8, page 80. Italics added.]

Why does external restraint over behaviour provide this immunity? As the degree to which behaviour is determined and controlled by the demands and expectations of others increases, the share of others in responsibility for the consequences of the behaviour also increases. If a person commits an act primarily because others want him to commit it, others must share in the responsibility for the consequences of the act. The restraining persons can easily be blamed if the consequences of the act are unfortunate. But when an act is determined exclusively by the self and is independent of the wishes and expectations of others, the self must bear sole responsibility if it results in frustration. Others cannot be blamed since others were not involved in the determination of the act.

We have noted elsewhere that homicide, in contrast with suicide, tends to occur among those groups where behaviour typically is subject to high levels of external restraint. If suicide is the result of aggression flowing inwardly against the self and if homicide results from the outward discharge of aggression against others when aggression is aroused by frustration, it will tend to flow inwardly against the self when the source of the frustration is the self and outwardly against others when the source of frustration is viewed as lying outside the self. The likelihood that the source of frustration will be perceived as lying outside the self is high when a wide sphere of the person's total behaviour is determined by the demands and expectations of others. The likelihood that the self will be blamed is high when a person's behaviour is determined by his own demands and expectations. Aggression will flow against the perceived source of frustration. When external restraints are strong, others will be perceived as the source of frustration, and aggression consequent to frustration will flow outwardly. When external restraints are weak, the self will be perceived as the source of frustration, and the aggression consequent to it will flow inwardly against the self. In extreme cases, it will produce suicide.

If suicide is a form of aggression and if aggression is one consequence of frustration, the suicide rate should increase with increase in frustration and decrease with decrease in frustration. A major source of frustration in the United States is the decline in income experienced during economic depressions. Therefore, we would expect the suicide rate to rise during business depression and to fall during business prosperity. This relationship is so strong, in fact, that about two-thirds of the variation in the suicide rate through time in the United States can be accounted for by economic fluctuations.

Ogburn,[11] Thomas,[16] Dublin and Bunzel,[2] and Henry[7] all have demonstrated the existence of this high negative relationship between suicide and the business cycle in the United States, in England, and Wales. The fact that this relationship has been demonstrated with the use of a variety of business and suicide indices during different time periods and in different countries firmly establishes the finding in empirical fact.

Economic data suggest that high income groups suffer the greatest relative loss of income when the business cycle turns downward.[9] If we assume that frustration accompanying business cycles are generated by failure to maintain a constant or rising position in the status hierarchy relative to the status position of others in the same status reference system—and if the upper status groups experience these frustrations more than lower status groups—we would expect suicide of upper status groups to be more sensitive to changes in economic conditions than suicide of lower status groups. Henry has shown this to be the case.[7] Suicide of males is more sensitive to the business cycle than suicide of females; suicide of whites is more sensitives than suicide of nonwhites; suicide of persons living in high-median-rental census tracts in Chicago is more sensitive than suicide of persons living in low rental tracts. Finally, suicide of persons in the young and middle age groups is more sensitive to business fluctuation than suicide of those subject to the relatively low status position of the older age groups in American society.

In each of these four cases, the suicide rate of the higher status category fluctuates with economic conditions more closely than the suicide rate of the lower status category with which it is compared.

It is necessary to point out that the homicide rate also fluctuates with economic conditions. Since homicide also is a form of aggression, the frustration-aggression theory would require that murder rates should respond to frustrations accompanying business cycles in the same way as suicide rates. Persons who commit homicide are, on the average, from low status groups. And since the sharpness of relative loss of income during depression is lower for low status than for high status groups, we are not surprised that the homicide rate is less sensitive to depression than the suicide rate. Among white persons, homicide does increase along with suicide during business depression.[8] But among Negroes, the homicide rate *decreases* during business depression and increases during business prosperity. Negroes who commit homicide represent probably the lowest point in the status hierarchy in the United States. We have noted that suicide of Negroes rises less during depression than suicide of whites, and have argued that this results from the fact that Negroes suffer less frustration (as defined)* during business contraction. Low status Negroes suffer frustration not during business contraction. Low status Negroes suffer frustration not during business contraction but during business expansion. Lying at the very bottom of the status hierarchy, they experience a gain of status *relative* to whites when whites, through economic misfortune, lose their relative position of superiority during business contraction. Distinctions between the races become blurred when there are representatives of each in the bread lines. Frustration comes to the low status Negro when business starts to improve and the whites are able to regain

---

* The frustration to which we refer is that resulting from interference with the assumed "goal response" of maintaining a constant or rising in the status hierarchy relative to the status position of others in the same status reference system.

their position of relative superiority. Whites relative to Negroes experience more frustration during business contraction and less frustration during business expansion, and this fact is reflected in both the suicide and homicide rates of these groups as they are affected by business cycles. Both suicide and homicide are acts of aggression and both increase with frustration.

CONCLUSION

The sociological evidence suggests that suicide is a form of aggression against the self aroused by some frustration, the cause of which is perceived by the person as lying within the self. Failure to maintain a constant or rising position in the status hierarchy relative to others in the same status reference system is one—but by no means the only—important frustration arousing aggression. When this frustration is perceived as being the fault of the self, the aroused aggression may flow against the self. This is most likely when the person is relatively freed from the requirement that his behaviour conform to the demands and expectations of others. Persons of high status and those isolated from meaningful relationships are most likely to blame themselves and commit suicide when frustration occurs, since their behaviour is relatively independent of the demands and expectations of others.

NOTES

1 Ruth S. Cavan, *Suicide*. Chicago: University of Chicago Press, 1928.
2 Louis I. Dublin, and B. Bunzel, *To Be or Not to Be*. New York: Random House, Inc., 1933.
3 Émile Durkheim, *Le Suicide*. Paris: Librairie Felix Alcan, 1897. (Translated by John A. Spaulding and George Simpson, and published as *Suicide*. Glencoe, Ill.: Free Press, 1951.)
4 Norman L. Farberow, 'Personality patterns of suicidal mental hospital patients', *Genetic Psychology Monographs*, 42: 3–79, 1950.
5 William J. Goode, *After Divorce*. Glencoe, Ill.: Free Press, 1956.
6 Maurice Halbwachs, *Les Causes de suicide*. Paris: Librairie Felix Alcan, 1930.
7 Andrew F. Henry, 'The Nature of the Relation between Suicide and the Business Cycle.' (Unpublished Ph.D. dissertation, Department of Sociology, University of Chicago, 1950.)
8 —— and James F. Short, Jr., *Suicide and Homicide: Some Economic, Sociological and Psychological Aspects of Aggression*. Glencoe, Ill.: Free Press, 1951.
9 Horst Mendershausen, *Changes in Income during the Great Depression*. New York: National Bureau of Economical Research, Inc., 1946.
10 F. Ivan Nye, 'Child adjustment in various types of broken homes and in unhappy unbroken homes'. (Paper prepared for the Annual Meeting of the American Sociological Society, 1956.)

11 William F. Ogburn, and Dorothy S. Thomas, 'The influence of the business cycle on certain social conditions', *Journal of the American Statistical Association,* 18 : 305–50, 1942.
12 Albert Rosen, William M. Hales, and Werner Simon. 'Classification of "suicidal" patients', *Journal of Consulting Psychology,* 18 : 359–62, 1954.
13 Peter Sainsbury *Suicide in London: An Ecological Study.* London : Chapman & Hall, Lt., 1955.
14 Calvin F. Schmid, *Suicide in Seattle, 1914–25: An Ecological and Behavioristic Study.* (University of Washington Publications in the Social Sciences.) Seattle University of Washington Press, 1928.
15 —— and M. D. Van Arsdol, Jr., 'Completed and attempted suicides'. *American Sociological Review,* 20 : 273–83, 1955.
16 Dorothy S. Thomas, *Social Aspects of the Business Cycle.* New York : Alfred A. Knopf, Inc., 1927.
17 National Office of Vital Statistics, *Vital Statistics of the United States,* Vol. I, table 8.43, pp. 209–216. U.S. Public Health Service, 1950.
18 National Office of Vital Statistics, Vital Statistics of the United States, Vol. III, table 56. U.S. Public Health Service, 1950.

CHAPTER 8

Status Integration and Suicide*

Jack P. Gibbs and Walter T. Martin

It is for good reason that many students have looked to Durkheim as a source of explanation for the empirical facts of suicide. His work offers the most promising point of departure for anyone interested in developing a theory concerned with differences in suicide rates. This is especially true of his statement that suicide rates vary inversely with the degree of social integration. Indeed, the sole objection to this assertion as a theoretical statement is that the concept of social integration is not clearly defined and consequently cannot be measured. By specifying the empirical referents of integration in terms subject to measurement, Durkheim's statement would be transformed into an empirical proposition capable of being subjected to a variety of tests. This appears to be the logical next step in advancing beyond Durkheim's work, and it is to this problem that this chapter is devoted.

TYPES OF INTREGRATION

The concept of integration has come to have a general meaning, but there is as yet no commonly accepted specific meaning. The highly abstract nature of the general meaning poses difficulties for the researcher attempting to deal with specific empirical variables and leads to consideration of various types of integration.

Virtually everyone who has subjected the term "integration" to conceptual analysis has concluded that several different variables are involved. Gillin, for example, suggests four kinds of integration: relatedness, functional linkage, consistency, and balance among the components of a culture system.[1] Landecker also describes four types of integration: cultural (consistency among the standards of a culture); normative (conformity of the conduct of the group to cultural standards); communicative (exchange of meanings throughout

* Reprinted by permission of University of Oregon Books from *Status Integration and Suicide* by Jack P. Gibbs and Walter T. Martin, 1964, pp. 14–31.

the group); and functional (interdependence among group members through the division of labour).[2]

An analysis of types of integration does not facilitate the testing of Durkheim's theory. In the first place, assuming that the types are exhaustive and mutually exclusive, there is no suggestion as to which is the crucial one for differences in suicide rates. This problem might not be serious if we know that there was a high intercorrelation among the different types of integration, but there is no concrete evidence of this.

The problem of selecting one type of integration as opposed to another for a test of Durkheim's theory is posed in any suggestion which links the concept to empirical variables. Linton's classification of cultural traits suggests a definition of integration: "While the Universals and Specialties within any culture normally form a fairly consistent and well-integrated unit, the Alternatives necessarily lack such consistency and integration."[3] According to Landecker, Linton's observation provides a rationale for measurement: "Thus cultural integration can be measured by determining the proportion of alternatives in relation to universals and specialties. The lower the proportion of alternatives, the higher the degree of cultural integration."[4]

Assuming that it is possible to gauge cultural integration in the manner suggested by Landecker, there is still no suitable theoretical rationale for expecting it to be related to differences in suicide rates. The same may be said, of course, for almost all of the types of integration that have been suggested. Types of integration without solid connection to substantive theory appear to offer limited usefulness for testing Durkheim's theory.

It is most important, when using Durkheim's theory as a point of departure, to make a careful selection of the type of integration and the empirical variables for its measurement; the selection of the type and the operations for its measurement should be governed, by, or at least linked to, Durkheim's observations.

Landecker's normative integration (conformity of the conduct of the group of cultural standards) was considered on the grounds that it reflected Durkheim's emphasis on the consensual nature of integration; but it was rejected in view of the prior observation that suicide rates have been known to vary independently of other forms of deviant behaviour, and because it appeared to be limited in its ability to explain age and sex differentials within a society. In addition, empirical observations arising from the extensive research of Robert C. Angell[5] seem to cast doubt on normative or consensual integration as the key to differences in suicide rates. In preparing an index of integration for selected American cities, Angell used empirical variables that, according to Landecker, are measures of normative integration. Through component measures based on the incidence of selected types of crimes and contributions to community welfare drives, Angell arrived at a composite index of both the degrees of conformity and consensus on values. Although Angell's measure was in many respects crude, one woud expect his index of integration to bear some relationship to suicide rates; however, such is not the case. Porterfield notes that "suicide rates are in no way correlated with [Angell's] indices of social integration";[6] and though it would be foolhardy to cite this as conclusive proof that suicide is not linked to the normative or consensual dimension of integration, it is one reason why we have concentrated on a different conception of integration, which we call "status integration".

INTEGRATION AND SOCIAL RELATIONSHIPS

Throughout Durkheim's comments on the nature of integration there is a constant suggestion that it has to do, in the final analysis, with the strength of the ties of individuals to society. In formal terms, then, it may be said that the stronger such ties are, the lower will be the suicide rate for a society. However, the proposition is only of heuristic value—one does not see individuals tied to a society in any physical sense. To create a testable proposition, it is necessary to establish the equivalent of a physical tie in social life. Such an equivalent is found in social relationships, and the strength of physical ties finds its counterpart in the degree to which these relationships are stable and durable. Thus, the first postulate of the theory of status integration reads: *The suicide rate of a population varies inversely with the stability and durability of social relationships within that population.*

THE DETERMINANT OF THE STABILITY AND DURABILITY OF SOCIAL RELATIONSHIPS

The first postulate is potentially testable in a direct approach. Since social relationships come into being only through social interaction, it is conceivable that the behavioural patterns of each individual in a population could be analyzed in terms of the frequency of interaction with others, the length of time spent in interaction with others, the regularity of the interaction with others, and the length of the individual's life spent in his present pattern of interaction.[7]

Two problems, however, make a direct test of the first postulate impossible at the present time: the present state of sociological knowledge, concepts, and theory regarding social relationships is not adequate for an attempt to make a direct measure of such dimensions as stability and durability; and the amount and type of data needed for measurements of this sort are beyond the scope of existing sources. In the face of these problems, a choice was made not to attempt a direct measure of the stability and durability of social relationships. If the first postulate is accepted, it follows that a statement of the conditions under which the stability and durability of social relationships will be at a maximum is in turn a statement of the conditions under which the suicide rate will be at a minimum.

In Weber's analysis of social relationships, it is suggested that the fundamental condition for the maintenance of a social relationship is the requirements of conformity to the demands and expectations of others.[8] Though Weber's insight deserves recognition, his orientation in the direction of voluntaristic nominalism is not conducive to generalizations about the conditions under which the stability and durability of social relationships will be at a maximum. For the observation to be fruitful, it must be coupled with Durkheim's social realism, which stresses the source of the demands and expectations individuals place on each other and the authority that underlies the requirement for conformity.

Although social relationships are observed and experienced in the form of interaction, on a higher level of abstraction they typically are governed by an authority independent of the particular individuals involved in them. The demands and expectations to which persons must conform if they are to maintain social relationships exist for the most part independently of the will of individuals; unless demands and expectations are sanctioned by an impersonal authority external to the interacting parties, the necessity for conformity is fortuitous. The social sanctions governing social relationships come into being through social identification of the interacting parties in terms of the status occupied by each. The predominant type of social relationship found in a population is thus one in which the status of an individual, his social identification, determines the demands and expectations to which he must conform in order to maintain interaction and his rights (the demands and expectations his society permits him to make of others).

With the above comments serving to emphasize the social character of human relationships, Weber's observation is converted into the second postulate of the theory: *The stability and durability of social relationships within a population vary directly with the extent to which individuals in that population conform to the patterned and socially sanctioned demands and expectations placed upon them by others.*[9]

CONFORMITY TO DEMANDS AND EXPECTATIONS AND ROLE CONFLICT

Although there is little or no relevant evidence, it seems likely that there is considerable difference among populations in the extent to which persons conform to patterned and socially sanctioned demands and expectations. Assuming this to be true, an attempt will be made to postulate the conditions that determine the extent of such conformity in a population.

In sociological terms, the rights of persons occupying a certain status and the demands and expectations that can be placed upon them by others constitute the roles of the status. In other words, along with the social identification of a person's status in a society there is associated a certain configuration of rights, duties, and obligations. These constitute the roles to which an individual with a particular status must conform if he is to maintain stable and durable social relationships.

Conformity to the roles of a particular status would not be difficult if it were not for the fact that each person in a population occupies several statuses simultaneously. Thus, a person is never simply a carpenter and nothing more—he is also a single, married, widowed, or divorced carpenter. In abstract terms, the consequences of this is that a person's social relationships do not stem from his occupancy of only one status. It is the fact that individuals occupy several statuses simultaneously, each of which has numerous roles that bring him into contact with other persons, which binds him to social life.

> Social roles are the institutionally proper ways for an individual to participate in his society and thus satisfy his needs and wants. But roles are also *demands* upon the individual, norms which prescribe certain acts and forbid others. These demands come from the various groups in which the individual holds memberships: his family, peer group, social class, occupational group, and so on.[10]

A man may have numerous social relationships as a consequence of his occupation, but conformity to the roles of his occupational status alone will not maintain his social relationships with his wife and children; the latter can only be maintained by conforming to the roles of husband and father. Conformity to the roles of one status alone is not ordinarily difficult. It is only when conformity to the roles of one status tends to interfere with conformity to the roles of one or more of the other statuses that the individual finds it difficult to maintain his social relationships.

The extent of variability in the stability and durability in social relationships as anticipated by the postulates may best be explained through a consideration of individuals attempting to conform to conflicting roles. For large and consistent differences in this respect to be present among populations, there must be something in the nature of social life other than purely individual choice. We thus arrive at the third postulate of the theory: *The extent to which individuals in a population conform to patterned and socially sanctioned demands and expectations placed upon them by others varies inversely with the extent to which individuals in that population are confronted with role conflicts.*

Ideally, a theory should tie in whenever and wherever possible with existing theory and research findings. Considering that the concept of role is central to sociology, one would expect to find that it has received a great deal of attention. Although this is to some extent true, it has unfortunately played a surprisingly small part in the generation of testable, empirical propositions. As Neiman and Hughes remark, "There are few, if any, predictive studies of human behaviour involving the concept role. If predictive ability is one measure of a scientific construct, this is a telling criticism of the construct."[11] Equally unfortunate is the failure of sociologists taking a macroscopic approach to social life and society to bring the concept into play either directly or, as it is used here, inferentially.

Actually, the concept of role has received considered attention from sociologists. As Neiman and Hughes' survey of the literature shows, the concept has been subjected to analysis by many sociologists, not to mention anthropologists and social psychologists, but this attention not withstanding, "The concept role is at present still rather vague, nebulous and nondefinitive".[12]

The major difference in opinion about empirical referents for "role" lies in whether the term refers to actual behaviour or, as we believe, to norms that prescibe or proscribe behaviour, and which take the form of patterned and socially sanctioned rights, duties, and obligations. The fact that norms are not palpable makes it difficult to deal with roles directly, but does not prevent dealing with them on an inferential level.

A rather surprising amount of theory and research has been devoted to role conflict, a dimension of role central to the present study, and there seems to be general agreement as to what is involved. Laulicht, in his definition, amplifies Seeman's (partially quoted):

> A role conflict situation is one in which a person occupying a given social position is exposed to "incompatible behavioural expectations. Though an apparent incompatibility may be resolved, avoided, or minimized in various ways, the conflicting demands cannot be completely and realistically fulfilled."[13]

Getzel and Guba also agree: "Role conflicts ensure whenever an actor is required to fill two or more roles whose expectations are in some particular inconsistent."[14]

Despite a consensus as to the nature of role conflict, the theory and research that have been devoted to it are not suggestive regarding a crucial question: under what conditions will a large proportion of a population be confronted with a conflict in roles? The failure of existing theory and research to provide an answer to this question lies in a psychological orientation to the phenomenon and the manner in which it has been analyzed. For the most part, studies have dealt with real or alleged conflicts among particular roles: military chaplains,[15] women in the United States,[16] leaders,[17] and military instructors.[18] Related observations, though not dealing directly and explicity with role conflict, may be found in Cottrell's study of the adjustment of the individual to his age and sex role[19] and Parsons observations on the roles associated with age and sex in the United States.[20] The methods employed to identify role conflict, the techniques used to analyse the phenomenon once isolated, and the conclusions reached in these studies do not lend themselves to a theory concerning the conditions which determine or reflect the amount of role conflict that will prevail in a population. It is not even correct to say that studies have produced a testable theory about role conflict as a general phenomenon, on a population level or otherwise. The same may be said for the more experimental studies, in which individuals are called upon to resolve alleged role conflicts in hypothetical situations.[21]

By and large, it would appear that most studies have concentrated less on the prevalence of role conflict within populations than on particular role conflicts, the perception of norms by the individual, conceptual analysis of the different types of role conflict, and the manner or means by which role conflicts can be resolved.[22] A notable exception is Warren's attempt to link role conflict to the concept of social disorganization.[23] However, since he links the two only on a conceptual level without specifying empirical referents for social disorganization, his study does not lend itself to a statement about conditions indicative of a high level of role conflict.

Investigations of role conflict among particular groups of people have, however, overlooked a significant point. Most investigations have concentrated, not on conflicts between the several roles of one status (intra-status roles), but rather on those conflicts arising between a role of one status and another role or roles of one or more other statuses. In Getzel and Guba's study, where the concept of status is ignored, the real or alleged role conflicts encountered by military instructors seem to arise from the fact that they are at once officers and teachers. Similarly, it would appear from Komarov-sky's description that the real or alleged role conflicts of college women arise from the fact that the women must conform simultane-ously to the roles of student and unmarried female,[24] and the role conflicts of military chaplains as described by Burchard may be attributed to the chaplains' attempts to conform to the various roles of military officer and spiritual leader. An awareness of inter-status role conflicts is implicit in the above investigations; our intent is only to make it explicit.

STATUS INCOMPATIBILITY AND ROLE CONFLICT

We have suggested that the condtions which determine the pre-valence of role conflict in a population remain unknown. An ap-proach to the problem necessitates a shift in current emphasis on the psychological dimension of role to its societal correlates. From the sociological point of view, the concept of role is inseparably bound up with the concept of status: "There is an increasing trend toward associating the concept role with that of status. Here per-haps is the most definitive use of the concept, and the one about which there is most consensus."[25]

A role was previously referred to as a socially sanctioned right, obligation, or duty that determines what demands and expectations will be placed upon a person and what demands and expectations that person can make of others. The question as to whom such rights duties, and obligations apply is largely a question of status. The more commonly accepted definitions of status, while not necessarily contradictory or inconsistent, never go beyond linking the term with the concept of position. Linton says, "A status, in the abstract, is a position in a particular pattern",[26] and Hiller defines it as "a place or position in the scheme of social relations".[27]

These definitions capture the general or commonly accepted meaning of "status" but, unfortunately for precise communication, position is a far broader concept than status.[28] For research purposes, we have found it more useful to conceive of a status as a social identification. Every person in a society is socially identified by inclusion in recognized categories to which particular descriptive terms are applied. The status of an individual is thus not revealed by his position in a pattern of social relations (which is first and foremost a highly abstract idea in the mind of a sociologist), but by statements of persons who have knowledge of the individual from interaction with him; these statements to the effect that the person is a man, a barber, a married man, a Negro, a father, are desig-nations of his statuses. All statements, however, which identify him with a recognized category are not status designations, because status implies socially sanctioned rights, duties, and obligations. Thus, a status is a recognized category of persons to which particular socially sanctioned rights, duties, and obligations apply: and these rights, duties, and obligations are the roles of the status.[29]

One crucial assumption made in the present theory is that in any society, given a collection of statuses and their corresponding roles, there is always the potential of conflict among the roles. The roles of any status are such that success in conforming to these roles is contingent upon the nature of the roles of the other statuses that a person occupies. If conforming to the roles of one status interferes with conforming to the roles of another status, an individual is confronted with an incompatibility in statuses. It is of particular importance to note that while this changes the referent of the present analysis from role to status, two statuses are incompatible only in the sense that conformity to one or more roles of one status interferes with conformity to one or more roles of other status. Consequently, two statuses with conflicting roles are incompatible from the behavioural point of view only when they are occupied simultaneously. For example, to pose a hypothetical situation, the fact that conformity to role A of status X tends to interfere with conformity to role B of status Y poses no problem as long as the two statuses are not occupied simultaneously by one and the same individual.

This reasoning results in the fourth postulate of the present theory: *The extent to which individuals in a population are confronted with role conflicts varies directly with the extent to which individuals occupy incompatible statuses in that population.*

STATUS INTEGRATION AND STATUS INCOMPATIBILITY

Since two statuses with conflicting roles are incompatible only insofar as individuals attempt to occupy them simultaneously, the incompatibility of statuses cannot be analyzed directly. What is needed is an observable and measurable phenomenon that reflects the extent to which the occupancy of incompatible statuses prevails in a population. As with role conflict, existing theory and research on status have concentrated on other problems. Although Adams' study of status congruency,[30] Slotkin's on the status of the marginal man,[31] Gold's on the status of the janitor,[32] Schuetz's on the status of the stranger,[33] and Devereaux and Weiner's on the status of nurses[34] all in one way or another touch on the idea of incompatibility,[35] none of them is primarily concerned with that problem.

The inability to closely link the idea of status incompatibility to other studies stems from the fact that sociologists have come to have a somewhat narrow conception of status. It would appear, particularly in American sociology, that there is implicit in the concept an hierarchial connotation which dominates current research and theory. In its concern with stratification and social class, contemporary sociological theory sometimes forgets that status has a meaning independent of hierarchy.[36]

A crucial assumption made in the present theory is that the patterns formed by the occupancy of statuses are indicative of the extent to which the occupancy of incompatible statuses prevails in a population. More specifically, it is assumed that the behaviour of persons moving in and out of statuses is closely related to the compatability of various combinations of statuses. In this connection, it should be obvious that the assumption is only valid when one or both of two statuses is achieved. That is, the scarcity of Chinese males in the continental United States is not assumed to result from an incompatibility between the status male and the status Chinese, but the relatively small proportion of Chinese-Americans who become government officials is assumed to be a case of status incompatibility.

If two statuses have conflicting roles, making them incompatible statuses when occupied simultaneously, it is assumed that they will be less frequently occupied simultaneously than will two statuses with roles that do not conflict. There are three reasons for this. In some cases, the incompatibility is recognized to the point where occupancy is socially discouraged; an example of this is the treatment afforded women who aspire to be airline pilots. In other cases, the person occupying two statuses that are incompatible will give up one or both because of dissatisfaction arising out of attempts to conform to conflicting roles (the large number of divorced bartenders suggests how the demands of an occupational status may create dissatisfaction with a particular marital status). In still other cases, inability to conform to the roles of one or both of the statuses leads to the person's being deprived of one or both statuses; an example is a person who, too old to meet the demands of his occupation, is deprived of that status.

Assuming that the actual occupancy of statuses in a society reflects status compatibility, it follows that the degree of compatibility between two statuses is directly proportional to the extent to which they are occupied simultaneously. As a simple example, consider a hypothetical population in which 75% of the persons with occupation X are married, while only 35% of the persons with occupation Y are married; these two figures constitute a measure of the degree to which being married and having certain specified occupations are compatible.[37] For occupation Y, marriage is far less compatible than it is for occupation X. We must stress, before, proceeding further, that although the extent to which two statuses are occupied simultaneously is taken to be a measure of the degree to which the two are compatible, the mere frequency of occupancy is not what makes them compatible or incompatible. Rather, the degree of compatibility is a function of the extent to which their roles conflict, and the extent to which they are occupied simultaneously follows from this.

It must be emphasized that incompatible statuses are those configurations[38] that are infrequently occupied. In terms of the examples given above, "occupation X-married" is a status configuration that is frequently occupied, while the status configuration "occupation Y-married" is one which is infrequently occupied.[39] The relative frequency with which a status configuration is occupied will henceforth be referred to as the *degree of integration* among the statuses in the configuration or simply as the degree of status integration. Thus, to return to the examples again, if 100% of the persons with occupation X were married persons, there would be maximum integration between this occupational status and marital status. Since every individual occupies a status configuration, the extent to which persons occupy compatible statuses in a population is a function of the degree to which the occupied status configurations conform to a pattern. The pattern of maximum status integration would be found in a population where knowledge of one status of an individual would enable an investigator to predict with certainty all undisclosed statuses. We thus reach the fifth and final postulate of the present theory: *The extent to which individuals occupy incompatible statuses in a population varies inversely with the degree of status integration in that population.*

A REVIEW OF THE POSTULATES

Although the problem of measuring the degree of status integration in a population is a complex one, as the following chapter will show, we have in the concept something that is observable and mensurable. The set of postulates that links status integration to variability in suicide rates is reviewed below.

Postulates No. 1: The suicide rate of a population varies inversely with the stability and durability of social relationships within that population.

Postulate No 2: The stability and durability of social relationships within a population vary directly with the extent to which individuals in that population conform to the patterned and socially sanctioned demands and expectations placed upon them by others.

Postulate No. 3: The extent to which individuals in a population conform to patterned and socially sanctioned demands and expectations placed upon them by others varies inversely with the extent to which individuals in that population are confronted with role conflicts.

Postulate No. 4: The extent to which individuals in a population are confronted with role conflicts varies directly with the extent to which individuals occupy incompatible statuses in that population.

Postulate No. 5: The extent to which individuals occupy incompatible statuses in a population varies inversely with the degree of status integration in that population.

From the above postulation there follows the major theorem: *The suicide rate of a population varies inversely with the degree of status integration in that population.* This theorem is central to the present study. In the following chapter, examples will be given of the type of hypotheses to be tested in line with the theorem, and the operations necessary for the measurement of status integration will be specified.

QUESTIONS REGARDING THE THEORY

One of the major assumptions made in the present theory is that the movement of persons in and out of statuses is indicative of the degree of role conflict in the different status configurations. Perhaps the most serious question that can be raised regarding this assumption relates to the prestige value of statuses. It is possible to conceive of two statuses with conflicting roles having such a high prestige value that individuals persist in attempting to occupy them despite their conflicting roles. The fact that these two statuses are frequently occupied simultanteously would tend to give the impression that they are compatible. If such a factor is present, it can only be assumed that a strain towards consistency is also operating in such a way as to bring about an eventual modification of the roles so as to reduce their conflict.

As a criticism of the theory, it can be suggested that the roles connected with the status of businessman conflict with the roles of the status husband in the United States, but despite this a large proportion of businessmen are married. This frequent occupancy of two allegedly incompatible statuses appears to directly contradict the assumptions of the theory. However, this high degree of integration does not indicate complete compatibility; rather, it means that, in spite of the observations of mutually interfering roles for the statuses of businessman and husband, these two statuses are more compatible than are the configurations businessman-single, businessman-widower, or businessman-divorced. That is, the measure of status integration is a *relative* measure which expresses "more" or "less" compatibility rather than all or none. Thus, the fact that businessmen are typically married does not mean a complete absence of incompatibility between these two statuses.

Another serious question regarding the theory is the obvious inability of status integration to reflect role conflicts among ascribed statuses. Since the movement of individuals in and out of statuses constitutes an underlying assumption, the theory is not applicable to configurations of ascribed statuses.[40] This would not create a problem if ascribed statuses did not have roles associated with them. Such is not the case and the possibility of a configuration of ascribed statuses being incompatible is a reality. However, it is possible that a strain towards consistency is particularly operative for ascribed statuses and that differences among populations with regard to role conflicts among ascribed statuses is negligible.

Throughout the presentation of the theory one salient fact regarding the concept of role was ignored. Conformity to roles involves a range of behaviour. By this fact it can be argued that conflicting roles can be resolved (without a disturbance of the stability and durability of social relationships) through deviation from the type of behaviour that represents maximum conformity to a role. Though the idea is accepted that conformity always involves a range of behaviour, this does not mean that a person may behave in whatever way he pleases and still retain his statuses. It does not follow that conformity to one role interferes no more or no less with conformity to all other roles simply because a range of behaviour is involved. Furthermore, since every role of a status involves a range of permitted behaviour, the factor is a constant from one status to the next. If it is claimed, on the other hand, that some statuses have roles with a wider range of permitted behaviour than others, the fact of the wider range is a part of the roles. This observation applies equally well to the compartmentalization of roles.

An objection to the present theory could be based on the fact that it does not explain why some roles conflict and others do not. In terms of content this is obviously always relative to the specific roles being considered. It is not necessary to single out the roles of each and every status in a population, even if this were possible, and subject them to a type of analysis that would reveal the sources of conflict. It is only necessary as far as the present theory is concerned to assume that when two statuses are infrequently occupied there is something about the two sets of corresponding roles that makes conformity to both difficult. Research in the future may reveal the nature of the conflict between particular roles; for the time being, however, the validity of the theory is not contingent upon such a demonstration.

An appropriate question in a discussion of incompatible statuses is why they come to be occupied at all. Since the present theory does not seek to establish ultimate causes, the observations that follow are at best not suggestive. In the first place, it should be made clear that the theory does not separate and label status configurations as being either compatible or incompatible; compatibility is always a matter of degree. The theory does not hold that it is a physical impossibility to simultaneously occupy statuses with highly conflicting roles; it is possible to maintain occupancy, but the consequences will entail a considerable loss as far as the stability and durability of social relationships are concerned. Thus, the answer to the question as to why some statuses are infrequently occupied must be sought elsewhere.

One very important factor lies in the problematical nature of the effectiveness of social control. Although the degree of incompatibility between two statuses may be socially recognized and their simultaneous occupancy discouraged, this does not prevent all individuals, particularly those confronted with fortuitous circumstances, from making the attempt, any more than the proscription of incest by law and mores makes incest a physical impossibility. Nor is it realistic to say that the social control system in all societies operates to discourage the occupancy of incompatible statuses to an equal degree, be the incompatibility socially recognized, ignored, or undetected. On the contrary, in a society where the value system places an emphasis on romantic marriage, material success, vertical mobility, and individual freedom, the conditions are conducive for the attempt to occupy statuses without consideration of probable consequences.

The most serious reservation regarding the theory is its failure to take into account factors of a more psychological nature. It could be argued that the consequences of a loss of social relationships is a feeling of frustration and isolation from social control, both of which could result in forms of deviant behaviour other than suicide. This would mean that the degree of status integration in a population might well fix the magnitude of total deviancy in a population but not the magnitude of the suicide rate. Only research in the future, in which a measure of the degree of status integration in a population is correlated with the incidence of forms of deviancy other than suicide, can hold the answer to this question. For the purposes of this study it will be assumed that the loss of social relationships has a specific as opposed to a general consequence.

METHODOLOGICAL OBSERVATIONS IN DEFENCE OF THE THEORY

The theory is obviously highly abstract, and many of the objections which can be raised against them primarily from the inherently vague concepts that play a role in the derivation of the major theorem. Such theories abound, however, in any science; and, providing they are capable of generating testable, empirical propositions, they are undoubtedly justifiable. As suggested by the major theorem, the present theory does lead to a testable proposition, and so has something more than argumentation to offer as evidence of validity.

The set of postulates from which the major theorem was derived may appear to be a somewhat tortuous line of reasoning; this can only be justified on the grounds that it generates a theorem which can be linked to empirical variables. However, the set of postulates does provide a means for gauging the validity of the theory apart from the major theorem. With the future development of new sources of data and techniques of analysis, it will be possible to test some of the postulates directly and to derive other testable theorems. If, for example, it were possible to measure the degree of stability and durability of the social relationships within a large number of populations, the first postulate could be tested directly, as well as a theorem linking status integration with stability and durability of social relationships.

Another fruitful approach would be to derive from the postulate a thorem linking status integration and role conflict. To test this theorem, reports by individuals of their experienced difficulties in conforming to roles would be linked to their status configurations. Although such reports are not conclusive proof of the presence of role conflict, the theory would expect persons in infrequently occupied status configurations to experience more difficulty in attempting to conform to their roles. The same would be true for actual failure to conform to roles.

With the fifth postulate, the theory would anticipate that individuals occupying status configurations characterized by a low degree of integration (i.e. infrequently occupied) would express a greater degree of dissatisfaction with one or all of their statuses and a greater willingness to change one or all of their statuses. The theory also anticipates that such a status configuration would be characterized by a higher rate of turnover in occupancy.

There are, in fact, numerous potentialities for future research as far as the set of postulates is concerned, and the writers are cognizant that only through the full development of these potentialities will a thorough evaluation of the theory be achieved. Such a development must of necessity await access to certain types of data, the perfection of techniques, and a sharpening of the concepts "role" and "status".

In conclusion, the set of postulates involves concepts that do not denote readily observable or mensurable phenomena; but it functions to link two phenomena, suicide rates and status integration, that do possess these characteristics, and points to the types of relationships that should hold for other phenomena once they become amenable to empirical analysis.

SUPPORT OF THE THEORY IN SUBSTANTIVE TERMS

Traditionally, most abstract theories in sociology are supported by argumentation or the citation of illustrative examples. It would be possible to cite numerous peculiarities and uniformities in suicide rates that tend to support the present theory. Such illustrations would be a poor second, however, to systematic tests of the major theorem.

Without considering specific illustrative evidence which supports the theory, there is one characteristic of variability in suicide rates that does deserve recognition. One of the most baffling aspects of this variability is that while the suicide rates of persons in different statuses do differ considerably, no status known to date provides absolute immunity to suicide[41] or a stable relative immunity within a society or among societies. Consider, for example, the immunity of the female relative to the male. In Sweden, during the period 1901–5, there were only 21.8 female per 100 male suicides; in Bengal, for the year 1907, there were 177.1 female per 100 male suicides.[42] In the United States, 1949–51, the mean annual suicide rate of widowed persons in the age group, 20-24, was 440% higher than that of married persons, but in the age group, 70-74, the suicide rate of the widowed was 2% less than that of the married.[43] In terms of the present theory, this becomes understandable because the degree of immunity to suicide enjoyed by persons is always a matter of status configurations and not particular statuses. In general terms, then, the present theory is in line with a fundamental characteristic of variability in suicide rates.

As for the matter of argumentation, it is obviously desirable to show wherever and whenever possible how a new theory ties in with existing knowledge. Throughout the formulation of the present theory, it was repeatedly noted that it is linked only to Durkheim's observations. This is particularly unfortunate for the assumption that the actual pattern of status occupancy is indicative of the degree of incompatibility among statuses. As evidence that the assumption is based on something more than the writers' credulity, however, the following points should be considered. First, as either general observations or formal analysis reveal, the occupancy of statuses in any society does not conform to a purely random pattern. Something beyond mere chance expectancy operates to link the occupancy of one status with another particular status. There is as yet no formal theory regarding this non-random pattern, much less a formal theory with empirical evidence to support it. Thus, with regard to the assumption, there is no formal evidence to the contrary. Though the assumption is not entirely justified on the grounds of the absence of evidence to the contrary, this is no small factor in its tentative acceptance.

A second reason for considering the assumption warranted is that it is not completely alien to prior observations. In an analysis of the "dilemmas" and "contradictions" of status, Hughes notes that the occupancy of one particular status in the United States tends to be associated with the occupancy of certain other statuses (the latter being "auxiliary characteristics"). He describes certain commonly-found status configurations and how persons who do not conform to the pattern are faced with adjustment problems, citing as an example the case of a woman engineer who was excluded by her male colleagues from the social life associated with her work. Later, in commenting on the status of physicians in the United States, Hughes says:

> ... it remains probably true that the white, male, Protestant physician of old American stock, although he may easily fail to get any clientele at all, is categorically acceptable to a greater variety of patients than is he who departs, in one or more particulars, from the type.[44]

These observations, and others, led Hughes to conclude that not only is it difficult for persons who deviate from particular status configurations to reconcile their roles, but also their deviation is a problem for persons who enter into a social relationship with them; the reluctance of persons to accept the deviant is reflected in such epithets as "hen doctor", "boy wonder", "bright young man", and "brain trust". What is most important for the present theory is the fact that the status configurations which (according to Hughes) pose adjustment problems are infrequently occupied in the United States, and the reverse is true for those that are described as posing no adjustment problems. Thus, the assumption in the present theory is only an extrapolation of observations such as Hughes recorded.

It would be possible to argue further for the assumption by citing a series of instances where the actual occupancy of certain status configurations conforms to perceptions of status incompatibility on an impressionistic level. Such illustrations, however, would not constitute proof. In final analysis, only a series of studies approaching the theory from several different directions will constitute formal evidence for or against the acceptance of the assumption.

NOTES

1 John Gillin, *The Ways of Men,* New York, 1948, pp. 515–31.
2 Werner S. Landecker, 'Types of Integration and Their Measurement', *American Journal of Sociology,* LVI, January 1951, 340.
3 Ralph Linton, *The Study of Man,* New York, 1936, p. 282, quoted in Landecker, p. 333.
4 Landecker, p. 333.
5 See Robert C. Angell, 'The Social Integration of American Cities of More Than 100,000 Population', *American Sociological Review,* XII, June 1947, 335–342; 'The Moral Integration of American Cities', *American Journal of Sociology,* VII, Part II, July 1951, 1–140.
6 Austin L. Porterfield, 'Indices of Suicide and Homocide by States and Cities', *American Sociological Review,* XIV, August 1949, 489.
7 All of these attributes of interaction are taken to be the variables in terms of which the stability and durability of social relationships would be defined in operational terms.
8 Max Weber, *The Theory of Social and Economic Organization,* trans. A. M. Henderson and Talcott Parsons, New York, 1947, pp. 118, 126.
9 This postulate contains a fundamental departure from Durkheim. Whereas Durkheim appeared to stress the consensual nature of the ties of the individual to social life, the present theory holds that the ties of the individual to social life are to be found in actual behaviour that creates and/or maintains social relationships. In short, consensus and behaviour are not identical, and it is the latter which in final analysis determines the existence and maintenance of social relationships.
10 Jackson Toby, 'Some Variables in Role Conflict Analysis', *Social Forces,* XIX, March 1952, 323.
11 Lionel J. Neiman and James W. Hughes, 'The Problem of the Concept of Role—A Re-Survey of the Literature', *Social Forces,* XXX, December, 1951, 149.
12 Neiman and Hughes, p. 149.
13 Jerome Laulicht, 'Role Conflict, the Pattern Variable Theory, and Scalogram Analysis', *Social Forces,* XXXIII, March, 1955, 250. The portion within quotation marks is from Melvin Seeman, 'Role Conflict and Ambivalence in Leadership', *American Sociological Review* XVIII, August, 1953, 373.
14 J. W. Getzel and E. G. Guba, 'Role, Role Conflict, and Effectiveness: An Empirical Study', *American Sociological Review,* XIX, April, 1954, 166.

15 Waldo W. Burchard, 'Role Conflicts of Military Chaplains', *American Sociological Review*, XIX, October 1954, 528–35.
16 Mirra Komarovsky, 'Cultural Contradictions and Sex Roles', *American Journal of Sociology*, LII, November 1946, 184–9; 'Functional Analysis of Sex Roles', *American Sociological Review*, XV, August 1950, 508–16.
17 Seeman, pp. 373–80.
18 See note 14 above.
19 See Leonard S. Cottrell, Jr., 'The Adjustment of the Individual to His Age and Sex Role', *American Sociological Review*, VII, October 1942, 617–20.
20 See Talcott Parsons, 'Age and Sex in the Social Structure of the United States', *American Sociological Review*, VII, October 1942, 604–16.
21 As examples, see Samuel A. Stouffer, 'An Analysis of Conflicting Social Norms', *American Sociological Review*, XIV, December 1949, 707–17; Samuel A. Stouffer and Jackson Toby, 'Role Conflicts and Personality', *American Journal of Sociology*, LVI, March 1951, 395–405; and Laulicht (note 13 above).
22 With reference to the manner or means by which role conflicts can be resolved, the most typical manner or means suggested in observations on the question would appear to involve the termination of social relationships. See Stouffer, Toby, and Getzel and Guba.
23 Roland L. Warren, 'Social Disorganization and the Interrelationship of Cultural Roles', *American Sociological Review*, XIV, February, 1949, 83–7.
24 Komarovsky, 'Cultural Contradictions and Sex Roles'.
25 Neiman and Hughes, p. 149.
26 Linton, *The Study of Man*, p. 113.
27 E. T. Hiller, *Social Relations and Social Structure*, New York, 1947, p. 235.
28 See Emile Benoit-Smullyan, 'Status, Status Types, and Status Interrelations', *American Sociological Review*, IX, April 1944, 151.
29 The definition of concepts is always at least partially relative to the problem at hand, and the present problem does not call for either a psychological or a hierarchial conception of status. Role and role conflict are dealt with inferentially so that our definition of these terms need not go beyond a general statement of what is involved. For a more elaborate conceptual analysis and classification that treats these concepts somewhat differently see Neal Gross, Ward S. Mason, and Alexander W. McEachern, *Explorations in Role Analysis*, New York, 1958.
30 Stuart Adams, 'Status Congruency as a Variable in Small Group Performance', *Social Forces*, XXXII, October 1953, 16–22.
31 J. S. Slotkin, 'Status of the Marginal Man', Socioligy and Social Research, XXVIII, September-October 1943, 47–54.
32 Ray Gold, 'Janitors Versus Tenants: A Status-Income Dilemma', *American Journal of Sociology*, LVII, March 1952, 486–93.
33 Alfred Scheutz, 'The Stranger: An Essay in Social Psychology', *American Journal of Sociology*, XLIX, May 1944, 499–507.
34 George Devereaux and Florence R. Weiner, 'The Occupational Status of Nurses', *American Sociological Review*, XV, October 1950, 628–34.
35 The same may be said for most of the studies and observations on role conflict which have been said for most of the studies and observations on role conflict which have been previously cited. In these studies however, the emphasis is upon roles with little treatment of the concept of status.

36 As examples of the scant attention given to the nonhierarchical dimension of status, see Samuel C. Ratcliffe, 'Social Structure and Status', *Sociology and Social Research,* XIV, November–December 1929, 156–62; Seymour M. Lipset and Reinhard Bendix, 'Social Status and Social Structure: I, British Journal of Sociology, II, June 1951, 150–68.

37 It should be emphasized that the example given here is only for the purpose of illustration. The example is over simplified because it tends to ignore all other statuses. In actual practice, the compatibility or incompatibility of statuses is a matter of the compatibility between one status and a configuration of statuses.

38 A status configuration is two or more statuses that theoretically could be occupied simultaneously. An example of a status configuration in the United States would be "male-carpenter". A more complex status configuration would be "male-carpenter-married-Negro-parent".

39 The frequency with which a status configuration is occupied is, of course, always relative. Thus, in the example given above, the status configuration "occupation X-married" is more frequently occupied than is the status configuration "occupation Y-widowed".

40 Similarly, the theory could not be expected to hold in a population where the possibility of shifting statuses is at a minimum. There is no evidence at the moment, but this basic assumption of inter-status mobility would appear to be drastically violated in the case of a population of bedridden, widowed, females all of age eighty-five or older. Members of this population have almost no opportunity to change their labour force, marital, occupational, educational, or parental statuses.

41 Two possible exceptions are tied in with age—infancy and extreme old age.

42 Both sets of figures from John Rice Miner, 'Suicide and Its Relation to Climatic and Other Factors', *American Journal of Hygiene,* Monographic Series No. 2, 1922, pp. 30, 31.

43 U.S. Department of Health, Education, and Welfare, *Vital Statistics— Special Reports,* No. 39, Washington, 1956, p. 426.

44 Everett C. Hughes, 'Dilemmas and Contradictions of Status', *American Journal of Sociology,* L. March 1945, 354.

CHAPTER 9

Suicide Statistics*

J. Maxwell Atkinson

Since Durkheim's *Suicide*,[1] sociological studies of suicide in Europe and the United States have focused almost exclusively on the problem of explaining suicide rates, and the following remarks, and one by an American, and one by a Dutchman, are illustrative of the fact that this has been seen as the major, if not the only, sociological approach to the study of suicide.

> "the foremost task of sociological studies of suicide is to explain differences in rates".[2]
> "the problem is approached from the sociological angle, which means that the investigator has concentrated on the underlying reasons for differences in the suicide rates."[3]

Like Durkheim, the majority of later sociologists interested in suicide have turned to data derived from official sources both for the "facts" to be explained (i.e. the rates) and for the evidence with which to test their theories. Some recent works, however, suggest that a number of sociologists have begun to question this, the most usual approach to suicide,[4] and I want here to look at some of the assumptions involved in the traditional approach, and then to consider the relevance of the recent developments for the sociology of suicide. Finally, I shall outline an approach to suicide research, which represents an attempt to draw together the implications of these observations.

OFFICIAL STATISTICS AND SUICIDE

Official statistics are compiled by "persons other than sociologists for purposes other than scientific research",[5] yet rarely are the problems involved in using them given more than a passing mention in those works on suicide which rely on them.[6] One is regularly left to infer that some consideration was given to such problems from explicit discussion leaves the rationale behind the decision to use

---

* Retitled and reprinted by permission of the *Sociological Review* from 'On the Sociology of Suicide', in the *Sociological Review*, Vol. 16, No. 1, March 1968, pp. 83–92.

the fact that official statistics were used at all, and this absence of them obscure. The implication of this is that either such problems have been seen as minimal or that sociologists who have used the suicide statistics have considered any problems to have been adequately overcome in the past.[7]

The process of determining whether or not to use official statistics in sociological research involves two separate decisions. An investigator must first decide to accept or reject the official categories as valid indicators of his theoretical concepts.[8] If he decides to accept them, then he must make a second decision about the efficiency and accuracy of the officials in classifying units in their appropriate categories. The fact that official statistics have been so widely used in studies of suicide implies that sociologists have decided that the death registration category "suicide" is defined in a similar way to their own theoretical concept of suicide, and is, therefore, an acceptable indicator. It implies further that they have been satisfied that officials apply this official definition consistently, so that all, or at least most eligible deaths are included in the category "suicide", while all ineligible deaths are excluded. Yet the rationale behind these decisions is not made clear, and it appears that no sociologist has made any attempt to examine the relationship between the official definition of suicide and any theoretical definition, which makes it impossible to see how the argument in favour of the appropriateness of the categories can be sustained.

The second decision is referred to more often and the accuracy of the statistics is usually defended on the grounds that, even if they are not perfect, there is no reason to believe that any systematic bias is present.[9] The death registration procedures have, however, rarely been closely examined by sociologists with a view to determining how consistent officials are in classifying eligible deaths as suicides.[10] Here again, then, the rationale for the decision to use the official statistics is unsatisfactory, as there is, as yet, no evidence, of the kind needed to make the decision, available.

The fact that sociologists have, for the most part, been ready to test hypotheses about suicide on the basis of data, about which little is known, suggests that, before any more testing of Durkheim's or anyone else's theories of suicide is carried out by reference to official statistics, there is a need for a close examination of the compilers' definitions of suicide, and of the way in which they categorize deaths as suicides. At present, there is no justification for the assumption that the problems involved in using data derived from official sources are minimal, or that they have been adequately overcome in the past.

It was an appreciation of these kinds of problem which led Kitsuse and Cicourel to propose an alternative approach to the use of official statistics in the sociology of deviant behaviour.

"We suggest that the question of the theoretical significance of the official statistics can be re-phrased by shifting the focus of investigation from the processes by which certain forms of behaviour are culturally and socially generated to the processes by which rates of deviant behaviour are produced ... Thus the explanation of rates of deviant behaviour would be concerned specifically with the processes of rate construction ... The theoretical conception which guides us is that the rates of deviant behaviour are produced by the actions taken by persons in the social system which define, classify and record certain behaviours as deviant ... From this point of view, deviant behaviour is behaviour which is organizationally defined, processed and treated as 'strange', 'abnormal', 'theft', 'delinquent', etc. by the personnel in the social system which has produced the rate."[11]

They go on to point out four consequences of this approach. In the first place, the specification of definitions immediately becomes an empirical problem. Secondly, the problem of whether or not the categories represent identical forms of behaviour is raised. Third, it provides a different perspective on the question of "unreliability" and official statistics, as they can now be seen as accurate records of the numbers of officially defined deviants. Finally, the fact that the rates are constructed by identifiable organisations means that the relevant structure which produces them can be clearly specified and therefore examined. That such an approach can be effectively applied has been illustrated in their own work on education,[12] and elsewhere in the field of criminal justice.[13] It is interesting to note, however, that Kitsuse and Cicourel make no reference to suicide as an example of deviance, and, while this may be a chance omission, it could be interpreted as meaning that their approach is less appropriate for the study of suicide.

Though the case for this kind of approach to the use of official statistics is, in many ways, a convincing one, there are at least two problems raised by it, one a general one, and the other specifically related to the study of suicide. In the first place, they are, by their own admission, moving away from an attempt from explaining how certain individuals come to engage in various forms of behaviour. It could, therefore, be argued that, by shifting the focus to the organisational processes which produce the rates, one would be making a contribution to the sociology of organizations, rather than to the sociology of deviant behaviour. The concept of "deviance", however is itself problematic, and the traditional "positive" approach to deviance has been subjected to a great deal of powerful criticism,[14] especially by those who, like Kitsuse and Cicourel, stress the significance of societal reaction and the process of labelling individuals as "deviant" for the sociology of deviance.[15] It can be argued, for example, that all individuals behave in ways which would make them eligible to be labelled "deviant" at one time or another, and that it is only the unlucky few who become officially labelled so. If this is the case, then the aims and assumptions of the more traditional approach to the sociology of deviant behaviour do stand in need of drastic revision, as it has taken the proposition that only a few individuals indulge in a particular form of behaviour as given, and the explanation of this "fact" as its objective.

While it is possible, on these grounds, to defend the shift in focus to the organizational processes which lead certain individuals to be labelled as "deviants" when talking about crime or madness, it is less easy to apply the same arguments in relation to suicide. If there is one thing about suicide of which we can be sure, it is that no living person is eligible to be officially labelled a sucide. Similarly, we can be reasonably sure that the vast majority of the population of corpses is not eligible to be so defined, which makes the situation rather different from that where the majority of the living population are eligible for official labelling as, for example, "Law breakers". To focus exclusively on the organizational processes whereby individual deaths are officially labelled "suicides", therefore, would be to ignore the fact that suicide is a minority form of behaviour, which means that the problem of explaining how and why certain individuals act in this way is a very real one. This is not to say that the societal reaction approach to deviance has no place in the study of suicide, even though sociologists have paid little or no attention to its significance in this context. Nor should it be thought that the inadequate consideration given to official statistics is the only, or even the major, omission from sociological studies of suicide.

SOCIETAL REACTION AND SUICIDE

That sociologists interested in the effect of societal response to deviance on the subsequent behaviour of those individuals labelled deviant have focused on areas other than suicide may well be a result of the fact that the label "suicide" presupposes that no further behaviour is to be expected from the person so labelled. It is, however, possible to be labelled "potential suicide", and a recent work on this subject by two psychiatrists suggests that the response of others to such individuals may be an important determinant of whether or not a suicidal act takes place.[16] The evidence they describe suggests that, if the response to a suicidal warning is such that the potential suicide is led to believe that others expect him to commit suicide (e.g. because elaborate anti-suicide precautions are taken), it is likely that a suicidal act will follow. If, however, the response is interpreted as hopeful and the potential suicide believes that others do not expect him to commit suicide, it is less likely that an attempt will be made. Other studies of suicide have shown that the majority of those in the samples had given some kind of warning of their intentions prior to the act.[17] Thus, if the way in which others respond to these warnings is a crucial determinant of whether or not an individual commits suicide, and, if most or all suicides do give some kind of warning, these findings may represent a major advance in the study of suicide to suggest that suicide can be usefully studied in terms of societal reaction, and sociologists can ill afford to ignore the potential of this approach.

SUICIDE AND ATTEMPTED SUICIDE

Wilkins noted recently that sociologists have given little or no attention to the place of attempted suicide in the suicide process,[18] in spite of the fact that there is considerable evidence to show that the proportion of suicidal acts which result in death, is very small. That sociologists have been preoccupied with only the fatal outcomes of suicidal acts is all the more surprising in view of the observations, made in a number of works, which show social action to be a significant determinant of whether or not a suicidal act results in death. Firth showed how the outcome of suicidal acts in Tikopia was largely dependent on what he called the society's 'rescue services', and argued that these may well play a crucial part in determining suicide rates in all societies.[19] In England, Stengel and Cook have noted that intervention by others in the suicidal act is much more frequent in cases of attempted suicide than it is in cases of suicide,[20] while elsewhere it has been suggested that differences in the suicide rate may be explained, at least in part, in terms of different intervention patterns.[21] Observations like these make it difficult to see how suicide can be studied in isolation, without any consideration of the many non-fatal outcomes of acts of self-injury, and, as Wilkins has put it:

> "Little more can be learned about suicide by adhering to the traditional methods and assumptions for its study—especially those which prohibit or discourage analysis of attempted suicide and suicidal communication."[22]

RECORDED SUICIDE AS THE RESULT OF A PROCESS

Recent works on suicide by sociologists, then, suggest that some of them have begun to face up to problems which, in the past, were largely ignored. It still remains, however to develop an approach to suicide which takes into account the various factors outlined above. This is what both Douglas and Wilkins claim to have done, yet they advocate different approaches, which may reflect the fact that it is easier to point to the shortcomings of the Durkheimian approach than to overcome them.

Douglas's case for abandoning the traditional approach and focussing instead on the social meanings of suicide presupposes that his arguments against the use of official statistics are accepted.[23] It was noted earlier, however, that there is as yet no evidence suitable for making a decision about the appropriateness of the suicide statistics, and Douglas admits a need for such evidence. Until we have data of this kind, therefore, to reject the statistics is no more justifiable than to accept them, which means that, at present, the unqualified adoption of the Douglas approach would be premature.

The approach suggested by Wilkins sees suicide as the result of a series of selection processes leading towards or away from suicide:

> "An improved theory of suicide would (1) deal with conditions
> that predispose to suicide ... with due recognition that these
> predispositions may be halted in their course ; and (2) deal with
> those conditions under which a distinct and particular minority
> of such persons are permitted to complete their intentions."[24]

The process, then, consists of two stages, that prior to the suicidal act, and that between the act and its outcome. His case is convincing as far as it goes, but in the light of what has been said about official statistics, it does not go far enough, as it fails to take into account the possibility of the registration processes affecting the statistics of fatal outcomes. By arguing that the suicide rates result from the processes of selection leading up to death, he implies that the process by which the rates are produced does not continue after death.

On the basis of what has been said, however, it would seem more reasonable to postulate a suicide process consisting of three stages, each of which plays a part in determining the final population of recorded suicides.

1. *The period leading up to and including the suicidal act.* It is here that the observations about warnings and societal reaction to them are particularly relevant.
2. *The period between the suicidal act and death or other out-*

come, where intervention could make the difference between life and death.

3. *The period between death and registration as a suicide,* where the organizational processes for registering deaths may have an effect on which deaths come to be recorded as suicides.

Figure 1. is a diagrammatic representation of the three stages in the process, and is designed to show how, at each stage, some potential members of the population of recorded suicides (3B) are eleminated (i.e. the "A" populations).

FIGURE 1

The Three Stages in the Processes leading to Suicides being recorded as such

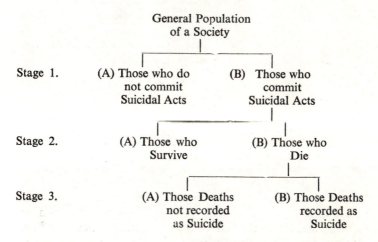

In the past, sociologists have been interested in the characteristics of population 2(B), and in comparing these with those of population 1(A), yet they have turned to population 3(B) for their data, and have ignored the importance of the A/B differences at each stage.[25] In particular, they have noted that more members of population 3(B) were "isolated" than are those in population 1(A), and, as a result, most sociological explanations of suicide have been little more than variations of Durkheim's theory of social integration and suicide. On the basis of the evidence cited earlier, one can hypothesize that isolation plays a significant part at *each* stage in the process. For there to be any response to warnings, others must be present; intervention is unlikely in the absence of others; and the absence of anyone who cares about what verdict is returned at the inquest may well be an important feature of the registration stage. If social isolation does discriminate between the A and B populations at each stage in the suicide process, then the earlier sociologists' readiness to infer a causal relationship between isolation and suicide may have been over-hasty, as they ignored the existence, let alone the possible significance of these three stages.

Yet to present such a model of the suicide process and to argue the case for studying suicide by reference to it is easier than to over-come the practical research problems it raises. There is the constant danger of making similar errors to those made in previous sociological works on suicide. How, for example, does one select indicators for concepts like "warning", "societal reaction", "intervention", "isolation", and, perhaps most difficult of all, "suicidal act"? How does one go about drawing samples from populations about which so little is known? And can one come to terms with the severe ethical and practical problems raised by the prospect of interviewing some of the people involved in the process? These are the kinds of question which need to be clarified before any research along the lines suggested can be contemplated.

NOTES

1 E. Durkheim, *Le Suicide,* Paris: Alcan, 1897.
2 J. P. Gibbs, 'Suicide', in R. K. Merton and R. A. Nisbet (Eds.): *Contemporary Social Problems,* New York: Harcourt Brace, 1961, p. 228.
3 C. S. Kruijt, 'Suicide: A Sociological and Statistical Investigation', *Sociologica Nederlandica,* 1965–6, Vol. 3, p. 44.
4 J. D. Douglas, *The Sociological Study of Suicide,* Ph.D. dissertation University of Princeton, 1965, and 'The Sociological Analysis of Social Meanings of Suicide', *European Journal of Sociology,* 1966, Vol. 7, pp. 249–98. (Reprinted in this volume, pp. 121–154.)

J. Dalgaard, 'Om international Sammenligning of selvmordsfrekvenser', (Critical remarks on the international comparison of suicide rates), *Sociologiske Meddelelser,* 1962, Vol. 7, pp. 53–60.

K. Rudfeld, 'Sprang han eller feldt han? In Bidgag til belysting af graenseomradet mellan selvmord og ulikker' (Did he jump or fall? Investigation at the borderline between suicide and accidents), *Sociologiske Meddelelser,* 1962, Vol. 7, pp. 3–24.

J. Wilkins and I. Goffman, 'Accomplishing Suicide', paper read at the annual meeting of the American Sociological Association, Miami, 1966.

J. Wilkins, 'Suicidal Behaviour', *American Sociological Review,* 1967, Vol. 32, pp. 286–298.
5 A. V. Cicourel and J. I. Kitsuse, *The Educational Decision Makers,* Bobbs Merril, Indianapolis, 1963, p. 8.
6 It is interesting to note that no mention at all is made of these problems in a recent book which claims to test a theory explaining suicide rates entirely on the basis of official statistics. See J. P. Gibbs and W. T.

Martin: *Status Integration and Suicide,* University of Oregon Press, 1964.

7 The fact that Durkheim's *Suicide* has been seen as a methodological landmark may have led sociologists to believe that to use the official statistics without questioning them must be in order, or the "master" would not have done so.

8 For an extended discussion of the problem of selecting indicators see P. F. Lazarsfeld: 'Problems in Methodology', in R. K. Merton *et al.* (Eds.): *Sociology Today,* New York: Basic Books, 1959, pp. 39–78.

9 As an example, see J. P. Gibbs: op. cit., 1961.

10 In England, the death registration processes have been examined by lawyers and doctors. See *Deaths in the Community,* British Medical Association, London, 1964; J. D. Havard: *The Detection of Secret Homicide,* Macmillan, London, 1960. In Denmark, sociologists have shown more interest in the subject, examples being the works by Dalgaard and Rudfeld cited in note 4. This may be a result of the fact that Denmark has one of the highest suicide rates in the world, which could have led Danes to seek alternative explanations of the suicide rates. In this context, it is worth noting that, in a recent Danish article, the use of official statistics to test Durkheim's theories was justified on the grounds that suicides are recorded more accurately in Denmark than in many other countries. See H. P. Weiss: 'Durkheim, Denmark and Suicide; A Sociological Interpretation of Statistical Data', *Acta Sociologica,* 1964, Vol. 7, pp. 264–278. In the U.S.A. a large scale survey of the death registration processes has started recently at the Bureau of Social Science Research Inc., Washington, D.C. under the direction of Ivor Wayne (personal communication, 1967).

11 J. I. Kitsuse and A. V. Cicourel: 'A Note on the Uses of Official Statistics', *Social Problems,* 1963, Vol. II, pp. 134–5.

12 *The Educational Decision Makers,* op. cit.

13 D. J. Newman: 'The Effect of Accommodations in Justice Administration on Criminal Statistics', in A. W. Gouldner and S. M. Miller (Eds.): *Applied Sociology,* New York: Free Press, 1965, pp. 163–79.

14 Especially notable is the critique of positive criminology in D. Matza: *Delinquency and Drift,* New York, 1964.

15 This position is well represented in the collection of papers in H. Becker (Ed.): *The Other Side: Perspectives on Deviance,* Free Press, New York, 1964; see also E. Lemert: *Social Pathology,* McGraw Hill, New York, 1961 and H. Becker: *Outsiders,* New York: Free Press, 1963.

16 A. L. Kobler and E. Stotland: *The End of Hope,* New York: Free Press, 1964.

17 E. Robbins, *et al.:* 'The Communication of Suicidal Intent—A study of 134 consecutive cases of successful suicide', *American Journal of Psychiatry,* 1959, Vol. 115, p. 724–733;

W. B. Delong and E. Robbins: 'The Communication of Suicidal Intent prior to Psychiatric Hospitalization', *American Journal of Psychiatry,* 1961, Vol. 117, pp. 695–705.

18 J. Wilkins: 'Suicidal Behaviour', op. cit.

19 R. Firth, 'Suicide and Risk-Taking in Tikopia Society', *Psychiatry,* 1961, Vol. 24, pp. 1–17.

20 E. Stengel and N. G. Cook, *Attempted Suicide: Its Social Significance and Effects,* London: Oxford University Press, 1958.

21 Wilkins and Goffman: op. cit., 1966.

22 Wilkins, op. cit., 1967.
23 *The Sociological Study of Suicide,* op. cit.
24 Wilkins, op. cit., 1967, p. 297.
25 Wilkins, on the other hand, has noted the significance of the A/B differences at stages 1 and 2, but has assumed that the population 2B is adequately represented by population 3B.

CHAPTER 10

A Typology of Suicide*

Anthony Giddens

The "objective" study of suicide as a social and psychological phenomenon dates back to the eighteenth century.[1] Since that time a very
extensive literature on the subject has built up. H. Rost's *Bibliographie des Selbstmords*, published in 1927, lists well over 3,000
items in the major European languages; and it is not complete.[2] Today the total must be at least twice as great.[3] The reader surveying
this voluminous literature, however, is impressed by certain notable
lacunae. Firstly, most of the literature is primarily descriptive in
character; the great bulk of it consists of surveys of the distribution
of suicide, or of clinical descriptions of individual cases.[4] Secondly,
there are two traditions of research which have remained largely
distinct from one another,[5] both in terms of their methodology and
their theoretical conclusions.[6] These are, on the one hand, the statistical approach which has been particularly favoured by sociologists;
and, on the other, the case-study method which has been the basis
of psychological theories of suicide. In this paper I shall not discuss
directly the methodological issues involved in research on suicide;
what I do want to do is to work out some theoretical ties between
the notions which have been developed in sociological studies of
suicide, and those which have emerged from the second tradition,
the psychological.

In the sociology of suicide, Durkheim's *Suicide* has provided a
model for most subsequent research. The most significant work
specifically focused on Durkheim's conclusions is Halbwachs' *Les
Causes du suicide*.[7] The careful statistical analysis pursued by Halbwachs substantiated Durkheim's empirical generalizations with few
exceptions.[8] Other statistical surveys have provided further confirmation.[9]

Durkheim's types of "egoistic" and "anomic" suicide, which are
the two most relevant to suicide in modern societies, have not been
developed, however, by later sociologists *as a typology*. Those writers
interested in the sociology of suicide as such have primarily been

---

* Reprinted by permission from the *European Journal of Sociology*, Vol
VII, 1966, pp. 276–95.

concerned with "self-ish" or egoistic suicide, although very few have retained the term itself. Since Durkheim's discussion of egoistic suicide is complicated and sometimes ambiguous, it is arguable that those who have linked suicide to "social isolation" have done no more than to draw out one element among the several factors Durkheim intended to group together as egoistic suicide. It is certainly true that writers, like Halbwachs, who have attributed suicide to social isolation have given much less attention than Durkheim to the broad structural conditions producing such isolation.[10] But their position is in a basic sense compatible with Durkheim's. Durkheim made it clear that "excessive individualism" is a general condition of modern societies leading to the isolation of individuals from closely-knit relationships with others.[11]

The concept of "anomie" has had a different history. Later sociologists have quite rightly regarded the notion of anomie as of central importance to Durkhem's sociology. But this has meant that they have sought to use the concept in relation to a broad range of problems, and not specifically with regard to suicide. Anomie has formed the conceptual mainspring of a general theory of "deviance" in which suicide appears only marginally.[12] Those sociologists who have studied suicide have, however, tended to make little use of the concept of anomie, or to regard anomic suicide as to all intents and purposes as indistinguishable from egoistic suicide.[13]

It is not my intention here to discuss the very considerable difficulties involved in interpreting Durkheim's various writings bearing upon the distinction which he intended to draw between egostic and anomic suicide. Suffice it to say that the discussion in *Suicide* relates to some very basic conceptions underlying Durkheim's theory of the division of labour in modern societies. The importance of egoistic suicide is related to the "cult of the personality" which develops in modern complex social structures; anomic suicide reflects the lack of moral controls characteristic of certain sectors of contemporary societies.

I have drawn upon Durkheim's discussion in what follows, and I believe that my analysis is, by and large, not inconsistent with his[14] but it is not important in this context just how far my account fully represents Durkheim's position. I have sought to conceptualize the distinction between "egoistic" and "anomic" suicide in a way which is clear and internally coherent, and which is consistent with recent research.

"Egoism" is bound up with institutionalized social conditions which "loosen" or "dilute" social ties binding the members of a group to one-another. This is, of course, a question of degree, and not an all-or-nothing matter. A major source of such "dilution" in modern society is to be found in the existence of social values promoting individualism, personal initiative and responsibility in important spheres of social activity. Thus, for example, values which place stress upon romantic love as a basis for marriage thereby place the onus on each individual to search out and win a partner through his own efforts. This position stands in constrast to one in which the arrangement of the marriage contract is made relatively independently of the wishes of the partners themselves. Even more important is the fact that, in the former type of system, fewer defined duties, obligations and reciprocal relationships tend to stem from the marital role itself. Values which promote individual initiative or responsibility, or which specifically leave a given sphere of social life "open", can be contrasted with those governing social structures in which the formation and definition of social ties is "taken out of the hands" of the individuals involved.

There is a considerable amount of evidence showing a general relationship between the degree to which personal initiative and individual freedom in role-obligations are institutionalized, and the suicide rate. The most thorough data are given in the recent work of Gibbs and Martin.[15]

While, as Durkheim recognized, it is impossible to draw an absolute line between them, it is not difficult to separate "egoism" from anomie as general conditions of social structure. Durkheim distinguished two main types of situation as leading to defined states of anomie. Anomie may occur as the result of rapid economic change; or it may exist in a more chronic state in some sectors of the occupational structure. The common element in both of these is that in each case social norms come to exercise only a low level of regulatory control over behaviour.[16] Social norms govern the objectives and motivations of individuals in two ways: they influence the actual setting of goals, defining what is appropriate and legitimate; but, as Durkheim emphasized above all, they also thereby limit and restrict aspiration. When social norms for any reason provide no clear definition of aspiration, or where norms produce disparity between aspirations and the possibility of their implementation, a state of anomie exists. Such a state no doubt characterises all social systems to a greater or lesser degree. The limiting cases of "perfect normative integration" on the one hand, and complete "normlessness" on the other, are never found in actual social structures. Anomie embraces spheres of social activity which stretch far beyond those actually discussed by Durkheim, including most situations in which socially defined "failure" is possible.[17] We can call the degree of structural anomie in a social system the degree of normative integration in that system, distinguishing this from "egoism", which we can say relates to the degree of social integration in the system. Empirically, of course, the extent of independent variation along these two dimensions is limited; nevertheless, a low degree of social integration in a social system is not incompatible with a high degree of normative integration, nor vice versa.

There is a good deal of research which indicates that there exists a connection between anomie and the suicide rate, and that this relationship is at least partly independent of that between egoism and suicide.[18]

This typology of suicide thus provides a viable basis for the analysis of macro-social conditions relevant to the aetiology of suicide in modern societies and it has received a certain amount of empirical verification in later research. But the psychological ideas which Durkheim attempted to link up with it, characteristically penetrating as they are, are fragmentary and inadequate, and for theoretical insights into the psychology of suicide we must look elsewhere.

The most significant theory of suicide which has been developed in psychology, and the only theory which goes beyond common-sense observations, is based on the psychoanalytic theory of depression.[19] In his original formulation of the theory, Freud draws an illuminating comparison between depressive states and grief produced by the death of a loved person. When such a person dies, or is suddenly removed through some other cause, the individual has to withdraw his emotional ties to that person and develop new ones elsewhere. This cannot be done immediately, and emotional energy is typically withdrawn from the external world and incorporated into the ego; the individual continues to identify with an introjected image of the other, and much interest in the external world is correspondingly lost. Now all love relations involve some ambivalence, and the individual has a fund of repressed hostile feelings about the object. The bereaved individual unconsciously feels he has been abandoned by the lost object: the aggressive feelings which this stimulates become the focus of the previously existing reservoir of hostile impulses. Feelings of dejection and lack of interest in life are based upon the retroflexion of these hostile impulses against the introjected object in the ego.

Both grief and depression originate in feelings stimulated by another person which become redirected against the self. However, while grief is a normal process of adjustment to the death of a loved one, in some individuals the tendency to depression is chronic. The key to differences between grief and states of depressive disorder is that "melancholia is in some way related to an object-loss which is withdrawn from consciousness, in contradistinction to mourning, in which there is nothing about the loss which is unconscious (...) (in grief) it is the world which has become poor and empty; in melancholia it is the ego itself".[20] The depressive individual is characterized by an abnormally rigid and punitive super-ego, which causes him to refer hostile impulses back against himself. The stronger the super-ego, the greater the tendency to invert hostile feelings, stimulated by others, against the self. The frustrations generating these aggressive impulses are not confined to actual object-loss, but "extend for the most part beyond the clear case of loss by death, and include all those situations of being slighted, neglected or disappointed, which can import opposed feelings of love and hate into the relationship or reinforce an already existing ambivalence (...)".[21] The self-accusations and feelings of worthlessness which characterize depression are thus sentiments which really refer to another person, and are stimulated by the real or imagined behaviour of another or others. The reason for the close connection between depression and suicide is now evident: suicide represents an extreme on a range of possible forms of self-aggression, which extends from relatively minor forms such as verbal self-deprecation to actual self-destruction.[22] Suicide presupposes a highly ambivalent object-relationship, in which the ego directs against itself "hostility which relates to an object and which represents the ego's original reaction to objects in the external world (...). In the opposed situations of being most intensely in love and of suicide the ego is overwhelmed by the object, though in totally different ways."[23]

The main deficiency of the theory is that empirically the correspondence between depression and suicide is not complete. There appears to be no strict continuum between the self-deprecations which typically characterize depression, and actual physical self-aggression: people suffering from extreme states of depressive disorder are not necessarily more prone to suicide than those experiencing an isolated depressive mood which is traceable to some defined precipitating event. Thus, while there is an intimate connection between depression and suicide, it is by no means established what are the specific characteristics of those depressive states producing direct attempts at self-destruction. It was probable, however, that one factor of considerable importance is the conscious and unconscious meaning which death has for the individual: suicidal acts are likely to accompany depression when death is invested with an instrumental significance—as a "magical" solution to problems, or a weapon that can be used to secure a desired end.[24]

In spite of its partial character, the psychoanalytic theory of depression is, as a theory of suicide, simple and powerful. Many cases of suicide seem to fit within this general framework. Suicide is probably almost universally preceded by some form of depression, and depressive disorder is far more commonly associated with suicide than are any of the other major types of mental disorder. On the other hand, it is not difficult to find cases which do not fit easily within such a pattern. The difference between the following two summary case-history is illustrative: the first seems to fit the character type and life-history which would be expected according to the theory, while the second does not.

Case 1. Suicide attempt. (Method: barbiturate poisoning).
   G. S. lost her father when she was three. Her mother spent several periods in mental hospitals, during which time G. S. was cared for by relatives. G. S. was stated to be moody and withdrawn, and had no close friends. At the age of twenty-five she married: her husband left her seven months later, and this precipitated her suicide attempt.

Case 2. Suicide. (Method: hanging).
   T. W. was the son of a successful advertising executive. His childhood was apparently uneventful. T. W. had poor results at school, but his father, who was determined that he should "do well", got him a job as a management trainee in his firm. He married at twenty-two, and had three children, aged two, three and five at the time of his death. He was a sociable individual, and had a close circle of friends. Precipitating cause of suicide: his application for promotion to a higher grade was rejected.

Even in these two very short case-histories, several differences are evident. G. S. lost a parent at an early age, and her relationship with her mother was rather unstable. As a person, she was withdrawn and friendless. Her suicide attempt was precipitated by an object-loss—the departure of her husband. T. W., on the other hand, had no apparent disruption in his relationships with his parents in childhood. His family life was, to outward appearances at least, happy. He was sociable and had many friends. The suicide attempt of G. C. followed the breaking of an important love relationship; T.W.'s suicide followed a failure to achieve a desired objective.

In Freud's analysis of depression, an indication is in fact given of a type of suicide rather different from that which is directly covered in the standard theory. Freud mentions that a psychological equivalent for the frustrating object can be "highly cherished ideal" which becomes unobtainable.[25] Other writers have also linked suicide with "failure" and a "sense of inferiority", but little attempt has been made to set up a psychological type which might embrace such cases of suicide more easily than the conventional theory is able to do. There are, however, concepts and ideas in the repertoire of psychoanalytic theory which can provide the basis of such a type.

In his initial formulation of the "superstructure" of the ego, Freud used the term "ego-ideal". He later distinguished the ego-ideal from the super-ego, and by far the great bulk of writing in psycho-analysis has been devoted to the functions of the latter. The positive goals and objectives which individuals strive for nevertheless clearly form a highly important sector of personality, as has always been stressed in academic psychology. The super-ego and ego-ideal, as Piers has pointed out, can be regarded as having different generic sources and different integrative tasks in personality; and each may be a partially independent source of tension and anxiety.[26] The ego-ideal, which "is in continuous interaction with the conscious and unconscious awareness of the ego's potentialities", is the critical agency besides the super-ego which governs the individual's self-esteem.[27]

Overwhelming concern with the functions of the super-ego in psychoanalysis is connected, Piers has suggested, with a corresponding over-emphasis upon guilt at the expense of other forms of tension which may frequently play an important role in personality. If guilt can be conceived as deriving from a tension between super-ego and ego, a second major source of anxiety can be differentiated as stemming from friction between ego-ideal and ego. Shame is anxiety generated when the goals and self-conception embodied in the ego-ideal diverge from the actual performance of the ego.

Just as in many cases of suicide guilt is the dominant source of motivation to the act, in others it is logical to assume that shame may be the main mobilizing energy. In the normal personality there can be assumed to be a fairly high degree of "fit" between the position and the attainments of the ego, and the demands and conception of self set by the ego-ideal. The normal individual presumably identifies with figures who set "realistic" and fairly well-defined levels of attainment which are consonant with his objective circumstances. In pathological cases, however, the ego-ideal may impose demands which can come to place great strain upon the capabilities of the ego to achieve an identity which will satisfy them. Such individuals will be abnormally vulnerable to shame anxiety and must constantly be sensitive to "validation" of their worth from the external world. Any change in their external circumstances can threaten the insecure position of the ego *vis-à-vis* the ego-ideal. This is particularly true if the ego-ideal is at the same time both demanding and non-specific, i.e. if the individual internalizes powerful motivations which are not linked to defined absolute goals, but which demand that he should continually prove himself "worthier" than, or "superior" to, others, or which produce in him a general "rest-lessness". The condition for the development of such a demanding ego-ideal is probably that the child is exposed to generalized "shame oriented" techniques of socialization, such that he is teased, ridiculed, or even ignored, rather than scolded or threatened for his misdemeanours. These imply to the child that he is "not good enough" and constantly menace him with feelings of inferiority and worthlessness. At the back of shame there is, as Piers puts it, not fear of hatred (punishment) but fear of contempt, or "death by emotional starvation".[28]

In such a pattern, masochistic tendencies are based upon shame. Frustration generated by disjunction between ego-ideal and ego provides the basis for aggression turned against the "inadequate" ego-identity. In suicide of this type, the self-destructive act represents an attempt to destroy the unsatisfactory ego which has shown itself incapable of acquiring an identity adequate to the ego-ideal. The situations giving rise to such a disparity can include all those which the individual may perceive as "failure". Suicide probably in most cases follows a long-term and cumulative process: there are various psychological mechanisms whereby the ego can temporarily protect or shelter itself from overweening demands of the ego-ideal. The individual may, for example, continually project his hopes in the future, convincing himself that others will one day appreciate his true worth, or that one day he will be a success. The rebuttal which finally precipitates suicide may be an apparently minor one.[29]

There are many clinical descriptions of suicide in the literature which seem to fit within this hypothetical framework. Hendin, for example, describes the case of a lawyer who was not doing well in his career, and who made a suicide attempt:

> His dreams under hypnosis were of the most elemental kind, In one instance they revealed him running to catch a boat and just missing it. In his associations "missing the boat" symbolized the low opinion which he had of his entire career. His legal ambitions were excessive and he found it impossible to compromise with his grandiose success fantasies. The aggressiveness which stemmed from this grandiosity interfered with his actual performance, a constellation frequently observed in male patients with extremely high and rigid standards for themselves. What is seen as failure causes an enormous amount of self-hatred, and suicide amounts to a self-inflicted punishment for having failed.[30]

Now there are good reasons to suppose that, as Freud put it, "the unconscious does not believe in its own death". Suicide has various possible unconscious or only partly conscious symbolic meanings where death is not treated simply as an end to existence. Hendin distinguishes, among others, the following meanings which death may have in acts of suicide: 1. "Retaliatory abandonment": a person who has, or considers himself to have been, abandoned by a friend or loved one, kills himself as an act of retaliation, thus abandoning him in his turn. 2. Reunion: the suicide is a mode of reuniting with a loved one who has died or left. 3. Revenge: suicide is an aggressive act against another person who has wronged the individual involved. 4. Rebirth: suicide is a means of changing identity, of being born anew. 5. Self-indictment: A man who feels himself to be a failure punishes himself by suicide.[31] There are two main elements present in these five forms of conceptions of death: the first three all refer to hopes and fantasies linked directly to another person or other persons (abandonment of the other; reunion with the other; revenge against the other); the second two refer more immediately to the identity of the suicidal individual himself.

This offers an evident connection to the two psychological types of suicide discussed previously. Thus the unconscious objectives of suicide where shame is the dominant mobilizing agency could be seen as involving the self-condemnation of the individual and the replacement of his unsatisfactory identity by one more consonant with the demands of the ego-ideal—in other words, the rebirth of the chastened ego in a new guise. Where guilt is the driving energy, on the other hand—for reasons to be elucidated subsequently—the unconscious objectives behind suicide would embody a desire for retaliation, reunion, or revenge, but most likely a mixture of the three. Since the first type of suicide would normally involve some decisive attempt to destroy the existing identity in order to be "reborn", we could regard this type as "more genuinely suicidal" than the other. Menninger has suggested a threefold division of suicidal motivations: the "wish to kill", the "wish to be killed", and the "wish to die", considering that these are present in differential degree in different cases of suicide.[32] According to Freud's theory, suicide is retroflexed aggression: We can therefore presume that the "wish to kill" is always an underlying factor in suicide. But in suicide deriving from shame, where the object is the destruction of the unsatisfactory self-identity, we could, in Menninger's terminology, say the "wish to die" is predominant; while in the other type it would be the "wish to be killed" which combines with the "wish to kill" as the dominant impulsion.

In *Suicide*, while he stressed the value of psychological studies, Durkheim argued that these aspects of suicide are "obviously quite distinct" from the factors of social structure producing a given *pattern* or distribution of suicide in a group.[33] Now if it were the case that personality (or more specifically, suicidal tendencies in personality) were simply a biological given, and every population had the same quantum of potential suicides in it, then this would be a defensible position. The social factors Durkheim isolated might then be supposed to act "directly" to either curb or exacerbate these pre-existing tendencies. Since, however, personality develops largely in and through society, the conditions which Durkheim analysed as acting "directly" to produce a given rate of suicide cannot be supposed to be separate from those which influence the formation and distribution of suicidal personality types in a population.[34] The relationship between social and psychological factors in the actiology of suicide should therefore be as follows:

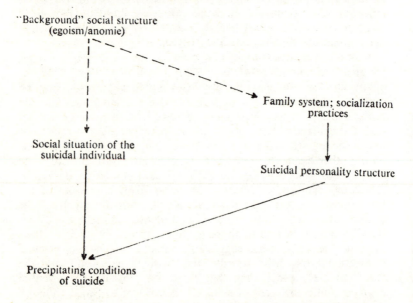

This is simply a schematic outline of relationships which are in actuality very much more complicated. There is, in fact, a continual *interaction* between the various sets of factors involved here. But for purposes of theoretical analysis this scheme identifies the major directions of relationship leading to suicide. The social conditions of a broad kind which Durkheim distinguished (egoism/anomie) influence the causation of suicide in two ways: via the organization of relationships in the family and other agencies shaping personality development; and more "directly" in affecting the social position of the potentially suicidal individual.

The typology outlined below indicates what seem to be clear relations between the psychological types previously outlined, and Durkheim's structural types. A general correspondence is assumed between the two types of structural condition and the variables governing the development of each psychological type, without assuming complete isomorphism. In other words, while the psychological types of suicidal personality are not simply "derivable" by induction from the structural typology, at least some degree of "overlap" is assumed, yielding two partially separable psycho-social types. The development of a highly punitive super-ego, for example, presupposes that a child is disciplined to maintain powerful constraints over his impulses from an early age. Such a discipline is likely to be operative when the parents are influenced by values stressing the desirability of personal responsibility and self-reliance. Although a broad correspondence—i.e. some degree of "overlap" of this kind—is assumed in the case of both egoism and anomie, it is neither plausible nor necessary to assume complete "closure".

"Egoism", as a general condition of social structure, sets a broad "background" making for the diminution of structured social ties

EGOISTIC SUICIDE

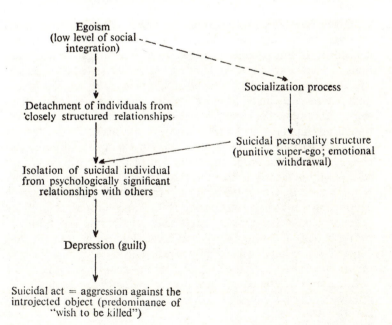

Egoism
(low level of social
integration)

↓

Detachment of individuals from
closely structured relationships

↓

Isolation of suicidal individual
from psychologically significant
relationships with others

↓

Socialization process

↓

Suicidal personality structure
(punitive super-ego; emotional
withdrawal)

Depression (guilt)

↓

Suicidal act = aggression against the
introjected object (predominance of
"wish to be killed")

binding individuals to one-another in established relationships. In specific sectors of social life, individuals are thus relatively free of role obligations which necessarily involve them in prescribed relationships with others. "Egoism" tends towards the isolation of individuals from closely defined ties with others. People are not, however, placid reflections of social forces, but autonomous actors who in part activity create their own social environments. Now the personality type described in Freud's theory of depression is characterized by a propensity to introvert feelings, and consequently by a low capacity to form stable emotional attachments to others. This type of individual tends to be extremely dependent upon an established relationship, but finds it difficult to function satisfactorily within it; and he has great difficulty in breaking relationships with former objects and in forming new object-attachments.

The essential point of linkage between social and psychological factors in egoistic suicide can therefore be said to be in the reciprocal "push" towards *the isolation of the suicidal individual from relationships that are significant to him and on which he is highly dependent.* Social factors may act to isolate large numbers of individuals from closely-knit relationships with others: but in certain instances their influence will interact with the personality dispositions of individuals who "create their own social isolation"—in other words, who find it difficult to develop and maintain lasting and close affective relationships with others. The new result is the detachment of certain individuals from relationships on which they are extremely dependent. In this process many possible "weightings" or combinations of factors are possible. However, it can be stated as a general rule that the less the degree to which the potentially suicidal individual is necessarily involved in a closely structured system of relationships with others, the more his dependency needs will become frustrated, and his restricted ability to form and maintain satisfactory object relations will come to the fore. An example will make this clear. In Western Europe the formation of the courtship-marriage relationship is largely left to the responsibility of every individual. Now, in such a system, the kind of person who is disadvantaged in contracting a marriage relationship is the one who is already highly dependent upon one already established relationship (i.e. normally with a parent) and who finds it very difficult to form close affective contacts with others. In a system where arranged marriage is the rule, on the other hand, such a person will tend to be necessarily involved in a marriage relationship, since the formation of the contract will not depend basically upon his own ability to form and maintain an affective tie.

In many instances, however, isolation may be phenomenal rather than actual: the individual, in other words, is involved in a closely defined relationship with another, but is unable to make of it a stable and satisfying social tie. Such a situation may indeed result when a highly dependent individual has made the transition from the parental family into a marriage relationship. Even here, however, the external social context in which the relationship is embedded may affect the nature of the adjustment which the individual makes to the relationship. In a society where there are many other obligation and reciprocal relationships which stem from the marital role in an extended kinship group, some of the individual's dependency needs can be taken out of the marriage tie itself.

It is important to note that, in Freud's theory, depression and the suicidal act have intrinsically social nature. Depression and suicide, which in an obvious aspect go together with withdrawal from the social world, are also seen to represent hostile impulses directed *towards another*. The depressive state, which appears simply to entail a withdrawal from others, is at the same time in an inverted fashion aimed at others. The dependency orientation which goes hand in hand with the tendency to depression means, as various observers have pointed out, that the actions of the suicidal depressive represent both aggressive impulses towards the other, turned back against the self, and also an attempt to regain the affection of the object.[35] Suicidal behaviour, as the extreme form of self-directed aggression, is both a hostile act against the others, and an appeal for love and forgiveness, having the goal of expiation. As Fenichel has written, suicidal acts thus represent:

> desperate attempts to enforce, at any cost, the cessation of the pressure of the super-ego. They are the most extreme acts of ingratiatory submission to punishment and to the super-ego's cruelty; simultaneously they are also the most extreme acts of rebellion, that is murder—murder of the original objects whose incorporation created the super-ego, murder, it is true, of the kind of Dorian Gray's murder of his image. This mixture of submission and rebellion is the climax of the accusatory demonstration for the purpose of coercing forgiveness: "Look what you have done to me; now you have to be good again".[36]

The connection between social isolation and suicide now can be made clear: *egoistic suicide represents an expiatory attempt at or appeal for reintegration within a relationship or a group*. The possible permutation of hostile and expiatory motives in this appear to be many. Thus any of the three meanings distinguished previously may be dominant in any given act of suicide. The aggressive connotation against the other may be marked, in which case the suicide approxi-

mates either to an act of "revenge" or of "retaliatory abandonment";
if "reunion" is the dominant *motif*, then the act will have a less
"externalized" aggressive character. In a given range of cases, the
appeal for response from others may be non-specific: the individual
may perpetrate a suicidal attempt, for example, in a public place.
In most cases, the suicidal act seems to be aimed at a specific object
upon whom the individual's dependency needs are focused. But
in some instances, the appeal for love may be directed at a different
object from the introverted aggressive response: the individual
simultaneously rejects one person and appeals to another. In all
cases the presumption must be that the act has some unconscious
reference to the persons who formed the original identifications
upon which the super-ego was built: the parental figures. As Hendin
has observed:

> the act of dying itself can be conceived as pleasurably in-
> corporated into the reunion fantasy. Most frequently the em-
> phasis is not placed upon the dying but upon the gratification
> to follow, with the mood in such reunion dreams being quite
> pleasant. In the overwhelming majority the gratification is on
> an extremely dependent variety, either directly with parental
> figures or with wives, husbands or siblings substituting as
> parents.[37]

There is no doubt that some suicidal attempts or threats of suicide
are consciously used as a sanction with the aim of influencing others
in a desired direction. However, in most suicidal acts, while there
is always a confusion of conscious and unconscious motivations, the
most important meanings are probably unconscious. It seems obvious
enough that where the suicidal act is used as a conscious sanction
on others, it is unlikely to be a "serious" attempt: i.e. little or no risk
of death is entailed. Where more deep-lying motivations are involved, the "risk-taking" aspect of egoistic suicide becomes more pronounced. In a very real sense, the individual stakes his life against
receiving a timely response from others.[38] Suicide from this aspect
is a kind of behavioural "leap into the unknown". Kierkegaard
wrote of the "leap into the unknown": "Earthly hope must be
killed; only then can be saved by true hope". The same thinking is
present in acts of suicide where the "risk-taking" element occurs:
a man offers himself up to the fates, apparently in order to end his
existence; but his act is at the same time an appeal which can be
answered and thereby provide him with a new faith in life.
Studies of attempted suicide indicate that the suicidal act which
does not eventuate in death usually does serve in part to reintegrate
the individual within a social unit, drawing some response from
others. Even the fact that the person is placed in a hospital ward,

and that some special attention is paid to him, may go some way towards achieving this objective.[39]

ANOMIC SUICIDE

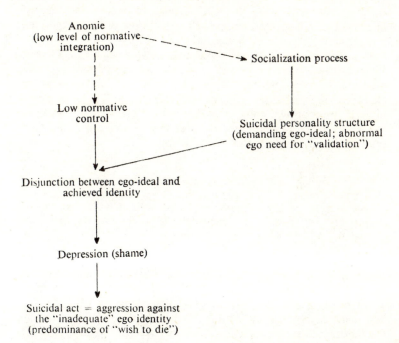

The same pattern holds for anomic suicide. Anomie, as a general condition of social structure, sets a social "background" making for disjunction between social norms and the goals and aspirations which individuals hold. In specific sectors of social activity, individuals are thus provided with ill-defined objectives or with goals which make the possibility of "failure" high. As in the case of "egoism", we can thus trace a "direct" relation between the structural condition and the precipitating circumstances of suicide. The "indirect" relation is represented by the assumed "overlap" between anomic social structure and the socialization process producing the second suicidal personality type described previously.

In anomic suicide, the essential point of conjuncture between social and psychological factors comes in the "push" towards *the detachment of the individual from defined and realisable goals which enable him to "relate himself to life" in a meaningful way.* Again, a range of possible "weightings" can be envisaged. However much standards of success and failure are dependent upon social definition, the experience of anomie depends also upon the individual's own perception of his situation. But the greater the degree to which the individual is involved in a social system which sets him clearly specified and realisable goals, the less the chance of pathological discrepancy between the aspirations and self-conception set by the ego-ideal and the actual accomplishments of the ego.

In a certain sense it must be true that anomic suicide also has an "internalized object reference" with, at a fundamental level, the introjected parental figures playing a key role. But here the expiatory character of "vindication through self-punishment" is transformed into a more thorough-going overthrow of the ego-identity. As Lynd has pointed out, shame demands a change in the ego rather than offering the possibility of atonement or appeal:

> Because of this over-all character, an experience of shame can be altered or transcended only insofar as there is some change in the whole self. No single, specific thing we can do can rectify or mitigate such an experience. Unlike guilt it is—in specific terms—irreversible. "In shame there is no comfort but to be beyond all bounds of shame."[40]

Anomic suicide represents the most desperate attempt to a man to place himself beyond these bounds. Anomic suicide therefore entails a transformation of identity. It thus could be said to combine, again in degree varying according to the particular case, the last two meanings previously identified: it is an act of self-indictment for failure, but also an act of expiatory "rebirth". The underlying conception could be expressed in Goethe's words *Stirb und werde*: die and come to life.

Depression of some kind is probably an almost universal affective state preceding suicide. Depression in anomic suicide may, however, have rather different features to the classical syndrome of depression, since guilt is not the dominant tension. Something like this was in fact recognized by Durkheim in his discussion of the "individual forms" of his social types. Egoistic suicide is characterized by "a condition of melancholic langour which relaxes all the springs of action".[41] Anomic suicide, by contrast, where it is traceable to some sudden and radical reversal of fortune, derives from "anger and all the emotions customarily associated with disappointment". In more chronic cases: "There are yet others who, having no complaint to make of men or circumstances, automatically weary of a palpably hopeless pursuit, which only irritates rather than appeases their desires. They turn against life in general and accuse it of having deceived them."[42] These latter descriptions are not too far removed from that loosely-defined syndrome which is sometimes identified as "anxiety depression". This pattern is often not characterised by the marked withdrawal characteristics found in classical depressive states. The primary dynamic is a more "active" anxiety focused on perceived inadequacies of performance or attainment[43] A typical case is described by Flind:

> Occasionally the whole clinical picture seems dominated by anxiety, a point mentioned by some writers. This was demonstrated in a case seen recently by me: a man aged forty-four who fairly suddenly developed numerous anxiety symptoms following a difficult time in his business in which he had worked excessively hard. In addition, he experienced headaches of the tension type, and gave a good description of what in fact was a degree of retardation, and complained of early waking. Throughout his illness he denied being depressed, and indeed he did not strike one as being so to any appreciable degree ... He described himself as normally placid and good-natured, and he was in effect a little obsessional and unbending. He had always been a very hard worker and a successful planning executive in business.[44]

In terms of being involved in established relationships with others, such as an individual may be a well-integrated member of a group. He may, in fact, hide his depressive feelings from others as far as possible: to show them would be to reinforce his feelings of inferiority. He is unlikely to parade his suicidal intentions in front of others; his suicide may come as a surprise and a shock to relatives and friends. If life seems meaningless to him, it is not because he is separated from others, but because his activity is not structured by aspirations which accord with the identity which he has achieved.

One implication of the conception developed here is that suicide, both anomic and egoistic, is in an inverted way an attempt at *mastery*: an attempt to control and rectify an intolerable state of affairs. Suicide is a grasping towards omnipotence in a situation in which the influence of the individual, as he may realise on a conscious level, is pathetically inadequate. His world has slipped away from him, and yet in the very act of denying that world he attempts to encompass and change it as well as to change himself. But the effort at mastery takes on different forms. In egoistic suicide it is an attempt to influence others through self-punishment, and thereby to escape from social isolation. In anomic suicide, the attempt is more radical: to effect a change in identity, a transformation of self, and thereby to escape a situation of meaninglessness.

It should be made clear, however, that these distinctions are made for the purpose of analysis. Actual cases of suicide may involve elements of both, and must be judged according to how far they tend towards one type rather than the other. As has been indicated previously, "egoism" and anomie are not necessarily exclusive as general conditions of social structure: the existence of values promoting individualistic action in a given sphere of social life can itself produce a strain to anomie. Social isolation and anomie are intimately related. As Durkheim wrote:

> We know that (egoism and anomie) are usually merely two different aspects of one social state; thus it is not surprising that they should be found in the same individual. It is, indeed, almost inevitable that the egoist should have some tendency to non-regulation; for, since he is detached from society, it has not sufficient hold upon him to regulate him.[45]

The goals and objectives after which men strive are not separate from the stability and closeness of the social relationships in which they are involved: the responses of others are a primary criterion by reference to which individuals evaluate their attainments, and in terms of which their identities are structured. Finally, as Piers has pointed out, there may be complicated interconnections between shame and guilt in personality, whereby the arousal of one leads to behaviour producing the other, beginning a chain-reaction between the two.[46]

CONCLUSION

The typology developed in this paper is quite complicated, and highly generalized, and the empirical exploration of it is difficult. It nevertheless indicates a number of fairly specific propositions which can be approached, it not "tested", in a concrete fashion.[47] These bear most directly upon the relationship between suicide and attempted suicide (i.e. suicidal acts which do not terminate in death). Now in virtually all sociological studies of suicide, the authors have based their ideas solely upon analysis of completed suicides, the implication being that "unsuccessful" suicide attempts are the same in all significant respects as actual suicides, and that no special additional study need be made of them. A conclusion of the theory set out in this paper, however, would be that attempted suicide cannot simply be regarded as "failed" suicide, but as an act which has different characteristics. It would follow from it that suicidal acts which tend towards the egoistic type are most likely to eventuate in an "attempt"—i.e. not to terminate in death. In suicidal behaviour of this type there may be, in what is psychologically a highly significant sense, no "wish to die". As Menninger has written:

> Anyone who has sat by the bedside of a patient dying of a self-inflicted wound and listened to pleading that the physician save his life which only a few hours or minutes before the patient had attempted to destroy, must be impressed by the paradox that one who wished to kill himself does not wish to die.[48]

Since egoistic suicide has the expiatory objective of direct appeal to others, it follows that the individual (not necessarily with conscious intent) will tend to dramatize his plight *through using a "risk-taking" method of suicide* which provides some opportunity for others to respond. The taking of a drug which has a comatose effect, for example, is one such method. In suicide by shooting, hanging or drowning, on the other hand, unless the individual very consciously structures the situation so as to make the act ineffective, death is more immediate and inevitable.

There is a good deal of evidence supporting the notion that most attempted suicides differ in important respects from most completed suicides. A high proportion of suicide attempts are made in situations in which the intervention of others is inevitable or highly probable, and where this must be known to the individual who makes the attempt.[49] A woman waits, for example, until around the hour when a friend usually calls, before taking an overdose of barbiturates; a man threatens to jump from a building overlooking a busy street, rather than choosing a deserted height nearer at hand. Follow-up studies of attempted suicides indicate that only a small proportion of individuals who attempt suicide actually kill themselves at a later date. Moreover, there are several notable differences in the relative distribution of suicide and attempted suicide which have been reliably established. Male rates of suicide usually outrank female rates by a ratio of two or three to one; women attempt suicide, however, two or three times more frequently than men. Suicide rates tend to increase with advancing age; but rates of attempted suicide are highest in the 20–40 year-old age-group[50].

Examination of these differentials does suggest that a good case can be made for the hypothesis that anomie is most likely to be more developed in those circumstances associated with a high ratio of suicide to attempted suicide. It seems legitimate to presume that, in most modern societies, men are in general more exposed to situations of potential anomie than women are. Women tend to have more clearly defined and restricted normatively sanctioned aspirations than men, however much the sex difference in this respect is diminishing. The case of suicide in old age is more difficult. Old people tend often to be isolated from regular ties with others. But it is nevertheless time that in old age a person is placed, often quite suddenly, in a position where he feels himself no longer a useful member of society; and where the norms of behaviour which he was accustomed to follow are no longer appropriate. The jump in the male suicide rate at retirement age might be explicable in these terms. However, a further complicating factor in the case of old age is that any method of suicide used is likely to have more serious and immediate consequences than with a younger person. No doubt many "risk-taking" attempts which a more youthful individual would survive actually lead to death in the case of elderly persons.

There is a third circumstance producing a high ratio of completed to attempted suicide. This is suicide of the seriously or fatally ill. It will not do in explaining such suicides simply to hold that when a person who is seriously ill kills himself it is to escape from the physical pain which he suffers. Many people in such a situation put up with very great pain without any serious inclination towards suicide. Study of cases of suicide connected with physical illness show that the vast majority are much more concerned with the incapacitation which is usually involved. In most cases, where an individual is bed-ridden or perhaps suffers some obvious physical deformities as a result of such illness, he is placed in a situation which is definitely "anomic": where he must adjust to a social and physical condition demanding radical changes in his habits and conception of self.

I have not so far mentioned in this paper the third type of suicide which Durkheim discussed at length in *Suicide*: the "altruistic" type. My main justification for this omission is that I intend the typology developed in the paper to apply only in the first instance to modern or "industrial" societies. While Durkheim considered that examples of altruistic suicide could be found in advanced societies, it is, according to him, a type characteristic of more traditional ones. "Obligatory" altruistic suicide takes the form of a duty: a person placed in a certain social position has an obligation to kill himself. (as in *suttee*, for example). Durkheim distinguished this from a second sub-type, "optional" (*faculatif*) altruistic suicide, which involves no definite form of obligation, and where a person kills himself in such a way as to bring honour to his name. But the anthropological evidence which Durkheim had to rely on was, by modern standards, insubstantial and no doubt partly apocryphal. More recent anthropological research shows that suicide in traditional societies only rarely fits readily within Durkheim's altruistic category: most cases approximate much more closely to the egoistic/anomic types[51]. Moreover, as Halbwachs pointed out, it hardly seems appropriate to regard some of the instances Durkheim classed as altruistic suicide as cases of suicide at all. In many of these cases it would seem reasonable to class the act as one of "sacrifice", and to regard this as separate from suicide proper. In other cases which might be labelled as "altruistic" suicide, there are elements present which suggest that they could be treated within the context of the typology set out in this paper. Consider the case of the Buddhist monk who consigns himself to the flames in a public and deliberate fashion. Durkheim would no doubt regard this as an instance of altruistic suicide; but very evident in this form of suicide are similar characteristics to those which are found, usually in a less open form, in suicides discussed in this paper: the act represents an accusation, a protest, against some wrongdoing on the part of others.[52]

NOTES

1 An early bibliography of suicide is given in E. Motta, *Bibliographia del suicidio*, Bellinzona, 1890.

2 H. Rost, *Bibliographie des Selbstmords*, Augsburg, 1927.

3 *i.e.*, items in English, French and German. The latest comprehensive bibliography of suicide is in N. L. Farberow and E. S. Shneidman, *The Cry for Help*, New York: McGraw-Hill, 1961, pp. 325–88.

4 There is also a very large literature on moral aspects of suicide, which stretches right back to classical times. A few works of this kind are noted in Farberow and Shneidman, ibid, pp. 387–8.

5 This was recognized, in effect, by the earliest writers on suicide, who commonly distinguished between the "internal", and "external" or social, causes of suicide.

6 An important exception to this is A. F. Henry and J. F. Short, *Suicide and Homicide*, Glencoe: Free Press, 1954.

7 M. Halbwachs, *Les Causes du suicide*, Paris: Alcan, 1930.

8 Perhaps the most important respect in which Halbwachs failed to confirm Durkheim's findings was in his findings that suicide rates do not rise, but tend to drop, during period of marked economic prosperity. See pp. 362–74.

9 A useful statistical source-book is L. I. Dublin and B. Bunzel, *To Be Or Not to Be*, New York: Smith and Haas, 1933. The results of various ecological studies of suicide in urban areas also basically support Durkheim's general position. See R. S. Caven, *Suicide*, Chicago: University of Chicago Press, 1928; C. F. Schmid, *Suicide in Seattle*, Seattle: University of Washington Publications, No. 5, 1928; P. Sainsbury, *Suicide in London*, London: Chapman and Hall, 1955; also cf: R. E. L. Faris, *Social Disorganisation*, New York: Ronald Press, 1955.

10 Cf. Halbwachs, op. cit., p. 480 et. seq.

11 E. Durkheim, *Suicide*, translated J. A. Spaulding and G. Simpson, London, Routledge and Kegan Paul, 1952, pp. 208–16.

12 R. K. Merton, 'Social structure and anomie', in *Social Theory and Social Structure*, Glencoe: Free Press, 1957. An inventory of subsequent studies

using the concept of anomie is given in M. B. Clinard, *Anomie and Deviant Behaviour,* Glencoe: Free Press, 1964.

13. See e.g. Sainsbury, op. cit., p. 22.

14 Durkheim, op. cit., pp. 208–16, and 246–57. Cf. Also Parsons' comments: T. Parsons, *The Structure of Social Action,* Glencoe: Free Press, 1937, pp. 332–8, and 'The Integration of Social Systems', in K. Wolff (ed.), *Emile Durkheim,* Glencoe: Free Press, 1962, pp. 118–53. Johnson has recently pointed out certain ambiguities in Durkheim's discussion of the types of suicide. He argues that the types which Durkheim claims to distinguish can all be reduced to a single structural dimension—that Durkheim in fact isolated just one structural cause of suicide. I do not agree with this interpretation; but in any case this does not affect the logic of the typology presented in this paper. See B. Johnson, 'Durkheim's one cause of suicide', *American Sociological Review,* XXX, 1965, pp. 875–86.

15 J. P. Gibbs and W. T. Martin, *Status Integration and Suicide,* Eugene: University of Oregon Press, 1964.

16 Cf. B. P. Dohrenwend, 'Egoism, altruism, anomie and fatalism: a conceptual analysis of Durkheim's types', *American Sociological Review,* XXIV, 1959, pp. 466–72.

17 It should be emphasized, that I do not intend to use "anomie" and "failure" as synonymous terms. Anomie, both structural and psychological, is however, frequently consequential upon a situation where potentialities for "failure" in certain sectors of social activity are built into the social structure.

18 The evidence cannot be presented in detail here. One of the most recent relevant studies is W. Breed, 'Occupational mobility and suicide among white males', *American Sociological Review,* XXVIII, 1963, pp. 179–88. (Reprinted in this volume, pp. 280–297.)

19 S. Freud, *Mourning and melancholia* (Standard Edition), London: Hogarth Press, 1955, Vol. XVII. Also *The Ego and the Id* (Standard Edition), Vol. XIX. A description of psychoanalytic ideas on suicide is given in D. D. Jackson: 'Theories of suicide' in E. S. Schneidman and N. L. Farberow, *Clues to Suicide,* New York: MacGraw-Hill, 1957, pp. 11–21. Throughout this article I have used the term "depression" generically in a very wide sense, to include both neurotic and psychotic depression. While there are several partially distinct psychoanalytic theories of depression, I have confined the account mainly to Freud's classical statement of the nature of melancolia, since the other theories are basically elaborations of the fundamental ideas set out there.

20 Freud, *Mourning and melancholia,* p. 246.

21 Ibid., p. 251.

22 Cf. K. Menninger, *Man Against Himself,* New York: Harcourt Brace, 1938.

23 Freud, op. cit., p. 252.

24 Cf. C. W. Wahl: 'Suicide as a magical act', in Shneidman and Farberow, op. cit., pp. 22–30.

25 Freud, op. cit., p. 245.

26 In this analysis I have followed the basic distinctions set out by Piers. See Piers and M. B. Singer, *Shame and Guilt,* Springfield: G. C. Thomas, 1953.

27 Ibid., p. 23 etc. It should, of course, be understood that the "super-ego" and "ego-ideal" are "ordering constructs" and not in any sense discrete "entities".

28 Ibid., p. 16. Most psychoanalists, following Freud, have regarded shame as being linked specifically to fear of genital exposure, and thus to anxiety over bodily "appearance" more generally. The phenomenon of shame is, in fact, much more pervasive than this in human experience. That this is so is shown by the frequency with which "feeling ashamed" and synonymous phrases (e.g. "feeling humiliated") occur in the course of everyday speech. While anthropologists have pointed to the importance of shame as a social and psychological mechanism in traditional and primitive societies, little has been written of shame in W. European societies. Indeed some anthropologists have sought to contrast the "guilt cultures" of W. Europe with "shame cultures". But, although shame may have a more "external" aspect in societies in which tight formalised standards of expected accomplishment prevail, the phenomena of shame and shaming are ubiquitous. Shame is evidently closely related to embarrassment, which may be nothing more than a mild sense of shame. Both shame and embarrassment stem from a questioning of the appropriateness of an identity which an individual is attempting to maintain. The more deep-rooted nature of shame is indicated by the fact that, while we can "be embarrassed *for* another", we are "ashamed *of* another": in the second instance, the behaviour of the other casts a slur upon *ourself*, while in the first we feel in an empathic way that he is showing himself in a bad light. Cf. E. Goffman, *The Presentation of Self in Everyday Life*, New York: Doubleday, 1959, p. 58 et seq., and *Stigma*, Englewood Cliffs: Prentice Hall, 1963. Cf. also K. Riezler, 'Comment on the social psychology of shame', *American Journal of Sociology*, XLVIII, 1943, pp. 457–65.

29 Menninger describes cases of suicide following the most trivial of setbacks. Cf. K. Menninger, op. cit., pp. 35–36.

30 H. Hendin, *Suicide and Scandinavia*, New York. Doubleday, 1965, p. 26.

31 Ibid., pp. 19–28.

32 Menninger, op. cit., pp. 23–71.

33 Durkheim, op. cit., p. 51.

34 Cf. Anthony Giddens, 'Theoretical problems in the sociology of suicide', *Advancement of Science*, XXI, 1965, pp. 522–6; and 'The suicide problem in French sociology', *British Journal of Sociology*, XVI, 1965, pp. 3–18. (Reprinted in this volume, pp. 36–51.)

35 This double aspect of depression was pointed out by Rado S. Rado, 'Psychodynamics of depression from the aetiological point of view', *Collected Papers*, New York: Grune and Stratton, 1956, Vol. I, pp. 235–42.

36 Fenichel, op. cit., p. 400.

37 Hendin, op. cit., p. 24.

38 E. Stengel, *Suicide and Attempted Suicide*, London: Penguin, 1964, pp. 103–7. J. Cohen, *Behaviour in Uncertainty*, London: Allen and Unwin, 1964. Cf. also R. Firth, 'Suicide and risk-taking in Tikopian Society', *Psychiatry*, XXIV, 1961, pp. 1–17. (Reprinted in this volume, pp. 197–222.)

39 E. Stengel and N. G. Cook, *Attempted Suicide*, London: Oxford U.P., 1958, p. 144 et seq.

40 H. M. Lynd, *On Shame and the Search for Identity*, London: Routledge and Kegan Paul, 1958, p. 50.

41 Durkheim, op. cit., p. 278.

42 Ibid., p. 286.

43 Cf. Hendin's discussion of suicide in Sweden: Hendin, op. cit., pp 51–87.

44 E. Beresford Davies (ed)., *Depression*, New York: Cambridge U.P., 1964, pp. 22–3. Such states are not necessarily suicidal. As in the case of "classical depressive states, a key factor may be how far death is invested with instrumental significance as a "means to an end".

45 Durkheim, op. cit., p. 288.

46 Piers and Singer, op. cit., p. 16 et seq.

47 A note is necessary on the relationship between mental ilness and suicide. Mental disorder is often regarded as a "cause" of suicide, with the implication that other suicides are "caused" by other factors. The reason for the close relationship between mental disorder and suicide is, however, rather that certain types of mental disorder—and, of course, in particular the depressive disorders—provide "suicidogenic" psychological conditions. These include: 1. a high level of emotional conflict and anxiety; 2. a tendency to extreme states of depression; 3. specific ideas about the nature of death. Thus suicide of the mentally ill does not fall outside the general framework developed in this paper. The causes of suicide overlap with, but do not correspond to, the causes of mental illness. N. L. Farberow and E. S. Schneidman, 'Suicide among schizophrenic mental hospital patients', in Farberow and Schneidman, op. cit., pp. 78–109.

48 K. Menninger, 'Psychoanalytic aspects of suicide', *International Journal of Psychoanalysis*, XIV, 1933, pp. 376–90.

49 Stengel and Cook, op. cit., pp. 119–21.

50 E. S. Shneidman and N. L. Farberow, 'Statistical Comparisons between attempted and committed suicides', in Shneidman and Farberow, op. cit., pp. 28–9.

51 See, for example, P. Bohannan, *African Homicide and Suicide*, Princeton: Princeton U.P., 1960.

52 Anthony Giddens, 'Suicide, attempted suicide and the suicidal threat', Man, LVI (1964) pp. 115–16; and M. D. W. Jeffreys, 'Samsonic suicide or suicide or revenge among Africans', *African Studies*, XI, 1952, pp. 77–85.

CHAPTER 11

The Sociological Analysis of Social Meanings of Suicide*

Jack D. Douglas

The history of ideas demonstrates conclusively that certain ideas can become so pervasive and central to the thought of a culture that over many centuries the members of that culture unquestioningly apply these ideas in many different ways to new fields of experience.[1] Such ideas are what we shall call *metaphysical ideas*. Such metaphysical ideas normally form the ground for common-sense discourse. The history of ideas has shown that they also form the ground for, and frequently constitute much of the substance of, serious intellectual works. Though science in the western world was born and developed partly as an explicit revolution against all such unexamined, "unempirical" ideas, recent work in the history of science has led to the conclusion that scientific thought is largely the result of and partly constituted by just such metaphysical ideas.[2] Moreover, more recent work in the history of science has led to the conclusion that once scientific ideas have been accepted by the members of a scientific discipline, these ideas in turn come to form the unexamined ground and substance of the *normal* scientific works within that discipline. Though these ideas thus have far more in common with common-sense and humanistic discourse than most scientists would ever care to admit, there are some important differences which are taken into consideration by giving the established, unexamined ideas of sciences a different name—that of paradigmatic ideas.[3]

Though sociological thought is still to some extent in a non paradigmatic stage of thought construction, it does seem reasonably clear that since about the middle of the nineteenth century sociological thought has been constructed both of unexamined or metaphysical ideas and of paradigmatic ideas. Insofar as sociological thought has been paradigmatic, it has been *multiply paradigmatic*: that is, sociological thought has since that time normally been intentionally constructed in such a way that it will be seen by members of the (roughly

* Reprinted by permission from the *European Journal of Sociology*, Vol. VII, 1966, pp. 249–75.

defined) discipline to fit certain (multiple) ideas held by those members to constitute "sociological thought".[4] These paradigmatic ideas were the foundations upon which whole works were constructed. Sometimes one or two paradigmatic ideas formed the basis for a sociologist's lifetime work.[5] In general, however, those works were constructed around a number of paradigmatic ideas, even though these ideas often conflicted with each other when they were examined in relation to each other.[6]

Most of the twentieth century sociologists who have done works on suicide have taken Durkheim's *Suicide* as their major paradigm: that is, they have constructed their works in such a way that members of the discipline will see[7] their works as being further expositions of the fundamental (paradigmatic) ideas in Durkheim's *Suicide*. In doing so, they have implicitly assumed that the fundamental questions concerning the proper nature of a sociological investigation of suicide have already been answered in *Suicide*. This means that the fundamental ideas of these twentieth-century works are not at all apparent. One must certainly see them in the context of Durkheim's *Suicide* if he is to adequately understand them. Once again, however, the fundamental or paradigmatic ideas of Durkheim's *Suicide* cannot be very adequately understood until one puts it in the context of the many nineteenth-century works on suicide which Durkheim used to construct his own work.

For these reasons, our investigation of the sociological methods of analysing social meanings of suicide must begin with an investigation of the metaphysical and paradigmatic ideas of the nineteenth-century works which formed the context of Durkheim's *Suicide*. We shall then be ready to critically examine these ideas as they are found in their most developed form in Durkheim's *Suicide*. From this critical examination we shall be able to proceed to our exposition of what now seems to be the best sociological method of analysing social meanings of suicide.

NINETEENTH CENTURY SOCIOLOGICAL THOUGHT CONCERNING SUICIDE

The metaphysical ideas of the nineteenth-century sociologists were very close to the metaphysical ideas of common-sense, especially as they found these common-sense ideas expressed by literary and philosophical authors involved in the practical activities of administering public health programmes and government bureaus of vital statistics.

Throughout the entire nineteenth century, there was a great profusion of literary and philosophical works on suicide. This great interest of the intellectuals in suicide had begun in the eighteenth century when the ethics of suicide became a fundamental issue in the great debate over the real and proper nature(s) of society.[8] This concern with suicide as a social problem grew rapidly in the nineteenth century, eventually reaching a point at which a large segment of the population seems to have believed that there was a veritable "mania" for suicide sweeping Europe.[9]

This great concern with suicide led to the publication of a huge number of works on suicide which expressed the metaphysical ideas concerning suicide of common sense and which directly influenced the works of the sociologists. The works of Buonafède, Bourquelot, des Etangs, Debreyne, Lisle, de Boismont, and Legoyt were all quite important in this respect.[10]

From these many works, and probably from their own direct common-sense experience as well, the sociologists derived (or "absorbed") their most important metaphysical ideas for their works on suicide. Though by no means the only important metaphysical ideas in their works,[11] the three most important of these for our purpose are the following:

(1) Social actions are in some way caused (or motivated) by meanings held by the individual and shared by other members of the society.[12] This idea was and is one of the most fundamental common-sense ideas concerning persons. It was accepted and used by the sociologists even when certain of their paradigmatic ideas conflicted with it; and it remained very largely unexamined among the French and Italian sociologists who were most important in constructing sociological thought on suicide, even when the German sociologists began to consider the problem of determining social meanings to be the most fundamental problem of sociological thought. Though I do not think such a fundamental proposition should go unexamined, space limitations will prevent our treating it as problematic here; it will remain a metaphysical idea for our purpose in this essay.

(2) Individuals know the meanings of their own actions and they also know the meanings of other individual's actions. The first half of this metaphysical idea was denied by one of the paradigmatic ideas of sociological works in the later half of the nineteenth century (see below), but the second half, the ability of the observer (the sociologist) to understand the meanings of the actions of others, was retained.

(3) Meaningful social actions, especially actions which are moral or immoral, are just as subject to counting and quantitative analyses as are physical objects and properties. This idea, which was first clearly stated by certain philosophers at the end of the seventeenth century and first used in the analysis of social statistics by Süssmilch in the eighteenth century[13], remained very largely unexamined throughout the nineteenth century and the first half of the twentieth

century. (This particular idea is to some degree paradigmatic, in that it was quite explicitly stated by the moral statisticians and others and in that they sometimes examined the ways in which one should go about quantifying. However, it is treated here as being primarily a metaphysical idea because the sociologists never really questioned it and, therefore, never really attempted to establish or demonstrate its validity. From the seventeenth century on, men of practical affairs, such as government officials and physicians, had come to assume that the social world, like all the rest of the world, was subject to quantitative precision[14]. By the nineteenth century the only questions concerned matters of how one could most effectively quantify the social world.)

These metaphysical ideas pervade the sociological works of the nineteenth century—and most of those of the twentieth century. They were, however, most influential in determining the specific forms of thought in the sociological works through both their influence on the paradigmatic ideas of the sociological work and their combinations with the paradigmatic ideas in these works. The most important paradigmatic ideas of the nineteenth century sociological works on suicide (and on most other social phenomena) are the following:

(1) The stability of suicide rates proves that the official suicide statistics (from which these rates were taken) are reliable and valid. As de Guerry had said, such regularity could not be the result of chance:

> La statistique criminelle devient aussi positive, aussi certaine que les autres sciences d'observation lorsqu'on sait s'arrêter aux faits bien constatés, et les grouper de manière à les dégager de ce qu'ils offrent d'accidental. Ses résultats généraux se présentent alors avec une si grande régularité qu'il est impossible de les attribuer au hasard. Chaque année voit se reproduire le même nombre de crimes dans le même ordre, dan les mêmes régions ; chaque classe de crimes a sa distribution particulière et invariable, par âge, par saison ; tous sont accompagnés, dans des proportions pareilles, de faits accessories, indifférents en apparence, et dont rien encore n'explique le retour.[15]

(2) The stability of suicide rates indicates that these actions are caused by some lawful factors external to or not controlled by the individuals committing them. Again, de Guerry had stated the case rather well:

> Si nous considérons maintenant le nombre infini de circonstances qui peuvent faire commettre un crime, les influences extérieures ou purement personnelles qui en déterminent le caractère, nous ne saurons comment concevoir, qu'en dernier

résultat, leur concours amène des effets si constants, que les actes d'une volonté libre viennent ainsi se développer dans un ordre fixe, se resserrer dans des limites si étroites. Nous serons forcés de reconnaître que les faits de l'ordre moral sont soumis, comme ceux de l'ordre physique, à des lois invariables, et qu'à plusieurs égards, la statistique judiciaire présente une certitude complète.[16]

(3) The most important external factors causing these actions are social factors[17]

(4) The most important social factors in the causation of social rates of suicide are the social meanings, especially the "moral customs" of the social groups. This paradigmatic idea was clearly an explicit formulation of one of the most important metaphysical ideas.[18]

(5) There exists a reasonably small set of highly abstract social meanings (called the "social system" or the "social structure") which are the causes of specific patterns of social actions such as suicide rates; and the only valid sociological theory of such patterns (or suicide rates) will be one in terms of states of this set of abstract meanings. Unlike the other paradigmatic ideas, this idea was not fully developed until Durkheim's *Suicide*.[19] As we shall show further below, however, this idea, in the specific form used by Durkheim, had slowly developed throughout the century.

THE CONFLICT OF METHODS

These metaphysical and paradigmatic ideas, especially when combined with a few lesser paradigmatic ideas (see below), formed the basis for two fundamentally different methods for analysing the social meanings of suicidal actions. At first, these two methods were pretty well combined, at least syncretistically, in the works of *statistical medicine*.[20] As the nineteenth century progressed, however, these two traditions of methodological analysis, the *case study method* and the *(moral) statistical method*, came into increasing conflict. Out of this conflict the moral statisticians created certain paradigmatic ideas to justify their own method and to "invalidate" the case study method. These paradigmatic ideas, combined with the more general metaphysical and paradigmatic ideas already discussed, came to constitute the distinctive ideas of Durkheim's *sociologistic* position.[21]

THE CASE STUDY METHOD

The method of determining the meanings causing suicidal actions by studying the individual cases of suicide was firmly grounded in the metaphysical ideas that actions are caused by meanings shared and understood by all members of the society. Given these two ideas, it was apparent that to explain suicide, one had to know its meanings and that one could best know these meanings by self-reports of meanings. The increasing use, primarily by doctors, of the ideas of scientific induction in explaining any actions led to the development of this common-sensical method into an attempt to provide more abstract explanations by observing a number of cases of suicide. This *informal statistical method* (or *method of analytic induction*)[22] was increasingly formalized. It developed from a simple, unstructured review of the classical literary cases of suicide in such works as those of Montaigne[23] and Voltaire[24] into the careful counting by Brierre de Boismont[25] and others of the number of suicide notes giving certain motives for the ensuing suicidal actions. The methods used by the members of this methodological tradition for determining the meanings of suicide, however, did not become formalized along the lines of the statistical method. These researchers and theorists did not attempt to impose any sets of predetermined categories upon these meanings, rather, their analyses stayed close to the linguistic categories used by the suicides themselves. Nor did they make much attempt to analyse the meanings by any more formal methods.

Though, as we shall shortly argue, this case study method was in certain respects more valid than the statistical method used by the sociologists of the latter part of the nineteenth century, still the method involved far too simplistic a view of social meanings. For our purposes here, it is sufficient to note that the method failed to consider the complexity and difficulty of understanding one's self. It assumed far too high a degree of self-awareness, rationality, and honesty on the part of social actors. It was in part because of their realization of this that the moral statisticians and, subsequently, the Durkheimian sociologists rejected the case study method of determining and analysing the social meanings of suicide. This was shown in two specific paradigmatic ideas they both adopted and created in their analyses of the works based on the case study method:

(a) suicide itself is an irrational action, so that individuals who commit suicide cannot be presumed to understand the meanings of their own actions;[26]

(b) men are in general infinitely complex and/or irrational, so that the whole case study method of analysing meanings by taking the statement and actions of individuals as the fundamental data is invalid.

There were, however, other reasons, probably more important reasons, for the rejection of the case study method by these groups of sociologists. For one thing, some of them were anxious to create their own professional and academic discipline, and this seemed to demand a method that was distinct from the common-sense methods still used by the (philosophical and psychological) case study method-ologists. As Durkheim said, "[. . .] if there is to be social science, we shall expect it not merely to paraphrase the traditional prejudices of the common man but to give us a new and different view of them".[27] Even more importantly, however, there was the distinctive mathematical method, the statistical method, to which the moral statisticians had become increasingly committed. The fundamental idea of this whole mathematical method was that individual differ-ences must, for certain purposes, be eliminated or overlooked. Quetelet had, to some extent, attempted to salvage consideration of individuals by his *average man theory;* but data on individuals was increasingly rejected until the fundamental paradigm of the sociolo-gistic position almost[28] completely eliminated such data:

(c) society must be considered to be a different level of reality from individuals, so that analysing data from individuals is invalid.[29]

Unfortunately, as we shall see, this paradigmatic idea had as one of its consequences the elimination of all scientific means of deter-mining and analysing the social meanings of suicide.

THE STATISTICAL METHOD OF ANALYSING THE SOCIAL MEANINGS OF SUICIDE

Though it extends back to the works of the political arithmeticians and Süssmilch by direct lines of influence, the statistical method of the sociologists in the nineteenth century developed primarily in three major, interrelated schools of thought, each making somewhat differ-ent use of the fundamental metaphysical and paradigmatic ideas: the medical statisticans and medical hygienists, deriving largely from the French "idéologues",[30] and best represented by Villerne and Parent Duchatelet; the probability theorists, deriving largely from the direct influence of Laplace on Quetelet, who in turn influenced the works of all the traditions; and the demographic works, deriving from many different sources, including Süssmilch through his influ-ence on Malthus and others. These traditions of thought were in-creasingly synthesized and carried forward during the century by the *moral statisticians,* especially by the works of Guerry, Etoc-Demazy,[31] de Boismont, Lisle,[32] Morselli, Œttingen,[33] Wappaus, Masaryk, Wagner,[34] and Bertillon.[35] At the end of the century stands the great attempt at a synthesis of the fundamental metaphysical and paradigmatic ideas of these traditions of thought, Durkheim's *Suicide.*[36] Since Durkheim's work is the best of these moral statistical works[37] and since it is this work which still serves as the sociological paradigm for research and theory on suicide, we must briefly examine Durkheim's methods of determining and analysing the social meanings of suicide.

On the most general level, the task which Durkheim set himself in *Suicide* was that of *systematically relating the already established statistical relations between certain official statistics on official categorizations of individuals (such as married, divorced, etc.) and certain official statistics on suicide rates to the egoist-anomie theory of immoral actions developed by certain Romantic authors*,[38] and previously applied only partially to the statistics on suicide by Boismont and Morselli.[39]

The official statistics on suicide were treated as being almost completely non-problematic (except in the instance of official categorizations of motives, which conflicted with Durkheim's whole theory of suicide). In writing *Suicide* Durkheim accepted as valid Morselli's idea that "A corpse is a corpse", by which Morselli meant that an official categorizer of the causes of death could very reliably and validly tell if an individual had committed suicide.

There was actually no adequate justification for this assumption. The medical examiners and theorists of suicide, including Esquirol, had long been aware of the great difficulty of determining whether or not a corpse was the result of a suicide.[40] Most importantly of all, these problems were the direct result of the *social meanings of suicide* shared by various groups of vital statisticians. Unfortunately for Durkheim's own arguments, the official categorizations of a death as caused by "suicide" were generally most dependent on their imputations of an *intention to die by one's own action: since one of the critical dimensions of meanings involved in the statutory definitions of "suicide" as a cause of death and in the general common-sense meanings of "suicide" in the Western World is precisely that of "intention to die"*,[41] the official categorizations of "suicide" can in general be only as valid and reliable as official categorizations of "intention". Since Durkheim thought official categories of intentions or motives to be completely invalid and unreliable, he should have concluded the same thing about official statistics on suicide. (The *essentially problematic* nature of the social meanings of "suicide" is a far more important reason for considering the official statistics on suicide to have unknown—and possibly unknowable—meanings, but we shall deal with this below.)

Durkheim probably believed to some extent that the stability of the official statistics on suicide meant that they could not to any significant degree be the result of errors. This view had been expressed much earlier by Guerry, was used intermittently throughout the

nineteenth century, and was ultimately given its most brilliant exposition by Halbwachs in *Les Causes de suicide*.[42] The argument is
invalid, even in its most brilliant form, two reasons which these
theories failed to consider: even "errors" are normally found to fit
certain stable patterns;[43] and the complex nature of the social meanings of suicide which lead to a greater number of different ways of
categorizing suicide, actually lead one to expect highly stable probability distributions in the official categorizations of suicide.[44]

Besides this fundamental problem with the official statistics on
suicide, there are a large number of biases in the official statistics
that parallel the official categories of social structure (class, occupation, age, etc.) in such a way as to greatly bias any theory constructed
from or tested by them. Most importantly, it seems most reasonable
to expect that in societies, such as the Western World, in which some
groups morally stigmatize suicides and their families, there will be
both differential tendencies on the parts of members of different
(official) categories to have any "suspicious" deaths within their
families categorized as something other than "suicide" and differential degrees of success in these attempts. Moreover, it seems most
reasonable to expect that the attempts and the frequencies of success
will be greatest precisely in those groups which are most "integrated"
in the society. The general implication of this very involved argument is that the greater the degree of social "integration" of a group,
the lower will be its official suicide rate *as a result of the nature of the
official categorization process itself.* Consequently, one can explain
the fundamental correlations in Durkheim's argument in terms of
the nature of the *official categorization processes.*[45]

In general, the use of official statistics on suicide to derive and
test sociological theories of suicide was based on fallacious assumptions and arguments. Moreover, the failure of the sociologists using
the statistical method of analysing social meanings to see this was
the direct result of their failure to see the importance of social meanings in determining the official statistics and of their whole statistical
method of analysing social meanings.

On the one side of Durkheim's general argument were the official
statistics on suicide. On the other side were the official statistics on
other official categories such as marriage, divorce, education, etc.
Durkheim by no means assumed that correlation constituted causality
or explanation. The explanation of these statistical relations in terms
of social meanings was provided by Durkheim in different ways: (1)
his causal (or backward) definitions of suicide types provided him
with some social meanings; (2) he derived the meanings of the other
official categories from his common-sense observations and reason-
ings; (3) he inferred social meanings from the juristic norms or

laws of the society; (4) he inferred *post hoc* some meanings of these other categories from their relative associations with the statistics on types of suicide (which had been given meanings by definition, though these definitions really were partly descriptive definitions derived from Durkheim's knowledge of the works using the case study method of analysing social meanings;[46] and (5) he inferred the meanings of the relations from many different *petitio principii* created for the purpose.

Durkheim's *petitio principii* method of argument has been very well criticized by both Alpert and Needham and will not concern us here.[47] Durkheim's *post hoc* or causal definitions of the suicide types actually added little social meaning to the rest of his analyses. The critical aspect of his whole method of determining and analysing social meanings of suicide was the method he used to determine and analyse the meanings of the official categories other than suicide. Bayet, in his great work on *Le suicide et la morale*, was the first sociologist to see clearly that Durkheim's whole method of determining and analysing the meanings of these categories (and, one should add, of the types of suicide as well) was common-sensical:

> En tout cas, ce qui est grave, c'est qu'il faut croire l'auteur sur parole. Où sont les usages prouvant que les protestants "punissent le suicide"? Par quoi s'exprime "l'éloignement" pour ceux qui touchent au suidicé? Quels faits permettent de dire que la morale commune réprouve le suicide? Durkheim ne le dit pas. Sans doute est-il d'avis que la morale de son temps est la sienne et qu'il la connaît. Mais on peut supposer aussi, sans aucun paradoxe, que notre propre morale nous est en un sens fort étrangére. Le témoignage du plus grand philosophe ne peut remplacer, au point de vue scientifique, des observations soumises au contrôle à la critique.[48]

Durkheim did not clearly see the need for any scientific method of determining and analysing meanings: probably because he started *Suicide* with a positivistic method which emphasized external (morphological) factors as the causes of social actions such as suicide.[49] In the course of the work he came increasingly to see the social meanings of such categories or factors as being the critical causes or explanations of the suicide rates, but he had no objective method of determining social meanings other than the use of common-sense and the existing juristic norms. In one part of *Suicide* he argued, as he had earlier, that only the juristic norms were an adequate indication of the moral meanings, since they were not subject to individual variations.[50] His whole argument, however, rested on the absolutely fundamental assumption that the moral meanings of suicide do not vary within Western cultures, since, otherwise, variations in suicide rates could be explained by his own theory in terms of variations in these moral meanings rather than in terms of variations in the social meanings of anomie-fatalism and egoism-altruism. (Bayet saw how fundamental Durkheim's assumption of the invariance in moral meanings was to Durkheim's whole argument and proceeded to demonstrate in immense detail just how unjustified Durkheim's assumption was for his own society, France.) This meant that he was left with nothing but common sense to determine and analyse the variations in the social meanings of the categories which he was using to explain variations in the suicide rates.

To adequately demonstrate that Durkheim did rely almost exclusively upon his common-sense understandings of the official categories of social relations to derive or impute the critical meanings between these official categories of social relations and his general, meaningful causes of anomie-fatalism and egoism-altruism would demand an extremely long argument. Since, moreover, this argument has already been presented elsewhere, we shall content ourselves with one instance of this critical flaw in Durkheim's argument. When Durkheim invoked the supposed differences between the masculine mind and the feminine mind to explain the less "constraining" effect on women of marriage, he was merely following the established practice among students of suicide. Morselli had argued, for example, that men are, by their nature, much more subject to "egoistical motives" than women:

> As to her causes (physical and moral) the greatest excess of men is found in the group of vices, in that of financial embarrassments, and in weariness of life, that is to say, amongst the egoistical motives, whilst among women, after mental diseases, there predominate passions, domestic troubles, shame and remorse (especially in cases of illegitimate pregnancy). Among the causes which urge them to leave this life woman always exhibits that spirit of self-denial, that delicacy of feeling and of love, which, inspire all her acts.[51]

Now, Durkheim does not at all dispute the greater egoistic suicide rate of men. Largely working with the same statistics on family associations and suicide that Morselli used, Durkheim found more or less the same statistical relations and, working in the same theoretical tradition, he agreed, in his own way, that the difference was man's greater egoism. But he then supplies a completely contrary (and very complex) common-sense interpretation of this supposedly greater masculine egoism, an interpretation that happens to fit all of the details of his own theory:

> This is also why woman can endure life in isolation more easily

than man. When a widow is seen to endure her condition much better than a widower and desires marriage less passionately, one is led to consider this ease in dispensing with family a mark of superiority ; it is said that woman's affective faculties, being very intense, are easily employed outside the domestic circle, while her devotion is indispensable to man to help him endure life. Actually, if this is her privilege it is because her sensibility is rudimentary rather than highly developed. As she lives outside of community existence more than man, she is less penetrated by it ; society is less necessary to her because she is less impregnated with sociability. She has few needs in this direction and satisfies them easily. With a few devotional practices and some animals to care for, the old unmarried woman's life is full. If she remains faithfully attached to religious traditions and thus finds ready protection against suicide, it is because these very simple social forms satisfy all her needs. Man, on the contrary, is hard beset in this respect. As his thought and activity develop, they increasingly overflow these antiquated forms. But then he needs others. Because he is a more complex social being, he can maintain his equilibrium only by finding more points of support outside himself, and it is because his moral balance depends on a larger number of conditions that it is more easily disturbed.[52]

Even when he was aware of common-sense interpretations that were completely contrary to his own, he continued to use his common-sense interpretations with complete confidence.

THE METHOD OF USING SYSTEMATIC COMPARISONS OF SITUATED COMMUNICATIONS TO DETERMINE AND ANALYSE THE SOCIAL MEANINGS OF SUICIDE[53]

The logical outcome of the paradigmatic ideas of those works using the statistical method of determining and analysing social meanings is that found in Durkheim's sociologistic theory : *they have no scientific means of determining and analysing social meanings in terms of real-world events that can be objectively observed and replicated because they have denied all epistemological value to such forms of data.* They must, however, have social meanings to explain the suicide rates. Consequently, they must use their common sense ideas (their *deus ex machina data*) about the meanings of certain categories. Being unconstrained by any methods of observations for arriving at such meanings, they use their common-sense ideas to impute those meanings to the category which their abstract theories have predicted. The argument has now come full circle and appears very convincing until one considers the nature of the critical evidence, the social meanings.[54]

Though the details are very difficult, the general nature of the remedy is clear: in order to determine and analyse the social meanings of suicide, and thence, to be able to determine what causal relations exist between these meanings and the various types of suicidal actions, sociologists must develop scientific methods of observing, describing and analysing communicative actions concerning real-world cases of suicide. Since we have already seen the fundamental weaknesses of the early case study method, this earlier method will not help much. The twentieth century case study methods of psychiatry and psychology are also of little use, since they are based primarily on certain abstract, predetermined, genetic theories of action[55] which leave out of consideration almost all aspects of social meanings and, thereby, falsify the nature of human action.

What is called for is a whole new sociological method for determining and analysing the communicative actions which can be observed and replicated in real-world cases of suicide. This method must retain the emphasis on observation and description of the earlier case-study methods, but it must also retain the emphasis on comparative studies of patterns of meanings of the statistical method.

The ideal method would involve, at the first step of observation, the exact recording of all verbal and non-verbal communicative acts involved in a case of suicide. The next step would be the preliminary analysis of the patterns of invariant *linguistic items* (i.e. words, phrases, sentences, facial expressions, etc.). Following this, one would next analyse such communications to determine the *varying structures* in which these linguistic items appear: that is, one would determine the *usages* (or *constructions*—see below) made with these linguistic items. One would then attempt to determine the relations between the general *situations* or contexts of the social actors, as defined by the actors, and the constructions appearing. Lastly, one would be ready to attempt a more general theory relating meanings to each other and to actions.

We need hardly point out that this ideal is quite utopian at this time. At the present time the best approximation to the ideal method which is practicable involves the careful use of the best cases of suicidal communications and actions recorded by psychiatrists and other persons involved, such as the persons committing the actions, analysed by one's common-sense understandings of the meanings of such communicative acts in our society.[56] Such analyses of cases must be comparative and must not be predetermined by some set of personality or society categories *assumed* to be the only right categories for understanding the social world.

Such an analysis is clearly a very lengthy one that we cannot possibly fully undertake here, even though the details of the method will not be clear until one can actually see a number of cases being comparatively analysed. However, my previous analyses of just this sort have led to conclusions which have fundamental implications for all sociological investigations and theory and which, consequently, are especially worth summarising here.[57] Following the brief statement of these general conclusions, we shall briefly analyse a few cases of "revenge suicide" to demonstrate some of the fundamental details of this method of determining and analysing the social meanings of suicide.

The sociologist who begins to consider the actual ways in which officials go about deciding that a given instance of death is a "suicide" soon discovers a startling fact about "suicide" in the Western World. First of all, one discovers that the term "suicide" does not have any clear and distinct meanings in the Western World, not even in terms of the formal definitions proposed by theorists or those decreed by law for the officials charged with categorizing the "causes of death". The following are the most common dimensions of meanings found in different combinations in the formal and legal definitions of "suicide":

(1) the *initiation* of an act that leads to the death of the initiator;
(2) the *willing* of an act that leads to the death of the willer;
(3) the willing of self-destruction;
(4) the loss of will;
(5) the motivation to be dead (or to die, or to be killed) which leads to the initiation of an act that leads to the death of the initiator;
(6) the *knowledge* of an actor concerning the relations between his acts and the objective state of death;
(7) the degree of *central integration of the decisions* of an actor who decides to initiate an action that leads to the death of the actor;
(8) the *degree of firmness or persistence of the decision* (or *willing*) to initiate an act that leads to the death of the initiator;
(9) the *degree of effectiveness* of the actions in producing death.[58]

The profusion and complexity of different definitions of suicide certainly makes it apparent that different official statistics on suicide cannot be comparable. But, far more importantly, it indicates that "suicide" is an *essentially problematic conception*: that is, "suicide" is not a socially meaningful linguistic category that is *either* applied rightly *or* wrongly to any given instance of social action; rather, it is a category with different (abstract) meaning that can rightfully *either* be applied *or not* applied to certain types of actions. Whether or not the category is actually imputed in a given situation is dependent on factors that are partially independent of the meanings of the term itself. Most especially, whether or not the category is imputed in a given situation is dependent upon the *argument processes* that take place between the participants in the situation. (For example, it is most common for members of the family and friends to argue with the official categorizers to the effect that this instance of death should not be categorized as a "suicide".)

This essentially problematic nature of the social meanings of "suicide" means, for one thing, that there is no such thing as one definite, necessarily valid (socially meaningful) "Suicide rate". The whole idea of a given, necessarily valid (or invalid) "Suicide rate" for a Western society is a complete misconception of the meaningful nature of "suicide" in Western societies, *even* if one is only concerned with the categorizations made by officials. (One would expect, however, that the meanings are less essentially problematic among one group with a high degree of shared experience than between different groups of this nature.) Whatever the state of reality, the "facts", one can construct many different, equally "valid", socially meaningful counts of "suicide", and this is true even if, for some totally arbitrary reasons, one attends only to the categorizations of officials. The problem with statistics on suicide, therefore, is not at all one of simply devising more accurate measurements. The fundamental problem of determining and analysing the social meanings of suicide must be solved *before* one can attempt any quantitative analyses.

However, it is even more important to discover that, aside from being essentially problematic, "suicide" is also *situationally* (or pragmatically) *problematic*. That is, regardless of the abstract social meanings given to the category of "suicide", the actual or realized imputations of the category in any given instance of death are dependent upon many other factors, most especially upon the intentions of the participants. (An obvious instance of this which illustrates the difference between the two types of problems of meanings is the individual who specifically intends to commit what he imputes the category of "suicide" but does it in such a way that the local officials will categorize it as an "accident".)

Since there are no specific meanings imputed to all (or even most) suicidal actions, the meanings of such actions must be *constructed* by the individuals committing them and by the others involved *through their interactions with each other*. Just what specific meanings are realized or actually imputed will depend on the *intentions* of the various actors, the *socially perceived* ways in which the actions are committed, the specific *patterns of suicidal meanings* (see below) which are realized, and the whole *argument processes*, before, during, and after the "suicidal actions". (It should be clearly noted that whether or not actions are socially categorized as "suicidal" depends on precisely the same sort of process. That is, individuals construct arguments involving behaviour and statements in order to communicate to other arguers the meanings which best fit their intentions. The obvious examples are those individuals who construct situations which they believe will be categorized as "accidents", with the intentions of avoiding "embarrassment" for their families, stigmatization of their character, loss of insurance money, etc.)

The study of suicide in terms of specific situations or real-world instances of "suicide" leads one to see that the meanings imputed to "suicide" by individuals not involved in a concrete, real-world situation of suicidal actions are very different from the meanings imputed to "suicide" by individuals who are involved in a concrete situation of suicidal action at the time of the communication. This means that *the situated meanings are very different from the abstract meanings*. This finding has two fundamental implications for all investigations of the social meanings of suicide and, most likely, for all of sociology. First of all, it is not possible to predict or explain types of social events, such as suicide, in terms of abstract social meanings such as egoism or general social values against suicide. This is a denial of both the fundamental paradigmatic idea of Durkheim's sociologistic theory and of the (derivative) fundamental paradigmatic idea of most general theories in sociology today. Secondly, *it is not possible to study the situated social meanings of suicide, which are more important in the causation of suicide, by any means (such as questionnaires or laboratory experiments) which involve abstracting the communicators from concrete instances of suicide in which they are involved.* This generalization leads one to question the value of any method of investigation of any realm of social action which attempts to abstract the members of the society from the involvements of their everyday lives.

This does not mean that there are not patterns of meanings common to those events imputed the category of "suicide" or "suicidal" by members of the society. When one looks at the meanings imputed in concrete situations one does find certain *general dimensions of meanings* occurring in almost all cases. Most importantly, any suicidal action is believed to mean something fundamental (or *substantial*) about the self of the individual committing it, or about the situation (especially the significant others) in which he committed the action, or about some combination of the self and the situation. Whether the specific meaning realized (see below) will be directed to the self or to the situation of the actor will depend on the *imputations of causality* made by the various interactors: that is, will they see the individual as the cause (or "responsible") for his own actions or will they see him as having been caused ("driven") to do it by the situation (loss of job, family trouble, etc.). The individual committing the suicidal action very generally attempts to place one of those two general *constructions of meanings* upon the action by making use of such devices as pointing out the external cause which is to be imputed causality (or blame) for his suicide.

It is not possible for individuals to construct just any meanings whatsoever for their actions, though individual creativity does extend the limits immensely and all cases include imponderable idiosyncrasies. There are, first of all, the various criteria determining the *plausibility of arguments,* which limit very greatly the meanings which can be realized, though it is even most likely that in some instances individuals even intend to have their arguments considered to be implausible or irrational ("insane", "senseless", etc.). There are, secondly, relatively few patterns of situated meanings which one finds playing important parts in most of the realized meanings concerning "suicidal actions" and which, consequently, are very generally used by individuals to intentionally construct certain overall meanings. (Because of their frequency it seems most likely that individuals must take these patterns into consideration in some way in their attempts to construct the meanings of their actions for others.) The most common patterns of meanings of this sort in the Western World are those involving "revenge",[59] "the search for help",[60] "sympathy", "escape", "repentance", "expiation of guilt", "self-punishment", and "seriousness".[61]

We can best illustrate a part of the method of analysing such meanings of suicide[62] by briefly presenting a few comparative case analyses. For this purpose we shall analyse the "revenge" meanings of suicide.

As we have noted above, suicidal actions have, as one of their potential dimensions of meaning, the meaning that *something is fundamentally wrong* with this situation. This means that suicidal actions can be used *reflexively* to say that something is fundamentally to blame for their situation. Because of the generally shared values against hurting others, especially against pushing another person too far ("to the brink"), individuals can use such reflexive meanings to achieve goals while still alive through attempting suicide but "failing" to die (or succeeding in not dying, depending on just what their goal is). We can see this use of the reflexive meaning of suicide rather clearly in the following case:

Mr. F. B., born 1902, had for several years before his admission to hospital shown increasing irritability, suspiciousness and lack of inhibition. In 1945 he became openly paranoid and de-

> pressed, and at the same time made excessive sexual demands. He was afraid of committing suicide (three members of his family had killed themselves), and threatened his wife and child. When his wife started separation proceedings he became extremely depressed and self-accusatory. One evening he drank acid with suicidal intent and told his wife that he had done so. He was immediately admitted to a general hospital and thence transferred to the observation ward and finally to a mental hospital. His paranoid and depressive symptoms remained stationary and he settled down to a dull retarded state. His wife did not continue with the separation proceedings, but visited him regularly, and said that she would not divorce him as he might try again to take his life. At the time of the follow-up interview, seven years after the suicidal attempt, he was still in the hospital [. . .].[63]

In this case we can see quite clearly that the wife interpreted her husband's suicidal actions as being a direct result of her separation proceedings, that is, it was clear to her that this particular, immediately preceding situation was a "cause" of his suicidal actions. In line with her interpretation of his suicidal actions and her desire that he not commit suicide, she changed the situation back to what it had been before the "causing" situation.

However, there is also an "aggressive" possibility in this general reflexive meaning of suicidal actions.[64] By using various methods of pointing out who or what is the cause (i.e. "to blame") for one's suicidal actions one can produce negative social sanctions and self-blame against specific entities and persons.[65] In analysing such meanings it seems essential to begin comparing the more culturally obvious instances and only after understanding the many details of these to proceed to the more culturally involved, subtle cases. One of the more culturally obvious cases of revenging oneself upon some specific person(s) is the following:

> A young clerk twenty-two years old killed himself because his bride of four months was not in love with him but with his elder brother and wanted a divorce so that she could marry the brother. The letters he left showed plainly the suicide's desire to bring unpleasant notoriety upon his brother and his wife, and to attract attention to himself. In them he described his shattered romance and advised reporters to see a friend to whom he had forwarded diaries for further details. The first sentence in a special message to his wife read: "I used to love you; but I die hating you and my brother, too." This was written in a firm hand; but as his suicide diary progressed, the handwriting became erratic and then almost unintelligible as he lapsed into unconsciousness. Some time after turning on the

gas he wrote: "Took my 'panacea' for all human ills. It won't
be long now." An hour later he continues: "Still the same, hope
I pass out by 2 a.m. Gee, I love you so much, Florence. I feel
very tired and a bit dizzy. My brain is very clear. I can see
that my hand is shaking—it is hard to die when one is young.
Now I wish oblivion would hurry"—the note ended there.

Another note regretted the inconvenience to the landlady
for using her premises as a death-house. Still another read:
" 'To whom it may interest: The cause of it all: I loved and
trusted my wife and trusted my brother. Now I hate my wife,
despise my brother and sentence myself to die for having
been fool enough to have ever loved any one as contemptible
as my wife has proven to be. Both she and her lover (my
brother) knew this afternoon that I intended to die tonight.
They were quite pleased at the prospect and did not trouble to
conceal their elation. They had good reason to know that I was
not jesting.' "

The brother who is twenty-three years old spoke frankly to
the police about his friendship with his brother's wife. Though
separated in childhood when the parents had drifted apart,
the two brothers had later on become inseparable companions
until shortly before the tragedy, when both fell in love with
the same girl. The younger man attempted suicide when his love
was not returned and upon his recovery, the girl agreed to
marry him out of pity—but later on she found she could not
live up to her bargain. After a few weeks of married life, the
husband discovered the relationship existing between his wife
and his brother. He became much depressed and threatened
suicide. The day before his death, there was a scene and when
assured that the two were really deeply in love with each other,
the clerk retorted: "All right, I can do you more harm dead
than alive.[66]

This case shows very clearly the general structure of "revenge"
meanings that suicidal actions are very generally intended to construct in the minds of others and in the individual committing the
suicidal action. First of all, and most strikingly clear in this case, is
the importance of *pointing-out* the person one thinks is to blame,
the person whom one intends to be held responsible for the suicidal
action by others *and by the person blamed*. The general problem
of analysing such meanings is that of determining how it is that individuals in our culture go about imputing *causality* of social actions
and what it means (normatively, especially) to be the cause of this
type of action.[67] In the present case the pointing-out of whom the
actor takes to be to blame and whom he thinks should be blamed by
others (and by themselves) is very clear: he left many notes and
made many statements so that those whom he blamed would be

perfectly clear. But the pointing-out of those he wants to be taken as the culprits is not enough: to have them defined as the causes by others (or by themselves) he has to show that there exists some typical situation which is typically believed to cause a typical motive, which in turn is believed to cause certain typical actions (such as suicidal actions). In this case he did these things by trying to show that he had been betrayed by the immoral action of his brother and his wife.

Now, since the construction of such a meaning is clearly dependent upon much more evidence than simply his own statements, the meaning that is created in other minds is partly dependent upon the meaningful responses to this blaming by those pointed-out by him as to blame. In this case they tried to appear sincere (freely talking with the police) and show that she never *really* had loved him, was simply doing him a kind deed, and could not help herself from betraying him because of the force of love (i.e. it was not "really" a betrayal at all, though it might be admitted that it looked that way from his standpoint). The problem which such strategies face is that the committing of a suicidal action also means that one is highly committed to what he says (that he is serious and sincere, as this action of ultimate commitment shows) and that he is deserving of "sympathy" because of what the external situation has forced him to do.[68] In such a situation those who are blamed have a very difficult time of it trying to define things in a way more acceptable to themselves (especially if they "know" that what he says is "true"). And they can hardly argue that they are more right or that they are more sympathetic. They would seem to have only two courses of action that promise any success: that of redefining what happened (it wasn't "really" the way he said it was), which is the path chosen by the brother and wife in this case, and that of redefining the person who committed the suicidal action—he was "crazy" or he was *just* trying to harm us, so that he is not so sympathetic after all. This might well help to explain why it is that so many individuals who attempt suicidal actions are treated as "crazy" (sent to psychiatrists, etc.) by their significant others and why individuals who intend their suicidal actions to blame others use less direct means of blaming (i.e. so that they won't be clearly *just* "aggressive").[69]

This analysis has also led us to see that social causality or "blame", like "suicide" itself, is the result of *suicidal argument processes* between the many participants, real and imagined.[70] (It also leads us to expect that society as a whole must eventually be analysed in terms of such *meaningful conflicts* rather than in terms of assumed patterns of shared meanings as is generally done today.)

As an example of the far more involved, subtle "revenge" meanings that can be constructed for suicidal actions, we shall present and briefly analyse the case of Marguerite as reported in Deshaies excellent work:

Thirty-eight years of age, divorced for several years, Marguerite S. had lost her parents and a child. She lived alone and worked as a saleswoman in a Parisian department store. Very pretty, refined, well-balanced, not at all emotional, she had never had the least psychopathic trouble. Of normal intelligence, she was very affectionate, obliging, gentle, devoid of all aggressiveness, on the whole passive and somewhat listless. She had a coquetterie, self-confidence, and the simpering, slightly childish manner common to pretty women. She scarcely exploited her charms, and lived rather turned in upon herself, waiting for events instead of preparing for them.

In 1938 there came an event. Chance linked her with an engineer, Guy, two years younger than she. She became his mistress. Their liaison was not interrupted by the war, on the contrary—it reinforced it, at least on Marguerite's part. And then, these were the sad years of the occupation, with their anxieties and common hopes. Even though they didn't live together, Marguerite strained her ingenuity to better Guy's existence; their sexual understanding was perfect. Marguerite was happy and loved passionately, without reserve, without after-thought, with no eye to the future—even though their liaison was without a formal engagement. (Guy, a methodical and prudent fellow, had taken care to make this clear from the beginning.)

For Marguerite, Guy represented the universe. He was at the same time child and lover, family and master, the reason for living and the aim of living. He had bound up all her capacity for affection, filled the emptiness of an incomplete existence, and made the ideal teacher around whom her deeper personality could develop. It was not a matter of a thunderbolt, but of a slow, steady, building up of layers which united her indissolubly to her object. The hold of the object manifested itself in everything though without being anything of an obsession, for the self had no place to struggle, its adhesion was complete. To give oneself body and soul is not a vain image, the oblative form of love, the purest perhaps, the proof, as in the present case, a fortunate passion, a normal passion. Why must it be so rarely given out?

A November evening in 1943 produced the catastrophe. With consideration, but with decision, Guy announced to her the end of their liaison. Marguerite experienced an intense emotion, with cardiac pain, facial congestion, tears, astenia. "It's impossible, oh! no, it isn't true! Tell me it's a nightmare! My Guy, my Guy, you are everything for me, you are my God, you are

my soul! Can one live without his soul? It's not possible.
You're all my life, everything [...]. To whom will I tell my
troubles, my thoughts? It's horrible! You are my sole reason
for living, without you I no longer have anything. I feel as if
my head will burst. Must I pay with all the tortures of the heart
and mind for the few hours of joy I've known? My darling,
if you go away it's either madness or death for me [...] I don't
wish it, but I wouldn't have the strength to bear [...]"

Destroyed, poor Marguerite stopped working, stayed inside,
and lost interest in everything that wasn't the object of her
passion. Her disarray was total, a veritable cataclysm in which,
at one blow, all the affective organization of her life foundered,
all her attachments were broken, all her interests vanished,
her whole future dissolved. The duration stopped at the thres-
hold of the present, burdened with a past which could no longer
lead to anything. The weeks rolled by, their alternative hope
and despair determined by the attitude of Guy, who was sometimes softened and charitable, sometimes hardened and pitiless
according to the predominance of his tender feelings or his
rational will to carry out his plan.

[...] Meanwhile Marguerite had gone back to work and was
striving to reconquer her lover. She was calm, with a normal
deportment, no longer emotional; nevertheless, her passion
remained unchanged. After a sad Christmastime, cruelly
nourished by the tender memories of the past, she appeared for
the first time animated by an aggressive tendency which gave
to the idea of suicide the character of vengeance. "I am suffering, I can't stand it any longer, I wish to die. I wish I were
able to hate you! I have given you everything and you have
given me a hard heart. Why haven't I met another man who
had a heart less hard? Why do I love you so much? I would
like to hate, I would like to hate you. I would like to kill you
and then myself [...] Have pity!" "But I know what I will
do: it isn't you who will leave me, it is I. I shall die before
you, under your eyes, I want you to see me die. I want you to
see me dead and I want the image of me always between that
woman and you." Jealousy explodes and works against the unknown rival: "I will scratch that woman's eyes out. I will kill
her. I will kill her. She has no right to marry you. You are my
whole life, without you it's the end of the world, without you
I can't go on living." This aggressiveness was transitory and
suicide continued to be seen as a liberation from suffering
and also a way to free Guy from the problems and boredom
she had created for him.

The idea of suicide was active and accepted, but Marguerite
still hesitated, perhaps from a lack of courage, but especially
because a vague hope persisted, since Guy continued to see her.
Her sleep was troubled by expressive nightmares: train acci-

dents, falls down precipices; she is going to hide herself under the water, deeper and deeper and she suffocates; she throws herself out the window of Guy's building; Guy suddenly appears at her home and she tells him: "I shall remain with you always"; sometimes some sexual dreams, exceptionally dreams of war (bombing at which she is impassively present).

Then all hope disappeared. Guy definitively maintained his decision and told her to "remake her life" without him. And then since she could no longer live either with him or without him, she decided to kill herself. She still loved Guy as much, and in a letter which she addressed to him on 29 April 1944, she told him again all her love, and very tenderly, with neither irony nor complaints, she wished him happiness before telling him adieu. The next day they took her body from the Seine.[71]

The thing that seems most striking about Marguerite's suicide is the great difference in the general "tone" or over-all meaning (that is, the context of meaning determined by the dominant meanings) of the last communication with her lover, her "farewell" letter, from the earlier communications about her intention to commit suicide. In the earlier stages of the struggle it was clear that she was fighting and that suicide was being used as a "weapon", a threat of making the other responsible for the grave and immoral injury to herself. In the last communication, which, most unfortunately, Deshaies did not reproduce, she was, providing Deshaies' interpretation is correct, not at all "aggressive", quite to the contrary, she was kind and loving towards him. It is, of course, quite possible on the surface of it to believe that she had a "change of heart" and decided not to blame her lover for her death. But, even if this were what she had intended, this is probably not the meaning of such a communication, or not the sole communication, to someone, such as the lover himself, who looks at it. The meaning to an observer, especially one involved with her in such a way as to be somewhat sympathetic, is that she has at the very end expressed her deepest love for him and has been so forgiving as to wish him only the greatest happiness. This not only makes her more dependent upon him, because of the great love, and, therefore, makes him more the cause of her suicidal action; but it also makes her far more "sympathetic". The over-all result of her change in tone in her communications is to make her lover even more "guilty" or to "blame" for her terrible action, probably even in his own eyes. (It is, however, entirely possible that her lover, being subjected to blame, might still see it in terms of the first tone of her communications, especially since the first parts of a sequence of communications tends to strongly determine the context of the latter parts of the communications.[72] If so, then he would quite possibly interpret her "farewell" as being just such an indirect form of "aggression".) The expression of "sympathy" can itself be an action intended, or in fact even if not intended, to produce the greatest injury; and it seems especially possible to do this when one commits a suicidal action, so that the only "aggression" expressed is that turned upon oneself in such a way as to make the other, whom one expresses only love for, appear to be the one "really" responsible for the injury.[73]

This last analysis is clearly dependent primarily upon the common-sense understanding of the sociological observers. As such, it is clearly less replicative or scientific. Such analyses as these can only be verified after the more objective, replicative, comparative studies of the actual, direct statements of the social actors have led to highly verifiable results. The immediate goals of sociological investigations of suicide must be to provide the necessary descriptive material and the analyses of such material. A very great deal of further careful descriptions and analyses of the whole *suicidal processes* remains to be done. However, the basic problems and the methods for solving them now seem clear.

NOTES

1 Lovejoy's classic study of the *Great Chain of Being* idea in Western culture is one such conclusive demonstration.
2 E. A. Burth's classical work was one of the first to clearly apply this general idea to science. See his *The Metaphysical Foundations of Modern Science*, New York: Doubleday, 1954.
3 See Thomas S. Kuhn, *The Structure of Scientific Revolutions*, Chicago: The University of Chicago Press, 1962.
4 Until the latter part of the nineteenth century the terms used instead of "sociology" were "moral statistics", "public hygiene", "medical statistics", "social statistics", etc. Since these various disciplines of thought actually constituted the paradigmatic works for those works (such as Durkheim's *Suicide*) still treated as sociological paradigms by sociologists, it seems apparent that one should use the term "sociological" in referring to them, even though the earlier authors did not meet that often used rule-of-thumb test of the self-imputation of the name "sociology". This whole problem of naming brings into sharp focus the whole question of the processes by which this many faceted set of disciplines came to share the one name of "sociology". It is clear that there was much conflict over the whole question of naming that there was vacillation on the part of some. Why did "sociology" win out over the others, at least in France? Did its generality allow its proponents to gain the support of more traditions of thought in their political struggles to found an independent profession in the academic setting? Was it the failure to achieve such a general name that led to the death of moral statistics in Germany? This whole critical question of *the naming of disciplines* awaits serious investigation.
5 Halbwachs has previously argued that this is the key to understanding

Quetelet's many works. See *La Théorie de l'homme moyen: Essai sur Quetelet et la statistique morale*, Paris, 1913.

6 Rather than any synthesis of the paradigmatic ideas, the early sociologists were normally content to provide a *unifying theme* to their work, which usually consisted of some general goal of social welfare, such as national power, alleviating suffering, or eradicating evil.

7 It must be specifically noted here that sociologists have often used many devices for *presenting* their works as more in agreement with the professionally accepted paradigm, Durkheim's *Suicide*, than they in fact were. Halbwachs', for example, tried to show that his work, *Les causes du suicide*, was in agreement "in principle" with Durkheim's *Suicide* even though he in fact rejected much of Durkheim's basic argument.

8 See L. G. Crocker, Discussion of Suicide in the Eighteenth Century, *Journal of the History of Ideas*, XIII, 1952, pp. 47–72.

The importance of suicide in French thought of this period was in turn probably partly the result of the importance of the subject in English thought in the seventeenth century. See S. E. Sprott, *The English Debate on Suicide*, La Salle, Illinois: Open Court Press, 1961.

9 Tissot wrote a very influential work expressing both this idea and the idea that an increasing "spirit of revolt" was responsible for such social actions, an idea which became more important in the sociological works as the century progressed. (See *De la manie du suicide*, Paris, 1841.) The same idea was expressed in the far more balanced work of T. G. Masaryk: 'Die Selbstmordneigung tritt gegenwärtig in allen civilisirten Ländern mit erschreckender Intensität auf . . .' (See *Der Selbstmord als Sociale Massenerscheinung der Modernen Civilisation*, Wien, 1881.)

Much of this belief in the spreading "mania" of suicide was probably the result of the great importance of suicide in romantic literature. (See, for example, Maigron's attack on the romantics, *Le romantisme et les mœurs*, Paris, 1910.) But the feeling of certainty that the quantity of suicide was steadily increasing was probably the result of the steady increase in the official registrations of deaths caused by suicide. This steady rise in the official counts was most likely the result of a steady growth in the registration activities of the officials, but there was little critical attitude towards the statistics except on the part of doctors who were involved in the problems of trying to categorize the causes of death.

(Though we shall not be directly concerned with recent literary and philosophical works on suicide in this essay, it is important here to note that this concern with *suicide as a problem* is still very great in the Western world today. In fact, though it may have been a temporary result of the Second World War, there is every indication that the last few decades has been a period in which suicide was considered to be a more serious philosophical and moral problem than at any time in the last century. Albert Camus great work, *The Myth of Sisyphus*, begins with the brutal assertion that "there is but one truly serious philosophical problem, and that is suicide". For other important examples see P. L. Landsberg, *The Experience of Death: the Moral Problem of Suicide*, New York: The Philosophical Library, 1953; Léon Meynard, *Le suicide, étude, morale et métaphysique*, Paris: Presses Universitaires de France, 1954, and Georg Siegmund, *Sein oder Nichtsein: Die Frage des Selbstmordes*, Trier: Paulinus-Verlag, 1961.

10 Many of the most important works forming the link between philosophical, literary, and common-sense works and the sociological works were

quoted extensively (and referred to in the bibliography) in Legoyt's very influential work, *Le suicide ancien et moderne,* Paris, 1881.

11 One of the most important metaphysical ideas in these sociological works will not be directly dealt with here at all. This is their universally shared idea that *suicidal actions* are "immoral" actions, both in an absolute sense (as in Durkheim's conception of "social pathology") and in the sense that this is a universally shared social meaning of suicide in Western societies. This idea was behind the explicit theoretical idea that a breakdown or decrease in "social constraint" (or "social organization", etc.) was in some way the cause of the increasing suicide rates in Western societies.

12 This metaphysical idea sharply distinguished sociological thought from the paradigmatic thought of the "social mechanists" and some of the more extreme positivists who simply sought to use the theories of the natural sciences as paradigms for analysing social actions. For an excellent treatment of the "social mechanists", see Pitirim A. Sorokin, *Contemporary Sociological Theories,* New York: Harper, 1928, pp, 3–63.

13 Johann Peter Süssmilch, *Die Göttliche Ordnung in den Veränderungen des Menschlichen Geschlechts,* Berlin, 1761.

14 For an excellent treatment of the general cultural development in the Western World, of the ideas and values of quantitative precision see G. N. Clark, *Science and Social Welfare in the Age of Newton,* Oxford: Clarendon Press, 1949.

15 A. M. Guerry, *Essai sur la statistique morale de la France,* Paris, 1833, p. 9.

16 Ibid. p. 11.

17 Both de Guerry and Quetelet expressed this position well. Consider, for example, the following statement by Quetelet: 'Society includes within itself the germs of all the crimes committed, and at the same time the necessary facilities for their development. It is the social state, in some measure, which prepares these crimes, and the criminal is merely the instrument to execute them. Every social state supposes, then, a certain number and a certain order of crimes, these being merely the necessary consequences of its organization." (*A Treatise on Man,* Edinburgh, 1842, p. 6, originally published as *Sur l'homme* in Paris in 1835.)

18 This idea was clearly developed by the time of Morselli's, *Suicide: An Essay on Comparative Moral Statistics,* New York, 1882.

19 Morselli seems to have shared much of this idea, but his greater caution in constructing statistical arguments between the external categories and the internal, meaningful states seems to have dissuaded him from developing the idea. See, for example, his excellent statement of this position on page 114 of Ibid.

20 The most important work in this school of thought is Esquirol's *Maladies mentales,* Paris, 1838.

21 Though our discussion of sociologism is somewhat different, distinctive aspects of Durkheim's sociologism have previously been well discussed by Edward Tiryakian in *Sociologism and Existentialism,* Englewood Cliffs, N. J.: Prentice-Hall, 1962.

22 One of the finest discussions of this method in relation to other methods used by sociologists is by L. L. Bernard *in* The Development of Methods in Sociology, *The Monist,* XXXVIII (1928), 292–320. Montaigne discussed suicide at length in 'Custom of the Island of Cea'. It should be stressed that the use of literary and historical cases of suicide remained

very important throughout the nineteenth century. Such works as that of Legoyt were largely based on historical material and in certain fundamental respects this form of data was far more reliable and valid than that of twentieth-century sociologists. (See the extensive criticisms of official statistics below.) Historical and literary case material still remains, of course, the best source for studies of changes in the moral meanings of suicide. Such material was used very well for this purpose by W. E. H. Lecky in *History of European Morals from Augustus to Charlemagne*, 2 vols., New York, 1869. It was used excellently in the finest study done thus far on the moral meanings of suicide, A. Bayet's *Le suicide et la morale*, Paris, Alcan, 1922.

Durkheim himself relied almost entirely on literary cases taken from the Romantics to construct his types of suicide. E. Durkheim, *Suicide*, Glencoe: The Free Press, 1951, pp. 227–94.

24 Voltaire's essay on suicide in the *Philosophical Dictionary* made use not only of the traditional historical cases but also of contemporary newspaper cases. From such sources he attempted to arrive at certain scientific conclusions about suicide: 1. suicide is more frequent in cities than in rural regions; 2. the explanation of the greater urban frequency of suicide is that cities produce more melancholia (or depression) in individuals because they have more free time from physical labour to think; 3. suicide can be physically inherited because moral character is inherited (an idea which Morselli and many others most emphatically accepted); and 4, some suicides, such as Euripide's Phaedra, commit suicide in order to get revenge against someone (an idea which became of great importance only in the twentieth-century works on suicide).

25 Brierre de Boismont, *Du suicide et de la folie suicide*, Paris, 1856.

26 This idea was largely adopted from the psychiatric theorists, especially from Esquirol's work (op. cit.) in which suicide was considered to be a symptom of insanity.

27 *The Rules of Sociological Method* (Glencoe: The Free Press, 1962), XXXVII.

The importance of the new method for the new academic discipline (or the other way around) was indicated by Durkheim himself in his Introduction to *The Rules of Sociological Method:* "A happy combination of circumstances, among the more important of which may rightly be placed the proposal to establish a regular course in sociology in the Faculty of Letters at Bordeaux, enabled us to devote ourselves early to the study of social science and, indeed, to make it our vocation. Therefore, we have been able to abandon these general questions (of philosophical sociology) and to attack a certain number of definite problems. The very force of events has thus led us to construct a method that is, we believe, more precise and more exactly adapted to the distinctive characteristics of social phenomena" (Ibid. p. IX.).

28 Durkheim did not actually completely eliminate data on individuals, even when consistency called for this. Through his Aristotelian ideas concerning causality, Durkheim retained a form of negative (nay-saying) causality for individuals. This was a form of material causality whereas the efficient causality, which is what concerns science, was society. For an analysis of such aspects of Durkheim's argument see Appendix II, 'The Individual and Society in Durkheim's *Suicide*', of Jack D. Douglas,

The Social Meanings of Suicide, Princeton University Press 1967.

29 The statistical method of argument would surely not be sufficient in itself to explain this elimination of data on individuals. Besides the factors of founding an independent profession, there were other intellectual forces leading in the same direction: political theory had come to treat the nation state as independent of the individual members; race psychology had developed ideas of extra-individual, meaningful forces causing actions by individuals: and the *organic analogy* was a powerful one throughout the nineteenth century.

30 See F. Picavet, *Les idéologues,* Paris, 1891.

31 *Recherches statistiques sur le suicide,* Paris, 1844.

32 *Du suicide,* Paris, 1856.

33 *Die Moralstatistik,* Erlangen, 1882.

34 *Die Gesetzmässigkeit in den scheinbar willkurlichen menschlichen Handlungen,* Hamberg, 1864.

35 *Cours élémentaires de statistique,* Paris, 1895.

36 This interpretation of Durkheim's *Suicide* has previously been established in the author's *The Social Meanings of Suicide,* Part I, chap. 1 and 2. The whole history of the social research of these many schools has been dealt with in *The Rise of Social Research,* ed. by Anthony Oberschall and Jack D. Douglas, forthcoming by Harper and Row.

37 Since there are some who would probably dispute calling Durkheim's *Suicide* a work of moral statistics we should point out that *Suicide* was reviewed in the first volume of *L'Année sociologique* (1896–1897), 397–406, under the general category of "Statistique morale". We might also point out that the unnamed author of this review was very critical of Durkheim's "denying" all causal significance to individual factors.

38 Chateaubriand was especially important in this respect. For some of the details on this relationship see Jack D. Douglas, *The Sociological Study of Suicide: Suicidal Actions as Socially Meaningful Actions* (unpublished Ph.D. thesis, Princeton University, Princeton), pp. 20–6.

39 This formulation of Durkheim's task leaves out of consideration the very important intellectual warfare aspect of *Suicide,* that is, the task of justifying the independent existence of a profession of sociology. This is very important for understanding the whole work but not for understanding that part of it which concerns us here.

40 Especially valuable in this respect is H. W. Rumsey, *Essays and Papers on Some Fallacies of Statistics,* London, 1875.

41 For a consideration of the many dimensions of meaning involved in attempts to formally define "suicide" and of the implications of this for determining the common-sense meanings of suicide, see Jack Douglas, 'The Social Aspects of Suicide', in volume IX of the new *International Encyclopedia of the Social Sciences;* and Appendix I of *The Social Meanings of Suicide,* op. cit.

42 M. Halbwachs, *Les Causes du suicide,* Paris, 1930. (The author is currently preparing an English edition of *The Causes of Suicide,* to be published by the University of California Press.)

43 This had in fact been noted by Buckle in a footnote concerning errors in the addresses of London mail, but he failed to draw the general implication.

44 The whole argument and mass of data against the validity and reliability of official statistics on suicide has been dealt with in great detail in

Part III of Jack D. Douglas, *The Sociological Study of Suicide,* op. cit., pp. 259–406.

45 Ibid.

Most of the previous arguments against the use of official statistics have been by psychiatrists. (See, especially, the fine work by F. Achille-Delmas, *Psychologie pathologique du suicide,* Paris, Alcan, 1933. Though these works have often been right in particulars, they have never tried to show that there exist (systematic) biases in the statistics and that these biases are related to the social structure and the official categorization processes in specific ways.

46 De Boismont was especially important in this manner and probably provided most of Durkheim's knowledge of individual cases of suicide. See Jack D. Douglas, ibid., pp. 20–112.

47 See, especially, Rodney Needham's, 'Introduction' to E. Durkheim and M. Mauss, *Primitive Classification,* Chicago: The University of Chicago Press, 1963, pp. XIII–XV.

48 A. Bayet, *Le suicide et la morale,* Paris, Alcan, 1922, p. 3.

49 Roger Lacombe, in his excellent general critique of *La méthode sociologique de Durkheim,* Paris, Alcan, 1926, has argued that the fundamental weakness of Durkheim's whole method was his failure to recognize the need for any scientific means of determining the inner (psychological) meanings which Durkheim believed to be the causes of social actions. Lacombe did not, however, see the reasons for this in the very nature of Durkheim's positivistic method nor did he have a specific solution to offer to the problem.

50 As Bayet (op. cit.) argued so excellently, Durkheim's whole "realist" conception of law and its relations to morality and actions is completely untenable. Bayet, however, did not see that this method of analysing moral meanings was a necessary outcome of Durkheim's whole method.

51 H. Morselli, *Suicide,* op. cit. p. 305.

52 E. Durkheim, *Suicide,* op. cit., pp. 215–6.

53 The whole argument concerning this interpretation of *Suicide* can be found in Part I of Jack D. Douglas, *The Social Meanings of Suicide,* by Princeton University Press, 1967.

54 Though being very cautious in criticizing the master of the French school, Halbwachs clearly saw the reliance of *Suicide* upon the "dialectique":

"En fermant cet ouvrage, plus d'un lecteur, surtout plus d'un lecteur philosophe, a sans doute eu le sentiment que le problème du suicide ne se posait plus, et qu'on connaissait désormais la solution. Est-ce la dialectique, sont-ce les statistiques qui emportaient la convictions? L'un et l'autre sans qu'on sût bien toujours distinguer ce qui était l'autre. Quelquefois la dialectique plus que les faits, non par la faute de Durkheim d'ailleurs. Mais cela présentait plus d'un inconvénient. On ne s'apercevait pas que l'édifice reposait sur des fondements qui n'étaient point partout aussi solides. Comment en eût-il été autrement? Il n'y a pas d'œuvre scientifique de nouvelles expériences n'obligent à réviser et compléter." M. Halbwachs, *Les Causes du suicide,* op. cit., p. 3.

55 The inadequacies and the limits of usefulness of psychological and psychiatric case studies of suicide have been analysed at length in Jack D. Douglas, *The Sociological Study of Suicide,* op. cit., pp. 337–406.

56 The determination and analysis of the social meanings of suicide in other cultures poses very difficult problems. The best attempt to do so thus

far is G. Devereux's *Mohave Ethnopsychiatry and Suicide* (Washington, U.S. Govt. Printing Office, 1961.)

57 See Jack D. Douglas, *The Social Meanings of Suicide,* op. cit., Part IV.

58 For a detailed presentation of the various formal, theoretical definitions of "suicide" see P. B. Schneider, *La tentative de suicide,* Paris, Delachaux, 1954, pp. 9–59. For an analysis of these dimensions of meanings in the formal definitions, see Jack D. Douglas, Appendix II, *The Social Meanings of Suicide,* op. cit.

59 The author is currently analysing the cross-cultural "revenge" meanings of suicide in a work entitled *Revenge Suicide,* to be published by Prentice-Hall.

60 Harvey Sacks has previously analysed these patterns of meanings in 'No One to Turn to', in E. Schneidman, ed., *Essays in Self-Destruction,* to be published by Holt, Rinehart, and Winston.

61 See Jack D. Douglas, *The Sociological Study of Suicide,* op. cit., pp. 440–511.

62 We should point out that throughout this paper we have discussed and concentrated on "suicide" rather than on the very broad spectrum of different social categories of "suicidal" phenomena in the Western world. The reason for this is simply one of simplification. We could not discuss other categories in any detail in such a brief work. The general properties of "suicide" probably hold for these other categories, but there are many important, specific differences. (Some of these have been discussed briefly in Jack D. Douglas, *The Social Meanings of Suicide,* op. cit.)

63 Quoted from Stengel and Cook, *Attempted Suicide,* London: Oxford University Press, 1958, p. 56.

64 Psychologists and sociologists have very generally come to consider "suicide" to be one form of "aggression". See, for example, A. F. Henry and J. F. Short, *Suicide and Homicide: Some Economic, Sociological and Psychological Aspects of Aggression,* Glencoe: The Free Press, 1954. They have not seen however, that the success of such an aggressive intent is due to the reflexive nature of the social meanings of suicide. They have really missed the whole social nature of such an action.

65 One can construct the meanings of his suicidal actions in such a way as to "blame the world" or "blame Hollywood" (as seems to have been partially true in the death of Marilyn Monroe) and so on. However, because our commonsense theories of persons tend to strongly emphasize persons as the causal factors in explaining our actions, it is especially easy to see other individuals as the something that is to blame for a suicidal action.

66 This case is quoted from Louis I. Dublin and Bessie Bunzel, *To Be or Not To Be,* New York: Smith and Haas, 1933, pp. 294–5.

67 Hendin has tried to show that in Denmark persons are believed to be not only a fundamental cause of the actions of others, as they are in the whole Western World, but that they should be held responsible for the actions of others far more than is the case in most of the United States. It would thus seem that the fundamental difference, a difference which makes it far more possible to use suicidal actions as a threat (thus to achieve whatever one wants to achieve) and as revenge, is due to a difference in the social definition of "responsibility" for the actions (welfare, etc.) of others, rather than in any difference in definitions of the causality of such events. See Hendin, *Suicide and Scandinavia,* New York: Grune and Stratton, 1964, pp. 28–29.

This example brings up the whole problem of subcultural patterning in the meanings of suicide. Clearly there are such patternings, some of which are national. ("Romantic suicide" in Germany would be another instance.) However, though little is known about them as yet, they seem to be variations on the generally shared patterns.

68 Here we have had to bring in some of the other dimensions and patterns of the social meanings of suicide. This shows the fundamental need for a general comparative approach in which one sees each pattern or dimension *in the context* of all the others. Any other approach completely distorts the meanings. (This has been done in Part IV of Jack D. Douglas *The Social Meanings of Suicide,* op. cit.)

69 This whole analysis has been taken from *The Social Meanings of Suicide.*

70 An extensive analysis of such a *suicidal process* has been given in Chap. V of Part IV in Ibid.

71 G. Deshaies, *Psychologie du suicide,* Paris: Presses Universitaires de France, 1947. (This case has been translated by the author of this essay.)

72 This suggested "primacy effect" is one of the very many properties of communications which one would have to understand quite well before he could give any nearly definitive interpretations of the meanings of suicidal phenomena.

73 This analysis has been taken from Part IV of Jack D. Douglas, *The Social Meanings of Suicide,* op. cit.

PART III

CHAPTER 12

Suicide in Non-Western Societies

At the time when Durkheim published his *Suicide*, anthropologists were engaged in a controversy over the frequency of suicide in the "lower" societies. Durkheim himself, in advancing his conception of altruistic suicide, rejected the view that suicide is virtually unknown in traditional forms of society. But even today it is difficult to reach a firm conclusion on this issue. The difficulties inherent in assessing the significance of suicide rates in the developed societies have already been referred to, and it is plain that to calculate even gross estimates of rates in traditional societies is normally quite impracticable; the most that can be said is that there is probably a large amount of variability in the frequency of suicide between different societies.

Diversity in frequency of suicide is also associated with considerable variation in forms of suicide. The cases discussed in Bohannan's *African Homicide and Suicide*, for instance (from which the article by La Fontaine on the Gisu is taken) in some ways resemble typical European patterns. However, suicide in such societies is inevitably usually bound up with religious or magical beliefs. Thus among the Gisu, who live on the borders of Uganda, suicide is embedded within a set of beliefs linking it to the power of the ancestors. While a non-suicidal death may be explained in terms of hostile acts of sorcery on the part of other men, suicide is believed to result only from the intervention of dead ancestors. But La Fontaine concludes that Gisu suicide does not show any characteristics readily classifiable as "altruistic" suicide in Durkheim's sense.

Forms of suicide which do more closely approach the "altruistic" type can readily be found in the anthropological literature. Thus Leighton and Hughes describe instances of the suicide of old people among the Eskimos which could plausibly be said to fall into this category. The most common situation leading to suicide in old people among the Eskimos, according to Leighton and Hughes, is "being no longer a useful and productive member of the group". However, in virtue of the relative scarcity of such instances, it is clear that Durkheim's theory of altruistic suicide does not provide a satisfactory interpretation of suicide as a whole in traditional societies.

This should not be taken to imply that it is impossible to bring the various sorts of suicide described by anthropologists within the purview of an overall theory of suicide. On the contrary, it should be pointed out that there are certain important similarities between many of the forms of suicide found in traditional cultures, and those characteristic of modern European societies. Jeffreys, for instance, provides various examples of "revenge" suicide, which in his view forms a type of suicide equivalent to, although distinct from, Durkheim's types. But, in fact, the use of suicidal actions and threats as a mode of sanction, of which the "revenge" *motif* is a specific form, is a common feature of suicide in many different societies. Thus, for instance, Malinowski notes that, in the Trobriands, there is an accepted form of attempted suicide which is used as a sanction in matrimonial disputes: the suicidal action represents an indictment of the spouse who has wronged.[1] Similarly, among the Kuma of New Guinea, suicide attempts, which are always by drowning, form a method of protest by newly married women when they are unhappy with the match which has been made for them.[2] A further example can be found in Dobu. Here suicide attempts are also made in the context of marital quarrels: the attempt is made in the other spouse's home village, and registers a protest, in front of the relatives, against the other's conduct.[3]

In all these cases, including those of "revenge" suicide, the act of suicide is a sanction, a method of bringing pressure to bear upon others to act in a desired way. There are obvious parallels here with suicide in modern Western societies.[4] These similarities are illustrated with particular clarity in Firth's discussion of "risk-taking" suicide in Tikopia. There are three usual methods of committing suicide in Tikopia: hanging, swimming out to sea, and putting out to sea by canoe (*forau*). Both of the first two methods normally lead to death with some degree of rapidity. But the practice of putting out to sea by canoe is less unequivocal in this respect. *Forau* can be interpreted as an exposure to risk whereby the individual makes public his dissatisfaction with some aspect of his life, and demands that others respond in an appropriate way; if the individual survives, as Firth suggests, he is "re-integrated" into the community.

Japan is the only country in the world which has industrialized with a minimum of Western influence; and as a *locus classicus* of ritual suicide it is of particular interest. There are certainly some significant differences between suicide in Japan and suicide in Western societies. The distribution of suicide according to age is perhaps the most obvious difference: in Japan, in contrast to Western societies, suicide is extremely frequent among adolescents and young adults. But ritual suicide, if indeed it ever was the predominant kind of suicide, is no longer so; and, as Iga and Okara are concerned to show, suicide in Japan probably is today essentially similar to the forms found in the West.

NOTES

1 B. Malinowski, *Crime and Custom in Savage Society*, London, 1949, p. 94ff.
2 M. Reay, *The Kuma*, Melbourne, 1959, pp. 178–81.
3 R. F. Fortune, *Sorcerers of Dobu*, London, 1932, pp. 91–3. For further examples, see Anthony Giddens: 'Suicide, attempted suicide, and the suicidal threat', *Man*, July-August, 1964, No. 136, pp. 115–6.

CHAPTER 13

Notes on Eskimo Patterns of Suicide*

Alexander H. Leighton and Charles C. Hughes

GENERAL CHARACTERISTICS OF ESKIMO SUICIDE

Among all Eskimo from Greenland to Alaska suicide[1] was apparently in former times supported by fundamental cultural values. Rasmussen[2] records a succinct expression of this point of view as uttered by a Netsilik Eskimo: "For our custom up here is that all old people who can do no more, and whom death will not take, help death to take them. And they do this not merely to be rid of a life that is no longer a pleasure, but also to relieve their nearest relations of the trouble they give them." An important reinforcement of this clearly expressed function was the common belief that the souls of people who had died by suicide went to the best of the afterworlds, along with those who had been murdered or who had met other forms of violent death.

The means of self destruction were various and included stabbing with a knife or spear, shooting, hanging, strangulation, jumping off a cliff, drowning, and starvation. Weyer has summarized most of the methods in his statement:

> On King William Island, old folks no longer able to provide for themselves generally hang themselves. Among the Iglulik Eskimos suicide by hanging or drowning is rather common. The act must be performed while the hut is empty and a lamp must be left burning so that one entering will see the body. Suicide is stated to be fairly common among the Koksoagmiut, south of Hudson Strait; remorse and disappointed love are the only causes, death being sought either by strangulation, by pitching one's self over a cliff, or by shooting. Also the Tahagmiut to the west not infrequently commit suicide, strangulation and shooting being the common methods. A native of Angmagasalik will throw himself into the sea, often prompted by the admonition from his relatives that he has nothing to live for. The Copper Eskimos, however, resort to suicide but rarely, according to Jenness. This observer remembers hearing of only one

* Reprinted by permission from the *Southwestern Journal of Anthropology*, Vol. 11, 1955, pp. 327–38.

case and that was due not to any morbid weariness of life, but to terror of the revenge that might be expected for a crime that the man had committed.[3]

An important characteristic of most of these Eskimo patterns is that they were relatively non-ritualized. They *tended* to be individually-performed events, only occasionally supported by incipient social rules and prescriptions as to *how* the suicide should be accomplished (although there was considerable social agreement on the motives). Thus, in terms of the traditional behaviour involved, most of the Eskimo patterns fall somewhere in the centre of the range between extensively patterned suicides, such as the Japanese, and individualistic types, such as those in contemporary American society. A second generalization is that the usual motives prompting suicide were suffering (physical and mental) and being no longer a useful and productive member of the group. In this connection, Weyer recalls a vivid incident told to him in his own field work:

> A hunter living on the Diomede Islands related to the writer how he killed his own father, at the latter's request. The old Eskimo was failing, he could no longer contribute what he thought should be his share as member of the group so he asked his son, then a lad about twelve years old, to sharpen the big hunting knife. Then he indicated the vulnerable spot over his heart, where his son should stab him. The boy plunged the knife deep, but the stroke failed to take effect. The old father suggested with dignity and resignation, "Try it a little higher, my son." The second stab was effective. . . .[4]

Illustrations of a similar nature can be found in most of the Eskimo literature for the killing of aged or infirm parents by dutiful children was evidently a common occurrence.[5] Perhaps the epitome of this pattern with respect to the aged is expressed when Weyer says:

> The Eskimos of Baffin Island have great respect for the aged and treat them well. But when a woman becomes so old that she is a burden, she may calmly resign herself to death, allowing herself to be walled into a snowhut and left to die. She thinks it is better ; the tribe agrees.[6]

Suicides motivated by starvation were apparently not common except in areas subject to stringent local conditions (e.g. the Netsilik area).

There are, then, several points to be noted in the general Eskimo pattern of suicide: (1) it was relatively non-ritualized; (2) there was considerable variability in method; (3) the usual reasons for giving up one's life were sickness, suffering, and the feeling of uselessness (which may have been in large part a reflection of attitudes from the individual's social environment).

SUICIDE PATTERNS ON ST LAWRENCE ISLAND

The suicide episodes mentioned by your Yuit informants on St Lawrence Island differ from the general Eskimo practice by having more elaborate patterning and by involving a larger number of people in the event. In this way they apparently resemble the customs that have been described for the Chukchee on the neighbouring mainland of Siberia.

Our information was gathered primarily from three male informants, with supplementary descriptions given by five other individuals[7] The youngest of the principal informants was approximately forty-eight years old. Of the other two, one was sixty-three (as nearly as can be determined), and the other was of unknown age but seemed to be the oldest of the three.

The data upon which our discussion of the suicide pattern is based can be classified roughly into fifteen fairly complete specific episodes, and at least twenty-nine fragments or mentions of individuals who died by suicide. Twelve of these episodes and twenty-one of the incomplete histories were reported as having been observed by the informant himself, though not all of them took place on St Lawrence Island, some being among people of the same culture across the water in Siberia. The remaining episodes and references (which consist of either brief aspects of the patterns, or listings of names) were not seen by the informant, but were events reported to him by other individuals. In addition there are two general descriptions of the pattern, one by an informant who said he had witnessed suicides and one by an informant who said he had not.

As nearly as can be determined from our field notes, the last suicide occurred in 1902. The death record compiled by Dr E. O. Campbell, a missionary on the island from 1900–11, lists one man, age forty-five, who shot himself and left a wife, three children, and a brother as survivors. During the previous year an elderly woman had been hung by her sons. These two suicides were apparently the last successful attempts, for although another was tried sometime between 1900–4 (the dating is extremely vague), it was stopped by Dr Campbell. A man suffering from "measles" decided he wanted to be hung, but Dr Campbell broke up the funeral party at the place of execution and took charge of the ailing man.

Three methods of ritual suicide were mentioned as having existed on St Lawrence: hanging, shooting with a rifle, and stabbing with spear or knife. Hanging was the most, and stabbing the least, common. The victim himself apparently had his choice.

It would be interesting to know the actual frequency of suicide, but our data do not permit even a crude estimate. As far as sex difference goes, it is noteworthy that in our total list of episodes, men predominate. There is also a suggestion that possibly the self-inflicted suicides were fewer than the cases in which the "victim" had himself killed by others. On the other hand, our data contain no indication of a connection between high status and self-inflicted death.

The general procedure for suicide was the same, no matter whether the blow was self-administered or given by someone else. Once having decided to do away with himself, the individual initiated the process by asking his relatives to kill him or at least help in the suicide. As a rule they would not consent at first, but rather tried to dissuade him from his intentions.[8] One of the St Lawrence informants said that among their ethnic counterparts at Indian Point (Siberia) the custom was for the prospective suicide to ask three times for someone to help him, the third request being one that could not be refused. There was no indication of limits to the number of requests at Gambell.

The requirement that the prospective suicide warn his relatives of his intentions is one of the most significant aspects of the pattern, for it is here that the *group* involvement begins to emerge. Unfortunately, however, there are as yet no adequate data on whether an individual could ever "legitimately" commit suicide by himself without first warning his relatives of his plans; or whether he always had to implicate the wider social group in his demise. Probably it was the latter, however, for an informant questioned on this point by CCH on a visit to the island in 1954 said that it simply never happened that a person would go off and kill himself all alone—"always lots of people around".

The reasons given by our informants to explain why the relatives tried to dissuade a person from suicide were that his family loved him and did not want him to die. One may conjecture that contributing factors may have been the existence of values strongly opposed to harming a family member and the necessity for the executioner to undergo a severe piacular ritual after the death.

If the prospective suicide continued to ask among his relatives for death they finally had to agree. He would then dress himself in his house as one already dead, i.e. with his clothing turned inside out. Presently a group of relatives would arrive and carry him seated on a reindeer skin to the "Destroying Place." This was the spot where in any regular funeral some of the deceased's property was broken. There were two such places on the edge of Gambell village.

Sometimes, particularly if the man were sacrificing himself to save someone else, he would walk to his death. This was considered an especially praiseworthy act.

Before his death at the Destroying Place, the prospective suicide commonly addressed his relatives, giving them advice about life, and his reflections upon parting from this world. Informants describe this speech somewhat as follows: "Sometimes he say 'You big enough. You know what you can do. Older people must teach younger ones. And after me you won't need me any more. You can defend you self.' Because our custom is: anything when we couldn't think clear, we had to come to older people." And another excerpt: "He says 'My time is up, so I couldn't tell you anything more to what to do. So you be think you selves and you almost grown man now.' "

If a man were to be killed with a rifle by an assistant, the latter was usually his wife, but in one case at least a female cousin performed the act. If hanging were the method chosen, one of the wooden supports of the old-style skin covered house was taken in the procession from the victim's home. A walrus skin rope with a loop was fastened through a hole in one end of the post which was placed at the suicide's back and held more or less vertically by relatives, the ground as a rule being so frozen that a socket for the post could not be dug. When the moment for death arrived, the suicide pulled his parka over his face, while others put the loop around his neck. Then either the victim was pulled upwards by the rope and strangled in the process, or (and this was more common) he was lifted up on the reindeer skin by the assistants, the rope was drawn tight, and the skin lowered away. According to the informants it often took longer than half an hour for death to be accomplished by this method and during this time the victim's hands might be held to prevent his thrashing about.

There are no data for the details of the procedure if the suicide were stabbed by an assistant. However, in one case where the wound was self-administered it was reported that the man sat on a reindeer skin, fastened a knife to his leg, and bent forward, forcing the blade into his heart. If the person killed himself by shooting, he sat on a deerskin facing the village so the bullet would go in the opposite direction. He placed one end of a walrus rope around the trigger, the other about his toes, pointed the gun to his forehead, and pulled the trigger with his foot.

After death, the corpse was bundled up with walrus lashings in the same deerskin that had been used for the trip to the Destroying Place and it was taken to the mountain behind the village for disposal. On arrival at the final resting place the body was treated in the manner traditional for all corpses. The clothing and lashings which covered the body were cut. If the man had been shot, his relatives were not allowed to see the bullet hole and the body was placed face down on the earth. If he had been hung, the body was placed face upwards. Regardless of the manner of death, some sort of stick was always taken to the Destroying Place and included in the deerskin bundle to make it rigid for easier carrying. If the death had been by hanging, the stick was placed along the front of the body which lay face upwards; if by shooting, it was laid along the back.

Once the decision and arrangements for the death had been made by an individual, retraction was very difficult, but among the neighbouring Chukchee it was believed that all forms of bad fortune would ensue unless the retractor made a heavy sacrifice to the "Outer Being", an important deity in the Chukchee supernatural hierarchy.[9] It was, however, mentioned on St Lawrence Island that in at least two cases dogs were killed after a suicide vow had been retracted, presumably in the attempt to have them substitute for the human being.

The treatment accorded the relative who acted as executioner is particularly interesting as illustrating a case in which the necessary violation of a basic and deeply held value is followed by ritual activities which seem to constitute both symbolic punishment and exorcism of any evil that might arise from the killing. The prevailing attitude seems to have been, as one informant expressed it, "No one likes to kill anyone; people usually kill themselves when they want death." This informant himself put forward the suggestion that the treatment of the killer was some form of punishment.

The executioner was confined to his or her house for a period of twenty days. During this time he was not allowed to go outside for fresh air; he could not change his clothes; and he could not do any sort of work in the house. He always wore his clothes with the hair turned inward, and his head and eyebrows were shaved without water. A small net made of baleen was placed over his head or parka hood. He could not wash himself nor use his fingernails for scratching, though he was allowed to use a stick or comb for the latter purpose. For picking up meat he had to use a pointed knife rather than his fingers. After this initial twenty-day confinement, he was free to go outside, but still could not engage in constructive labour for another (unspecified) period of time.

The severity of this treatment can be judged by comparison with the usual period of ritual confinement for the family of a deceased person. This was five days if the deceased had been a male, ten days if a female. For each of these cases there was also an approximately equal period of somewhat less restricted activity during which the mourner was not confined to the house and the most stringent proscriptions were relinquished. Possibly the ritual confinement for the family of a deceased person was also considered a form of punishment, but there are no data on this point.

When death was by hanging, several relatives participated in holding the post, and in raising and lowering the deerskin. It was apparently felt that in such an operation no single individual was responsible for the death and as a result none had to undergo the severe treatment accorded a person who alone caused a death. It is likely that they nevertheless had to carry out some ritual limitations of activity, similar to those described above for ordinary mourning. Adequate information on this point is unfortunately lacking.

The commonest reason given for suicide was suffering due to physical sickness. A second cause was prolonged grief over the death of a loved one; another was pervasive despondency without apparent cause. The latter, as described by the informants, seemed to be very similar to the clinical depressions known in our culture. A motive mentioned only once was the suffering caused by prolonged starvation.

The above motives are found in other Eskimo groups. On St Lawrence there was one additional reason not found in these groups nor in the Chukchee culture, as far as the evidence at hand indicates. This was the belief that a man, by giving his own life, could thereby save the life of an ill son or grandson. In the words of one informant, "My own parents, father and brother (sic), they been hang. I know my father very well that time. We was both sick, myself and my father same time. Maybe my father was think 'If I die myself maybe he (son) get well'." And a similar case at Indian Point was related: "Seems to me he wasn't very sick. He shot because he want to save son who was sick. Shot by own son (other son). . . . He was talking aloud before shot him. Say, 'I want to be shot because I want my son to live so I take his place to die'."

Suicides based on this motive seem to have been at least as common as those due to sickness, although it is, of course, difficult to be sure of any such estimate. It is not known whether a man would sacrifice himself for his daughter or granddaughter, or whether a woman ever performed this sacrificial act. The specific rationale advanced for the action was that the offering of a life would appease the "devils" who were causing the illness of the son, and they would cease to torment him. This is indicated in the following: "(Q.) Why do people think that by taking their own lives this will save their son? (Informant) They believe that a person who shot himself puts all the sickness on him and when he dies there is none left behind for the family. He sacrifices himself to save the family."

Usually it was old men who committed suicide, but occasionally elderly women and people in the prime of life did so too. No clear-

cut information on patterns of abandoning the aged (which, if prac-
ticed, might have increased the prevalence of suicides, especially
among old women) is available, although the practice probably did
exist. When it was a case of saving somebody else, it was often the
able-bodied men in their most productive years who sacrificed themselves. Those who committed suicide were thought very brave and
courageous; they, along with people who were murdered were said
to go to heaven—to a "place where they would be happier". It was
particularly proper, according to one of the early ethnographers,[10]
for what the St Lawrence Islanders termed an "athletic man" (i.e.
the strong, able, aggressive individual who dominated his fellows) to
kill himself rather than die a natural death. One reason for this may
be, as Margaret Lantis has suggested[11] that the prestige and high
social evaluation accorded a good hunter in this culture was greatly
enhanced by this ultimate act of killing—the killing of oneself. Thus,
rather than suffer the social decline concomitant with waning physical powers, the athletic man and hunter often chose to destroy
himself while still enjoying a large measure of prestige.

A brief comparison of the St Lawrence patterns with those of the
Chukchee[12] may be interesting, since the two cultures share many
other items in common and Chukchee suicide is often mentioned in
the literature. Among the Chukchee, in contrast to the St Lawrence
Islanders, self-administered suicide was a much less honoured form
of death than was dying at the hands of another. A person would
kill himself only when he was young and could persuade no one else
to deliver the blow. Death was inflicted by friends as well as relatives,
whereas on St Lawrence only a family member could do the killing.

The reasons for suicide also show both differences and similarities:
in Siberia (as on St Lawrence) suffering from sickness was a paramount motive, but in Siberia the motive of sacrifice to save someone else's life was apparently lacking. On the other hand, death
accomplished to spite someone or to make him regret his culture
nor is it mentioned for other Eskimo groups.

In Siberia, as on St Lawrence, suicide was sometimes considered
a legacy passed down from father to son, but it was usually thought
of as more exemplary than obligatory. Among the Chukchee, and in
common with most of the other Eskimo groups, people who died
by suicide were believed to go to the best of the after-worlds. In
both St Lawrence and Chukchee cultures, retraction of the death
vow after it was accepted by the group was impossible without
either serious misfortune or heavy sacrifice. In both places relatives
tried to dissuade the person bent on death before group acceptance
took place.

In contrast to the St Lawrence pattern, the Chukchee death usually occurred inside the house, there being no mention of a Destroying Place. The same three methods were known in the two areas: death by stabbing with either knife or spear, death by strangulation (in Siberia garrotting, rather than hanging) and death by shooting with the rifle. The most noticeable difference is that the person to be strangled lay with his head in his wife's lap, while two relatives pulled a rope from either side and his wife held his hands to prevent involuntary struggling. In Siberia the death was usually accomplished on the same day that the vow was uttered, and the person destined to die was feted with fine reindeer meat and shown extraordinary kindness. In St Lawrence, the death did not usually occur on the same day and there is no mention of special treatment before it.

SOME FUNCTIONAL ASPECTS OF SUICIDE ON ST LAWRENCE ISLAND

Although the main purpose of this paper is to make an ethnographic contribution, we wish to offer by way of conclusion some observations of a functional nature. The Eskimo values and practices in regard to suicide are apt to strike members of our society as exceedingly curious and to excite speculation as to how they could come into existence and be perpetuated. Some of the most interesting questions in this regard are at the level of individual psychology, since the act appears to be a contradiction of the fundamental self-preserving characteristics of the human organism. However, an adequate explanation, even if entirely theoretical, would involve a review of the concepts of unconscious motivation, learning theory and related fields, a task which extends far beyond the limits of this article.

At the level of group behaviour, the problem has many interesting aspects. It may be recalled that Durkheim[13] examined several different forms of suicide, and one generalization he reached was that the form which he called "altruistic suicide" occurs "when social integration is too strong". It would seem that Eskimo suicide can be placed in this general class, although one can leave off, for scientific purposes, the value assumption implied in the phrase, "too strong".

Suicide is of interest, then, from the point of view of social behaviour; and its functional implications may perhaps be more easily described in terms of such group phenomena than is possible in terms of intra-psychic processes. Along these lines Merton[14] offers a framework for functional analysis which can be applied without too much elaboration to our data and can at the same time yield some additional understanding. He defines the "function" of an item as the "observed consequences which make for the adaptation or adjustment of a given system". There are also "dysfunctions", which are "those observed consequences which lessen the adaptation or adjustment of the system". He draws an important distinction between the "manifest" and the "latent" functions or dysfunctions of any item: "Manifest functions are those objective consequences contributing to the adjustment or adaptation of the system which are intended and recognized by participants in the system; latent functions, correlatively being those which are neither intended nor recognized."[15] The specification of the system to which a function or dysfunction is imputed is crucial in Merton's scheme.

When the principal individual (that is, the "victim") is considered as the system in question, it is evident, at the very least, that the suicide pattern serves to end physical, psychological, or social suffering. A latent function would be that death by suicide gives prestige and high valuation to the individual, especially if it is a sacrificial suicide, and possibly to his surviving family (data on this point are lacking). An element in the motivational complex behind the suicide, having to do with anxiety and defences against it, is the expectation of achieving a quick transformation into a happier existence. Although in a strict sense this cannot be a "function" of suicide (i.e. an "objective consequence"), a happy-afterlife is defined by the system of belief as the consequence of killing oneself. We may also note the possibility of unconscious wishes for death, either innate or as the result of personality development and experience.

If the group (in this case, the individual's kinship group) is chosen as the unit for analysis, a manifest function of suicide is that the unit is relieved of the drain on its resources caused by an economically and socially disruptive member. This is achieved by an institutionalized pattern which not only disposes of him, but at the same time constantly imposes obstacles to the encouragement of sheer murder as a way to accomplish the same purpose. The emphasis seems always to be maintained on the voluntary decision of the individual. By this means it would appear that the potential group destructiveness of murder which can easily become cantagious is not allowed to develop. Wanton destruction of human life is also further blocked by the numerous proscriptions in the suicide ritual itself, such as the requirement that the executioner always be a relative, and the long period of exculpation. By the former, the usual norms requiring retributive blood vengeance if someone is killed by a member of another family are nullified, and thus a potential chain of compensatory killings is precluded.

A latent function may consist in reinforcing the kinship bonds by implicating the kinship group in the arrangements for the killing and the funeral. These are not only reinforced by the sheer interaction involved, but more explicitly in the final speech of the suicide. If the death is a sacrifice, the basic sentiment of helping one's relatives and sharing with them is dramatically and vividly emphasized. The ritual "punishment" of an executioner and the mourning restraints on the surviving relatives also underline group solidarity and the seriousness of losing a member. In particular cases, a manifest dysfunction of the suicide pattern for the kinship group lies in the destruction of a member who was perhaps well-beloved and who could still contribute his wisdom and advice, even if infirm physically. And when the suicide is sacrificial, an exteremly important dysfunction lies in the destruction of a productive, useful member of the group who is in the prime of life.

If we now consider the larger society, the village, as the unit for functional analysis, it is possible to see a manifest function again in dissipating drains on its resources, and more broadly, in ridding the society of unhappy people. A function at the latent level is perhaps in the entertainment aspect: suicide provides a spectacle for other members of the social group, much as public executions once did in our culture. Of course a manifest dysfunction for the larger society as well as for the kinship group is found in the destruction of a member insofar as he contributes to the group. At the same time, however, the overall rate of suicides in the group is in effect institutionally controlled so that the security and well-being of the social group as a whole is never seriously endangered by the practice.

For the last unit which Merton suggests, the cultural system, several preliminary points can be set forth. A manifest function which is served by the ritual punishment aspect of the pattern is that the condemnation of killing an in-group member, especially a relative, is dramatized, and group cohesion is emphasized. Again, in the actual suicide pattern itself, traditional methods of social control are reinforced in the final departing speech of the suicide, where he reiterates the importance of listening to the elders and abiding by their advice and by the old ways. There are probably also significant manifest religious aspects but our data are too scant to permit much speculation on this point.

Latent functions of the sacrificial suicide would appear to be quite important: dramatizing and emphasizing belief in the powers of the spiritual world; reinforcing belief in the worth of the individual member of the society—for instance, that the beneficiary is worthy of the sacrifice; extremely vivid and powerful dramatization of the sentiments of mutual help and concern. No manifest dysfunctions to the cultural system (as distinct from the society) appear evident to us, but a latent dysfunction is engendered by retarding the development of other means of solving the problem, such as empirical medical techniques, and hence the enrichment of the cultural system. It is suggested that as the cultural as well as at the individual level, suicide avoids rather than solves the problems.

NOTES

1 "Suicide" here will include both those forms in which an individual delivers the death blow against his person—as by shooting, jumping off a cliff, or starving—and those in which the principal individual procures the help of another person who is the executioner, as in voluntary hanging. This paper will not discuss related patterns such as infanticide, or the sanctioned killing of an anti-social member of the group. For a comparative treatment of these topics see E. A. Hoebel, 'Law-ways of the Primitive Eskimos' *Journal of Criminal Law and Criminology*, Vol. 31, pp. 663–83 1941.

2 Knud Rasmussen, *The Netsilik Eskimos*, Report, Fifth Thule Expedition, Vol. 8, pp. 1–542, Copenhagen, 1931, p. 144.

3 Edward C. Weyer, *The Eskimos*, New Haven: Yale University Press, 1932, p. 248.

4 Idem, p. 138.

5 Cf., for instance, Knud Rasmussen, *Across Arctic America*, New York: G. P. Putnam's Sons, 1927; Kaj Birket-Smith, *The Caribou Eskimos*, Report, Fifth Thule Expedition, Vol. 5, pp. 1–725, Copenhagen, 1929; Franz Boas, *The Central Eskimo*, Sixth Annual Report, Bureau of [American] Ethnology, pp. 399–669, Washington, 1888; William Thalbitzer, ed., *The Ammassalik Eskimo*, Meddelelser om Gronland, Vol. 39, Copenhagen, 1914, and others.

6 Weyer, *The Eskimos*, p. 138.

7 The authors wish to acknowledge their gratitude for the use of supplementary data on the suicide pattern which were gathered on St. Lawrence Island by Dorothea C. Leighton and the late Frederick C. Cross, Jr.

8 This contrasts markedly with the practice reported among the Ammassalik: "When people fall seriously ill and there is no prospect of their recovery, they get tired of their sufferings, and then they often put an end to their lives by throwing themselves into the sea. They are often prompted to take this step by a word of admonition from their relatives, telling them that 'they have no longer anything to live for' " (Thalbitzer, *The Ammassalik Eskimo*, p. 74.)

9 Waldemar Bogoras, *The Chukchee*, Memoirs, American Museum of Natural History, Vol. 11, 2 parts, New York, 1904–9, p. 566.

10 Riley D. Moore, 'Social Life of the Eskimo of St. Lawrence Island', *American Anthropologist*, Vol. 25, pp. 339–75, 1923.

11 Correspondence, 1954.

12 Cf. Bogoras, *The Chukchee*, pp. 560–7.

13 Emile Durkheim, *Suicide*, Glencoe: Free Press, 1951.

14 Robert Merton, *Social Theory and Social Structure*, Glencoe: Free Press, 1949, pp. 50–4.

15 In his complete paradigm, he suggests several other aspects which should be discussed in functional analysis—such as functional alternatives, concepts of dynamics and change, problems of validation of functional analysis, and concepts of mechanisms through which functions are fulfilled, etc.—Our discussion, which is intended to be merely suggestive, will not attempt to encompass these other aspects.

CHAPTER 14

Suicide Among the Gisu*

Jean La Fontaine

"A person commits suicide if he finds too much trouble" Gisu say Suicide, in their eyes, is a choice between the alternatives of life and death. Mental illness or insanity is not therefore considered to be a cause of suicide. A mentally unsound person is thought to be incapable of weighing the pros and cons of living and could have no inducement to commit suicide.

However, suicide is not entirely a reasoned decision. It is also a manifestation of *litima*, which is best translated "temper". This is a personal characteristic which, Gisu say, results in the possessor's being liable to fits of anger or violence, or unreasonable jealousy and spite. Gisu believe that traits of character are inherited and therefore a whole lineage or a group of kinsmen may be referred to as bad-tempered, in the sense of possessing *litima*, although they are reluctant to push the argument to its logical conclusion and say that a tendency to commit suicide may be inherited. They are equally reluctant to admit that a member of their own lineage or a close kinsman has committed suicide. Suicide is considered to be evil, for it results from strife, from bad relations between men, or between men and the ancestors.

Suicide is also thought to be contagious in the sense that physical contact with the body or surroundings of a suicide may cause the person who suffered contagion to commit suicide. For this reason the dead body must be removed from the place of death by someone entirely unrelated to the dead man and his kin; the service is repaid by the gift of a bull. A sheep must also be killed to pacify the spirit of the suicide, which is evil. A suicide's hut may be pulled down; it will certainly be smeared with the content's of a sheep's stomach, which is the material used for purification in all cases of ritual defilement. The chyme will be smeared on the agent of death (usually a rope or cord) and thrown round about the spot where the

* Reprinted by permission of Princeton University Press from 'Homicide and Suicide Among the Gisu' by Jean La Fontaine, in *African Homicide and Suicide*, edited by Paul Bohannan. Copyright © 1960 by Princeton University Press.

suicide took place. If the suicide hanged himself on a tree, it will be cut down and burnt. Nothing must be left which might cause another suicide by its contagious evil. Relatives of the dead man and his close patrilineal kinsmen are particularly susceptible to the evil influence for two reasons. The *litima* which was the precipitating cause of the suicide is also dormant in their natures and therefore the contagion of a suicide may make this quality active. Also, the suicide may have been a form of ancestral vengeance directed against the lineage group as a whole. The wrath of the ancestors, if not appeased, may cause another member of the lineage to commit suicide.

It is only the ancestors that can make a man kill himself. Witchcraft and sorcery can impel a man to kill another but not himself. This belief is connected with the idea that the measurer of a man's allotted span of existence, who metes out life and death, is the creator-god, Nabende or Were, who may work through the ancestors. The ancestors are thus intermediaries between him and the patrilineal descent groups whose founders they are. The ancestors can cause a man to commit suicide in one of two ways: either they may cause him to feel such shame at some anti-social act that he will kill himself, or they may involve him with hostilities with his close kinsfolk so that he commits suicide out of *litima*. Gisu do not formulate their ideas in quite this way. They say, "What makes one man in a certain situation commit suicide, while another, in an identical situation does not? It must be the anger of the ancestors.[1] Thus, most men will say that an immediate sacrific to the ancestors is one of the essential precautions to take when cleansing the community after a suicide.

Suicide, then, causes a state of ritual uncleanliness which must be purged or more evil will follow. This fact is also emphasized in the lack of ritual surrounding the disposal of the body. Gisu say that no one except very close kin will go to the funeral of a suicide; this is unusual, for there are strong obligations on neighbours, maternal kin, and affines to attend mortuary ceremonies. By their presence they show that they are not guilty of causing the man's death by witchcraft or sorcery.[2] No drums are beaten for the burial and no mourning observances are carried out. No one must name a child after a suicide victim, and his name is not mentioned in sacrifices to the ancestors. Formerly, before the introduction of burial practices, the corpse was thrown into thick bush where no one would be likely to come across the bones, for they, too, were ritually dangerous. The skull was not placed in the lineage depository with the skulls of honoured men and women of the lineage. The net result was to blot out as quickly as possible all memory of the person who brought the evil of suicide into the community.

In part, the refusal of the wider community to attend the funeral of a suicide is a reflection of the idea that the people in daily contact with the dead man were responsible for the death. The most frequently cited cause of suicide is quarrelling with those people whose hostility makes an individual feel that life is no longer worth living. That is, those people with whom, in the Gisu social system, a man must be on good terms. One's father and brothers, one's spouse, should be loyal and appreciative and, at the very last, fulfil their obligations towards one. Thus, when a suicide takes place there is a feeling, not usually formulated precisely, that these people are to blame.

A threat of suicide may occasionally be used to impose demands on relatives. One such threat came to my notice, which I will give in detail: Wosukira,[3] the son, by a young wife, of an influential minor chief, was at secondary school. He had already been expelled from two schools for making girls pregnant and this was his last chance. After two defections, his father refused to pay further school-fees, but would permit him to continue at school if his mother paid the fees out of what she could earn in agricultural work. Then he made a third girl pregnant and wanted to marry her, in part to pacify the school authorities. His father refused to pay the bride-wealth and expressed his disapproval of the whole affair. At this, Wosukira threatened suicide and left his father's homestead. His mother was worried and sent his sister to find him; she also did her best to persuade the father to relent. Wosukira did not carry out his threat, but had he done so, his mother, and probably others, would have blamed his father.

Gisu say that suicide must be prevented if possible, but this does not mean that the threat of suicide is either condoned or often used as a weapon to enforce one's demands. In the sample of cases which we will examine here,[4] there are only four in which previous threats of suicide were mentioned. Gisu do not hold the idea that by committing suicide a man may revenge himself on others by releasing an evil spirit to attack them. The spirit of a suicide is thought to be evil, but rather in the way that the spirits of anyone who dies an untimely death is evil.

Gisu will readily construct a hypothetical situation to illustrate common motives for suicides. The reasons given for men and women differ slightly, but there are three broad categories: failure to have children, quarrels with close relatives or spouse, or the death of several children or siblings. Each of these situations is found among the cases in this sample.

Gisu say that if a man has no children and particularly no sons, or if he has a series of unsuccessful marriages and can get no woman to stay with him long enough for him to achieve a stable family unit, his state is indeed bad. At beer parties he will be chaffed or ridiculed, at councils no one will listen to him; generally, he will count for nothing. This will cause him to feel bitter against fate and jealous of others who are more fortunate; he will feel *litima*, and may well commit suicide. Case 1 is an example of this, in a more dramatic form than usual.

Case No. 1. Wangobi, son of Mafwabi, aged about 35, had not been able to marry until this, by Gisu standards, late age; he had remained a virgin until his marriage. When he did marry, he proved to be impotent. His wife said that he had been in despair and had tried several remedies, but to no avail. Talking over this case with informants, I got a large measure of agreement that he had taken the only way out of an impossible situation.

A woman who is barren or whose children all die in infancy may suffer ill-treatment from her husband, even if he does not divorce her. Her co-wives and neighbours will treat her with contempt. This treatment may make her feel the *litima* that will cause her to kill herself.

Case No. 2. Lozita Nagudi was barren. Her husband had taken a second wife who had a child and Lozita was very jealous of her. The husband seems to have been fond of Lozita and was scrupulously fair in his treatment of both. On this occasion he brought back two pounds of meat from the market and divided it between them. Lozita refused to take her share saying: "Give it to your favourite wife, the mother of your child." He remonstrated with her, saying that they each had equal rights, but she persisted in her refusal. He got angry and boxed her ears, whereupon she tore herself away and ran towards a high cliff in the neighbourhood. Her husband followed her but, despite his efforts, she threw herself over the edge and was killed.

However, Gisu say that fewer women than men commit suicide because they are childless. This is related to the fact that a woman can escape from the situation by returning to her natal home, where her family will support her, and may even accuse her husband's lineage of bewitching her, for they will not believe that she is barren. Moreover, she has always the hope that taking a new partner may result in a more productive union. "A woman can always find a husband but a man who cannot keep a wife is indeed unfortunate" is a common saying.

But if a woman's natal family do not support her in quarrels with her husband and his lineage, whatever the cause, a woman is likely to kill herself. This is the type-situation for female suicide. One man gave me an example from his experience which I quote in full; it is not in the sample but is closely paralleled to one which is.

Case No. 3. A girl of my informant's acquaintance, from a hills area, was married to a man who lived at some distance from her home in the plains. There are more cattle in the plains than the hills and her father had been able to get a large number for her bride-wealth. The woman did not get on well with her husband who beat her and did not fulfil the obligations of a husband. She went home to her father. He was not pleased to see her for he had used the cows of her bride-wealth to marry a wife for her brother. He refused to let her stay with him, which would have signified his willingness to repay the bride-wealth and obtain a divorce for her. Her brother, naturally enough, was equally unsympathetic, and the two men told her to return to her husband and not leave him till she had proof that he had sent her away, an action which would mean that he forfeited the bride-wealth. She left her father's homestead and hanged herself.

It is clear that Gisu ideas on suicide do relate to the facts. One can pick actual cases which correspond exactly to the "ideal type". Moreover, there is an institutionalized way of committing suicide, by hanging. Of the 68 cases in this sample, an overwhelming majority used this method, as Table 1 indicates.

TABLE 1

Methods of Gisu Suicides

Hanging	64
Stabbing	1
Drowning	1
Setting fire to the house	1
Jumping over cliff	1

One can say, then, that suicide is a recognized, if not socially approved, course of action; it is a possible way out of certain difficult situations. The crucial point, however, is that Gisu do not win esteem by committing suicide. The "way out" is not thought to be the "noble way out." Gisu suicide cannot be classified in Durkheim's category of altruistic suicide.

TABLE 2

Alleged Motives in Gisu Suicides

Motive	Men Number	per cent of total	Women Number	per cent of total
Physical distress	16	40	8	28.5
Mental disorder	2	5	5	17.9
Quarrels with kin	–	–	3	10.4
Fear of results of own misdeed	10	25	3	10.4
Other	4	10	2	7.1
Not known	8	20	7	25.7
TOTAL	40	100	28	100

An examination of the alleged motives for the sixty-eight cases of suicide in our sample is set out in Table 2.

Two points emerge from a consideration of this table. The first is that a strikingly large number of suicides, both male and female, are attributed to the person's having a long-standing, painful, or incurable disease. Gisu ideas on suicide make no mention of this condition as a possible motive. This factor is intelligible in the light of the importance of physical fitness for participation in the social life of a society such as that of the Gisu. A man or woman who is ill is, to a large extent, outside the society, unable to take part in communal activity. When illness first attacks an individual, the support of the community is felt by him or her in the efforts that are made to cure the disease. If all remedies fail, the attitude changes; some people may even attribute the affliction to a supernatural punishment for evil doing. The isolation engendered by this situation may well lead to suicide.

However, the data provided by the analysis of alleged motives does not show clearly the sociological factor involved. Further, the attribution of seven suicides to mental disorder is quite contrary to Gisu theory and throws doubt on the reliability of the data.[5] In fact, the categories of motive show a marked similarity to those into which Durkheim divided the alleged motives for suicide in French society,[6] and one could hardly say that the structure of the two societies was the same. Durkheim himself discarded the analysis of individual "motives", and showed that suicide rates are determined by extra-individual forces. Let us turn to look at some economic and social factors which affect Gisu suicide.[7]

Sociological studies have related the variations in the incidence of suicide in a particular society to fluctuations in its economy. Durkheim found that dislocation of the economic organization, whether because of a sudden rise or depression, correlated with a rise in the suicide rate.[8]

Henry and Short[9] modified this theory, on evidence from their data that there is a negative correlation between the suicide rate and the business cycle. Both these studies deal with societies where the state of the economy is measurable in terms of a business cycle. In this essay, we are dealing with a society whose economy is, basically, a subsistence one. It is subject to sharp seasonal and local variations, and by its very nature cannot rise above a level which is marked by the greatest productivity of the soil under ideal climatic conditions. The problem is complicated by the fact that Gisu also participate in a money economy. They grow cash crops and buy articles which are the products of industrialized societies using a money economy. One might perhaps use these cash crops as an index of the prosperity of Gisu economy, for they represent a surplus over the basic subsistence needs of the society. However, the cultivation of cash crops has been steadily increasing and has not yet reached its maximum capacity. Fluctuation in the amount of these crops in any series of seasons is obscured by the fact that there are more and more producers entering the market. Moreover, the income from cash crops is used freely to supplement deficiencies in the food crops. This is made possible by the differing effect of seasonal changes on cash and food crops: one may be affected and not the other.

It is essential to attempt to assess to some degree the nature of the relationship of suicide to economic conditions in order to test the conclusions that have been drawn about their inter-connection. Gisu society, like that of industrialized societies, has a status hierarchy that is based on the use of wealth to gain power and prestige. In both types of society, an economic depression involves persons in the hierarchy in loss of status and hence in a situation of anomy. However, the data are such that only tentative conclusions may be drawn.

The quality of the harvests of both food crops and cash crops and the number of suicides for the same year are presented in Table 3.

The total incidence does not seem responsive to changes in the economy. However, if we separate male from female suicide, we can see that economic factors seem to have some significance; the incidence of suicide by males shows more coordination with economic changes. In the post-famine years of 1946 and 1949, and the year following a rapid rise in prosperity in 1952, the numbers of men who committed suicide increased, while those of women do not seem to have been affected. This difference between men and women

TABLE 3

Economic Conditions and Suicide in Bugisu

| Year | Economic Conditions | Total | Suicide | |
			Male	Female
1945	Famine relief necessary. Cotton crop poor	9	4	5
1946	Food still very short. Good coffee crop	9	7	2
1947	Bad year for both food and cash crops though not famine	3	2	1
1948	Bad food harvest. 22 tons of maize imported. Good coffee crop	5	2	3
1949	Food still short	4	3	1
1950	Economy returning to normal	7	6	1
1951	Good year for food and cash crops	5	1	4
1952	Not very good cotton year. Other crops normal	5	2	3
1953	Normal food harvest. Coffee good and prices high	11	8	3
1954	Very good year for both cash crops	0	0	0
1955	Harvest not yet in (suicides for half year)	10	5	5

can be related to their different roles in the economic structure of society, particularly with regard to the opportunity to use economic resources. Food over and above that for consumption and the money from cash crops is in the hands of men. It is the men who own land and cattle and can use these and surplus crops to achieve high status by using these means to create relations of economic interdependence with others or by marrying more wives. A woman, once she has fed her children and seen that they and she get a fair share of the husband's wealth for buying the necessities of life, has no further interest in wealth. Her position does not depend on wealth, although she gains in prestige if her husband is wealthy. A woman's primary task is to produce children, and her standing in the community depends on her achievement as the mother of many and healthy children.

Interesting results can be obtained from an analysis of suicides by age. Data is not available for all sixty-eight cases; the forty-four for which an age is given as summarized in Table 4.

The highest incidence of all suicides is found among the age

TABLE 4

Age of Gisu Suicides

Age	Total Suicides	Women	Men
Up to 15	4	0	4
16–20	3	0	3
21–25	3	2	1
26–30	7	2	5
31–35	7	2	5
36–40	5	4	1
41–45	2	2	0
46–50	2	0	2
51–55	2	2	0
56–60	2	1	1
61–65	2	0	2
66–70	3	0	3
71–75	0	0	0
76 +	2	0	2

groups 26-30 and 31-35, a fact which is in striking contrast to findings for other societies in which the tendency to commit suicide increases with age. This has been related to the weakening of the individual's ties to society,[10] and to the fall in prestige which individuals suffer in age.[11] We can relate the difference in the distribution of the Gisu figures to a difference in the position of the aged. Not only are they removed from the struggle for prestige and the necessity to maintain their status, they acquire a positive source of prestige in their age and experience.

In order to explain the peak in suicides between the ages of twenty-six and thirty-five, one must separate the figures for male and female suicides. Then it becomes apparent that it is the suicide of men that accounts for this rise. Nearly half the male suicides for which data on age are available are under thirty, and two-thirds are under forty. This fact can be related to the structural position of young men in Gisu society. In discussing homicide, we saw that there is tension in the relations between young men and seniors of their own lineage, who wield authority over them. This inter-personal hostility is a factor in the incidence of suicide as well.

There are two peaks in the suicide figures for men under thirty-five: there are seven suicides of youths under twenty,[12] and ten of young men between the ages of twenty-five and thirty-five. Each group forms nearly a quarter of the total for all ages.

Boys of the youngest group are not highly integrated into the society. They are of little importance, for they are usually not yet circumcised at this age. They cannot, therefore, take part in the economic or political activities of their elders; they are also cut off from the society of women and young girls who have their own task, in which boys play no part. Boys of this age are not essential to any of the major tasks of the community; those who go to school have little time for additional activities together with other members of the community. They also learn values and acquire knowledge which puts them in a still more isolated position vis-à-vis the rest of the society.

As the youths grow older,[13] circumcision appears as the passport to full participation in the world of men. The position of inferiority in which an uncircumcised youth finds himself appears easily surmountable. In theory, all circumcised men are equal in status; only the uncircumcised are inferior. Circumcision ceremonies involve the whole community and are a powerful force for strengthening the cohesion of groupings at all levels in Gisu society. The novice is the centre of attention and is made to feel that it is an integral and essential part of his lineage and of the community. His fortitude during the operation brings him praise and a high standing among his age-mates, with whom he has been made to feel the greatest solidarity. It is noticeable that the suicides of young men in the immediate post-circumcision years (20-25) drop suddenly from seven to one.

The circumcision ceremonies have the effect of strengthening the solidarity of the lineage group and emphasizing the ties between its members and the common interests, rights, and duties among them. The relation between the newly circumcised men and the fellow lineage members, and particularly seniors in the lineage, do not bear out this ideal. We have seen how the relations between successive generations of males become strained almost to breaking point after the young man has passed through circumcision. The formal inequality of rank which supported the asymmetrical father-son relationship has disappeared. Once the son has acquired a wife and family of his own, which he does soon after circumcision, the social distance between himself and his father is still further diminished. What distinguishes them at this point is that the older man still controls land, cattle and other economic resources that the younger man wants for himself. For the fifteen years after the age of about twenty-five a Gisu man is more involved in the business of raising his status than at any other time. The traditional status hierarchy was based on wealth; modern conditions have not altered this, but merely offer new opportunities for acquiring wealth.[14] If a young man wants to get ahead, either in the traditional system or in the hierarchy of new jobs, he must do it when still young, before he has growing sons for whom to provide.[15]

The newly-circumcised young man, then, views his elders as frustrating agents, who stand in his way of advancement. Although he is now the formal equal of any man in the society, his new status does not bring any material advantage of itself. He has to fight for his rights to land and to a wife, to complete with the older members of his lineage for control of economic resources. Land is extremely short in many areas and the prevention of inter-lineage warfare, which provided an outlet for feelings of aggression and a means by which the needs of an expanding lineage for more land might be met, means increasing conflicts between members of the same lineage. The ideals of mutual loyalty and cooperation between members that are the main emphasis of the circumcision ceremonies contrast sharply with the rivalry which characterizes the actual situation.

During their early twenties, many young men leave Gisuland and find work either in Kenya on European farms, or in Buganda on cotton plantations. In this way they can both escape the authority of their elders and hope to earn the money to pay bride-wealth for a wife and buy land, if their fathers refuse to do their duty and provide them with these two essentials. Emigration relieves the situation only temporarily, however. Most of the emigrants go for short periods, and few intend to do other than make money and return to their birthplace. Strong emotional ties bind a Mugisu to his lineage home, the place where he has *par excellence* a right to land. Title to a piece of land means also a right to citizenship and a place in the society; few Gisu willingly forego it. The return of young men aggravate the situation of conflict in yet another way. Having established themselves as independent, they are less willing than before to submit to the authority of their seniors. They are also, to a certain extent, strangers in the community and their ties with its members are not strong enough to counteract the influence of mutual hostility. Far from relieving the situation, the possibilities of emigration aggravate it.

Among females, there is a difference in the distribution of suicide by age. The figures are not large enough to warrant drawing far-reaching conclusions, but it is significant that the peak occurs at the age at which women are close to the menopause. There are two cases approximately in each of the age categories between twenty-one and sixty, with the exception of the 36–40 age group which contains double that number. We have already said that a woman's position in Gisu society depends on her fulfilment of the role of mother. While she is still capable of bearing children, a woman is of value in the community. Should her marriage break up she will readily find another husband and her family will generally support her in obtaining a divorce if she has no children by her husband. If she reaches the age at which all women stop being able to bear children, without having established herself as the mother of children in a stable marital union, she is liable to be rejected both by her husband and her family. She is no longer an asset to either group.

In the oldest age groups, the suicide of women appears less, in spite of their higher survival rate. This is largely because an elderly woman becomes closely associated with her son's family. She has a vital role as grandmother, whereas men cannot play a similar part in the household of their sons, as is shown by the avoidance between father-in-law and daughter-in-law. Elderly men do suffer some loss of status with the onset of old age, whereas women can achieve a higher status more like that of men. They take an increasing part in ritual affairs. Isolation is greatest for men in old age.

We have said that circumcision ceremonies are a powerful force making for social integration; the effects of this on young men can be seen in the lesser tendency of men to commit suicide in the immediate post-circumcision years. Their influence extends beyond this one category of members of the society. The ceremonies involve all members of the society who take part in the dancing and displays of group solidarity. In spite of this the over-all rates for years in which circumcision took place show little change over other years. Even allowing for a time lag before the effect of the ceremonies makes itself apparent, there is no marked effect.

If however, we separate the suicides by sex some effect is noticeable. In four of the five post-circumcision years, there is a decline in the number of female suicides. No change appears in male suicides, because other factors tend to counteract the integrative effect of the ceremonies on men. The rites mark a crisis for both the youths who are initiated and for their seniors who see a threat to their supremacy in the entrance of more competitors into the male adult world. For women there is no such crisis. The ritual emphasis on lineage solidarity entails no such conflict between ideal and actual behaviour as it does for men. Women cannot own or inherit property, so in this respect they are not in competition with other members of their lineage Their status depends on qualities other than the successful manipulation of the status system; their relations of rivalry are with their co-wives, members of other lineage groups. It is the marital situation which presents conflicts for a woman, and this has no reference in the rituals; a woman takes part as a valued member of her natal family.

In looking at suicide in Gisu society, the marked difference in the factors affecting the suicide of men and women is the most striking feature. It is related to the lesser involvement of women in the economic organization of the society and their status in the hierarchy of prestige-bearing roles. In this, the Gisu material bears out the conclusions of Henry and Short, who found that suicide of females is less sensitive to changes in the business cycle than is that of men, and related this fact to the situation described above for the Gisu, and, to a lesser degree, to the United States. As far as Gisu are concerned, however, the point is not that women have a lower status than men but that their status is based on a different scale of values. They do not enter into competition for prestige as men do. Consequently, they are less sensitive to changes in the economic state of the society and in old age do not suffer the isolation which inability to compete for power imposes on old men. The groups into which women are integrated by periodic rituals, such as those of circumcision, do not contain relationships which make for hostility. The anxieties of women are centred round their role as mother, on the successful performance of which their status depends. Thus, the suicide of women is greatest in those years when they must succeed as wives and mothers in order to establish themselves in a position which will guarantee security in old age and a respected position in the community. For men, membership in a corporate group with ideals of unity that conflict with the necessity to compete with fellow members in a status hierarchy based on wealth, means that they are more influenced by economic factors, less by the integrative force of ritual. Frustration or isolation engendered by the nature of the economic struggle causes men to commit suicide in early maturity.

In attempting to discover if there is any relationship that can be considered meaningful between homicide and suicide in Gisu society, one must again treat the sexes as separate categories. There appears to be a rough inverse correlation between murders and suicides for the years 1945–55 inclusive. A simple regression test indicates that the correlation is not significant; examination of the two phenomena by sex of the suicides shows clearly that no such correlation is observable.

One must notice, however, that although the absolute number of female suicides and murderers is less than those for men, a far greater proportion of women who commit violent acts kill themselves than kill others. Over a period of ten years, eleven women killed other people, twenty-eight killed themselves: more than twice as many committed suicide as murder. During the same period, 141 men committed murder and only forty committed suicide. In terms of the theory put forward by Henry and Short, this would seem to indicate that women have higher status than men and that they were also subject to fewer external restraints from a weaker relational system. We have seen that the first implication is not true. Women have lower status than men. However, this lower status does not really fit into the male status hierarchy; it is defined by other non-competitive criteria. I would suggest that it is the involvement of individuals in a competitive status hierarchy rather than the fact of relative status in a hierarchy that is a factor in the situation. This is consistent with the psychological determinants put forward by the same authors: they relate the tendency to commit homicide to the legitimization of other-oriented aggression and a weak internalization of restraints, consequent on discipline imposed by the father, which consists of corporal punishment rather than mental chastisement. This is true for Gisu men.

Aggressive behaviour is encouraged for men, discouraged for women. The Gisu boy is disciplined almost exclusively by his father, whose power of inflicting physical punishment reaches its extreme in the circumcision operation, to which the young man must submit in order to be able to take part in the adult world. This adult world in which the young man emerges is one of aggressive competition; the extreme expression of this was found, formerly, in the warfare that broke out sporadically between neighbouring groups. A woman's world is entirely different. Brought up by her mother, and discouraged to express her aggressive tendencies, she emerges into a world where her personal achievement depends on her own physical nature.

The second point, that homicide is correlated with strong external restraints from a stronger relational system and suicide with weak external restraints from a stronger relational system system and suicide with weak external restraints and a weak external system, also holds for the difference in acts of aggression between Gisu men and women. We have seen how men are members of a lineage, a corporate group with a strong hold over its members. The adult male must conform to their expectations of him if he is to achieve full membership and the prestige goods which bring higher status. Rejection from the group is the greatest disaster which can befall him; he loses a right to citizenship and a place in society. Moreover, he takes part in a competitive hierarchy in which the expectations of others play a great part in determining his status. He comes into conflict with those people with whom he is integrated in a corporate group—his lineage mates. A woman is marginal to this group organization. Her membership of the lineage is residual; she has no rights in the corporate group and as such is not subject to their demands to such an extent as her brothers. She forms an integral part, not of a lineage, but of domestic groupings. Her degree of involvement in social or cathectic relationships[16] is far less than that of a man; her status is thus far less determined by conformity or otherwise to the expectations of others.

Gisu society is in a state of change. Contact with Europeans has brought economic development as well as far-reaching social changes. Many of the factors which have been shown to act in determining the expression of aggression can be traced to the influence of these changes. To mention only one: the prevention of warfare, and thus the limitation placed on the area controlled by any one lineage, together with an increase in population, has caused a great change in the nature of relations among members of the land-controlling group, the lineage. It seems tenable, however, that the changes intensify strain at points in the social structure, relationships which by virtue of the type of social organization were always ambivalent.

NOTES

1 Of course, all Gisu theory on this subject is designed to explain individual cases of suicide, rather than suicide *per se*.

2 One cannot, as has been said, cause a suicide by the use of supernatural powers.

3 This is not his real name.

4 These cases are taken from the Police Death Enquiry Files for 1945 to 1955 inclusive. Any death in suspicious circumstances is investigated by the Police, and a report made. The cases examined are the total number recorded.

5 In the records, no indication is made of who was questioned about the suicide; the investigation is not designed to show motive, but to decide whether the case is one of suicide or murder.

6 Durkheim, *Le Suicide* (1897), Nouvelle ed. 1930, p. 146.

7 Although the following discussion is set forth in terms of the quantities available, the sample is inadequate for the use to which it has been put. However, the conclusions drawn about suicide and economy in Bugisu are based on a general knowledge of the society and not merely on the figures, which are used mainly in illustration. It has, thus, a certain validity in ethnographic observation which it lacks statistically.

8 Durkheim, op. cit., p. 264.

9 *Homicide and Suicide,* 1954, p. 23.

10 Durkheim, op. cit.

11 Henry and Short, p. 38.

12 Three of the under-fifteen suicides were of boys of fourteen; the other was a boy of twelve.

13 Circumcision in Bugisu takes place between the ages of sixteen and twenty.

14 See my article on Gisu chiefs in A. I. Richards (editor), *East African Chiefs: a Study of Political Development in some Uganda and Tanganyika Tribes,* London, 1959.

15 It would be interesting to see if the suicide of the 26–35 age group is more sensitive than others to economic change. Henry and Short (op. cit., p. 29) show that the two age groups 25–34 and 15–24 are the most highly sensitive to changes in the business cycle. Unfortunately, the Gisu data does not make such a close analysis feasible.

16 Henry and Short, op. cit., p. 16.

CHAPTER 15

Samsonic Suicides: or Suicides of Revenge Among Africans*

M. D. W. Jeffreys

INTRODUCTION

Though Westermark[1] in 1908 referred to suicides based on vengeance, so far I have not found any detailed discourse on this type or aspect of suicide. It is true that Hoebel,[2] quoting from Rattray's[3] study of the Ashanti, wrote: "Revenge–suicide could be achieved by cursing the king and putting the blame on someone who drove you to do the act. In a quarrel between two men one of them could reach the point where he felt the stand of the other went beyond all reason. Or, it could be that his own situation was untenable, and being unable to get out of it, he destroyed himself but also had the satisfaction of making a scapegoat out of his adversary by saying, 'I call upon such and such a god to kill the King, and I do so on your head, and after I am killed may you pay 100 pereguan (£800) to buy the Bongo's skin with which I shall be strangled.' Like the threat of suicide among the Trobriand Islanders and the Cheyennes, it should have served to check extreme and outrageous demands in the enforcement of what might have been legal rights by reason of the social injury suffered by the person who was blamed for pushing the suicide to his extreme act." Hoebel, however, does not develop the matter any further.

Durkheim[4] grouped European suicides under three headings: the Egoistic, the Altruistic and the Anomic, as characteristic of the types found in European culture. To these I suggested a fourth, namely suicides of revenge. This paper is an amplification of an article of mine[5] that appeared in 1952.

Bohannan,[6] however, remarked: "Jeffreys was, in my opinion, wrong however in saying that vengeance is a fourth 'type' to be classed with Durkheim's three types, because the criterion of vengeance suicide is not to be found in the degree and sort of integration

* Revised for this volume by the author from his original article of the same title in *African Studies*, Vol. 11, 1952, pp. 118–22, published by the Witwatersrand University Press.

of the social group, the primary criterion in the Durkheim classification. Vengeance suicide is, however, very difficult to evaluate in Durkheim's terms." In that case suicides of revenge become a type, *sui generis*.

African culture patterns are differently oriented and consequently different patterns of suicide forms are found therein. In Africa suicide as a form of revenge is quite frequent and in this paper I propose to call them Samsonic suicides, because the Biblical story of Samson's death gives the earliest historical description of a revenge type of suicide; "And Samson called unto the Lord, and said O Lord God, remember, I pray Thee and strengthen me, I pray Thee, only this once, O God, that I may be at once avenged of my two eyes. And Samson took hold of the two middle pillars upon which the house rested, and leaned upon them, the one with his right hand, and the other with his left. And Samson said let me die with the Philistines. And he bowed himself with all his might: and the house fell upon the lords and upon all the people that were therein. So the dead which he slew at his death were more than they which he slew in his life."[7]

This type of suicide with a reference to Samson was reported by Bosman[8] in 1700 from Axim on the Gold Coast "... I remember when I had the Government of *Axim*, a very Rich one [gold mine] was discovered; but we lost our Footing there in a very Tragical manner; For the Commander in chief of the *Negroes*, being closely Besieged by our Men, ... shot Gold instead of Bullets, hinting by Signs that he was ready to Treat, and afterwards Trade with the Besiegers, but in the midst of this Negotiation he blew up himself and all his Enemies at once, as Unfortunately as Bravely, putting an end to our Siege and his Life, and like *Samson* revenging his death upon his enemies."

This point of view of suicide, the Samsonic, where the suicide not only destroys himself but also his enemies was discussed in America in a symposium edited by Mannheim[9]: "Cases of aggression turned against the self are apt to be simple, since a certain amount of more or less direct aggression against others is likely to be involved. The hysteria with an ambivalent attitude of love and hate towards members of his family may have symptoms which injure them as well as himself. In American society suicide may harm others as well as the self. Among the Tikopia suicide is, according to Firth, the son's method of revenge, a threat which constantly serves to prevent tyrannical fathers from becoming too unjust."

Samson's suicide, though an act of revenge, does not conform strictly with the type of revenge suicide that I have in mind. The type I have in mind might be called institutionalized suicide. Krober[10] wrote that what he called "institutionalized suicide" depended upon culture: ". . . the culture not only defines certain situations that call for suicide but often indicate the correct way to execute it . . . The Japanese *harakiri* . . . immediately rises to mind. This, with special form of disembowelment, was formerly confined to nobles." Here is Japanese society prescribing a social sanction to avert shame and disgrace and the manner of carrying it out.

In the Trobriand Islands jumping from the top of coco-nut palm under the stimulus of shame was absurdly regarded by Malinowski, not as a social sanction enforced by the local social structure but as a legal institution, an act of law. For Malinowski suicide among the Trobriand islanders "is performed as an act of justice, not upon oneself, but upon some person of near kindred who has caused offence. As such it is one of the most important legal institutions among these natives." According to Malinowski[11] "taking the law into one's own hands", which to any lawyer means the breaking of the law, is a legal institution: however, such a suicide is not one of revenge in the sense I shall use the term even though Evans[12] wrote: "The old legal term 'self-murder' had some wisdom in it; the vengeful nature of many suicides is plainly indicated in the spiteful tone of the 'you'll be sorry!' notes left behind."

Suicide as an act of revenge has two origins one based on a belief, the other based on knowledge of the social organization or else on the laws of the society in which one lives.

SUICIDES BASED ON THE SUPERNATURAL VENGEANCE

Temple[13] gives a hint about this type of suicide: "The lengths to which sacerdotal vindictiveness has often gone in India, is indicated by the well established custom of ceremonial suicide, self-immolation, and self injury, in order to bring divine or supernatural wrath on an opponent or enemy." This attitude is based on a belief expressed by Hocart[14]: "the dead are universally treated as of higher rank than the living".

Sumner and Keller[15] noted that revengeful suicides based on a belief are motivated as follows: "It is quite logical for those who think that ghosts have great power, to wish to become ghosts in order to attain ability to wreak vengeance. Among the Tlinkit a man committed suicide simply to make trouble for one who offended him. According to native custom, if a person commits suicide because some one has offended him or opposed a wish of his, heavy damages or a life must be given to the tribe of the suicide by the tribe of the one giving the offence. So suicide is sometimes resorted to in order to harass and burden others. The threat of suicide is sometimes used as bluff in order to do pecuniary harm to their owners by way of revenge."

Frazer[16] remarks on a belief that the ghost of a suicide will wreak vengeance on the suicide's provokers: "In the East that indifference to human life which seems so strange to the Western mind often takes a peculiar form. A man will sometimes kill himself merely in order to be revenged on his foe, believing that his ghost will haunt and torment the survivor, or expecting that punishment of some sort will overtake the wretch who drove him to this extreme step." Vestiges of this type of belief in the malevolence of the ghost of a suicide persisted in England until 1823 when suicides were no longer buried at the cross-roads. Puckle[17] commenting on this ancient practice, wrote: "Various reasons for this strange custom have been given; knowing as we do, that one of the prominent features of the treatment of the dead is the terror which all ages and all peoples have shown at the possibility of the return of a revengeful spirit, we are justified in thinking that the real object was to confuse the mind of the departed as to the direction of his former home, and the fact that it was a common practice to anchor the body down by driving a wooden stake through the heart tends to support this theory."

Suicide as an act of ghostly revenge is recognized as a social sanction and this aspect is adumbrated by Sumner and Keller.[18] "A curious form of retaliation is suicide. To understand how anyone might take recourse to this method which seems to us with our ideas and traditions, exactly the way not to do it, one must bear in mind that all people do not share our convictions about the sanctity and worth of earthly existence, while they possess a faith in their beliefs about the next life which, however loudly we may profess it, we do not exhibit. Their faith is, at any rate, strong enough to act upon and it does not seem to them that they are taking chances. If a person is not powerful enough to avenge himself in life, he believes that as a ghost he will be able to do so; and thus believing, threatens suicide. Since the individual whom he menaces shares his beliefs quite unshakenly, the threat is often sufficient to secure redress; but if not there is no hesitancy about carrying it out. This is a sort of *post mortem* retaliation."

This attitude to suicide is found in Africa, hence the possibility of revenge by committing suicide is accepted in many African tribes. Leonard[19] reported the case of a Brass man attempting suicide at Opobo in the Calabar province. He had shot himself but the medical officer had saved his life. He told Leonard that "if he could not go back to Brass in the flesh he might get back to it in the spirit, and so pay off old scores". Vedder,[20] writing of the Herero of South West Africa, remarked: "Suicide may also be an act of revenge.

The person who commits suicide is actuated by the thought that the dead are capable of bringing about evil and death more effectively than the living." This belief is also found in Tanganyika territory thus Gouldsbury and Sheane[21] reported that: "When a man has a grievance, and received no redress, he will, as a final resort, go before the wrongdoer and say, I shall commit suicide, and rise up as an evil spirit to torment you."

From Rhodesia comes an indication that among the Shona certain cases of suicide can be attributed to a belief that the ghost of the deceased will take vengeance on the living. Crawford[22] remarked: "It has been suggested that among the Shona suicide is sometimes committed by a person in order to revenge himself on another by turning his spirit into an *ngozi* to avenge the wrong. This may be so; but I have found no evidence to support this save, perhaps, in one or two cases where a young person has killed him or herself wearing the clothes of a faithless lover. This is almost certainly intended to indicate the reason for the suicide; but whether it is intended to go further and put fear of spirit revenge into the person whose clothes were worn, is difficult to say." Bohannan[23] discussing suicide among the Bantu Kavirondo remarked: "There is no altruistic and as yet little anomic suicide amongst the Baluyia. M. D. W. Jeffreys has drawn attention to another type of suicide, which he calls *Samsonic suicide*—killing oneself to avenge oneself on others. He shows this form to be widespread in Africa; it is found among the Baluyia. They hesitate to refer to any specific suicide as having been motivated by revenge, but they do believe that the ghost of a suicide can be particularly potent in bringing trouble and difficulty and that there undoubtedly are people who commit suicide in order that their ghosts may trouble the husbands, fathers, or other persons who forced them into impossible situations. The *Samsonic* interpretation is, therefore, sometimes emphasized and sometimes not, in any specific case." Roscoe[24] reported that among the Bakitara of Uganda: "The ghost of anyone ... who had been wrongfully accused and had committed suicide was very dangerous, even ... a woman who had been wrongfully accused of adultery would go and hang herself, and her ghost would then be a malignant influence. Her body was buried as near the place of her death as possible that the ghost might be destroyed or confined to that locality. If she hanged herself on a tree, the body was buried just clear of the roots, the tree was cut down and its roots dug up; the whole was then burned to ashes and the relatives had to pay ample compensation to the chief on whose land the deed was done." In this instance in addition to the menace of the ghost there is a material penalty payable to the head of that society and this example leads to the next type of suicide of revenge.

SUICIDE BASED ON SOCIETAL REPRISALS

The efficacy of such suicides depends upon a belief but the vagueness of a ghostly reprisal is replaced by certain knowledge in those societies that inflict penalties on the provoker. In such societies the suicide knows that his death will be revenged on the alleged provoker by society mulcting the latter in damages or in compensation. Such societies provide a patterned suicide and, out of a motive of revenge, suicides arise which, but for this patterning would not otherwise occur.

Among the Kassema of the Northern Territories of the Gold Coast an instance where both ghostly and social vengeance arise as a result of suicide was reported by Cardinall[25]: "Cruel enough as they all are to thieves, they are not unkind to their wives or their children. Fear prompts this kindness. No one is afraid to die in a moment of temper, and a woman will frequently stab herself with a poisoned arrow. Such a catastrophe would almost ruin the husband. There are all manner of spirits to pacify, spirits to cleanse as well as the outraged relatives to appease."

The Gold Coast had a high incidence of tribes who practised Samsonic suicides. Among the Ashanti, because of a highly organized political structure, suicides of revenge were a recognized and common means of getting even with an enemy. Thus Bowditch[26] who was on the Gold Coast in 1817 writing of the Ashantee remarked: "If a man kills himself on the head of another, the other must kill himself also, or pay 20 oz. [of gold] to the family of the suicide: in Fantee the sum is indefinitely great: this is frequently resorted to, when there is no other prospect of revenge.

"Adumisa, an extraordinarily beautiful red skinned woman of Cape Coast Castle, possessed numerous admirers but rejected them all. One of them in despair, shot himself on her head close to her house. The family demanded satisfaction; to save her relations from a ruinous palaver, she resolved to shoot herself in expiation." Bowditch[27] then describes the type of suicide where the suicide among the Ashantee invokes the king's oath. "If a man swears on the king's head, that another man must kill him, which is understood to be invoking the king's death if he does not, the other man must do so, or forfeit the whole of his property, and generally his life. This very frequently occurs, for the blacks in their ardour for revenge, do not regard sacrificing their own lives to bring a palaver on their murderer, which their families are sure to do."

Dupuis[28] who was on the Gold Coast in 1819 stated: "Another description of suicide is when a man deprives himself of life in revenge against an opponent, while any matter where justice is concerned may be pending: in this case, the party is said to have killed himself upon the head of his oppressor, who seldom escapes the retaliation of the law without a pecuniary fine to the state, and other disbursements among the courtiers."

Ellis[29] in 1883 reported on much the same lines about Coomassie: "The queen-mother, who possessed enormous influence, threatened to commit suicide *on the heads** of the principal chiefs of the war-party if they persevered in their intentions, and this threat sealed the fate of their party.

Ellis[30] reported in 1887 much the same custom among the Tshi: "... should a person commit suicide, and before so doing attribute the act to the conduct of another person, that other person is required by native law to under-go a like fate. This practice is termed *killing oneself upon the head of another*, and the person whose conduct is supposed to have driven the suicide to commit the rash act, is visited with death of an exactly similar nature. Such suicides are rare and the family of the suicide generally forgo their right to the death of the person indicated as the cause of the calamity, receiving money damages instead." Among the Ewe of Togoland Manoukian[31] has reported a similar type of suicide. "In Ho, according to Spieth, suicide was believed to make the whole sub-tribe unclean, so that the suicide's relations had to pay a fine and undergo certain purification rites, in order to prevent drought, the occurrence of which was commonly regarded as a supernatural sanction in the dry Ho country."

Stone[32] in 1900 reported as follows: "To commit suicide in the presence of another is one of the ways the Yorubas have of revenging a gross insult offered to him by that person. This is called *dying on the neck*, though I was never able to find out the reason for this." Ajisafe[33], a Yoruba, supplies the reason: "Should a man or woman be provoked to commit suicide, the provoker is held responsible for same. The penalty is a very heavy fine to be paid to the family of the victim or forfeiture of the provoker's life. The corpse of the suicide is not buried, but is removed to the house of the

---

* To commit suicide *on the head of* a person means that the intending suicide invokes the name of that person before putting an end to his own life. The person whose name is thus invoked occupies, according to local custom, exactly the same position as if he had killed the suicide with his own hand, and is liable to be mulcted in damages and subjected to all the extortions of a family *palaver*."

provoker till the judgement shall have been satisfied; then the corpse is taken over by the family, who bury it according to the rites and ceremonies for the burial of suicides."

Among the Bafut in the west Cameroons the Ritzenthalers[34] reported suicides of revenge: "Suicide is relatively rare. One informant stated that during his life time he knew of only three . . . Some of these were girls who refused to be coerced into a marriage they did not like. One such girl hanged herself and had to be cut down by a special ju-ju man, one of the Council of Elders sent by the Fon. The father had to leave the compound and move to another place . . . He had to build a new house and acquire new possessions, since all the old ones were left behind to decay. No one can move into the old hut. This is true even of a compound where someone not belonging to the compound will come to hang himself. He will have to be cut down by special ju-ju and everyone has to abandon the premises. Indeed, one means of revenge upon an enemy is by hanging himself in his compound."

Weeks[35] reported from the Congo a type of suicide of revenge. "A man living at Nkondo, a village in the Ngombe district, was very ill, in fact near to death, and did not desire to leave his property—trade goods, cloths, guns, powder, etc.—to his relatives for he regarded them with much hatred. So he made up his mind to burn down the house containing his goods. He waited for an opportunity, and one night when five persons—three adults and two children—were sleeping in the house, he locked the door, set fire to the structure, and rolled himself in his blanket to await the end. The dry grass of the hut burned like tinder, and the powder, catching fire, caused a tremendous explosion. Only one man escaped. The family of the two children demanded and received compensation for their death from the suicide's family. The adults who were killed belonged to his family. Whatever the reason for his grievance against his family, he had a terrible revenge."

Dundas[36] reported that among the Wachagga of Kilimanjaro the mviyago, or dying curse, is supposed to be so powerful that it cannot be averted: "Curses, and dying curses in particular, are very commonly pronounced, more particularly by women against others of their sex. . . . When any two women quarrel they are always ready to threaten a dying curse on eath other. It is said, and I can well believe it, that women have committed suicide merely the sooner to be avenged in this way upon their hated enemies."

In east Africa Hobbly[37] has reported suicide as a means of revenge by starting a blood feud. "A young man one day had a violent quarrel with his own mother while cultivating, and eventually beat her with a stick. She ran crying to a village near by, and one of the elders came out and gave the young fellow a thrashing; to everyone's astonishment the young man hanged himself that afternoon, and the people of the vicinity told my agent, who went to enquire into it, that he had committed suicide so that his blood relations might lay his death at the door of the elder, and thus start a blood feud against him."

Stayt[38] reported that among the Bavenda of South Africa there exists a legal mechanism, the chief's court, which will punish the person alleged to be the cause of the suicide. "If a man commits suicide all the relatives are called to the chief's village to determine the cause of the *tragedy*. It is considered that no man would take his life without some outside provocation, and so the death is regarded as a form of murder. If no adequate explanation is forthcoming the suicide's wives and property are confiscated to protect the rest of the family and enforce the culprit to declare himself. If on consultation with a diviner, the death is discovered to be the work of a spirit, the property is returned, the chief keeping two oxen as payment for his trouble."

Suicide as an act of aggression against society is fairly common in Africa. Roscoe[39] in Uganda reported that: "If a Bagesu wife hanged herself in her house, her husband was accused of being the cause. He was despoiled of all his possessions and his house was broken down." It was quite clear that a threat of suicide by one of his wives acted as a strong deterrent towards a husband's unkindness or harshness.

Doke[40] remarked: "It is by no means an uncommon thing for a man among the Lamba when he has had a quarrel to go and commit suicide, knowing full well that his death will be requited by his relatives at the hand of the man with whom he quarrelled. The survivor, the cause of his death, is charged with murder. So that a threat of suicide is usually sufficient to cause one's opponent to desist." In these instances the threat of Samsonic suicide acts as a form of social control.

One of the most illuminating instances where society by providing a punishment for suicide and hence encouraging the Samsonic suicide comes from the Bamum tribe of the old German Cameroons. This tribe had a genius as a king, one Njoya,[41] who after inventing his own script set a number of his scribes to compile the Laws and History of the Bamum people.

I made an unpublished English translation of this document and now quote from Chapter XXXVIII thereof: "If a man hangs himself in a Bamum village then the village head must give a slave to the King, 3,000 cowries to Tangwa (a court official), and 600 to his assistant. The reason that a slave is given to the King is because the man, being under the control of the village head, must have suffered some injury from him, otherwise he would not have hanged himself. All people in the land belong to the King: so the giving of the slave is compensation for the loss of a subject of the King in the town of the village head. If a person hangs himself in a settlement of the King's slave then 10,000 cowries must be paid to the King; 3,000 to the people's intermediary: one fowl and a dagger to the Mungu house."

This attitude towards suicide that the person is the property of the king and hence someone must be held responsible for his death is also found among the Ewe of the Gold Coast. Ellis[42] remarked: "In Dahomi it is criminal to attempt to commit suicide, because every man is the property of the king. The bodies of suicides are exposed to public execration, and the head is always struck off and sent to Agbormi, at the expense of the family, if the suicide were a free man, and at that of the master if he were a slave."

This concept of suicide was parallelled at one time in the law of England where all persons are still the King's subjects and where suicide, so far from being "an important legal institution", was called *Felo de se*, that is a felon with respect to oneself. The body was disgraced by being buried at four cross roads with a stake through its heart, the object being to anchor the suicide's ghost. No burial service was conducted and, as a felon, the suicide's property was escheat to the Crown. Such legal consequences might induce a person to commit a revengeful suicide in order to bring disgrace upon his family and to deprive them of enjoying the succession of his property.

Though there is an article on suicide in *The Catholic Encyclopedia*, Vol. XIV of 1913, the Samsonic type of suicide is not recorded. An explanation for the absence of Samsonic suicides in Europe may be found in a cultural explanation, namely that in Christendom its members have been indoctrinated with the teaching that vengeance must be left to the supernatural as for instance in the *Epistle to the Romans* Chap. 19, R.V. "Avenge not yourselves, beloved, but give place unto the wrath of God: for it is written, Vengeance belongeth to Me: I will repay, saith the Lord." Whence it follows as Kroeber aptly observed: "In the last analysis, the motivations and methods of suicide seem very largely to be part of cultural patterns."

In conclusion Samsonic suicides, or suicides of revenge, would not occur (*a*) if a belief in the power of a ghost to torment the living did not exist; or (*b*) if either the social structure or the law of the chief's courts did not impose a penalty on the provoker.

NOTES

1 E. Westermark, 'Suicide, a chapter in Comparative Ethics', *Sociological Review*, January 1908, pp. 12–33.
2 E. A. Hoebel, *The Law of Primitive Man*, Cambridge, Mass., 1954, p. 242.
3 R. S. Rattray, *Ashanti Law and Constitution*, Oxford, 1929, p. 312.
4 E. Durkheim, *Suicide*, trans. by J. A. Spalding and G. Simpson, New York, 1951.
5 M. D. W. Jeffreys, 'Samsonic Suicides or Suicides of Revenge among Africans', *African Studies*, 1952, Vol. XI, No. 3, pp. 118–22.
6 P. Bohannan, *African Homicide and Suicide*, Princetown U.P., 1960, p. 12.
7 *The Bible*, Judges, Chap. 16, vv. 28 and 30.
8 W. Bosman, *A New and Accurate Description of the Coast of Guinea*, trans., London, 1705, p. 12.
9 K. Mannheim, Ed., *Frustration and Aggression*, Yale U.P., 1940, p. 47.
10 A. L. Kroeber, *Anthropology*, New York, 1948, p. 613.
11 B. Malinkowski, 'Baloma: The Spirits of the Dead in the Trobriand Islands', *Journal of the Royal Anthropological Institute*, 1916, Vol. XLVI, p. 360.
12 B. Evans, *The Natural History of Nonsense*, New York, 1959, p. 131.
13 R. C. Temple, 'Folklore in the Legends of the Punjab', *The Indian Antiquary*, June 1900, p. 167.
14 A. M. Hocart, 'Death Customs', *Encyclopedia of the Social Sciences*, Vol. 5, New York, 1948, p. 23.
15 W. G. Sumner and A. G. Keller, *The Science of Society*, Vol. IV, New York, 1942, p. 262.
16 J. G. Frazer, *The Dying God*, London, 1930, p. 141.
17 B. S. Puckle, *Funeral Customs: Their Origin and Development*, London, 1926, p. 152.
18 W. G. Sumner and A. G. Keller, *The Science of Society*, Vol. 1, New York, 1946, p. 641.
19 A. G. Leonard, *The Lower Niger and its Tribes*, London, 1906, p. 259.
20 H. Vedder, *The Heren, The Native Tribes of South West Africa*, Capetown, 1928, p. 198.
21 G. Gouldsbury and H. Sheane, *The Great Plateau of Northern Rhodesia*, London, 1911, p. 85.
22 J. R. Crawford, *Witchcraft and Sorcery in Rhodesia*, Oxford U.P., 1967, pp. 246, 247.
23 P. Bohannan, *African Homicide and Suicide*, Princetown U.P., 1960, p. 177.
24 J. Roscoe, *The Bakitara*, Cambridge, 1923, p. 42.
25 A. W. Cardinall, *Natives of the Northern Territories of the Gold Coast*, London, 1920, p. 77.
26 T. E. Bowdich, *Mission to Ashantee*, London, 1819, pp. 258, 259.
27 Op. cit., p. 256.
28 J. Dupuis, *Residence in Ashantee*, London, 1824, p. 238.
29 A. B. Ellis, *The Land of Felish*, London, 1883, p. 242.
30 A. B. Ellis, *The Tshi-speaking Peoples of the Slave Coast*, London, 1887, p. 302.
31 M. Manoukian, *The Ewe-speaking People of Togoland and the Gold Coast*, London, 1952, p. 38.

32 R. H. Stone, *In Africa's Forest and Jungle*, London, 1900, p. 248.
33 A. K. Ajisafe, *The Laws and Customs of the Yoruba People*, Lagos, Nigeria, 1924, p. 32.
34 R. and P. Ritzenthaler, *Cameroon Village*, Milwaukee, 1962, pp. 62, 63.
35 J. H. Weeks, *Among the Primitive Bakongo*, London, 1914, pp. 274, 275.
36 C. Dundas, *Kilimanjaro and its People*, London, 1924, p. 171.
37 C. W. 'Anthropological studies in Kavirondo and Nandi', *Journal of the Anthropological Institute*, 1923, Vol. XXXIII, p. 358.
38 H. A. Stayt, *The Bavenda*, Oxford, 1931, p. 163.
39 J. Roscoe, *The Bagesu*, London, 1924, p. 41.
40 C. M. Doke, 'Social Control among the Lambas', *Bantu Studies*, 1923–6, Vol. II, p. 39.
41 Njoya *The History and Customs of the Bamum*, 1913?, unpublished Ms.
42 A. B. Ellis, *The Ewe-speaking Peoples of the Slave Coast*, London, 1890, p. 224.
43 A. L. Kroeber, *Anthropology*, New York, 1948, p. 616.

CHAPTER 16

Suicide and Risk-taking in Tikopia Society*

Raymond Firth

Ever since Henry Morselli suggested that in the "so-called voluntary actions" of suicide there could be discerned regularities and uniformities which could be related to social factors, and Emile Durkheim brilliantly demonstrated some of the major relationships,[1] there have been many attempts to correlate suicide behaviour and frequencies with states of society. In the enormous literature that has grown up there have been a number of studies of specific anthropological interest, including the general works of Steinmetz and Wisse, and localized analyses of varying detail, such as those of Voegelin, Fenton, Elwin, Carstairs, and Bohannan—to mention only a few.[2] These studies contain very valuable material, especially on the etiology and mechanisms of suicide, its distribution, and the social reactions and events connected with it. But while one can accept Durkheim's general thesis about the social determination of suicide rates, there are still some difficulties—which I shall explore in this paper—about aspects of the theory which has been built upon it.

Durkheim's argument, in outline, was that in two types of suicide anomic suicide and egoistic suicide, the social controls have been weak—in the first type because the individual has become detached from social institutions, and in the second because society itself has left the resolution of his personal affairs to him as a voluntary matter. In a third type, the altruistic suicide, the controls of society have been so ordered as to encourage and virtually dictate the individual's action.

SUICIDE AND STRENGTH OF SOCIAL CONTROLS

One argument that subsequent theory has made is that suicidal behaviour is correlated positively with strength or completeness of social controls. Nadel[3] has argued with respect to the Nuba that where there is less latitude for misfits, the suicidal predisposition is

* Reprinted by permission from *Psychiatry*, Vol. 24, 1961, pp. 1–17. This article appears in Raymond Firth' *Tikopia Ritual and Belief* (London, 1967), pp. 116–40.

fostered; where individuals deviating by choice or accident from normality are least able to find legitimate alternative ways of living in the group, they must lean most strongly towards ultimate escape by suicide. Straus and Straus,[4] using a comparative case study from Ceylon, hold that in a closely structured society, where reciprocal rights and duties are stressed and enforced, the identity of the individual merges with the group, and altruistic suicide occurs, even for seemingly trivial causes. But in a loosely structured society an offender can be reabsorbed into the family group and the society, or at any rate interpersonal relations are not so rigid that suicide ensues.

I find such propositions superficially plausible but not entirely satisfactory. In effect they fail to utilize some of the distinctions and the flexibility which Durkheim introduced as regards categories of persons concerned, and combinations of suicide types. Nadel regards a correlation between social rigidity and suicide incidence as an "intrinsic and logical one". I regard it as a tautology. If by definition suicide is an escape from society and its judgements, and if the society is so rigid that no other avenues of deviance from normality are open, the two variables are already interdependent, and the correlation is spurious. The *behaviour* of suicide is an index of social rigidity, but *incidence*—that is, rate—of suicide is an index of the degree of deviance in the society. With societies of equivalent rigidity in norms of conduct, there may be different degrees of deviance, depending for example, upon the character of personal goals, variation in the resources available for satisfying them, and so forth. The model for theories of a direct relation between suicide and social rigidity seems to be of a rather simple mechanical kind—society is seen as a kind of vessel with apertures, and with a constant internal level of pressure from deviant behaviour. In the case of the most rigid system, only one aperture is open, and pressure can be reduced only by use of the single outlet—that is, suicide, which therefore has a high rate. In less rigid, more loosely structured systems, there are presumably more apertures, and the rate of outlet through the suicide aperture is correspondingly lower.

I do not think that this simple conceptual model is a travesty, but there are objections to it. The first is that the motion of a social system which is rigid overall in every particular of judging conduct and repressing deviance, seems unrealistic. Even in societies with a very elaborate and precise moral code, and very full mechanisms for dealing with breaches of the code, there still seem to be avenues for personal expression of deviant tendencies. Some of these may be in the direction of developing evasion techniques, or of the formation of deviationist subgroups, if the society has enough magnitude.

Others may be in the direction of more positive outlets, possibly of a sublimatory kind, in the fields of art or religion.

A second objection lies in the type of argument which has been put forward with some cogency by Henry and Short,[5] to the effect that suicide varies *inversely* with the strength of external restraint over behaviour. They point out, as did Morselli and Durkheim, that suicide is often a correlate of less responsibility—for example, of bachelors as against married men, of people of advancing age as against younger people. Even if it be found difficult to accept their general proposition comparatively, there is another alternative. In a society with more permissive, more flexible rules and treatment of deviance (and for brevity I am speaking here as if "deviance" can be used as a unitary term, despite the differences in kind and degree), suicide incidence may be a semi-independent variable. It is conceivable that for reasons unconnected with the rigidity of social norms, suicide might be a preferred way of dealing with a situation, because of its assumed finality. If the character of the problem for an individual be seen not in the rigidity of society but in the very fact of having to cope with existence in society, then however easygoing the society, the individual may still prefer to escape from it altogether. Moreover, it could be argued that of some types of individuals—for instance, adolescents—it is not the rigour of social norms that is appalling, but the lack of firmness. They may commit suicide because they lack guidance, not because they have too much of it. As Kluckhohn has pointed out, the speculation that adolescent suicide occurs more often where marriage is late and premarital sexual expression is severely punished would be vindicated only if examination of the facts proved a higher rate in the more repressive societies and a lower one in the more permissive[6] Empirical data may of course bear out the contention that lack of guidance leads to crime or some form of deviance other than suicide; yet though suicide and murder are usually seen in inverse relation, they are to some extent alternatives, as Elwin has mentioned for the Bison-horn Maria.[7]

Again, in a loosely structured society, in which considerable variation of individual behaviour in general is sanctioned, there may be different views about the propriety of suicide. In one such society suicide may be strongly condemned, or, as among the Zuñi or Tallensi,[8] it may be regarded as silly. In another, it may be tolerated, and if not actually praised, may be tacitly approved as a solution of personal difficulties. As Durkheim argued, the presence or absence of a religious sanction may not appear to affect greatly the actual volume of suicide. But it may be an indicator of the significance of more general social attitudes with more effect.

I put forward these views to indicate that it is logically possible for suicide to vary semi-independently with permissiveness, but I intend to offer later what may be concrete support for this theory. I would argue that the whole question of the incidence of suicide in relation to the state of society is much more complicated than is indicated by propositions such as I have cited earlier. Analysis is further complicated by one more element—the characterization of "suicide" itself. Most definitions of suicide refer to the death of a person through his intention to commit the act of self-destruction. Such a definition by intent is necessary for clear theoretical classification. Yet empirically the classification is in a sense *post hoc*. Where death has eventuated through an act initiated by the dead person, intention to self-destruction must be presumed. But where a similar act has been initiated, but for some reason death has not eventuated, there is often a question as to whether the person really intended to destroy himself and was prevented, or was feigning such intent and wished to be prevented. Some deaths classified as suicide were possible acts which their initiators hoped would be prevented, but through miscalculation or other accident were not. As Weiss has pointed out, attempted suicide is often a different type of action from successful suicide.[9] Such situations are well known—for example, the rate of attempted suicide is much higher for women than men in Western society, though the incidence of actual suicide by men is higher. Involved in the suicide attempt is a distinct element of risk-taking. It is part of my argument that such risk-taking may be built into the structure of ideas about suicide, and may then have a bearing on the sociological interpretation of the volume of suicide.

SUICIDE METHOD IN A "PRIMITIVE" COMMUNITY

I will illustrate this point of view by data from Tikopia, a Polynesian community in the Western Pacific.[10] With less than two thousand people in all, Tikopia is politically part of the British Solomon Islands Protectorate, but has been so isolated that until very recently little effective administration has been given it and social control has been the responsibility of the local chiefs. The rate of suicide in this community has been relatively high. My figures on incidence relate to the period between 1929, after my first expedition, and the end of 1951, shortly before my second expedition (in March 1952). Though not official, the figures may be taken as fairly accurate, since they were obtained primarily by comparison of the names in my sociological censuses at the two dates, and inquiry as to the cause of death of every person who appeared in the 1929 census but had not survived until 1952. The data on the second expedition were collected and analysed with the help of my colleague, James Spillius.

Many of the people concerned had been known by me personally very well, and information about their deaths was obtained not from a questionnaire but as ordinary news, with much descriptive detail. Uncertainty in the classification of a death as suicide is therefore not due to lack of information about manner of death, but to uncertainty as to whether the death was intentional. The special physical circumstances of Tikopia offer, as it were, a wider arc than usual within which the ascription of death as self-destruction or not may swing.

Tikopia attitudes towards suicide are closely connected with their attitudes towards death in general. Summarily stated, these attitudes express regret concerning death rather than fear of it; the Tikopia view death realistically, both as a social and a personal phenomenon. There appears to be much sincere feeling expressed at the loss of close kin, but there is also much mourning of a more formal kind. The absence of the dead person, the social loss, receive ample emphasis; the personal terrors of physical dissolution do not seem to occupy much attention. The transient character of human life is accepted together with the idea of the continuity of the soul, consequently the timing of the moment of cessation of bodily functioning is not necessarily treated as a manner of critical importance. To take one's own life is merely to anticipate the inevitable end. In some circumstances, death has an esthetic attraction. Judgement is primarily concerned with the circumstances of the death, rather than with the fact that it may have been self-inflicted.[11]

No term in Tikopia is the exact equivalent of "suicide", but the expression *fakamate* (causing to die) is used reflexively and conveys the idea of devoting oneself to death. The descriptive terms for the various ways of putting an end to one's life are commonly used. Tikopia have sometimes chosen odd ways to commit suicide. About the oddest was that chosen by Pu Sao, who having broken wind in a public gathering, in his shame climbed a coconut palm and sat down on the sharp-pointed, hard flower spathe, which pierced his fundament and killed him—a bizarre case of making the punishment fit the crime. But the normal Tikopia ways of committing suicide are three, differentiated broadly according to age and sex: hanging (mainly by middle-aged and elderly people); swimming out to sea (women only, especially young women); putting off to sea by canoe (men only, especially young men). Hanging (*noo ua*, tying the neck) is usually fatal. The person makes a noose in a fishline or other fairly thin cord, ties the other end to a house beam, and then rushes to the end of the house, the violence and tightness of the noose apparently bringing death very quickly. The method is not completely reliable. One man looped a noose around his neck at the top of a coconut palm and leapt off, but the rope broke; he fell, but lived. In swimming out to sea (*kau ki moana*), the women, though good swimmers, soon seem to be overcome by heavy seas or by the sharks that are common off the coast, and mortality from such suicide attempts appears frequent. In accounts of Tikopia's past this method is mentioned very often, and the laconic *ne kau* (swam) is often used in discussions of a genealogy, indicating the fate of many unmarried young women.

Resort to either hanging or swimming out to sea may be classed (with a qualification discussed later) as a suicide attempt, since if straightforwardly accomplished without interference the result is death. But resort to putting off to sea in a canoe (*forau*) is more difficult to interpret. The Tikopia term in general indicates a sea voyage, and any canoe voyage from Tikopia is a hazardous undertaking. Tikopia is a mere dot in 40,000 square miles of ocean, with the nearest land, Anuta, equally isolated—only half a mile across and 70 miles away; larger land is more than 100 miles away and in some directions many hundreds of miles. With the alternation of storm and calm, especially in the monsoon season, to try to make a landfall from Tikopia is a great risk. Many would-be voyagers fail, and the chances for survival average considerably less than even. Yet spurred on by the desire to see the outside world, Tikopia men, especially young men, have been ready to take a chance. In many cases it is difficult to separate an attempt to escape from Tikopia to see the world, with a serious chance of not surviving, from an attempt to escape from Tikopia society with an intent to perish or an attitude of not caring whether one perishes or not. All these cases covered by the term *forau* involve a fatalism which is very strange to the Westerner. In effect, judgement of the canoe attempt as a suicide attempt or not is based by the Tikopia primarily on the conditions in which the person puts off to sea. Secrecy—often helped by a night departure—at the start of most such voyages is normal, to avoid being stopped not only by sorrowing relatives, but also by the canoe owner, who does not want to lose his property. But if a person puts off alone, in a high sea, after a scene in which he has been enraged or gravely embarrassed, in a tiny canoe ordinarily used for lake traffic, with no sail or provisions, then the interpretation is that he is a probable suicide. If, in contrast, he puts off with other members of a crew, in a quiet sea, with no emotional scenes preceding his departure, in a large seagoing craft, with some sort of sail and provisions, then the interpretation is usually that he has made a deliberate ocean voyage. Yet it is possible for a man to take sail, club, bow and arrows, coconuts and other food, but not intend to use them. When far out at sea—perhaps having been afloat for days—and tired of life, he may overturn his canoe or break it with his club, and go down to death or be devoured by the sharks. The odds against survival, of the individual hothead especially, are so high that it is reasonable to characterize *forau* of this individual type from which young men did not return as "suicide-risk" or "suicidal" adventures in the pejorative sense of the term. But even in this connection there is a qualification, especially in relation to the Tikopia "rescue service", which will be discussed later.

In discussing Tikopia suicides, I give what seem to be predisposing conditions, but I am not implying thereby that I have provided all the elements for the final understanding of any case. Still, social factors are clearly apparent both in the choice of method and in the attendant circumstances. In suicide at sea, an almost complete sex differential is manifested: a woman swims to her death, a man takes a canoe. Yet Tikopia men in ordinary circumstances swim as well and as freely as do women. Again, by report a curious fastidiousness is sometimes displayed in committing suicide. A person dying by hanging, it is said, excretes freely. If the deed is committed without premeditation, the interior of the house is in a mess; in the person's dying struggles mats and the interior of the house become covered with excrement. People coming to release him are disgusted, and before mourning begins women must clean up the disorder. For this reason, I was told, a person who is thinking of suicide by hanging may refrain from food for a day or so, in order "that his excrement may not be laughed at". It may seem to us unnecessary to be so finicky about the manner of dying, yet this has a crude logic. If part of the reason for destroying the body is to preserve the social personality intact—by safeguarding it from disintegrating despair or shame—then the person does not want his reputation to suffer by his death. Suicide in Tikopia is thought to merit a certain dignity.

The physical details as such of the suicide do not seem to worry the Tikopia. For a suicide at sea, the common fate is often discussed thus: "The death of a woman, to be eaten by sharks; when a man voyages out in a canoe, he goes on and on, his canoe overturns, he too is eaten by sharks." The details may be quite horrible to westerners, but the Tikopia face them in a matter-of-fact way.

Attitudes Towards Suicide

The Tikopia attitude towards suicide of others is in general one of mild disapprobation. Among pagan Tikopia in 1952, according to information given by Pa Fenuatara, there was some religious sanction for this opinion. The gods dislike a man to kill himself by hanging, because their function is to take the soul at death, and a sudden death gives them no time for preparation. If a man commits suicide, his soul goes off and wanders about, and its ancestral spirits in the heavens must search for it to bring it safely to its spirit home. But if a man commits suicide by going off to sea in a canoe, or a woman by swimming out to sea, the result is "a splendid death", a "sweet death", to which the spirits do not object, and from which they can catch up the soul of the dead person. When the canoe of a man is engulfed at sea, he cries out to the spirits of his mother's lineage, who come and bear off his soul. The same is true for women, but in some groups there are special privileges. The Ariki Kafika—the chief—told me that when the women of his lineage swim out to sea they are clasped in the arms of their Female Deity, who pulls them down. They drown but are not eaten by sharks, while the goddess takes their souls. Similarly, the women of the allied lineage of Porima are protected by their Deity of the Woods, who spits in the eyes of the sharks.

Among Christian Tikopia in 1952 the orthodox view was that the soul of a suicide does not go to Paradise, but to Satan. The Bible says it is wrong for a man to die this way, and the church is opposed to the practice. But the common view seemed much more tolerant. Spillius was told that if a man commits suicide, the priest should make the proper prayers at the altar to insure that the soul goes to Heaven, but the families of suicides in fact seemed to go to little trouble to see that this was done. As Pa Raroifi said, the special prayers and services of the priest would cost the family a mat as a gift to the priest, and once the body of the man was in the ground people did not worry about him unless his ghost started to walk.[12] I myself have no record of any such special prayers.

In common with its condemnation of suicide, the church also condemned the *forau sora*, the secret voyage, holding that if a man wishes to undertake an overseas voyage he should wait for the Mission vessel or some other powered craft. The souls of people belong to God, and they should await the will of the Lord in respect to their time to die. Hence the more pious Christians held that the *forau* custom should be abandoned. Yet it is significant that the incidence of *forau* seemed to be much the same among Christian and pagan young men, and that among those who took canoes secretly in this way were two sons of the Mission priest, one of whom was lost at sea. In other words, the compulsive character of competitive adventure among the young men seemed to override all Christian teaching. The sanctions of the church had not yet been effectively internalized and integrated into the personality.

By 1952 no effective political sanction had been imposed on Tikopia canoe voyaging. But since at various times these voyages have given much trouble to the administration in searching for lost men and repatriating survivors, it is likely that before long some hindrances may be placed in the way of Tikopia risk-voyaging, and going off in a canoe may be declared an offence. Unless alternative outlets are provided at the same time, however, it may be very difficult to implement such a control.

In general, then, the Tikopia viewed suicide as no crime, and the church's doctrine that suicide was a sin was not influential enough to inhibit many Tikopia from risking their lives and some from deliberately sacrificing them. The disapprobation of suicide and the strenuous efforts to save those who had attempted it were based on social more than on religious reasons.

Suicide Rates

To consider Tikopia suicide rates more closely I give in the accompanying table the deaths between 1929 and 1951 from the three main methods as closely as could be ascertained by years.

Tikopia Suicides* and Possibly Suicidal Voyages, 1929–51

| Year | Suicides According to Method | | |
	Hanging	Swimming to sea	Canoe-voyaging
Unclassified	3	1	26
1929–42	0	0	7
1943	0	0	6
1944	0	1	10
1945	0	0	2
1946	0	0	1
1947	0	3	6
1948	0	0	11
1949	0	0	8
1950	1	7	4
1951	2	0	0
Total	6	12	81

* Occasional suicides by odd methods are not included in this table.

Disregarding for the time being the deaths from canoe-voyaging, and considering only the indubitable suicides from hanging and swimming out to sea, for a mean population of 1,500, over a period of twenty-three years, the annual rate of suicide was 0.8 persons, or for comparative purposes, 53 suicides per 100,000 population. Even if in a mass suicide of six girls in 1950 by swimming out to sea, only the principal girl be counted (and her followers be put down to mis-adventure), the rate would still be about thirty-seven per annum per 100,000 population, which is considerably higher than that for most Western countries, where the yearly rate is between about ten and thirty per 100,000 population.[13]

Now consider the deaths from sea-voyaging. The loss of 81 persons in twenty-three years includes four females who accompanied their male kin, either on an ordinary voyage overseas, or as part of a crew in a searching fleet, and at least five persons who died from exhaustion or other illness after landing on a foreign island. But the majority of those who perished must have set out under conditions so hazardous that their prospects of survival were slight, and their fear of self-destruction small. Since the Tikopia keep no precise annual records, a breakdown of the figures by years was not exact. But at least thirty, and probably considerably more, were in the five years 1944–8, when the new experiences of the war had stimulated a high level of interest in overseas adventure. Despite their intense, almost obsessive interest in the novel, scarce goods of the Western world, the Tikopia did not develop a millenarian movement of the kind known as a "cargo cult",[14] in which fantastic preparations were made to receive an expected bounty from heaven. A combination of reasons was probably responsible, but it may have been partly because of the outlet for their craving presented by the possibility of a voyage overseas. They could go to meet the millenium; they did not have to wait passively for it to arrive. In this connection it is significant that of the fifty-five persons whose loss could be dated with reasonable accuracy, about forty were probably under thirty years of age when they died. In such young men the lust for adventure was greatest. But they tended also to be the more easily emotionally disturbed. From evidence about the nature of the flight and the preceding circumstances, it is clear that probably at least a dozen of these *forau* were deliberate suicidal attempts, and that the rate of effective suicide should perhaps be put at between sixty and seventy persons per annum per 100,000 population.

Types of Suicidal Situations

I have no systematic material of a quantitative kind on the causes of suicide in Tikopia, mainly because in many cases, often long after the event, it was not possible to get from the surviving kin any very clear-cut statement of all the reasons which led a person to self-de-struction. It was evident, for instance, that many young men put off to sea following some degree of emotional disturbance, but the rela-tives and friends were not always sure exactly what the circumstances were leading up to this, and it was often impossible for me to discern how much shame, resentment, and frustration were intermingled. But the major types of situations apparently involved in suicide can be indicated, with ostensible cause.

One type of suicidal situation is that involving loss of spouse or other close relative. Pa Mukava, youngest son of the Ariki Tafua of 1929, some years after my first visit committed suicide on the death of his wife. "He killed himself for his wife; he hanged himself. When she died, he wailed and wailed that day, his grief was great; then he went to hang himself—on the same day." A similar case was that of Pa Nukusorokiraro; his wife died and he hanged himself on the same day. In 1929 I was told how one of my friends had earlier tried to commit suicide on the death of his son. In the darkness of the funeral house one of the mourners had felt someone crawl past. On inquiry, people discovered that the father was gone. One mourner, guessing that the father had gone to hang himself, ran out and saw him standing in a nearby canoe shed with a noose about his neck. The mourner dashed over, lifted him up, and yelled to the others, who released him, worked over him, and revived him. Three points characterizing this type of suicide are: action is taken by the grief-stricken person quite soon, with no more than a few hours for reflection; the method chosen is often hanging, which is fairly quick and certain; if the suicide is prevented, usually no further attempt is made.

Another type of situation is chronic or severe illness, including mental illness. In despair at the infirmities of old age (including, I was told, the disintegration of his body, so that his skin began to stick to the mat on which he lay), Pa Saukirima, the rather dour head of the lineage of Fusi in 1929, hanged himself in his house one evening, using a tough rope which had bound up a bundle of tobacco. Other suicides were by mentally ill people, as is illustrated by the following:

> The mother of Pa Ranginiumata was lunatic, and swam out to sea. A canoe party including the Ariki Kafika heard shrieks, eight or ten times, and then silence. Paddling to the spot, they found a basket with water bottles floating (a woman's equipment) and sharks poking up their heads from the water. The sea around was smooth and blood-stained, though waves were breaking elsewhere.

With regard to suicide from insanity, it is questionable how far the Tikopia would accept the old "suicide while of unsound mind" formula of the English coroner. In general, the Tikopia draw a definite distinction between the suicides of insane persons, and those of persons who in their view have made a free choice voluntarily and consciously to take their lives. Here is an illustration:

> Pa Rangitoko went crazy, chasing children, fighting people who tried to restrain him, and trying to enter houses at random. People tied him up at night by his wrists and ankles, and his wife, in fear of him, went to live with her daughter. This went on for a long time, with periods of lucidity intervening. At last his head cleared, and after living alone for a time, he wanted his wife to return. But his wife, still afraid that it might be a trick of the spirits to induce her to come back in order to wreak harm on her, did not come. His body pitiably wasted from lack of food, the man hanged himself, in the daytime, in his house.

I asked if his suicide had been brought about by spirits, since he had been so crazy. The reply was: "Oh! It was his own doing! His being affected by the spirits, his shrieking, his madness, were over. When we used to come to him, he threw things at us, he fought us. But when his mind cleared, his wife didn't come and prepare food for the two of them, so he became angry, hanged himself and died." Here then the Tikopia interpretation was that resentment against his wife took the form of an aggressive act against himself, a commingling of anger and despair. In such a case, too, the suicide is partly revenge against the person who has offended one.

But while the Tikopia distinguish suicides due to insanity from ordinary suicide, they are sometimes inclined to attribute the obsessional aspect of suicide to a temporary disturbance of the balance of the mind. They may even use the same expression (*vare*) as is used for insanity, although it is susceptible of a range of translation, and can also properly be interpreted in the relatively mild sense of plain silliness or stupidity. For instance, an old dirge voiced by a man for his sister can be rendered as follows:

> My sister, my nourisher
> You jumped into the sea
> Nor did you glance aside to shore
> The foolish thought was conveyed to your mind
> And you went to your death—whither?

Here the brother does not imply that the woman was actually insane, but stigmatizes her idea of taking her life as stupid. Akin to this is the view traditionally taken when Tikopia chiefs at times insist on risking their lives on overseas voyages. A chief, especially the Ariki Kafika, the premier chief, should not voyage abroad for trivial reasons, such as a lust for adventure. If such a chief will not be held back by pleading and argument, but determinedly goes on a *forau* and is lost at sea, then it is thought his mind has been made up for him by the spirits. The expression is, "His mind has been caused to be bound by the spirits." His mental balance has been disturbed and his judgement affected.

Another type of situation sometimes leading to suicide is domestic discord. Not long before 1928 Nau Saraniu hanged herself because her husband was guilty of continued infidelity with a widow. In another case, some time after 1929, Pa Korofatu took a second wife, but fought with her so strenuously that both of them rushed off in opposite directions and committed suicide separately, by hanging. After the death of the Ariki Taumako, some time in the 1940s, the wife of Pa Nukuvakai insisted on keeping all the food taboos of mourning rigorously. Her husband tried to feed her with pudding and other good quality foods, but she refused. He objected, saying, "Are we not married? And don't we eat together? Stay in your taboos. But I'm going, and you can stay and keep your taboos for me." By this he meant that she could now start mourning for him instead. He did not steal away secretly but ostensibly joined a searching fleet looking for three young women who had swum off to sea. Then he slipped away to pursue his own suicide attempt, and it was only discovered later that he had had a row with his wife. "It's not certain if he died at sea or if he died on shore—he went in a small canoe, and with no provisions.

The last case illustrates the pattern of many Tikopia suicides—the person feels himself or herself offended and frustrated, and flounces off in a rage, often hurling back some pointed "last words" to make the survivors regretful. I did not actually witness any such departure, and it was not clear to me how far the subsequent reports tended to dramatize the final situation, or simply to reproduce in brief form the admittedly dramatic quality of much Tikopia behaviour. While in general Tikopia manners are urbane, and the Tikopia are adept in concealing their thoughts, they often seem to lack self-control when frustrated. This is very much a matter of social conditioning, and their anger sometimes appears to an observer to be histrionic, and rapidly appeased by the recognized techniques of status enhancement. Yet they are capable in such conditions of radically destructive acts. The Tikopia well recognize and regret their propensity to take umbrage. As one of my informants said, "This land is bad. Someone is angry, he goes then and hangs himself. Someone else is scolded by his family, thereupon there's a hanging."

Under the general heading of suicides from domestic discord may be placed the consequences of revolt against parental authority. If a son is struck or strongly rebuked by his father, he may go off to sea with the intention of seeking his death. When the father finds out, he will wail for the son, and then go out to sea in search of him. If he finds the boy, he will bring him back, forgiven, the incident purged. If not, he may turn back to mourn in his house, or he may go on in his canoe to meet his own death. Such is the Tikopia stereotype. Actually, while most fathers go in search, few appear to have followed their missing sons to death. But by traditional account many sons have flung off in suicidal rage after reprimand from their fathers. Similarly, girls subjected to parental wrath are recorded to have reacted by swimming off to sea. Such suicide attempts by young people are part of the expected norms in Tikopia, and being feared by parents, help at times to mitigate parental discipline.[15]

Another type of suicide situation is shame at the unavoidable consequences of an act, which occasioned the curious death of Pu Sao, and also the mass swim out to sea, both mentioned earlier. The physical basis for the shame may vary through a wide range of circumstances. But with young women a common reason is pregnancy, if the lover either will not acknowledge himself as responsible, or will not marry his mistress. The circumstances of the mass swim were as follows.

> A granddaughter of the Ariki Kafika, Fakasuariki, "swam out to sea because she was pregnant and ashamed". She knew the father of her child, but, it was said, his family refused to allow him to marry her for reasons not known. She was afraid that if she revealed his name, he might be killed by the men of Kafika lineage, as was a commoner and she was a woman of a chiefly family. Her father and mother were ignorant of her pregnancy, but her companions among the unmarried girls knew. When she decided to swim off to sea, many of them followed her. From Tuatekoro, the base of the cliff between Ravenga and Namo, they plunged into the sea. Some of them, perhaps a score in all, were held back on the beach by brothers and fathers who had obviously been alerted by the unusual sight, and others were pulled out of the sea. But not all could be rescued. It was midmorning on a sunny day, but with a very high wind and heavy, breaking seas. Those girls who succeeded in getting out beyond the reef were soon lost. A searching fleet of ten canoes put out, but failed to find any of the girls who had evaded the first pursuit. One vessel of the fleet, containing three men and a girl as crew, was lost in the search, and one young man who had swum out to try to save his sister was also lost.

This tragedy cost eleven lives, six of them with intent. The cause of the suicide of the girls who followed Fakasuariki may be broadly set down as loyalty, although from another point of view it may be termed anticipatory grief. Such loyalty is a complicated sentiment. In part it rests upon the notion that a person of high status should have a *following* when entering upon a new and critical experience (such as a voyage abroad, or a religious conversion), and in part here upon the peer-group attachment which obtains among young men or young women. Loyalty in another form is demonstrated by the traditional accounts of the death of bond-friends at sea, in which one will tie his wrist to that of his friend so that they may both perish together.[16] Still another type of loyalty suicide, according to Tikopia account, occurs when a sick, elderly man, either because of food shortage, or because he believes that the time has come to hand over the responsibilities of office to his son, will refuse to take food, and starves himself (*fakapakupaku*) to death. It is difficult, however, to class such behaviour simply as suicide, if only because the Tikopia are very sentimental about family relationships and may be inclined to attribute to suicidal starvation what is in fact mere physical weakness or inability to take nourishment. A type of suicide which may be linked with this category is that carried out from respect for authority. Such cases have occurred when an offender is ordered off to sea in a canoe; or when a man of rank, confronted with a woman who does not wish to marry him, has ordered her to swim to her death rather than allow her to marry another man. Such virtual executions have been regarded by the Tikopia as justified, and even the victims have acquiesced with regret rather than protest against their enforced suicide.

In this analysis my aim is not to make any particular psychological contribution, but to try to relate individual action more closely to social process. One might classify the motives for suicide in Tikopia into four general categories of a psychological order: (1) grief or despair, such as in suicide because of unrequited love, or love for a dead spouse; (2) anger, such as that resulting from domestic discord, including revolts against parental authority; (3) shame, such as occurs in the case of pregnancy of an unmarried girl; and (4) loyalty, such as is evident in suicides from friendship and peer-group attachment. How far do these relate to the sociological categories, for example, of Durkheim? Tikopia suicides hitherto mentioned do not fall easily into his "anomic" type, characterized by loss of integration of the individual with society. Tikopia social values—as distinct from religious values—have been fairly well preserved, and even the upheavals consequent on the famine of 1952, or the loss of confidence in the state of Tikopia society when the division between paganism and Christianity seemed most acute, saw no outbreak of suicide. But anomic suicide is not unknown in Tikopia; at least one case is recorded in a previous famine of a man's taking his family in a canoe to sea rather than face starvation on shore. In general, suicides from motives of grief or anger may be regarded as falling under the heading of "egoistic"; with regard to those in the category of response to shame, although they are in part egoistic, the strength of the shame may be related to the strength of the identification with the norms of the society. Suicide of the loyalty type clearly comes under Durkheim's "altruistic" category.

Yet I find classification in his terms difficult. Every suicide is in some respects an egoistic act, yet nearly every suicide displays some regard for the norms of society, and a recognition that the person is not in a position or not willing to adapt to these norms. "Detachment from society" or "integration with society" seem very crude phrases, grossly oversimplified, for the description of states of interaction of the potential suicide with other members of his society.

Durkheim's notions of the relation of the suiciding individual to society are too naive. His statements, for example, about obligatory altruistic suicide, in which "society" compels some of its members to kill themselves, raise a question of basic classification. If the individual has no choice, but is forced to his death as a duty, as in the case of a Tikopia criminal ordered off to sea, would not this be classed as execution rather than suicide? Even with the voluntary or "optional" (*facultatif*) altruistic suicide, Durkheim misses an important point: that some *conflict* of obligations is usually involved. "Society" is not united in praising the suicide; some sections of it may praise him, others—for example, members of his family—may condemn him, or at least anxiously try to stop him. Out of such situations of conflict the suicidal intent and much of the drama of the event arise. I would argue that at least for societies of the primitive order of Tikopia the potential suicide situation is one of much greater flexibility and even uncertainty than is usually stated in the theory of the subject.

One may first look at the suicide situation of going off to sea, either by swimming of in a canoe. As Halbwachs did,[17] I have drawn attention to the difficulty of classifying the empirical material in terms of knowing the actual intention of the person who died. Somewhat the same difficulty arises about Durkheim's famous principle of detachment, insofar as it refers to the initiative taken by the person concerned. Successful suicide is the only real detachment from society. People commit suicide in order to become detached from society; they need not, as Durkheim seems at times to have argued, first become detached from society and then commit suicide. If a person makes an attempt and does not die, is it because he was detached and made an error of judgment, or because he was not sufficiently detached and his nerve failed? Something like this quandary exists with the Tikopia. The problem is connected with what Weiss has termed the "lethal probability" of the means used. For Tikopia the lethal probability of going off to die at sea, by either swimming or canoeing, is high, but not one hundred per cent. There are two major possibilities here. One is that the potential suicide has time, if not often much opportunity, to change his or her mind, and come back to shore. The Tikopia themselves are fully aware of this possibility, and take it into account in their calculation of motivation and outcome. One of my Tikopia friends put the matter in this form:

> This land is sacred [in respect of] the women—a man does not make fighting gestures to a women [this is not strictly true]. A woman who is reproved, scolded—an unmarried woman only is scolded by a man—desires to die, yet desires to live. Thereupon she goes to swim out to sea. Her thought is that she will go and swim, but be taken up in a canoe by men who will seek her out to find her. A woman desiring death swims to seawards; she acts to go out and die. But a woman who desires life swims within touch, behind the breakers. She goes and goes, and arrives at Tai here [the speaker was thinking of her starting from Ravenga a mile away] to emerge on shore. She then comes and deceives her relatives, "I went and swam, swam, swam, to seawards, there, but I did not die." Great is the mind of women!

The second major factor adding to the uncertainty of the situation is the searching fleet. The Tikopia have a very lively understanding of the whole situation of going off to sea, and a very energetic attitude towards rescue expeditions. As soon as news of a suicide swim or voyage is known, a searching fleet of canoes is organized and hastily paddles out in chase of the fugitive. If the attempt is really serious, the fleet's chances of success are not very high—the escapee goes off at night, or in a high wind, which militates against the likelihood of his beng spotted and caught in those huge ocean wastes. But if the potential suicide rushes off in a rage at once, when sea conditions are good, or if his or her absence is noticed at once, or if the searching fleet is lucky or guesses well the effects of wind and current, the person may be recovered. For many of these attempts, especially by people who set off in daylight or in good conditions of wind and sea, it is very difficult indeed to decide just what combination of motives and chances lay behind their calculations—or whether they made any conscious calculations at all. They may have thought that they stood a good chance of being picked up, and could return in restored equilibrium; they may have thought that their chances were slim, but were prepared to risk their lives for their reputations; or they may have thought that it was impossible for them to be located and stopped. All those who die are classed as suicides. Of those who are rescued, some can be classed almost certainly as intended suicides, some almost certainly as fakers; but for most of them the issue must remain very much in doubt is inherent also in the view of the escapee himself.

To illustrate these points, including the vivid appreciation of such a situation by the Tikopia themselves, I give the history of such a "suicide" attempt.

Rather than live with a wife who had been forced upon him because it was understood that he had made her pregnant, Faka-sauakipure, a man of Tafua in Namo, went off to sea in a commandeered canoe belonging to the Ariki Taumako. I was with the chief when the news came to him. He was sympathetic to the man, who was a matrilateral kinsman of his, and did not vent his displeasure upon the man's kinsfolk, as they had feared, but sent his son over to reassure them.[18] The Tikopia were sorry for the man on account of his flight to sea, but against him for the desertion of his wife. His family wept for him.

At this time the general fleet of canoes was engaged in diving for greensnail, and it was thought that the news had not reached them. In any case, since the Namo people had already sent out a searching fleet, it was thought by senior men with whom I talked that many of the other craft would not leave their work and in fact few, if any, did so. The Ariki Taumako showed an adequate practical grasp of the situation. He asked whether the searching fleet was large, and on learning that it was, commented, "Great is the number of the fleet! Oh! Then they will secure him." He said that if the canoes of the fleet would spread out, starting from different places, they would have a better chance of seeing the wanderer.

The man's flight and the search made good material for gossip, and people sat out on the beach until late that night discussing the case. The next day the chief and others were very ready to talk about such voyages and the action taken by the rest of the community in regard to them. First the constitution of the searching fleet was discussed. "The married men mingle at intervals", it was explained; when the fleet responds to the news that someone is missing, the canoes are not allowed to start with crews of bachelors only, "because their mind is different". If left to themselves, fired by the spirit of adventure, and stimulated by the example of the man who is gone, these young men might quite likely start off on a voyage of their own. Hence the married men interpose themselves in ones and twos in each crew. The bachelors try to dissuade them, saying, "Go and get a canoe for yourselves." But the married men insist for they know the minds of the young men. A very large fleet goes out in search only if the son of a chief has gone. In this case, "Not a person may remain on shore," say the Tikopia in hyperbole. When such a fleet goes out, a woman may sometimes go with it—for instance, a mother wailing for her son may jump aboard and sit in the bottom of the canoe. She does not paddle, but merely wails. If the man is found, she may be of use in inducing him to return, for often he objects strenuously to being brought back.

If the weather is uncertain, the searching fleet goes out until the cliffs are lost to sight and the hill of Korofau and the peak of Reani alone show above the sea. But if the weather is good and the sea is calm, they go out until Korofau is lost and Reani (about 1,200 feet high) alone remains. They do not go out of sight of land altogether. All day they search, but if the man has had a long start they may not find him; at nightfall they abandon the attempt and return.

The attitude of the fugitive was also analyzed by my informants. They gave three possible variations of motive for the voyage: an attempt to reach some other land in order to have the thrill of being a voyager and seeing the world; a deliberate attempt at suicide as a means of wiping out disgrace; or a feint at suicide, the man hoping to be pursued and caught before he got too far away. It was pointed out, too, that when a man is alone on the face of the ocean, anger and shame are apt to burn themselves out, and the initial urge to self-destruction might change to a desire for life. The putative change of such a fugitive was outlined thus: if the man has affection and sympathy towards his island and his parents, then when he is out at sea he thinks of them, rests on his paddle, and wails, "Oh! Alas, my land! Oh! Alas, my parents! Oh! Alas, my children!"—or similar thoughts. Then he stops his paddle and drifts, or starts to return. In this case he will probably be picked up by the searchers. But if a man is intent on his purpose he plies his paddle steadily, and soon gets beyond reach, so that he is not found.

There was much discussion of chances. It was said that Faka-sauakipure had supplies, two pairs of coconuts. The Ariki Taumako said that even if he stayed at sea for a couple of days, if he drank from time to time to clear his throat and to strengthen his arms for the paddle he might be all right. People had found him missing in the morning, and had sought for him on shore without success. When they discovered that the canoe was gone, they knew he was at sea. When it is known that for any reason a man has become angry, a watch is kept upon him; if he says he is going anywhere, another man follows to prevent him from taking a canoe. But in the present case, since the man had lived with his wife for some time, apparently amicably, and then had vanished suddenly without warning, no one was prepared.

Reference was also made to the actions of his kin on shore. Wailing was begun in his house after his departure was discovered, and should he finally not come back, the mourning ceremonies would follow a prescribed course, which was described to me. The *forau* continued to be a principal topic of conversation in the villages of the district, with much speculation on the man's fate. The Ariki Taumako said to me, "I have sympathy for him, for the man who is drifting. We do not know if he is paddling, or if he is sleeping." He illustrated each action in turn with his hands—paddling and then, with arms outflung, a man sleeping stretched over a thwart. General opinion was against the chances of his return. It was argued that if he had gone to the south, he might, considering the conditions of wind and sea, reach another land. But if he had gone to the west, he would simply drift in the ocean spaces. Discussion also turned on the action of the chief's son, who, sent by his father to Namo had gone in anger, inclined to smash one of the canoes there in revenge. Returning home without having done so (he discovered the canoe he proposed to smash belonged to his own clan), he was reproved by his mother, "Why do you show anger? Look at your father! He is full of sympathy for the man. Why should you be angry about the canoe? Is it a man?" It was reported that the allegation of the woman's pregnancy had been untrue, and to that extent the man had been justified in rejecting her; but she was not criticized for having been the cause of his going off to sea.

The return of the wanderer put an end to speculation. Shortly before sunset three days after he had gone, his canoe was sighted a long way off shore. There was great excitement. For a time he was lost to sight again, and it was not certain whether it was a canoe or a fish. The chief's wife said uncertainly, "Perhaps it's a spirit!" Finally Fakasauakipure's identity was established. Five canoes, hastily dragged down to the water's edge, ranged out for a couple of miles, with the rays of the setting sun full upon them, and at last they saw him. The nearest canoe closed in, and two of the crew jumped into his craft and paddled it back to shore. As they came into the shallows, people crowded down on to the beach, and some went into the water to press noses with the wanderer in greeting. He did not speak. He saw a chief, the Ariki Fangarere, seated near the edge of the beach, went over to him and pressed his nose to the chief's knee in token of abasement, was raised up by the chief, and pressed noses with him. The man who first reached the wanderer now led him off to his house by the wrist, in a conventional friendship sign, and put a new, dry, bark-cloth garment on him. The wanderer was then offered food, which he refused. Meanwhile the Ariki Taumako had been waiting in his canoe-yard to see the wanderer and hear his tale. He and his entourage examined the canoe, which had been carried up, and exclaimed about how the outrigger, which had been weak, had been strengthened with coconut fibre. They speculated whether the man had sat in the bow or the stern. Then the chief got impatient and angry at the delay, and stalked home, while children were hushed lest they annoy him further. The kind of remarks prevailing in the conversation were: "Our friend is alive! If he had disappeared it would have been bad." "It is good that the man has lived!" "It is good that he has come in."

Later the wanderer, accompanied by his brother and his friend, entered the chief's house. The chief greeted them crossly saying, "Why didn't you come before?" "Shall he come wet to you?" answered the friend (a cousin of the chief's) with spirit. As soon as they came in the door, the voyager and his brother began to wail. The voyager then crawled to the chief, who was seated in the centre of the house, lay at his knee, and pressed his nose against it. The chief raised up the bent head, and Fakasauakipure pressed his nose to the chief's face. Then, still lying at the chief's knee, he began to wail a dirge—the continuance of the formal token of abasement and apology. After a little the chief said, "Sit still! Sit Still!," and the man stopped and went to sit at the side of the house. By this time a crowd had assembled.

Then he began to talk. First he mentioned where he had been—out to the southeast—and then he spoke of the fish (he was not sure if they were sharks or not) which had come and rested their snouts on the canoe outrigger. First he called on the Eel-god to chase them away, and then on the Taumako ancestor, upon which the fish disappeared. "Ah! If you had called on him first!," said the chief's wife; and the chief added, "He it is who has given you to us again." One of the first questions the chief asked was whether the man had lost sight of land, to which he answered in the affirmative; later the chief asked if he had seen any of the searching fleet, to which the answer was no. There were also several practical questions about mending the canoe. I noted particularly that throughout this discussion, which lasted a long time, the whole attitude was of interest in the man's journey—there was no reproach for the desertion of his wife, or for the trouble he had caused. The man himself related his experiences with considerable dramatic flair, and the audience listened quietly, with the chief doing most of the questioning. There was perhaps a kind of personal identification for each of the audience with the man who had dared the unknown and suffered alone in the ocean wastes. A day or so later came a gift of atonement from the man's family to the chief for the abstraction of his canoe. I am not sure whether the customary rescue-payment was made to the first men to reach the wanderer and jump into his canoe.

Sociologically, two points of importance emerge from all this. The first is that the returned "suicide" voyager by these procedures is completely reintegrated with society. His effort at detachment has failed, but he has succeeded in resolving his problem. He is once again absorbed and an effective catharsis has been obtained. The second point is that since a returned adventurer becomes the centre of attention, a certain premium is attached to attempting a dramatic sea flight of this kind. The stakes are high: they involve a real gamble with death. But if a man can go out, stay away for a while, and then return, he has a windfall gain in immediate social status. Yet cases of return from a distance would appear to be very rare; usually if a man is not found in the course of the day, he is lost to Tikopia—although in rare instances he may fetch up on another island.

From the point of view of suicide interpretation, what such a person is doing is gambling on natural hazards and on his credit with society. If either nature or society is against him—if the weather is bad, or the searching fleet lethargic—he loses his life. As the figures on ocean voyages indicate about a four to one chance against survival in 1929–52, this is suicidal conduct, although not suicide in the accepted sense of the term.

What I am saying, then, amounts to this—that except where the lethal probability of the means employed is known to be almost complete (for example, with some poisons), there may not be a clear-cut line between the categories of suicide and nonsuicide, between intending to kill oneself and not. There may be instead a scale of intention-*cum*-risk-taking. At one end, no intention to lose one's life, and little risk; at the other end, the intention to kill oneself and the most grave risk of accomplishing it, or little risk of being prevented. In between there may be many degrees of partly formed intention mixed with reluctance to die and hope of being saved, with yet enough resolution to face the risk and abide by the outcome.

All this bears on the question of the rigidity or permissiveness of the society and the incidence of suicide. It is quite clear that no correlation between social rigidity and suicide rates can be affected without taking into consideration the efficiency of the rescue procedures. Whatever the rigidity of the society, if the rescue procedures are good, then the incidence of suicide may be relatively low, even though attempted suicides may be many. Moreover, the fact that the rescue procedures are good, and the suicide incidence low, may mean that the society is a firmly structured one. If the rescue procedures are poorly organized and ineffective, this may mean a more permissive, less rigid structuring of the society—associated with a higher, not a lower suicide rate.

Tikopia society may be regarded as firmly structured, even rigid, in some respects, as in the procedures concerned with lineage organization and chieftainship, and the sense of social obligation is high. Yet in other respects it may be seen as a fairly permissive, tolerant society, with many alternative avenues of escape for offenders. Some kind of outlet for deviance is provided by spirit mediumship, which allows considerable personal expression outside the overt structural framework. Where frustration and aggression emerge in social relations, the Tikopia have well-developed techniques for smoothing over difficult situations and allowing aggrieved persons to retain their status. The expression *fakamatamata laui* (making the face good) refers to such techniques, which soften the rigour of social rules. In pregnancy, an unmarried woman has precedents for abortion or infanticide, or for bringing up her child out of wedlock—although this last is not common. For offences against a chief, a man usually has the alternative of fleeing to another district and thence in time making his ceremonial apology. But the sea flight, with all its terrible risks, is part of the pattern of Tikopia behaviour, associated for men, at least, not only with adventure and freedom of a positive, praiseworthy kind and the fascination of pushing back the limits of their universe. It is a case not of there being no other avenues of self-expression or expiation, but rather almost of seeking this avenue as a first resort than a last.

There is also a further factor linking the incidence of suicide and the permissiveness of Tikopia society. According to traditional Tikopia custom, the punishment for the most extreme offences was for a chief's executive officer to drag the offender's canoe to the sea, and order him into it, to set out and either perish in the ocean or fetch up on a foreign land. The chances of survival being so small, the order was virtually equivalent to a demand for self-execution. Conversely, if a person offended a chief, he might announce or imply an intention to go off to sea. After allowing time for the intention to mature, a man of rank might step in and order the offender to stop. He could then acquiesce in obedience to the command, yet with the dignity of having been prepared to expiate his offence with his life. Into this situation enter some of the most delicate elements of Tikopia personal diplomacy. The person who had let it be known that he intended to put off to sea had no certaintly of being stopped. Perhaps no one would take the initiative in getting him to desist, either because the responsibility was left by each man of rank to the others, or because there was not enough enthusiasm for his retention. In essence, then, the person placed his future in the hands of society. To what extent a given offender relied on not being allowed to proceed, it is impossible to say. But the whole situation of suicide attempts has this uncertainty of intervention as one of its parameters.

This may be illustrated further by a case which occurred during my first visit to Tikopia. A son of the Ariki Tafua fell seriously ill, and for a few days showed no signs of recovery, despite strenuous efforts by his family and others. The Ariki Tafua then attempted to commit suicide by hanging, to try to compel the gods to pay attention to the plight of his son. He was prevented by two men, coming to him with a gift of food, who happened to enter the house just as the noose was settling over his head. They rushed to him, and while one supported him the other removed the fatal cord. I happened to visit the old chief shortly afterwards, and found the household plunged in gloom. The chief soon began to speak, addressing his gods, upbraiding them for not curing his son and asking them to take his life instead, since he was an old man and could be more easily spared. It was a very serious, dramatic occasion. Shortly afterwards the old man did fall ill, it was believed in response to his appeal to the gods. But he was finally cured, and meanwhile his son had recovered also. The attempted suicide and the illness of the chief were the talk of the community, and great attention was paid to him, including ceremonial visits to him by the other chiefs. But I found that while the attempted suicide was treated as a very grave matter, some people questioned whether the chief's action had perhaps been quite so spontaneous as it seemed—possibly he had chosen his time carefully, when the sound of approaching footsteps had notified him that rescue would be at hand. But this was no more than a breath of suspicion. Even had it been correct, the chief would have been taking a risk, since the newcomers might have been slow to take in the significance of the situation. But the mere existence of this suspicion indicates how far the notion of suicide as the outcome of a gamble is built into Tikopia conceptions.

In general, then, I would argue that the incidence of suicide is not a simple variable that can be correlated directly with another single feature of the society. From the Tikopia evidence it may be that not only the manner but also the fact of suicide is socially determined. The promptness of mobilization of other members of the society and the efficiency of their rescue organization have a definite bearing on the incidence of suicide. Moreover, the incidence of suicide is affected through the classification of acts. Where risk-taking assumes a proportion great enough to amount to a virtual throwing away of one's life, and there appears to be a complete intellectual and emotional acceptance of the virtual certainty of self-destruction, the sharpness of the boundaries of the suicide category become blurred. Rigidity or permissiveness of the society, alone, then have little meaning in the interpretation. The Tikopia have a propensity to violent conduct in a variety of social situations in which their social status is threatened. There are a number of alternatives for the resolution of these situations. Even where the initial move is left to the person primarily affected and is in the direction of self-destruction, there are still some alternatives open. These are a product of natural forces, social forces, and the decision of the individual himself. Suicide, even if narrowly defined as persistence in conduct calculated to lead to self-destruction, is not a simple response to lack of alternatives, but to a selection of one alternative against others, for a complex of social reasons. The suicide of a person is a social act, to be understood only in the context of other social acts both of the person himself and of other members of his society.

NOTES

1 Henry Morselli, *Suicide: An Essay on Comparative Moral Statistics*, London: Kegan Paul, 1881. Emile Durkheim, *Le Suicide: Etude de Sociologie;* Paris: Alcan, 1897 (trans. by John A. Spaulding and George Simpson as *Suicide: A Study in Sociology;* Glencoe, Ill.: Free Press, 1951).

2 S. R. Steinmetz, 'Suicide Among Primitive Peoples', *American Anthropologist* (1894) 7:53–60. *J. Wisse, Selbstmord und Todesfürcht bei den Naturvölkern;* Zutphen, W. J. Thieme, 1933. Erminie W. Voegelin, 'Suicide in Northeastern California', *American Anthropologist* (1937) 39:445–56. William N. Fenton, *Iroquois* Ethnology, Bull. No. 128, Anthrop. Papers No. 14, 1941. Verrier Elwin, *Maria Murder and Suicide,* Bombay, Oxford University Press, 1943. G. M. Carstairs, 'Attitudes to Death and Suicide

in an Indian Cultural Setting', *International J. Social Psychiatry* (1955)
1: Winter, 33–41. Paul Bohannan, editor, *African Homicide and Suicide;*
Princeton, Princeton University Press, 1960.

3 S. F. Nadel, *The Nuba;* London, Oxford University Press, 1947, pp. 172–174, 266, 480.

4 Jacqueline H. Straus and Murray A. Straus, 'Suicide, Homicide and Social Structure in Ceylon', *American J. Sociology* (1953) 58:461–469.

5 Andrew F. Henry and James F. Short, Jr., *Suicide and Homicide,* Glencoe, Ill.: Free Press, 1954.

6 Clyde Kluckhohn, *Mirror for Man,* New York: Whittlesey House, 1949, p. 170.

7 See Elwin, footnote 2.

8 M. Fortes, *The Web of Kinship Among the Tallensi,* London; Oxford University Press, 1949, p. 168. But some Tallensi do commit suicide, as from grief at the death of a favourite child; and some may threaten suicide as a means of compulsion (p. 91).

9 James M. A. Weiss, 'The Gamble With Death in Attempted Suicide', *Psychiatry,* 1957, 20: 17–25. (Reprinted in this volume, pp. 384–397.)

10 General data about Tikopia are given in Firth, *We, The Tikopia: A Sociological Study of Kinship in Primitive Polynesia,* London: Allen and Unwin, 1936 (2nd ed. with new introduction, 1958). For suicide, see this, pp. 473, 536; and Firth, *Social Change in Tikopia: Re-Study of a Polynesian Community After a Generation,* London: Allen and Unwin, 1959, pp. 55, 66, 309–10.

11 Tikopia attitudes towards death are illustrated in *We, The Tikopia* (footnote 10); pp. 20–1, 287ff. Attitudes towards homicide are illustrated by a case in Firth, *History and Traditions of Tikopia,* Wellington, New Zealand: The Polynesian Society, 1961, p. 149.

12 Firth, *The Fate of the Soul: An Interpretation of Some Primitive Concepts,* New York: Cambridge University Press, 1955.

13 For example: England and Wales, 10.6 (1947); United States, 11.5 (1946); Sweden, 15.0 (1930); Switzerland, 26.1 (1930); Austria, 39.9 (1930). From Straus and Straus, footnote 4, p. 462.

14 Firth, 'The Theory of "Cargo" Cults: A Note on Tipokia', *Man,* 1955, 55:130–2.

15 For details of parental-filial relations see *We, The Tikopia,* footnote 10, pp. 178–86.

16 Firth, 'Bond-Friendship in Tikopia', pp. 259–69; in *Custom is King: Essays Presented to R. R. Marett on his 70th Birthday,* edited by L. H. Dudley Buxton, London: Hutchinson's Scientific and Technical Publications, 1936.

17 Maurice Halbwachs, *Les Causes du suicide,* Paris: Alcan, 1930.

18 For more details on this case see *We, The Tikopia,* footnote 10; pp. 245–6.

CHAPTER 17

Suicide Attempts of Japanese Youth and Durkheim's Concept of Anomie*

Mamoru Iga and Kenshiro Ohara

The rapid increase in Japan suicide rates after the Second World War—from less than 20 per 100,000 population before, and less than 15 during the war to 25.3 in 1955[1]—suggests that the high suicide rates in 1955 may be attributed, at least partly, to *anomie* after the war. The effect of *anomie* seems to have been especially great on Japanese youth, whose suicide rates nearly doubled from those of pre-war periods for both sexes (Table 1). The purpose of this paper is (1) to ascertain the essential components of Durkheim's concept of *anomie*; (2) to apply them to the explanation of high suicide rates of Japanese youth; and (3) to apply them to suicide attempts by Japanese youth. Although Powell[2] and Gibbs and Martin[3] maintain that Durkheim's concepts are inapplicable to individual cases, we try to find components of the concepts, which may be applicable to individual cases. After all, as Durkheim recognized by referring to the suicidal individual's psychological conditions, the components of the "suicidal current" must converge upon suicidal individuals if they are to contribute to suicide rates. The difference between suicidal and non-suicidal individuals who are exposed to the same "suicidal current" will be due to the variation in the amount and intensity of each one of the components, and the interrelationship among them, within the individual. The amount, intensity, and inter-relationship will be largely determined by social conditions and their effects upon particular individuals. It is the usually accepted contention that *anomie* as a social condition must be distinguished from *anomie* as a psychological condition. We maintain, however that the two are expressions of the same force—*anomie*—in the different contexts of social structure and individual psychology. We follow Leslie White in his handling of the dichotomy of culture and behaviour.[4]

* Reprinted by permission of The Society for Applied Anthropology from *Human Organization*, Vol. 26, Spring/Summer 1967, pp. 59–68.

DURKHEIM'S TYPES OF SUICIDE: AN INTERPRETATION AND POSSIBLE APPLICATION TO MODERN JAPANESE YOUTH

Each of Durkheim's types of suicide may be viewed in four aspects: (1) value orientation, (2) social restraints, (3) major source of suicidal motivation, and (4) psychological condition of the individual (Table 2). An egoistic individual cherishes "excessively individualistic" goals, which cannot be attained by conforming to societal values. Although the egoist's values are nonconforming, he has an unconscious wish for sympathy because man cannot live without "attachment to some object which transcends and survives him." Without social attachment, the individual feels that his efforts will end in nothingness.[5] At a time of difficulty, he may lose "the courage to live" and suffer from "depression and melancholy",[6] which lead to "egoistic suicide".

TABLE 1

Suicide Rates for 20–24 Year-old Japanese by Sex
(Per 100,000 Population)

	1920	1925	1930	1935	1940	1950	1955
Male	37.4	42.1	44.3	47.8	30.4	44.9	84.8
Female	27.0	30.3	31.3	31.3	18.2	27.8	47.2

Source: Ayanori Okazaki, "Jisatsu no Jisshoteki Kenkyu, 2" "Empirical Study of Suicide,"2), *Jinko Mondai Kekyu (Study of Population Problems)*, Vol. 75 (March, 1959), p. 22.

The altruistic suicide is committed by persons who are under strong social restraints and whose individual goals are more or less identical with their group's goals. The major source of suicidal motivation in altruistic cases in the sense of obligation and the attitude of "renunciation and an unquestioned abnegation".[7] This makes for psychological conditions such as the mystical joy of self-sacrifice, shame, or guilt, any of which may lead to suicide. The altruistic person typically has no sense of deprivation even in his self-sacrifice because his actions are determined by society which offers no alternative for comparison. He therefore willingly accepts the social restraints without resentment. Self-sacrifice may seem to be the only way to "live".

The different categories of altruistic suicide proposed by Durkheim—mystical, optional, and obligatory—may be distinguished from each other by the degree of the internalization of social values.

TABLE 2

Components of Durkheim's Types of Suicide
(An Interpretation)*

Components		Type of Suicide		
	Egoistic	Altruistic	Fatalistic	Anomic
Value Orientation	Individual-istic values Noncon-forming to societal values	Conforming Identification of individual goals with group goals	Conforming	Conforming with respect to equiva-lence of achieve-ment Uncritical demand for equality as the only basis of egois-tic gratification
Social restraints	Weak	Strong Effective psychologi-cal struc-turalization by norms	Extremely strong	Extremely weak almost removed—loss of restraining power on aspiration
Major source of suicidal motivation	The desire for "meaning of life" which is ob-tainable only by social attachment (p. 212) Conflict be-tween non-conforming values and unconscious wish for sympathy (p. 211) Loss of the will to live	Sense of obligation (p. 221) Abnegation and the state of impersonality (p. 223)	Excessive physical and moral despotism The sense of "future blocked and passion choked" (p. 276)	Greater goal-means discrepancy (p. 246) Sense of relative deprivation (p. 253) Dependency Insecurity
Psychologi-cal condition	Depression and melancholy (p. 214)	Mystical joy (p. 223 Shame and guilt	Resentment, fear, resignation	Greed, fevered imagination Dis-illusionment (p. 256) Jealousy (p. 253)

* The numbers in the table refer to pages in Emile Durkheim, *Suicide*, trans. by J. A. Spaulding and G. Simpson from 2nd ed., 1930, The Free Press, Glencoe, Illinois, 1951.

Mystical suicide involves the perfect psychological structuralization by social norms, a situation in which death for group values is a means for self-actualization. Optional suicide implies a lesser degree of psychological structuralization, producing a certain amount of ambivalence between group-oriented and self-oriented goals, although the former eventually prevail. The obligatory suicide seems to indicate a greater degree of resistance to social pressure, although the person involved feels that he must yield to society, probably for fear of punishment should he violate social expectations.

Durkheim's concept of fatalistic suicide[8] seems to lie between the obligatory type of altruistic suicide and anomic suicide. Fatalistic suicide involves a much greater degree of resistance to group pressure than the obligatory one, but also much greater social restraints than anomic suicide. Fatalistic and altruistic suicides share strong social restraints and conforming values, but the former can be distinguished from the latter by the feeling of a "future blocked and passion choked" and "an excessive physical and moral depotism" rather than a sense of obligation and self-sacrifice. Fatalistic suicide is also marked by resentment, fear, and resignation rather than mystical joy or shame and guilt.

Anomic suicide implies the removal of social restraints and involves unrestrained, unrealistic aspirations for equality of goods and services irrespective of the adequacy of resources for achieving them. Important determinants of this type of suicide are goal-means discrepancies and a sense of relative deprivation from comparing one's own situation with that of others who are "successful". The typical psychological conditions for this type of suicide are "greed, fevered imagination, disillusionment and jealousy",[9] Summarizing, we interpret the major components of Durkheim's concept of *anomie* as:

(1) Egocentric aspirations ;
(2) Unrealistically high aspirations because of weakened social restraints making for a greater discrepancy between goals and available means ;
(3) Emotional dependency on significant others for security and self-esteem ;
(4) A sense of relative deprivation and jealousy (in terms of the ego's relationship to social objects) which, combined with the preceding factors, make for an intense insecurity.

The concept of egoistic suicide can hardly apply to suicides of Japanese youth of conformity and dependency are as widespread as Doi,[10] Caudill,[11] Vogel,[12] De Vos,[13] and others have suggested. The concept of altruistic suicide may have been applicable to the Japanese before the Second World War, when the cultural ideal was to merge into the group: "his ego was not his own property", and "the real goal of conduct was exterior to itself".[14] Today, few, if any, Japanese seem altruistic in this sense. Few will commit "obligatory suicide" out of a sense of duty; and few will commit "mystical suicide" for the "joy of sacrifice, because, even with no particular reason, renunciation itself is considered praiseworthy".[15] The typical young Japanese today does not seem to be trained to the "renunciation and unquestioned abnegation" which might lead to "optional suicide". Dore[16] and the Research Committee of Japanese National Character for the Institute of Statistical Mathematics[17] give ample evidence for the individuation of Japanese personality in goal orientation. The concept of the fatalistic suicide from "excessive regulation", which "blocks futures of persons pitifully and which chokes passion violently", also appears to be more relevant to Japanese suicides before the Second World War, although it may still be applicable to suicides of females and in rural areas in Japan to a certain extent. Rather, it is the concept of *anomie*, as interpreted as in the preceding section, that seems most applicable to suicides among Japanese youth after the war. It seems applicable not only to the understanding of the high suicide rates but also to individual cases of attempted suicide.

In order to determine the applicability of the components of *anomie* to suicide rates of Japanese youth, it is necessary to demonstrate two essential conditions: (1) that Japanese youth in general share the essential components of *anomie*; and (2) that there is a logical relationship between the components and Japanese social structure.

THE COMPONENTS OF ANOMIE AND JAPANESE YOUTH

The characteristic components of *anomie* (ego-centrism, goal-means discrepancy, emotional dependency, and insecurity) are marked among Japanese youth. Although Japanese in general are shifting from collectively-oriented to self-oriented goals, the change seems to be much greater among the youth than among the older generation. In 1958, 54% of the 20–9 age group were primarily concerned with the individual rather than family or nation in comparison with 37% who were more collectively-oriented. On the other hand, 22% of the sixty-and-over group were self-oriented compared with 56% who were collectively-oriented.[18] Japanese youths tend to be highly ambitious and to be optimistic about their success "without a definite idea of what to do about it".[19] indicating great goal-means discrepancies. They also show a "great tendency to be affected by the opinion of others"[20] suggesting emotional dependency—dependency on others' reactions for security and self-esteem. The insecurity of young Japanese is also revealed by Stoetzel's findings of passiveness and easy resignation,[21] escapism,[22] despair,[23] and fear of illness.[24]

Although the greater degree of self-orientation among young Japanese may appear incompatible with their dependency, both self-orientation and dependency may be rooted in the same egocentrism. It is entirely possible to be oriented to selfish goals and still be dependent on others for goal attainment. Comparing high-school students with their parents, Caudill and Scarr found individualism in political ideas among Japanese young people but collateral dependency in family and occupational affairs. The collateral (rather than lineal) dependency in work was even greater among the younger respondents than among the older respondents, who surprisingly showed a higher degree of individualism in work situations.[25] Apparently Japanese youths tend to be individualistic in the realm of abstract ideas but dependent in the actual work situation.

THE COMPONENTS OF ANOMIE AND JAPANESE SOCIAL STRUCTURE

Egoistic Goals. The individualistic tendency of the Japanese after the war is pointed out by Dore, who holds that "personal relations have become instrumentalized, or a mere means to further individual ends and they are maintained only as long as they continue to serve those ends".[26] The Japanese also show a strong tendency towards egocentrism in the form of a lack of public morality,[27] which is exemplified in a Japanese saying that *tabi no haji wa kakisute* ("We need not be concerned about a deed committed on a trip, even if the deed is a shameful one"). Ohara has contended that this egocentric lack of a sense of responsibility in public affairs is a major cause of the high rate of parent-child suicides (*oyako shinju*),[28] in which parents kill their children before committing suicide themselves; the parents fear leaving children without parental protection in a cold and cruel world. How can we explain such egocentrism in a people who are reputed to be collectively-oriented, polite, and hospitable? Four explanations seem to be relevant:

(1) Japanese have few universalistic values which might regulate natural egocentric tendencies.[29] Japanese religious teachings, whether Buddhism or Shintoism, are highly particularistic—oriented not towards a supernatural or superempirical entity but towards particular social objects, such as parents, group heads, or the Emperor. The ethical value of behaviour is determined by the interpretation of one's social superiors and the reaction of society. Therefore, even to deceive others is virtuous, if it helps one's group head.

social restraints as well as tension reduction, hope, and the meaning of life. Religious restraints, however, seem to be very weak among young Japanese. In 1958, 84% of a representative sample of Japanese aged 20–9 "did not believe in any religion" in contrast with 16% who did so.[30]

(3) A basic characteristic of Japanese personality is diffuse fear. John Fischer, editor of *Harper's*, noted three characteristics of Japanese intellectuals: "cliques", "soft edges", and the "dread of power".[31] The fact that even intellectuals, although expected to be more self-expressive, individualistic thinkers, have a marked dread of power, may represent the basic anxiety of the typical Japanese. The insecurity of the Japanese will be more fully discussed later. This anxiety prohibits the Japanese from becoming involved with the plights of others and with social problems, as represented by the Japanese saying, *sawaranu kami ni tatari nashi* ("Avoid any thing which might cause trouble"). Insecure persons become exclusively concerned with their own security even at the expense of others. Because of this insecurity, "most [Japanese] people feel no responsibility for helping or being kind to strangers".[32]

(4) The "immaturity" of Japanese (from the Western point of view) has been pointed out by Stoetzel[33] and Vogel.[34] This immaturity implies a lack of differentiation from the infantile objects of cathexis, especially from the mother and from oneself. In the earliest stages of child development, even the mother cathexis is instrumental for need gratification. Immaturity thus implies egocentrism.

Goal-Means Discrepancy. The discrepancy between goals and means is noticeable among normal Japanese largely because of traditional emphasis on "rising in the world" (*risshin shusse*). This emphasis is illustrated by the fact that more than 80% of a representative sample of Japanese in 1953 regarded Toyotomi Hideyoshi, who in the sixteenth century rose from peasantry to become conqueror of Japan by sheer military strength and strategy, as an example for children to emulate, in comparison with only 4% who did not.[35] Parents are highly competitive in striving to enhance their children's chances to "get ahead", as analysed by Vogel.[36]

On the other hand, channels for social mobility are limited in the society where particularistic values are emphasized. Abegglen points out that Japanese companies, in selecting new personnel, exhibit a great degree of dependence on "qualities of character and background not directly related to the work position".[37] These qualities include family background, personality, influential connections, and nepotism.[38] Mannari proved the particularistic nature of Japanese business and industries by finding a significantly higher correlation between the persons occupying managerial positions of large firms and their class origin (in terms of the father's occupation) in Japan than in the United States.[39] Virtually the only way for those in Japan who have no special personal connections to achieve social mobility to desired statuses is to graduate from one of a few elite institutions. Before the Second World War, graduates of Tokyo University almost completely monopolized important government positions—the most desired positions in a society where *kanson mimpi* ("Government is divine, the public base") has been the motto. The fact that even today only a small portion of young Japanese can enter the top universities results in a great goal-means discrepancy for ambitious persons.

Dependency. Historically, the economic and emotional dependency of the Japanese has been intense. Every family was, in plain fact, dependent on its neighbours:

> The right to irrigate its fields at the time which could be determined by lot or by regular roster, the right to cut undergrowth as fertilizer and fodder from land held in common by the village or owned by a rich landlord, the cooperation of other villagers in protecting crops from nocturnal theft, their help at house building or re-roofing, at funerals or after a fire; all these were essential for the livelihood of the family.[40]

The necessity for patronage and personal connections which were essential for success in the Meiji Era,[41] is still very important in occupational competition. The importance of the *oyabun-kobun* (parent-role-person and child-role-person) relationship is marked not only among gang members, artisans, labourers and politicians, but among academic professionals. The cliquishness of Japanese intellectuals, which Fischer found,[42] is both a cause and an effect of dependency.

Western culture developed from collectivism to individualism and then to a new type of collectivism with high industrialization. Japan, however, has simply developed from an old form of collectivism to a new form in its drastic and rapid change from a preindustrial to an industrialized society without experiencing any emancipation of the individual. The Japanese are highly dependent upon groups, whether the family, the school, or the big firm.

There are many mechanisms built into modern Japanese social structure for the maintenance of dependency. When group solidarity is the basic value and authority is "right", dependency is required for the individual's adjustment. The more independent person not only tends to be frustrated; his security is always in danger. He tends to be regarded by superiors as *namaiki* (bumptious) and *shinyonaranu* (untrustworthy).

The effect of social structure upon dependency is reinforced by the great sensitivity of Japanese to social pressures. De Vos interprets this sensitivity as derived from underlying "infantile fear of abandonment".[43] It is also due to the dim prospect of security once one becomes the object of social censure and the difficulty thereafter in finding a suitable job, since personal connections and recommendations are essential for higher-status positions. The person who changes his job tends to be regarded as untrustworthy. Japanese employers generally prefer a loyal follower to a competent worker; the competency to merge into a group is more important than technical competency.

Insecurity. The Japanese saying, "Opening lips, autumn wind is cold" (*mono ieba kuchibiru samushi aki no kaze*) teaches that any statement may be unfavourably interpreted; therefore, it is wisest to be silent. This fear is also represented by other Japanese sayings such as *nagai mono ni wa makareyo* and *naku ko to jito niwa katenu*, both implying "Don't kick against the pricks". This fear is considered by Muramatsu as a characteristic of the Japanese mind[44] which underlies the reticence, embarrassed smile, and withdrawal, by which Japanese in foreign countries are often characterized.

Japanese insecurity can be traced at least in part to the traditional fear of power and governmental authorities. The Japanese lived for a long time in a strict police state with collective responsibility not only among family members but also among neighbours and villagers. They were subjected to severe punishment under the elaborate system of espionage which characterized the Tokugawa administration. People were literally frightened into "taking their proper places". Japanese insecurity is also rooted in the child-rearing practices. Vogel mentions fear as the major technique for disciplining children in Japan.[45] The discontinuity and inconsistency of the cultural conditioning of Japanese children is also an important source of insecurity. "The undisciplined freedom of early childhood" is "replaced at about the age of ten by rigid repression" which "breaks the spirit and prepares for the strict formalism and obedience to convention of adult Japanese life".[46] Even before this change, there is strong competition among parents to show visitors how well their children have been trained in early infancy. This results in inconsistency and incongruence in disciplining. This disciplinary inconsistency and incongruence is aggravated by the tendency for the authoritarian father to take out his spite on his child on the alleged ground of disciplining for the future benefit of the child. When the autonomy such behaviour requires is imposed upon an infant before his neuro-muscular system is ready to assume it, he may develop a sense of inadequacy, doubt, and shame. Inconsistency and incongruence not only frustrate the infant but also foster basic mistrust and hostility towards parents, which, in turn may lead to ambivalence and further insecurity.

The economic insecurity which is also real to most Japanese directly affects youth. Lower-class people seldom have secure jobs. The middle-class husband may have a secure job, but chances for getting additional income are restricted because of limited job opportunities and the social stigma against work for the wife and children in a respectable family. Insecurity is further increased by health hazards and the lack of adequate governmental services.[47] This insecurity develops both utilitarian and aggressive attitudes in Japanese youth. The present writers believe that a major cause of students' participation in anti-governmental demonstrations is their insecurity about future jobs. Many of the participants seem to become conservative citizens when they obtain secure positions.

An important factor in Japanese social structure for the production of insecurity is the vital importance of passing entrance examinations to a "good" university. As Vogel states' "in a non-affluent society where one has no place to turn in time of need, and welfare is provided by neither the government, nor the family, nor personal connections, the large firm assumes a critical importance, because it provides security as well as income".[48] The entrance to a large firm is determined by graduation from a "good" university, which, in turn, requires a high class standing and the passing of entrance examinations at all school levels. Japanese children and youths are generally in incessant competition for a high standing; otherwise they suffer a feeling of failure. The competition among parents for a higher position for their children is extremely intense.[49] Often the mother's affection is contingent upon the child's standing at school.

Thus far we have discussed the application of our interpretation of Durkheim's concept of *anomie* to the understanding of high suicide rates among Japanese youth. We began by analysing the relationships between the components of *anomie*, the personality type of Japanese youth in general and Japanese social structure. The second proposition advanced at the beginning of the paper and examined more fully now is that Durkheim's concepts of *anomie* as defined here is applicable to individual cases.

TABLE 3

Yatabe-Guilford Test for Suicidal and Non-suicidal Groups

	Total	Average Age	D*	C	I	N	O	Co	Ag	G	R	-T	-A	-S
Suicidal Persons														
Total	55	22.2	3.64	3.71	3.42	3.36	36.4	3.69	3.31	3.11	3.23	3.05	3.02	2.92
Male	26	22.7	3.38	3.62	3.08	3.35	3.50	3.38	3.04	2.88	3.08	3.04	3.19	3.04
Female	29	21.3	3.86	3.79	3.72	3.38	3.76	3.97	3.55	3.31	3.38	3.07	2.86	2.83
Non-Suicidal Persons														
Air Force Personnel	85	22.3	2.86	2.82	2.65	2.62	3.00	3.06	3.01	3.14	2.84	2.71	2.84	2.92
Nurses	90	21.4	2.52	2.54	2.60	2.56	2.67	3.08	2.86	3.26	2.82	2.70	2.97	3.18
Ordinary citizens														
Male	99	23.9	2.24	2.68	2.56	2.69	2.65	2.77	2.84	3.08	2.79	2.52	2.75	2.77
Female	50	23.3	2.66	2.70	2.90	2.72	2.88	3.26	3.20	2.72	2.84	2.86	3.26	3.20

* D Depression
C Cyclic tendency
I Inferiority feelings
N Nervousness
O Lack of objectivity
Co Lack of cooperativeness
Ag Aggressiveness (lack of agreeableness)

G General activity
R Rhathymia (carefree, happy go lucky)
-T Thinking introversion
-A Opposite to ascendance (submissiveness)
-S Social introversion

Source: K. Ohara, 'Jisatsu, no Yoin ni kansuru Kenkyu' ('Factors in Suicide'), Seishni-Shinkeigaku-Zasshi (Psychiatria et Neurologia Iaponica), Vol. 63 (February 1961), p. 143.

APPLICATION OF ANOMIE TO SUICIDE-ATTEMPTING INDIVIDUALS

The data for this paper were collected between April 1951 and August 1958 by the junior author, a Japanese psychiatrist, in Kamakura, a city of about 100,000 population near Tokyo. Suicidal subjects were those taken to two receiving hospitals in Kamakura. Twenty-six suicide-attempting males (average age, 22.7) and twenty-nine suicide attempting females (average age, 21.3) were studied in comparison with the following non-suicidal groups: eighty-five Air Force personnel (average age, 22.3) ninety nurses (average age, 21.4), ninety-nine ordinary male citizens (average age, 23.9), fifty ordinary female citizens (average age, 23.3), 416 college students, 258 high school students, and 249 junior high students. The tools used for the survey included the *Shinjoshitsu Kensa* ("Temperament Test")—an adaptation from Dr Kurt Schneider's *Psychopathischen Persönlichkeiten* test—and the Yatabe-Guilford and Thurstone tests.

Egocentric Nature of Aspiration. Both Kato[50] and Ohara[51] regard *jiga no kyosho* ("smallness of ego") as the core of the suicidal tendency. Doi sees narcissism and *amae* (counting on others for selfish goal-attainment) as the common character of mental disturbance in Japan.[52] Ohara and Iga also maintain that, although a majority of Japanese suicides are related to family problems, family problems are caused in many cases by the suicidal individual's exclusive concern with his own selfish goals.[53] There is a vicious circle of egocentrism and insecurity in a society where family cooperation still is a basic ideal. This is especially so when the person is dependent, financially or otherwise, upon parents or other family members for the attainment of egoistic ends. The possible egocentric nature of aspiration among suicide-attempting persons is suggested by their high score, compared with non-suicidal subjects, on the Co (lack of cooperativeness) and the Ag (aggressiveness) scales of the Yatabe-Guilford test (Table 3). Both suicidal males and females showed significantly higher scores in *yokuutsu-sei* ("depressiveness") on the "Temperament Test" (*Shin-joshitsu Kensa*). The most frequently observable characteristic of this *yokuutsu-sei*, according to Kurt Schneider, the original formulator of this test, is an egoistic, complaining, and jealous personality, exhibiting pessimism, negativism, and the tendency to withdraw from unpredictable situations.[54]

When egoistic wishes cannot be satisfied, a possible consequence is an intense desire for self-assertion which may be groundless—"self-inflation".[55] Self-inflation requires another person to whom self-assertion can be made. When such a person is not available for whatever reasons, the twice-frustrated egoist may turn his hostility against himself.

Unrealistically High Aspiration and Goal-Means Discrepancy.
Unrealistically high aspiration and the discrepancy between one's
wish and his capability of achieving it was apparently greater in the
suicidal subjects than in others. Ohara's suicidal individuals have
a "strong wish for achievement" but show "lack of actual effort
for it". They reveal weak will-power and the "incapability of realistic definition of the situation".[56] Thurstone tests show significantly
lower scores for suicidal than for non-suicidal males on D (capability
of taking initiative and responsibility); and both suicidal males and
females show significantly lower scores on V (capability of enjoying
strenuous projects).[57] By the "Temperament Test" both suicidal
males and females are found significantly higher in *muryoku-sei*
(helplessness): (Chi Square = 15.0. P < .001 for males; 27.6
P < .001 for females). According to Dr Schneider, *muryoku-sei*
(*asthenikheit*) is characterized by "being oversensitive to unpleasant
experiences which are trivial to ordinary persons, resulting in the
malfunctioning of neuromuscular system," often indicated by "easy

TABLE 4

Percentage of Subjects Who Answered
that "Suicide is Bad, Because it makes
Parents and Siblings Sad"

	Suicidal subjects		Non-suicidal Subjects					
			College		High School		Junior High	
	No.	%	No.	%	No.	%	No.	%
'Suicide is good."	18	32.7	71	17.1	41	15.9	12	4.9
'Suicide is bad."	37	67.3	345	82.9	217	84.1	237	95.1
Totals	55	100.0	416	100.0	258	100.0	249	100.0
'Suicide is bad," because:								
Total	37	100.0	345	100.0	217	100.0	237	100.0
"It makes parents and siblings sad."	8	21.5	17	4.9*	14	6.4	38	16.1
Other reasons.†	29	78.5	328	85.1	203	93.6	199	83.9

* The chi square for the difference between suicidal subjects and age-
comparable college subjects is 19.6 P. < .001.

† Other reasons include (*a*) "It makes for social disorder," (*b*) "We should
find a significance of life", and the three combinations of (*a*) and (*b*) and
(*c*) "Suicide makes parents and siblings sad", i.e. (*a*) + (*c*); (*b*) + (*c*) and
(*a*) + (*b*) + (*c*).

Source: Ohara, 'Jisatsu no Yoin ni kansuru Kenkyu', op. cit., p. 137.

tendency to fatigue, difficulty in sleep, headache, decline in thinking ability, difficulty in concentration and poor memory",[58] indicating ineffective goal-oriented activities.

Emotional Dependency. More important than intellectual dependency (in task performance) in suicide cases seems to be emotional dependency. Emotional dependency upon family members seems to be indicated by answers to the question, "Why is suicide bad?" While only 4.9% of age-comparable college subjects and 6.4% of high school subjects, who thought suicide was bad, gave the answer that "it makes parents and siblings suffer", 16.1% of junior high subjects (average age fourteen and 21.5% of suicide attempters with the average age of twenty-two gave the same answer (Chi square = 19.6 P < .001). The similarity between the suicidal and junior high subjects is noticeable, probably suggesting the emotional immaturity and dependency of the suicidal persons.[59] (Table 4).

Insecurity. In addition to the economic insecurity of suicidal subjects as shown by their occupational distribution,[60] other aspects of their insecurity seem to be indicated by higher scores on D (worries over possible misfortune), C (frequent shift of mood), I (inferiority feelings), N (nervousness), and O (lack of objectiveness, taking things personally) of the Yatabe-Guilford test, and significantly lower scores in E (emotional stability) and S (sociability) of the Thurstone test (significant at the .001 level).[61]

SUMMARY AND CONCLUSION

After analysing Durkheim's types of suicide into components and identifying the essential distinctions among all types of suicide according to Durkheim's proposal, we have attempted to apply the characteristic components of *anomie* to the understanding of high suicide rates of Japanese youth after the Second World War, and then to a comparison of suicide-attempting and non-suicidal individuals. We believe that the comparison indicates that Durkheim's concepts may be applicable for more elaborate empirical research.

If *anomie* is responsible for high Japanese suicide rates after the war (25.7 per 100,000 population in 1958 compared with 20.5 in 1935), then lower suicide rates are expected when Japanese adjust to the social change since the war. The decline in the suicide rate in the 1960's (15.9 in 1963),[62] at least in part, suggests such adjustment. This lower 1963 figure may suggest not only the new adjustment but also the decline of suicides of more traditional Japanese types (e.g.

altruistic or fatalistic types). One of the key foci for future studies of Japanese suicides must be the determining of the distribution of suicide patterns (for example, anomic, fatalistic altruistic, and egoistic types) by means of some operational indices for the purpose of finding dominant and variant patterns, as Florence Kluckhohn analysed value orientations[63] We have attempted to show that the operational indices of Durkheim's types are obtainable, and they might be applicable to both suicide rates and individual cases. In future studies larger and more representative control groups need to be compared with suicide-attempting subjects. More extensive comparisons of suicidal and non-suicidal groups with the use of more rigorously scientific methods are also necessary. In addition, suicidal attempts should be compared with successful suicides by means of "psychological autopsy" method as developed at the Suicide Prevention Centre at Los Angeles.[64]

NOTES

1 Ayanori Okazaki, *Jisatsu no Shakai-tokei-teki Kenkyu* (Social Statistical Study of Suicide), Nippon Hyoronsha, Tokyo, 1960, p. 43.
2 Elwin R. Powell, 'Occupation, Status, and Suicide: Toward a Redefinition of Anomie', *American Sociological Review,* Vol. 23 (April 1958) pp. 131–40; 'Rejoinder to Dr. Cary-Lundberg', *American Sociological Review,* Vol. 24 (April 1959), pp. 250–3.
3 Jack P. Gibbs and W. T. Martin, 'Status Integration and Suicide', *American Sociological Review,* Vol. 23 (April 1958) pp. 140–7.
4 Leslie White, 'The Concept of Culture', *American Anthropologist,* Vol. 61, 1959, pp. 227–51.
5 Emile Durkheim, *Suicide,* trans. by J. A. Spaulding and G. Simpson from 2nd ed., 1930, The Free Press, Glencoe, Illinois, 1951, p. 210.
6 Ibid, p. 214.
7 Ibid., p. 223.
8 Ibid., p. 276.
9 Ibid., pp. 256, 253.
10 Takeo Doi, 'Jibun to Amae no Seishin Byori' ('Psychopathology of *Jibun* and *Amae*'), *Seishin-Shinkei-gaku Zasshi (Psychitria et Neurologia Japonica),* Vol. 62 (January 1960), pp. 149–62.
11 William Caudill, 'Observations on the Cultural Context of Japanese Psychiatry', in M. K. Opler (ed.), *Culture and Mental Health,* Macmillan, New York, 1959, p. 224.
12 Ezra F. Vogel and S. H. Vogel, 'Family Security, Personal Immaturity, and Emotional Health in Japanese Sample', *Marriage and Family Living,* Vol. 23 (May 1961), pp. 161–6.
13 George A. De Vos, 'The Relation of Guilt Toward Parents to Achievement and Arranged Marriage Among the Japanese', *Psychiatry,* Vol. 23 (August 1960), pp. 287–301.
14 Durkheim, op. cit., p. 221.
15 Ibid., p. 223.

16 R. P. Dore, *City Life in Japan*, Routledge and Kegan Paul, London, 1958, p. 390.
17 Research Committee of Japanese National Character, The Institute of Statistical Mathematics, *Nipponjin no Kokuminsei* (*Japanese National Character*) Shiseido Publishing Co., Tokyo, 1961, p. 287.
18 Ibid., p. 496.
19 J. Stoetzel, *Without the Chrysanthemum and the Sword*, A UNESCO Publication, Columbia University Press, New York, 1955, p. 207.
20 Ibid., p. 208.
21 Ibid., pp. 214–16.
22 Ibid., p. 220.
23 Ibid., p. 219.
24 Ibid.
25 W. Caudill and H. A. Scarr, 'Japanese Value Orientation and Cultural Change', *Ethnology*, Vol. I (January 1962), pp. 54–91.
26 Dore, op. cit., p. 390.
27 Lawrence Olson, *Dimensions of Japan*, American Universities Field Staff, Inc., New York, 1963, p. 133.
28 Kenshiro Ohara, *Nippon no Jisatsu* (*Japanese Suicide*), Seishin-Shobo, Tokyo, 1964, p. 266.
29 Ibid., p. 263.
30 Research Committee of Japanese National Character, op. cit., p. 478.
31 John Fischer, 'The Japanese Intellectuals: Cliques, Soft Edges, and the Dread of Power', *Harper's* (September 1963).
32 E. F. Vogel, *Japan's New Middle Class*, University of California Press, Berkeley, 1963, p. 153.
33 Stoetzel, op. cit., p. 233.
34 E. F. and S. H. Vogel, op. cit.
35 Research Committee of Japanese National Character, op. cit., p. 492.
36 E. F. Vogel, *Japan's New Middle Class*, p. 19.
37 James C. Abegglen, *The Japanese Factory*, The Free Press, Glencoe, Illinois, 1958, p. 26.
38 Ibid., p. 38.
39 Hiroshi Mannari, 'Nippon no Keieisha no Shakai-teki Seikaku' ('The Social Personality of Japanese Management'), *Shakai-gaku Hyron* (*Japanese Sociological Review*), Vol. 12 (September 1961), pp. 7–19.
40 Dore, op. cit., p. 377.
41 Ibid.
42 Fischer, op. cit.
43 De Vos, op. cit., p. 288.
44 Tsuneo Muramatsu, *Nipponjin* (*Japanese People*), Reimei Shobo, Tokyo, 1963, pp. 103–5.
45 Vogel, *Japan's New Middle Class*, pp. 249–50.
46 Dore, op. cit., p. 230.
47 Vogel, *Japan's New Middle Class*, p. 19.
48 Ibid.
49 E. F. Vogel, 'Entrance Examinations and Emotional Disturbances in Japan's New Middle Class', in R. J. Smith and R. K. Beardsley (eds.), *Japanese Culture*, Aldine Publishing Company, Chicago, 1962, p. 148.
50 Masaaki Kato, 'Jisatsu ni Itaru Michi' ('Ways to Suicide'), *Tokei* (*Statistics*), Vol. 8 (September 1959).
51 Kenshiro Ohama, 'Jisatsu no Yoin ni kansuru Kenkyu' ('A Study of Main Factors in Suicide'), *Seishin-Shinkei-gaku Zasshi* (*Psychiatria et Neuro-*

logia Japonica), Vol. 63 (February 1961), pp. 108–66.
52 Takeo Doi, '*Amae*—A Key Concept for Understanding Japanese Personality Structure', *Psychologia*, Vol. 5 (March 1962), pp. 1–7.
53 Kenshiro Ohara and Mamoru Iga, 'Family Problems in Suicide Attempts of Japanese Youth', *The Memorial Issue for Professor Takehisa Kora*, Jikei University School of Medicine, Tokyo, 1964.
54 Kurt Schneider, *Die Psychopathischen Personlichkeiten*, Franz Deuticke, Vienna, 1949, 9th ed., trans. by Kaketa and Hirezaki, Misuzu Shobo, Tokyo, 1964, pp. 118–121.
55 Karen Horney, *New Ways of Psychoanalysis*, Norton, New York, 1939, p. 99.
56 Ohara, 'Jisatsu no Yoin ni kansuru Kenkyu', p. 163.
57 Ibid., pp. 113, 114.
58 Schneider, op. cit., pp. 197–201.
59 Ohara, 'Jisatsu no Yoin ni kansuru Kenkyu', p. 137.
60 Ibid., p. 110; Seiken Kosaka and Nisho Usui, *Nipponjin no Jisatsu (Japanese Suicide)*, Sobun-sha, Tokyo, 1966, pp. 58, 61.
61 Ohara, 'Jisatsu no Yoin ni kansuru Kenkyu', p. 146.
62 *Nippon no Tokei (Statistics of Japan)*, Bureau of Statistics, The [Japanese] Premier's Office, 1964, p. 199.
63 Florence R. Kluckhohn, 'Dominant and Variant Value Orientation', in C. Kluckhohn and H. A. Murray, *Personality in Nature, Society, and Culture*, Alfred A. Knopf, New York, 1954, pp. 342–57.
64 R. E. Litman, T. Curphey, E. S. Shneidman, N. L. Farberow, and N. Tabachnick, 'Investigations of Equivocal Suicides', *The Journal of the American Medical Association*, Vol. 184 (22 June 1963) pp. 924–9.

PART IV

CHAPTER 18

Suicide in Relation to Social Factors

The papers which have been grouped together in this Part are inevitably somewhat heterogeneous in character. There is to be found in the literature upon suicide a very large number of statistical studies of the distribution of suicide in relation to various social factors. But much of this writing is repetitious, and it would be true to say that we know little more today about variations in suicide rates than was known one hundred years ago. I have therefore avoided including descriptive statistical articles in this book, and instead have abstracted basic statistical information on suicide and placed it in an Appendix.[1] The papers included in this section all have some interest over and above the simple documentation of rates of suicide.

There is one approach to the sociology of suicide which has developed partly independently of Durkheim's work: this is the "ecological" approach of the Chicago sociologists. It can easily be shown that, if neighbourhoods of differing social and economic characteristics are charted against suicide rates in any large city, suicide varies according to type of area. Schmid[2] and Cavan[3] documented this in detail for Seattle and Chicago respectively, showing that suicide rates are highest of all in areas of "social disorganization". These are neighbourhoods, normally situated near the centre of cities, where there is a great deal of lateral mobility, a high immigrant ratio, and where a large proportion of the population lives alone in lodgings or flats. In such areas, according to these authors, social life is generally unstable in character, and lacking in a coherent set of established norms.[4] Besides suicide, rates of divorce, delinquency, drug addiction, and certain forms of mental illness also tend to reach a peak in such areas. Sainsbury's study in London, the conclusions of which he summarizes in the selection reprinted here, follows the methodology of the American researches in most respects, except that Sainsbury relates the distribution of suicide not only to "social disorganization", but to socio-economic status conceived independently.

Ecological studies of the distribution of mental illness have shown stable differences in rates of schizophrenia between different areas inside cities.[5] But no such stable pattern has appeared in most research on the distribution of that form of mental illness which on the face of it appears most closely connected with suicide: the depressive disorders. Wechsler puts forward the hypothesis that the ecological distribution of depressive disorders is related to the disintegration of small communities as they become, or are absorbed by, expanding urbanism. This same disintegrative process would also be expected to produce high rates of suicide. Wechsler's results, derived from a study of fifty communities in Massachusetts which have undergone rapid growth, bear out both hypotheses.

The paper by Pierce takes up a problem which has been the subject of some controversy among previous writers: that of the relationship between suicide rates and the economic cycle. Durkheim's original contention that suicide rates rise not only in times of economic depression but also in periods of unusual prosperity has been rejected by several subsequent writers. Utilizing a relatively new statistical technique, Pierce shows decisive support for Durkheim's view. This finding is of considerable significance, since the thesis that suicide rates rise in times of marked prosperity (which Durkheim seems to have been the first to propose), constitutes the most striking evidence that he was able to offer in support of the theory of *anomie*.

Breed's paper is also directed towards a discussion of *anomie*. Abandoning the usual methodology, however, Breed bases his study upon interviews with those who had known men who had committed suicide. His specific interest is in the relationship between suicide and downward social mobility; but an interesting sidelight of his research is the finding of a whole series of errors in the official suicide statistics when they were compared with knowledge gained from the interview material which forms the substance of the study. His main conclusion is that, as compared with a matched control group, the suicides had experienced significantly greater downward mobility, together with a number of other economic difficulties.

Durkheim admitted that suicide rates vary seasonally; but he rejected the notion that climatic or weather conditions have any direct influence upon suicides. Other writers have nevertheless continued to postulate such a relationship. Connections have been claimed to exist between suicide and a broad range of climatic conditions, including, among others, barometric pressure, humidity, amount of rainfall and temperature. But the material bearing upon these problems is sketchy, and most research of this type has been inconclusive. Pokorny and his co-authors adopted a more intensive method than has normally been used in such research; their results show no connection between suicide or attempted suicide and any of the factors they examine, including the seasons.

A further problem which crops up with great frequency in the literature on suicide, and one which Durkheim also discussed at some length, concerns how far suicidal actions result from imitation. As Motto indicates, the view that imitation plays a role in the causation of suicide is an old one, and is prominent in some of the earliest works on suicide—especially in relation to the part which the reporting of suicides in the press is presumed to play as a source of information stimulating imitation and therefore further suicides. But very little evidence of a systematic kind has ever been produced to support this view. Motto accordingly studied suicide in periods when broad areas of the United States were without newspapers because of strikes, and compared rates of suicide during these periods with rates prior to the strike. His results show that, while in most of the cases he considers suicide rates do drop during the period without newspapers, in no instance is this a statistically significant difference. The author therefore concludes: "whatever deleterious effect newspapers may exert on their readers stems more from the implied and expressed attitudes and value system than from news content".

NOTES

1 Pp. 419–424 in this volume.
3 Ruth S. Cavan, *Suicide*, Chicago, 1928.
4 The efforts of some of these writers to use correlations between such rates as an index of "social disorganisation" has been criticised as involving fallacious statistical reasoning. For a brief discussion of the "ecological fallacy" in relation to the work of Cavan, Schmid and Sainsbury, cf. Douglas's *The Social Meaning of Suicide*, pp. 99 ff.
5 The best-known work in this connection is Robert Faris and H. Warren Dunham, *Mental Disorders in Urban Areas*, Chicago, 1939.

CHAPTER 19

Suicide in London*

Peter Sainsbury

The diversity of districts within London is the unplanned product of geographical, historical, economic and social causes. Since the Middle Ages there has been the major division of London into a commercial centre, the City, developing around the port in the east, and a political centre in the west at Westminster. In the former a zealous community of ambitious merchants pursued their trades, defying any interference from the court; and around this commercial hub were gathered the industries and the homes of the labourers. With increasing trade and industrialization, the working-class district expanded into the gargantuan slums of the present day Though bleak and grim, this district is comparatively settled socially, for it is a community which has arisen and is maintained in response to local industrial demands. The high proportion of London-born among the inhabitants of the East End boroughs is evidence of social stability.

In the environs of Westminster the more erratic world of the court and government developed. Here were provided the diversion of the momentarily privileged and the entertainment of the wealthy and leisured. This division of London has persisted: the restless, meretricious West End, and the settled East End where the Cockney, the hereditary Londoner, lives by the commerce of his port and City.

London's growth was greatly hastened by the industrial and technical developments of the nineteenth century, and the consequent construction of a system of rapid local transport. Out of this arose a second differentiation: highly mobile districts for business, commerce and shopping at the centre, and at the periphery "vast dormitories, an anonymous wilderness, neighbourhoods without neighbours"[1]. The early parochial character of London was obliterated, and the shifting impersonality of the modern city emerged, this being especially marked in West and Central London.

* Reprinted by permission of the author and the Institute of Psychiatry, Maudsley Hospital, from *Suicide in London: an Ecological Study*, London, 1955, pp. 68–79.

Finally, there has been the delimitation of a mosaic of smaller districts, each with characteristic populations and activities. These were manifest in the eighteenth century.[2] Today there are the one-room flat, boarding-house and hotel areas of Kensington, Bayswater and Bloomsbury which cater for the immigrant; social isolation is pronounced here. There are districts, notably Hampstead, to which aspire the commercially successful, where occupational mobility might be expected to be a special feature. Similarly, trades and professions gravitate to circumscribed districts; the doctors' mecca to the north of Wigmore Street has a quality as unmistakable as that of the artists' or greengrocers' headquarters in Chelsea and Covent Garden.

So London has developed "natural areas", such as have been described in Chicago, a fact recognized in the County of London plan;[3] they do not seem, however, to conform to the simple concentric pattern found in Chicago, although some characteristics, such as population density, are so arranged.[4]

A most important respect in which the social structure of London differs from that of Chicago or Minneapolis is that London's most mobile and apparently most socially disorganized districts do not coincide with those of greatest poverty. The prosperous north-western boroughs have the highest rates of mobility, isolation and social disorganization; the poor eastern boroughs the lowest. Moreover, in London the zones of transition are not the most mobile, nor do they appear to be the centres in which immigrants are absorbed; the statistics clearly show that immigrants settle first in the north-west, and next in the peripheral southern boroughs.[5]

In the following sections the relationship of the natural areas of London to the incidence of suicide will be discussed.

DISTINCTION BETWEEN POVERTY AND SOCIAL DISORGANIZATION

The separation in London of the districts of greatest poverty from those of social disorganization provides an opportunity to examine the importance of these separately in relation to suicide. For in the American studies the coincidence of poverty and social disorganization at the city centre left in doubt the role of each in producing the high central suicide rates. The findings in London unequivocally support the view that social disorganization, not poverty, is the paramount factor.

As the boroughs are administrative areas of recent origin it is preferable to consider borough divisions or groups, if these more nearly correspond to the social, cultural or physical unit.

A comparison of the suicide-rank order of the boroughs during

1919–23, 1929–33 and 1940–4 showed that each borough, especially those with high rates, preserved a fairly consistent position. This finding strongly supports the hypothesis that some social characteristic of the borough controls its suicide rate. It is fair to suppose that during the war the borough populations changed considerably because of evacuation, conscription, and so on, but nevertheless the boroughs preserved their social peculiarities and retained their usual relative rates of suicide. A striking example of the tenacity with which a borough maintains a high suicide rate is proved by Westminster. From the figures for suicide in Westminster given by Winslow a hundred years ago it appears that the suicide rate during 1832–6 was 15.7 per 100,000, which is five times the rate of London as a whole in 1831.[6]

The alliance of a high incidence of suicide with social mobility, isolation and disorganization in the north-western boroughs has been sufficiently stressed; but the social characteristic primarily responsible for a high rate varies from borough to borough. In Mayfair, for example, the impersonal, fleeting nature of relationships and the lack of a consistent and generally accepted set of values seem to be especially important. In the rented single rooms of South Kensington, Bayswater and Bloomsbury the untoward consequences of loneliness and anonymity seem to prevail; and a high suicide rate was actually found in the Bloomsbury district of St Pancras. In Hampstead the human problems to be expected are those of the parvenu adopting unaccustomed values and a new way of life, those of the immigrant adjusting to an unfamiliar culture, and those of the lonely boarding-house dweller. High suicide rates were observed in the two latter groups, and even the more prosperous tended to be over-represented among the suicides. The high mobility around the railway stations in the City and Paddington might well conduce to a high rate of suicide, such as was found in the districts adjoining the termini of St Pancras.

The remaining boroughs north of the river and adjoining the high-suicide-rate group, Hammersmith, Fulham and Islington, have intermediate suicide rates, just as in social characteristics they share many features of both the high- and low-rate boroughs.

Two working-class districts may be distinguished: the first, the East Central group, comprising Shoreditch, Finsbury, Bethnal Green and Southwark, has the higher suicide rate. Shoreditch, in fact, is among the ten boroughs with highest rates, although it shows few of the social features so evident in the other nine. Its high suicide rate seems less anomalous when one considers its central position adjoining the high-rate district, its high-mobility rating and the abundance of "black" streets on the survey maps. The second working-class group, Poplar, Deptford, Stepney and Bermondsey, is more to the east; its suicide rate is well below the average for London. Reasons have been adduced for supposing that these working-class districts form a stable well-knit community of perennial Londoners. Furthermore, these four boroughs have the four highest birth-rates of London.[7]

Wandsworth, Lewisham and Woolwich form the southern and outer ring of the county. They also have a low suicide rate. They comprise a socially homogeneous group of middle-class and skilled working-class residential boroughs. They show few signs of social disorganization; on the contrary, the impression is one of settled family life and owned homes; all three boroughs have an increasing population.[8]

In London, suicide rates seem therefore to vary with the social character of a district. This was so in Chicago,[9] in Minneapolis[10] and in Hamburg.[11] In London, the suicide rate was highest in the more mobile central district and in lodging-house areas; it was lower in the more stable boroughs and the peripheral suburbs.[12] What are the possible explanations for the distribution of suicide in the London boroughs?

As suicide is high in boroughs with a large immigrant population, is it that the immigrants are a selected, suicide-prone type? But the evidence is that urban immigrants from the country are a more socially desirable type than the city-born.[13] Booth, on the strength of his inquiries in London, described them as "often the cream of their native counties.[14] Nevertheless, there is also a tendency for large cities to attract psychopathic characters, such as addicts[15] and "drifters".[16]

Gruhle relates the geographical distribution of suicide in part to density of population and overcrowding, and in part to the way in which social classes are disposed in the city. The high suicide rate in the wealthiest quarter of Hamburg, and the low rate in the poorest, are attributed to the greater inclination to suicide of the wealthy. The findings in London partly support this view; but socio-economic status correlates with suicide to a smaller degree than do social mobility and isolation, which seem to be the ultimate processes responsible for local variations in suicide; they account for the differences both in neighbourhoods and in classes.

As mental illness is more prevalent in city localities where the suicide rate is high, may the distribution of suicide be explained on this basis? The problem then becomes one of explaining the pattern of mental disorder in the city. These questions wil be examined in subsequent sections.

There are obvious statistical pitfalls which I have tried to avoid.

By taking the suicides over a five-year period, a reasonably reliable borough rate is assured, and when the borough rates during three decades are compared, the fairly consistent pattern suggests that the differences are valid.[17] The age and sex incidence of the populations was not found to account for the differences, nor did the distribution of widowed, divorced or foreign-born in the boroughs, as their numbers were too small. The effect of transiency was largely removed by basing the rates on resident populations.

The contention that high rates occur because potential suicides are attracted to certain districts or, more generally, to a misanthropic, solitary way of life, is difficult to disprove. There is reason to suppose, however, that this does not provide the entire explanation; cities actively impose a sequestered, detached mode of living upon some, among whom will be individuals predisposed to succumb to such enforced solitude.

Not only Zorbaugh's studies[18] but the observations of anyone familiar with the life and inhabitants of such districts attest the demoralization and dejection attendant upon living in the obscurity of a city boarding-house.

The view must be sustained that the nature of community life, its cohesion and stability, and the opportunities it provides for satisfactory relationships, alone afford a comprehensive explanation of the variations in suicide rate of communities and other social groups.

POVERTY IN RELATION TO SUICIDE

In the published literature there is little precise information about the relationship of social status to suicide, so the findings in London merit further consideration.

In distribution, poverty and suicide are mutually exclusive, for it has been shown that the boroughs with highest suicide rates are also those with the highest proportion of middle-class, moderately well-to-do inhabitants, and the poorest boroughs, Shoreditch apart, have an average, or more commonly, a less-than-average suicide rate. From the exceptions it is evident, however, that the relationship is not a simple inverse one. For example, St Pancras with a suicide rate of 28.3 has a considerable poverty and a smaller middle-class component than the other high-rate boroughs. In Lewisham and Woolwich, with suicide rates of 14.3 and 15.5, 31% and 17% of the population respectively belong to the middle class; both are boroughs which combine a relatively high social status with low indices of mobility and isolation. A lack of consistency between social status and suicide is also evident in the findings for the borough subdivisions.

If the neighbourhood status is narrowed down to the more immediate milieu of the street of the suicide's home, the over-representation of suicides in the streets of a higher social grade and their under-representation in the lower grades is striking.

Similarly, suicide was proportionately greater in the upper occupational classes than in the lower. This finding is in keeping with the findings of the Registrar-General and of allied studies undertaken in America.[19] The Registrar-General's Tables and the official statistics of other countries show a higher rate of suicide among those engaged in the professions and among owners of businesses,[20] careers in which individuality, independence and personal responsibility for one's actions, are important—conditions for Durkheim's egoistic suicide. Among the case studies on suicide, only Stearns gives figures for social status. He found that 65% of suicides were well-to-do.[21]

But when the suicide's actual economic status at the time of his death is considered, a discrepancy becomes evident. It is then found that the proportion of suicides in poverty is much increased. This implies that among the suicides were many who had lost status, either through unemployment, illness, business failure or the poverty of old age. Unexpected poverty would seem to dispose to suicide to a greater extent than does habitual poverty.

The relationship between poverty and suicide is complex. The conclusions which may reasonably be deduced from this study are that indigenous poverty does not foster suicide. On the contrary, the suicide rate tends to increase with social status. On the other hand, poverty befalling those used to a better standard of living is a burden badly tolerated, and a factor predisposing to suicide; secondary poverty of this kind would account for the rise in the suicide rate in the upper occupational classes during the economic depression—and the discrepant finding that the incidence of suicides living in poverty is greater when the suicide's actual economic level at the time of death is the criterion, rather than the economic status that might be inferred from occupation and neighbourhood.

Poverty and contentment are by no means incompatible, as both Booth and Smith stressed in their Surveys.[22] There is a shared tradition and a neighbourly and cordial atmosphere in many of London's poor districts, which is in contrast to the cool formality of South Kensington and other more prosperous areas. A further important focus of community activity and feeling in London's working-class districts is the trade-union movement. The respective suicide rates reflect this difference.

The findings support the hypothesis that increased social mobility or isolation, whether of class, occupation or neighbourhood, conduces to suicide; for suicide prevails among the social classes and occupations which demand individuality, are less subject to group control, and have a high mobility of status (i.e. opportunity for changing status). The boroughs with the highest suicide rate have a high proportion of middle-class residents engaged in commercial occupations. They also have a high spatial mobility, with a consequent decrease in neighbourliness; and it is with these features that a high incidence of suicide seems to be associated.

It is interesting to compare the class status of the mentally disordered with that of suicides. Neustatter studied the effect of poor social conditions in producing neurosis among children. He concluded that low economic status did not directly determine neurosis among the poor children of South-East London, as the incidence was higher among the well-to-do children of the north-west boroughs.[23] American observations on mental disorder and neighbourhood have established that rates are higher in the slum districts,[24] and decrease with rising social and economic status.[25] In both these studies, however, the poorest parts of the city were found to be the most mobile, which makes comparisons with London difficult.

The occupational rates for mental disorder show that persons of higher status have a lower incidence of mental illness.[26] The economic status of patients has been shown to vary with the type of psychosis. Manic-depressives are over-represented in the well-off, and the organic psychotics in the "dependent"; the number of the former is increased in periods of economic conditions.[27] It may be concluded that those mental disorders in which environmental stresses play an important part in provoking illness most resemble suicide in their relation to social status.

UNEMPLOYMENT

From the low negative correlation found between unemployment and suicide in the London boroughs it seems probable that there are social factors more important than unemployment in determining suicide rates. Nevertheless, suicide and unemployment are regularly found to increase together during economic depressions. Stearns found that the two were closely correlated in Massachusetts.[28]

In London the unemployed had a much greater suicide rate than the corresponding employed population: in about a third unemployment was a principal cause of suicide. Other findings give similar results. Lendrum gave the following figures: the proportion of attempted suicides who were unemployed was 22.6%, but the proportion of unemployment in the population of which they were a sample was 6.4%.[29] Twenty-six per cent of Hopkin's cases of attempted suicide were unemployed; but in only 6% was this considered the cause of suicide.[30] Lastly, Stearns found that 50% of suicides were unemployed, but this was never found to be the cause of the suicide.[31] Is this increased rate of suicide among the unemployed attributable to poverty or to another concomitant of unemployment?

It was calculated in the New Survey that unemployment persisting over six weeks would reduce the average family below the poverty line.[32] The majority of the unemployed in this study, therefore, would have been in poverty. But two observations suggest that poverty may be a secondary consideration: (1) the negligible increase in suicide found in the lowest social class during the 1931 depression, (2) *the case studies indicate that aimlessness and hopelessness are the cause, not poverty.*[33]

So it would appear that the unemployed experience in an exaggerated form the disturbance found in all classes at times of economic upheaval. The latter is the common factor causing both suicide and unemployment and so, in some measure, accounting for the association between them.

OVERCROWDING

No consistent relationship between overcrowding and suicide was observed. It is probable that the overcrowding indices are measuring two opposing effects: (1) that of socio-economic status, in which case overcrowding might be expected to go with a low suicide rate, (2) that of propinquity, an effect possibly allied to social disorganization, in which case overcrowding might be expected to raise the suicide rate. Only in St Pancras was overcrowding associated with a high suicide rate, and this was in the socially disorganized district adjoining the railway stations. Of the remaining four boroughs in which the degree of overcrowding in the suicide's home was examined, the suicides were under-represented in the overcrowded districts.

It is sometimes alleged that suicide is in some way dependent upon density of population[34] or city size, *per se*. What in fact this means is that city life, where overcrowding is admittedly a feature is more inclined to foster suicide than is country life.

SOCIAL ISOLATION

"Hell is a city much like London": the impassive indifference of the metropolis and its capacity to engender feelings of insignificance and loneliness among its residents is a product of two major social processes: first, the differentiation of districts given over exclusively to lodging-houses, hotels and flatlets; and secondly, the isolation produced by a high mobility which debases human relationships to a formal level and compromises all values by offering so many alternatives.

In this investigation precise indices of solitary living have been correlated with suicide rates in different districts, to test the hypothesis that social isolation is a powerful cause of suicide.

The suicide rate was highest in those boroughs that provided ample opportunity for solitary living. Not only did these include by far the greater proportion of boarding-houses, but they showed a greater incidence of people living alone or as boarders than did the rest of London.

The purely statistical finding of a high correlation between suicide rates and rates of isolated living acquired more meaning when the results of the inquiry into the mode of living of 409 suicides were examined. In five London boroughs it was shown that: (a) the proportion of the suicides living alone was significantly greater than was the proportion of persons living alone in the corresponding borough populations, (b) the rank of the boroughs with respect to numbers living alone was similar to their suicide rates, and (c) the Bloomsbury lodging-house district of St Pancras had a higher incidence of suicide than had the rest of the borough.

The relationship between suicide and solitary mode of life is probably one of cause and effect, for the individual records indicated that in 10% of cases loneliness had been regarded as a factor contributing to suicide. Allowing for the nature of the records, this is a substantial fraction. Loneliness was especially evident among the aged.

Many sociological studies have emphasized the close association between social isolation and suicide. Nevertheless, there is seldom, in case-studies reported by physicians, any reference to the suicides' mode of living. Stearns, however, found that nearly a third of suicides admitted to Massachusetts General Hospital lived in boarding-houses.[35]

Social isolation is a wider concept than living alone. It includes: the social and cultural isolation of the immigrant; the solitude of old age arising from lack of contemporaries to share values and outlook; the unemployed's sense of social rejection; the ostracism resulting from infringement of a social taboo by divorce or a criminal act, or any similar activity that might diminish relatedness to the community. A high suicide rate is found in all these categories: only the concept of social isolation embraces and accounts for such a diversity of phenomena.

SOCIAL MOBILITY AND SUICIDE

I have frequently mentioned the social effects of mobility, both spatial, i.e. movement of populations between districts, and vertical, i.e. movement between classes or occupational groups. For the study of suicide, the most important consequence is that mobility promotes social and cultural isolation. The immigrant into one of the more mobile districts of a city has to contend with alien and contradictory values which tend to undermine his accepted beliefs (and traditions); this may conduce to an attitude in which life loses purpose and significance.

The percentage of the resident's of a borough entering and leaving it daily, and the proportion born outside London, when used as measures of mobility, correlated significantly with the borough's suicide rates. A further index, such as rate of change of address in a neighbourhood, would, of course, have been preferable but was impracticable.

Among the five boroughs studied in detail, Hampstead and St Pancras had a high mobility, and both had high suicide rates. Their mobilities differ in type. In Hampstead a high proportion of the residents were born outside London, including an important foreign-born element; secondly, there is a raised class mobility, for this is a district into which the economically successful migrate: it contains more business men than any other part of London. In St Pancras there is a high transiency in the neighbourhood of the railway stations, and a big daily turn-over of population. Suicides among transients cause a substantial rise in the suicide rates in the southern divisions of the borough, though the characteristically high rate of these divisions persists if the suicide rate is based on resident population only. About 12% of *all* suicides in the five boroughs were transients: by contrast, 14% of residents committed suicide away from their homes.

The studies of the distribution of suicides in Minneapolis, and of juvenile delinquency and mental disorder in Chicago, clearly indicate a close association with mobility. The present findings suggest a similar relationship between suicide and mobility in London.

London's immigrants differ from Chicago's in that they move into the better-class neighbourhoods, which suggests that the unsettled nature of a district where immigrants congregate is more important than its economic status.

The foreign-born immigrants in Hampstead had a disproportionately high suicide rate. High suicide rates among the foreign-born have also been recorded in New York[36] and in Chicago. In the latter town the foreign populations were not found to account for the differences in suicide rates between communities.[37]

Schmid found that in a group of American cities there was a positive correlation of 0.6 between the percentage of residents of the city who were born in some other state, and the cities' suicide rates.[38] But there seem to have been no studies relating suicide to mobility comparable to those obtained for mental disorder.[39] Tietze, studying the effect of mobility on the incidence of mental disorder, found that inter-city mobility was a better indicator of the disruptive effects of mobility than was intra-city mobility.[40] This is consistent with our finding that Deptford, Poplar, Bethnal Green and Hackney combine low suicide rates with a low percentage of immigrants from both outside London and other boroughs, and a high percentage of resisidents born in the boroughs.[41]

SOCIAL DISORGANIZATION AND SUICIDE

It might be expected that if social control and integration in a neighbourhood are diminished, the conduct of its residents would lack restraint and moderation, and the incidence not only of suicide but also of illegitimacy, divorce and crime would be increased.

As regards the distribution of divorce and illegitimacy in London this expectation was realized; they are both more prevalent in the socially mobile boroughs, and show significant correlations with suicide. These findings are similar to those described in Chicago.[42] Mowrer records a correlation of 0.89 between the community rates for suicide and divorce during 1929–35.

The fact that the divorced have a high suicide rate does not explain the association, as the number of divorced in any borough is too small to alter the rates appreciably. On the other hand, a careful inspection of many case studies in which the cause of suicide was given revealed that an illegitimate pregnancy was seldom mentioned as a reason for suicide. The present study included only two such instances. Divorce and illegitimacy cannot, then, be said to cause high suicide rates in a district; all that is apparent is that suicide, divorce and illegitimacy tend to increase together in areas with certain social characteristics. Thus the rates for all three are high in the West End, where, for instance, night-life, intemperance, and what might be called meretricious values exist. The findings are different in the working-class and the middle-class boroughs of South-East London where the informal community may reduce the incidence of suicide, divorce and illegitimacy. I calculated from the

Registrar-General's occupational tables a significant correlation ($\tau = 0.44$) between borough suicide rates and proportion of population professionally engaged in amusements—an occupational class closely associated with those aspects of city life which may connote social instability.

The lack of correlation between juvenile delinquency and suicide was unexpected; Shaw's work in Chicago made it seem probable that juvenile delinquency and social disorganization might also be found together in London. Burt in London and Shaw in Chicago had shown that poverty areas and delinquency areas were closely associated; but it has already been mentioned, when contrasting the social structures of London and Chicago, that areas of poverty and social disorganization are separated in the former, but coincide in the latter. Therefore, in Chicago, areas with high rates for suicide, delinquency, poverty and social disorganization are found together; in London, juvenile delinquency and poverty are associated, but not suicide which is highest in the disorganized areas.

The conclusion which it seems reasonable to draw from these facts is that economic factors may be of relatively greater importance in determining juvenile delinquency than is social disorganization; for if the two factors are separately correlated with juvenile delinquency, only the former shows a significant association.

The position as regards adult crime may well be different, because in this study it was found that streets described in the New Survey as criminal and degraded contributed four times their expected number of suicides. Mowrer found that in Chicago the community rates for suicide and juvenile delinquency correlated to the extent of 0.14, but that suicide and arrests had a correlation of 0.71. This suggests that crime may be more closely allied to social disorganization.[43]

NOTES

1 J. Summerson, *Georgian London*, London, 1945, 1st. ed., p. 7.

2 M. D. George, *London Life in the XVIIIth Century*, London, 1925, 1st ed., pp. 65–8.

3 J. H. Forshaw and P. Abercrombie, *County of London Plan*, London, 1943, 1st ed., pp. 21–9, 160–6.

4 R. E. Dickinson, *City Region and Regionalism*, London, 1947, 1st ed., pp. 128–58.

5 H. L. Smith, Ibid., 1934 d, pp. 262–5.

6 F. Winslow, *The Anatomy of Suicide*, London, 1840, 1st ed., p. 343.

7 H. L. Smith, Ibid, 1932 d, pp. 343–88; Ibid., 1934 b, pp. 379–450.

8 R.G. Ibid., 1935 e, p. 27.

9 E. R. Mowrer, *Disorganisation Personal and Social*, Philadelphia, 1942 a, 1st ed., pp. 347–50.

R. S. Cavan, *Suicide*, Chicago, 1928 a, 1st ed., pp. 77–105.

10 C. F. Schmid, *American Journal of Sociology*, 1933, 39, p. 30.
11 H. W. Gruhle, *Nervenarzt*, 1940, 13, p. 337.
12 R.G., *Statistical Review of England and Wales for the year 1935*, Text, H.M.S.O. London, 1938 a, p. 139.
13 R. E. L. Faris, Ibid., 1944 b, p. 738.
   H. L. Gruhle, *Nervenarzt*, 1940, 13, p. 337.
14 C. Booth, Ibid., 1889 c, p. 511. Ibid., 1889 d, pp. 524–30.
15 H. W. Gruhle, *Nervenarzt*, 1940, 13, p. 337.
16 C. Booth, Ibid., 1889 c, p. 511.
17 C. C. Peters, *American Journal of Sociology*, 1933, 39, p. 231.
18 H. W. Zorbaugh, *The Gold Coast and the Slum, a Sociological Study of Chicago's Near North Side*, Chicago, 1929, 1st ed., pp. 69–86.
19 R.G., *Decennial Supplement, England and Wales 1931*, Part IIa, H.M.S.O., London, 1938 d, p. 70.
   L. I. Dublin and B. C. Bunzel, Ibid., 1933 e, p. 402.
20 R.G., Ibid., 1938 e, pp. 76, 161.
   J. R. Miner, Ibid., 1922 d, pp. 47–54.
21 A. W. Stearns, *Mental Hygiene Concord*, 1921, 5, p. 752.
22 C. Booth, Ibid., 1889 a, pp. 524–30.
   H. L. Smith, *The New Survey London Life and Labour*, London, 1932 a, 1st ed., Vol. III, p. 98.
23 W. L. Neustatter, *Lancet*, 1938, 234, Part I, p. 1436.
24 R. E. L. Faris and H. W. Dunham, Ibid., 1939 d, pp. 54–6.
25 R. W. Hyde and L. V. Kingsley, *New England Journal of Medicine*, 1944 a, 231, p 542.
26 R. E. Clark, *Bulletin of the Society for Social Research*, Dec., 1939, p. 8, quoted by E. R. Mowrer, *Disorganisation Personal and Social*, Philadelphia, 1942, 1st ed., p. 383.
27 N. A. Dayton, Ibid., 1940 b, pp. 367–72.
   R. E. L. Faris and H. W. Dunham, Ibid., 1939 e, p. 243.
   B. Malzberg, *Social and Biological Aspects of Mental Disease*, New York, 1940, 1st ed., pp. 278–85.
28 A. W. Stearns, *Mental Hygiene Concord*, 1921, 5, p. 752.
29 F. C. Lendrum, *American Journal of Psychiatry*, 1933, 90, p. 479.
30 F. Hopkins, *Journal of Mental Science*, 1937, 83, p. 71.
31 A. W. Stearns, *Mental Hygiene Concord*, 1921, 5, p. 752.
32 H. L. Smith, Ibid. 1932 e, p. 158.
33 H. L. Smith, Ibid., 1932 i, pp. 177–81.
34 H. W. Gruhle, *Nervenarzt*, 1940, 13, p. 337.
35 A. W. Stearns, *Mental Hygiene Concord*, 1921, 5, p. 752.
36 J. R. Miner, *American Journal of Hygiene*, 1922 a, Monograph No. 2, p. 16.
37 R. S. Cavan, *Suicide*, Chicago, 1928 a, 1st ed., pp. 77–105.
38 C. F. Schmid, *American Journal of Sociology*, 1933, 39, p. 30.
39 R. E. L. Faris and H. W. Dunham, Ibid., 1939 b, p. 100
   S. A. Queen, *American Sociological Review*, 1940, 5, p. 201.
   C. W. Schroeder, *American Journal of Sociology*, 1942, 48, p. 40.
40 C. Tietze, P. Lemeau and M. Cooper, *American Journal of Sociology*, 1942, 48, p. 29.
41 H. L. Smith, Ibid., 1934 d, pp. 262–5.
42 E. R. Mowrer, Ibid., 1942 d, p. 663.
   R. S. Cavan, *Suicide*, Chicago, 1928 a, 1st ed., pp. 77–105.
43 E. R. Mowrer, Ibid., 1942 d, p. 663.

CHAPTER 20

Community Growth, Depressive Disorders, and Suicide*

Henry Wechsler

To date, ecological studies of mental illness have been concerned primarily with the relation of social conditions to the incidence of schizophrenia. Despite the lack of total agreement about the meaning of the findings,[1] higher rates of schizophrenia have been found in lower socioeconomic neighbourhoods and in the central high mobility areas of cities.[2] Many of these studies have failed to associate depressive disorders with the same social factors as schizophrenia Faris and Dunham, noting the total absence of any pattern in the distribution of manic-depressive cases in the Chicago study, offer the explanation that these psychoses are caused by certain precipitating factors which "occur in all social and economic levels of life and consequently are not so likely to have a definite connection with the community situation but rather with the interplay of personality and psychological factors of family relationships and intimate personal contacts. Such a theory tends to connect the manic-depressive disorder with extremely intimate, and intense social contacts."[3]

More recently, Hare[4] obtained similar findings in England. Other studies have consistently noted the distribution of depressive disorders among higher socioeconomic strata than is the case with schizophrenia.[5] Commenting on these differences, Arieti suggests that manic-depressive psychosis is connected with "a structured, well-organized ... milieu, removed from the disorganization or relative looseness of organization that we find ... in low economic or socially unstable elements of the population".[6]

Faris and Dunham and Arieti appear to base their explanations on the generally accepted assumption that depression is related to an ambivalent dependent relationship which has been severed or is threatened with termination. Individuals who become accustomed to and require constant supplies of self-esteem from their social en-

* Reprinted by permission of the University of Chicago Press from the *American Journal of Sociology*, Vol. 67, 1961, pp. 9–17.

vironments would become subject to depressive disorders when the source of the supplies is viewed as threatened.[7]

Such an etiological conception of depression was viewed as leading to the following hypothesis about the ecological distribution of depressive disorders in the community: Stable communities, where close, intimate interpersonal relations foster dependency, will exhibit high rates of depression when rapid change alters or threatens to alter their social organization. When a small community is undergoing rapid growth in population, the pattern of close interpersonal bonds is threatened. Rapidly growing suburban communities, therefore, would be expected to have disproportionately high rates of depression. In addition, the disorganization associated with the sudden growth should also be related to high rates of suicide.

A recent study by Gordon and Gordon[8] tends to support this hypothesis. In investigating in four large Middle Atlantic counties, they found the highest rates in the rapidly growing suburban county, particularly among women of childbearing age. Although the study dealt with emotional disorders in general, and not specifically with depression, it is particularly suggestive, since depressive disorders are usually prominent among women of this age group. The major defect in the study is the use of such large geographical units as counties and the assumption that four counties differ only in respect to growth and the rural-urban-suburban dimension. Gordon and Gordon interpret their results to mean that persons in a mobile suburban area are particularly susceptible to emotional disorders because of their upwardly mobile orientation and unrealistic striving for pseudo-independence. In another study,[9] they found high proportions of geographically, economically, and culturally mobile individuals among private-office patients of psychiatrists.

The present study concerns fifty Massachusetts communities, located within a radius of twenty-five miles from Boston and served by three state mental hospitals. Data were available from the state hospital records and from Massachusetts and United States population statistics.

COMMUNITY GROWTH

The community's growth was computed on the basis of per cent change between 1950 and 1960 United States census populations[10] and the communities were rank-ordered and pooled into quartiles on the basis of it. Fourteen communities were placed in the fastest growing quartile, with twelve in each of the other groups. The fastest growing Quartile (I) had a pooled 104% increase between the 1950

COMMUNITY GROWTH AND SUICIDE 261

and 1960 populations; Quartile II, a 52% increase; Quartile III, a 19% increase; and the lowest Quartile (IV), a 4% decrease. As might be expected, in addition to varying in rates of growth, the quartiles also differed as to actual population. The group of greatest growth was the smallest, since a community that doubles itself within ten years must have been small initially. Each successive quartile was approximately double the preceding one in size of population.

HOSPITALIZED MENTAL ILLNESS

Records of three state mental hospitals were studied for the fiscal year 1957–8. Information was gathered as to the residences, ages, sexes, and diagnoses of all patients admitted to the acute treatment services during that period, multiple admissions during the year being counted only once. A total of 1,800 individuals were admitted to the three hospitals and information was available on all but forty-seven. Since the hospitals legally serve fifty communities, only persons with last residences in them were studied. One hundred and eighty patients (10% of the total sample) resided outside these fifty communities and were eliminated from the study, leaving a total sample of 1,573 patients. Patients were divided into three age groups: 16–34; 35–49; and 50 and over, and they were classified into four diagnostic categories on the basis of the final hospital diagnoses: depression (including manic-depressive, involutional, psychotic and psychoneurotic depressive disorders), alcoholism, schizophrenia, and other psychopathology.

SUICIDE

Reported cases of suicide in the fifty communities for 1957 and 1958 were obtained from available state vital statistics.[11]

INCIDENCE RATES

Incidence rates for hospitalized mental illness and suicide were based on 1955 populations, specific as to sex and age,[12] since detailed 1960 figures were as yet not available. In all these rates, a correction was made to eliminate residents under sixteen years of age, since the mental hospitals do not admit them.

A. Hospitalized Mental Illness

Distribution of patients by community growth, diagnoses, and ages.—Table 1, which presents the distribution of populations and patients within the four growth groups by age, indicates that there is

TABLE 1

Distribution of Populations and Patients by Growth Quartiles, Diagnostic Categories, and Age

	I		II		III		IV		Total
	No.	Per Cent	No.	Per Cent	No.	Per Cent	No.	Per Cent	
Population:									
Ages 16–34	21,417	7	48,945	15	82,108	25	169,790	53	322,260
35–49	16,716	6	40,383	15	71,690	27	132,926	51	261,715
50 and over	16,249	5	41,785	13	90,796	27	181,781	55	330,611
Total	54,382	6	131,113	14	244,594	27	484,497	53	914,586
No. Depressed:									
Ages 16–34	3	9	7	21	12	36	11	33	33
35–49	13	20	14	22	15	23	22	34	64
50 and over	7	5	22	16	43	31	67	48	139
Total	23	10	43	18	70	30	100	42	236

No. Alcoholics:									
Ages 16–34	6	12	8	16	12	24	24	48	50
35–49	7	5	18	12	45	29	85	55	155
50 and over	9	7	28	21	33	25	63	47	133
Total	22	7	54	16	90	27	172	51	338
No. Schizophrenics:									
Ages 16–34	12	6	29	15	48	25	102	53	191
35–49	12	7	25	14	47	27	91	52	175
50 and over	2	2	13	14	23	25	53	58	91
Total	26	7	67	15	118	26	246	54	457
No. Other:									
Ages 16–34	8	5	23	15	38	25	81	54	150
35–49	4	5	8	9	24	28	49	58	85
50 and over	12	4	41	13	94	31	160	52	307
Total	24	4	72	13	156	29	290	54	542
Total:									
Ages 16–34	29	7	67	16	110	26	218	51	424
35–49	36	8	65	14	131	27	247	52	479
50 and over	30	5	104	16	193	29	343	51	670
Total	95	6	236	15	434	28	808	51	1,573

a higher concentration of depressed patients, particularly in the 35–49 age group, in the faster-growing quartiles than would be expected on the basis of population distributions. The pattern of distribution of alcoholic patients, although fluctuating somewhat within the different age groups, appears to be very similar to the distribution of general populations. The number of schizophrenic patients in the four growth groups is almost identical with the distribution of populations. The distribution of other psychiatric patients tends to be slightly more highly concentrated in the slower-growing quartiles than general populations would warrant.

A chi-square analysis of the distribution of patients by diagnostic category and quartiles of community growth indicates statistically significant results only in the case of depression (Tables 2 and 3).

TABLE 2

Chi Square: Depressed and Non-depressed Patients
by Community Growth

Quartile Growth	No. Depressed	No. Non depressed	Total
I	23	72	95
II	43	193	236
III	70	364	434
IV	100	708	808
Total	236	1,337	1,573
		$X^2 3\ df = 13.05$	$P = .01$

TABLE 3

Chi Square: Depressed and Non-Depressed Patients Ages
35–49 by Community Growth

Quartile Growth	No. Depressed	No. Non depressed	Total
I	13	23	36
II	14	51	65
III	15	116	131
IV	22	225	247
Total	64	415	479
		$X^2 3\ df = 22.28$	$P = .001$

Here the proportion of depressed patients of the total number of patients from each growth quartile is positively associated with growth at the .01 level. In the case of patients between the ages of thirty-five and forty-nine, the result is significant at the .001 level.

Rates per 100,000 of hospitalized mental illness and community growth.—When the numbers of patients within each diagnostic category for the four growth groups are converted into rates per 100,000, an even more striking difference emerges. Table 4 indicates that only

TABLE 4

Rates per 100,000 of Hospitalized Mental Illness
by Community Growth Quartiles

	I	II	III	VI	Total
Depressed	42.3	32.8	28.6	20.6	25.8
Alcoholics	40.4	41.2	36.8	35.5	37.0
Schizophrenia	47.8	51.1	48.2	50.8	50.0
Other	44.1	54.9	63.8	59.9	59.3
Total	174.7	180.0	177.4	166.8	172.0

TABLE 5

Age and Sex Specific Rates per 100,000 Hospitalized Depression by Community Growth Quartiles

	I			II			III			IV			*Total*		
	Male	Fe-male	Total	Male	Fe-male	Total	Male	Fe-male	Total	Male	Fe-male	Total	Male	Fe-male	Total
All ages	32.8	51.9	42.3	22.4	42.3	32.8	12.4	42.6	28.6	10.7	29.3	20.6	14.3	36.0	25.8
Ages 16–34	18.4	9.5	14.0	8.5	19.8	14.3	7.5	21.3	14.6	2.4	10.4	6.5	5.7	14.6	10.2
Ages 35–49	11.7	147.4	77.8	25.3	43.6	34.7	6.0	33.8	20.9	8.3	23.5	16.6	10.7	36.5	24.5
Ages 50 and over	72.3	12.1	43.1	36.6	66.2	52.7	22.4	67.1	47.4	20.9	49.8	36.9	26.3	54.9	42.0

in the case of depression is there a progressive decrease in incidence rates as the community declines in rate of growth. The rate changes from 42.3 in the fastest-growing quartile to 20.6 per 100,000 in the slowest. In the case of the other diagnostic categories, no such proportionately large differences may be seen. In alcoholism there is a very slight change; in schizophrenia, almost no change; and in other psychopathology, a change in the opposite direction.

Table 5 permits a closer inspection of rates of depression by age and sex. Here it may again be seen that the strongest relationship between growth of population and depression occurs in the 35–49 age group, and particularly in women. Quartile I has a 77.8 rate per 100,000 for both sexes, while Quartile IV has a rate of only 16.6. In women, Quartile I has a rate of 147.4, while for Quartile IV, it is 23.5.

Correlation of rates of hospitalized mental illness per 100,000 and per cent of community growth.—Thus far, the statistical analysis has dealt only with pooled quartiles and not the individual communities. When correlation coefficients were computed between percentage of growth of community and incidence of the different diagnostic categories in the fifty communities, the following results were obtained: growth and depression $r = .23$; growth and alcoholism $r = .12$; growth and schizophrenia $r = -.10$; growth and other illness $r = -.11$; growth total illness $r = .05$. None of these correlations were significant at the .05 level. However, in the case of growth and depression, the relationship was significant at the .10 level.

When the relationship of the community's growth and incidence of depression among persons aged from 35 to 49 was analysed, a correlation coefficient of .42 was obtained. This relationship was significant at beyond the .01 level.

Leading category of patients from a community and community growth.— When the fifty communities were analysed to find whether depression is the leading category of illness in each, it was found that in communities with great growth: depression was more often the major diagnostic category than in communities with less growth: in 48% of the communities above the median growth, depression was the leading category of mental illness, while it was the leading category in only 16% of those below the median. A chi square of 4.50 indicated that this relationship was significant at the .05 level.[13]

B. Incidence of Suicides and Community Growth

The number of suicides for the communities in each growth quartile was computed for the years 1957 and 1958. Incidence rates per 100,000 (Table 6) reveal that for both years the fastest-growing quartile has a rate almost three times as high as the slowest-growing one; thus, apparently, the distribution of suicides by growth of community is similar to the distribution of hospitalized depression.

All the results appear to indicate that the frequency of hospitalized depression and suicide is positively associated with a community's growth. A number of methodological points, however, may be raised concerning the data.

1. The use of hospital diagnoses may be questionable. However, the three hospitals here used are in the same state system, and all employ the American Psychiatric Association's diagnostic categories.

Furthermore, the hospitals are currently co-operating in a large research project on depression, and indications are that there is a substantial amount of agreement as to diagnoses. There is no reason to suspect that diagnoses of mental illness are differentially made of patients on the basis of the rates of growth of their home communities.

TABLE 6

Incidence Rates of Reported Suicides
by Community Growth Quartiles

	I	II	III	IV
Population	54,382	131,113	245,843	483,248
No. suicides, 1957	11	15	29	33
Incidence per 100,000, 1957	20.2	11.4	11.8	6.8
No. suicides, 1958	14	17	24	43
Incidence per 100,000, 1958	25.7	13.0	9.8	8.9

2. The study does not cover the incidence of mental illness, or even of all hospitalized mental illness. Patients from the fifty communities may go to other public or private hospitals, but for hospitalized cases of mental illness there is a limited number of other hospitals to which they may be sent. The admissions to the largest private psychiatric hospital in the area and to the local Veterans Administration Hospital include a very small number of patients from these fifty communities admitted in the same fiscal year. The acute treatment psychiatric wards of several general hospitals may have more patients from these communities. However, in view of the lack of geographical patterns of community growth, there is no reason to suspect that these facilities are more easily accessible to residents of fast-growing communities than to others.

3. Incidence rates were computed on the basis of 1955 age-corrected populations, These figures may consistently overestimate cases from fast-growing communities. Two counterarguments may serve to limit this possible source of error. First of all, incidences for several diagnostic categories were employed, which should have raised rates for all diagnostic categories in the faster-growth quartiles. This did not occur. Second, a number of statistical tests were employed which did not depend on the size of the growth quartiles but only on the distribution of psychiatric patients. The potential over-estimation of incidence rates in the rapidly growing communities is a greater danger in the case of suicides. Here, however, even if

1960 population bases are used to compute the rates, the faster-growing communities would still have rates twice as high as the others.

Although the findings have pointed out an apparently stable relationship between depression, suicide, and growth of community, questions may be raised about the interpretation of the results.

(a) The fastest-growing communities also happen to be the small towns. Are higher rates of depression and suicide related to small populations, to high rates of growth, or to both? Unfortunately, the sample of fifty communities does not permit large enough statistical cells to arrive at a definite conclusion.[14] It is suspected, however, that both size and growth may have influence.

TABLE 7

Community Growth and Social Class

Community Growth Quartiles	Social Class Quartiles								
	I	(Per cent)	II	(Per cent)	III	(Per cent)	IV	(Per cent)	Unknown
I	3	27	4	40	3	25	1	10	3
II	2	18	4	40	1	8	2	20	3
III	3	27	2	20	3	25	3	30	1
IV	3	27	0	—	5	42	4	40	0
Total	11	99	10	100	12	100	10	100	7

(b) Are there alternative explanations? Geographical patterning of the growth quartiles is absent and may be eliminated. The only other factor that was investigated was social class,[15] which was found not to be significantly associated with growth. Table 7 indicates that the communities of the highest social class were randomly distributed among the four growth groups. There is some tendency, however, for the slowest-growing communities to be also the lowest socioeconomically. An analysis of the relationship of social class to incidence of mental illness[16] reveals significant negative correlations between all categories of mental illness except depression. This would indicate that growth is not related to incidence of depression through social class.

PROBLEM OF INTERPRETATION

The hypothesis which led to the finding of a significantly higher distribution of depression and suicides in rapidly growing communities was based on the assumption that the depressive disorders were a function of the social disorganization of stable intimate communities. However, another explanation, analogous to the drift hypothesis in the ecology of schizophrenia, may account for the findings: that there may be a selective migration of depression-prone individuals to the rapidly growing suburban areas. Several papers have reported that individuals moving to the suburbs may be characterized by a high degree of homogeneity in terms of "background experiences, stage in the family cycle, and occupational roles"[17] as well as in predisposition to "neighbouring".[18] Highly mobile persons desiring close contacts in the community may be particularly depression-prone at the time of the disruptive experience of moving to a new area.

The unresolved question which could differentiate between the explanation of causal and of the selective migration is: Who becomes hospitalized for depression in the fast-growing communities—the original residents affected by the change in the nature of their community or the depression-prone newcomers? The present study was not set up to differentiate between these hypotheses. However, to accept the theory of selective migration, one would have to assume that newcomers to the fastest-growing suburbs are more depression-prone than newcomers to the slower-growing suburbs. At any event, a future study has been planned to investigate the patterns of movement and length of stay of the depressed patients from fast-growing communities.

Despite the lack of a single explanation of the findings, the phenomenon which has been revealed has important consequences for the ecology of mental illness. If growing suburban communities are producing higher rates of depression and suicide, the current decentralization of urban areas and the growth of the suburbs should cause this trend to continue for at least some time. The depressive disorders, which have lately been reported to have decreased in proportion to other psychiatric illnesses, may once again become a prominent category of mental illness. As a consequence, it is suggested that social scientists in the field of mental health should attempt to study the currently neglected field of depression, and some of the numerous research efforts in the area of schizophrenia should be diverted to that end.

NOTES

1 For a discussion of the alternative causal and "drift" interpretations in the ecology of schizophrenia see Rema LaPouse, Mary Monk, and Milton Terris, 'The Drift Hypothesis and Socio-economic Differentials in Schizophrenia', *American Journal of Public Health*, XLVI, 1956, 978–86.

2 For a review of these findings see Paul K. Benedict 'Socio-cultural Factors in Schizophrenia,' in Leopold Bellak (ed.), *Schizophrenia*, New York: Logos Press, 1958, chap. xvii. Also, e.g. see Robert Faris and H. Warren Dunham, *Mental Disorders in Urban Areas*, Chicago: University of Chicago Press, 1939; and E. H. Hare, 'Mental Illness and Social Conditions in Bristol', *Journal of Mental Science*, CII, 1956, 349–57; see also Hare, 'Family Setting and the Urban Distribution of Schizophrenia', ibid., pp. 753–60.

3 Faris and Dunham, op. cit., pp. 172–3.

4 'Mental Illness and Social Conditions in Bristol', op. cit.

5 See Benedict, op. cit., pp. 719–29.

6 Silvano Arieti, 'Manic-Depressive Psychosis', in Silvano Arieti (ed.), *American Handbook of Psychiatry*, I, New York: Basic Books, Inc., 1959, 443.

7 For theoretical statements about the etiology of depression see Arieti, op. cit., chap. xxii, and O. Fenichel, *The Psychoanalytic Theory of Neurosis*, New York: W. W. Norton Co., 1945, chap. xvii.

8 Richard E. Gordon and Katherine K. Gordon, 'Social Psychiatry of a Mobile Suburb', *International Journal of Social Psychiatry*, VI, Summer, 1960, 89–106.

9 Richard E. Gordon and Katherine K. Gordon, 'Psychiatric Problems of a Rapidly Growing Suburb', *Archives of Neurology and Psychiatry*, LXXIX, 1958, 543–8.

10 *1960 Census of Population, Advance Reports, Final Population Counts*, Pc(A1)-23, Washington D.C.: U.S. Department of Commerce, Bureau of the Census.

11 *Annual Report of the Vital Statistics of Massachusetts*, Public Document No. 1, Commonwealth of Massachusetts, Office of the Secretary, Division of Vital Statistics, 1957 and 1958.

12 *The Decennial Census*, Commonwealth of Massachusetts, Secretary of the Commonwealth, 1955, Table 16.

13 This analysis was based on whether depression, alcoholism, or schizophrenia was the leading category of patients in a community. In the case of ties between depression and one or more diagnostic categories, credit was given to depression.

14 Only one of the communities in the slowest-growing quartile had a population of less than 10,000. The fastest-growing quartile had 5 communities with more than 10,000 persons and 9 with fewer than 10,000, according to the 1960 census. When these two groups within Quartile I were compared as to proportion of depressed patients of all patients, a slight tendency appeared for the *smaller* towns of rapid growth to have a higher proportion of depressed patients than the *larger*. However, this trend was not significant at the .05 level (x^2 1 $df = 1.90$).

15 Social class was computed for each community by rank-ordering per cent in managerial, professional, and white-collar occupations and applying the weighted Hollingshead two-factor index of social class.

16 These findings are currenly being prepared for publication in a separate paper.

17 Walter T. Martin, 'The Structuring of Social Relationships Engendered by Suburban Residence,' *American Sociological Review*, XXI, 1956, 446–53.

18 Sylvia F. Fava, 'Suburbanism as a Way of Life,' *American Sociological Review*, XXI, 1956, 34–7.

CHAPTER 21

The Economic Cycle and the Social Suicide Rate*

Albert Pierce

A proposition of central importance to Durkheim's analysis of fluctuations and difference in the social suicide rate may be paraphrased as follows: [1]

> The social suicide rate varies directly as anomie and inversely as social cohesion. [2]

The truth or falsity of that statement has implications not only for the validity of Durkheim's monograph but for the whole question of what methodological foundations should properly undergird sociological theory. Such a broad formulation does not, of course, lend itself to direct confirmation but is, rather, a generalization of a variety of compatible propositions of lesser scope and greater tractability. These latter were not only well supported by the evidence that Durkheim adduced but they have been confirmed rather consistently by the data that has accumulated since that time. Suicide rates are higher among the divorced and widowed than among married persons, in areas with transient populations as opposed to those with an established communal life, among dominant majorities as compared with suppressed minorities, in peacetime as opposed to wartime, etc. [3] Unfortunately, however, there has been one major sector in which subsequent investigation not only has failed to confirm the general hypothesis but directly contradicts it. This is the sector that relates the economic cycle to the social suicide rate. Ironically, it was precisely in this context that the critically important concept of *anomie* received its fullest explication. The following passages in which Durkheim formulates the relationship are all from his chapter entitled "Anomic Suicide". [4]

> It is a well known fact that economic crises have an aggravating effect on the suicidal tendency. (241) ... But to what do these crises owe their influence? Is it because they increase poverty causing public wealth to fluctuate? Is life more readily renounced because it becomes more difficult? The explanation is

* Reprinted by permission of the American Sociological Association from the *American Sociological Review*, Vol. 32, 1967, pp. 457–62.

seductively simple; and it agrees with the popular idea of suicide. But it is contradicted by the facts. (242) ... So far is the increase in poverty from causing the increase in suicide that even fortunate crises, the effect of which is abruptly to enhance a country's prosperity, affect suicide like economic disasters. (243) ...

If therefore, industrial or financial crises increase suicides, this is not because they cause poverty, since crises of prosperity have the same result ; it is becaue they are crises ;[5] that is, disturbances of the collective order ... Whenever serious readjustments take place in the social order, whether or not due to sudden growth or an unexpected catastrophe, men are more inclined to self-destruction. (247).

Characteristically, Durkheim's view runs counter to the "common sense" notion that the high levels of "prosperity" should show low suicide rates and that economic depressions should show high ones. This latter hypothesis might be tested appropriately by correlating indices of eonomic levels with suicide rates. Indeed, this has been done by Henry and Short.[6] Durkheim is maintaining, however, that the factor elevating suicide rates is the relative state of disorganization induced by rapid economic *change* and that those rates are tempered by economic stability—regardless of the *level*s of economic activity. Even more striking is his claim that the *direction* of the change is of no consequence.

A test of Durkheim's hypothesis requires an investigation of the relationship between some measure of economic change and suicide rates. Henry and Short were well aware of this but evidently found that the correlation coefficients of the levels were so clearly more significant as to command a priority of interest. They, in fact, undertook to demonstrate by a straightforward counting of cases that "suicide increased only during those years when the rise in the business index was very slight but not during those years of 'abrupt growth of power and wealth' ".[7]

Warren Breed drew the logical conclusion from existing evidence. He stated :

> [Durkheim's] belief that "anomic" rates rise during prosperity as well as depression has been found incorrect by Henry and Short who also showed more clearly than Durkheim that economic depression is accompanied by higher rates, mostly among higher income groups.[8]

Henry and Short's investigations occurred prior to 1954 when their findings were first published. At that time certain important advances in the analysis of time series had not become very widely disseminated. Although theoretical statisticians had for some time been concerned with the phenomenon known as "autocorrelated perturbances", it was not until the appearance in 1951 and 1952 of a series of two-articles co-authored by the English statisticians J. Durbin and G. S. Watson that the substantive researcher had any feasible way to do much more about it than hope its effects on his data were negligible.[9] The important contribution of these authors was to provide a measure of the degree of autocorrelation of "error terms" in what has since become known as the Durbin-Watson d-statistic.[10]

The variables in regression and correlation models are, of course, implicitly related by specific mathematical functions—for example, they may be linear, exponential, logarithmic, quadratic, etc. However, for these models to be valid for time series, the so-called "error terms", which are the deviations of the observed values from those estimated from the function, must be stochastically independent. That is, the probability of occurrence of the value of any error term should be unaffected by the values of the temporally prior error terms. The absence of such independence implies that conditions exogenous to the model have a determinate effect on the observed values, and that the function does not therefore represent, the true relationship between the independent and dependent variables. In other words, owing to the influence of exogenous factors, the time of occurrence of the observation might be a better predictor of its value than the independent variable is. The d-statistic measures the tendency of time-adjacent values of the error terms to covary. An acceptable value of d permits one to accept the hypothesis that the error terms are randomly distributed about the regression function in the time dimension. Durbin and Watson have provided tables of critical values of d for various degrees of freedom.[11] A value of d in the unacceptable range indicates a condition of dependence in the values of the error terms which, in turn, tends to produce a speciously high correlation coefficient. The validity of the various ancillary tests —t-tests, F-tests, z-tests, confidence intervals, etc.—also becomes suspect. Moreover, it is not realistic to take refuge in the statement "assuming that autocorrelation is not present in serious amounts". It is well known among investigators with relevant experience—econometricians, for instance—that empirical time series for which this would be a valid assumption are extremely rare.[12]

It was not the objective of the present investigation to assess the validity of the Henry and Short study *per se*. Those writers did, however, rely primarily on Ayres Index of Industrial Activity as their economic measure. The segment of relevance to the present investigation proved to be severely deficient by the Durbin-Watson criterion. Moreover, the Ayres Index is a trend-adjusted series and there are a priori reasons to expect it to show poorly on that account.

The present study was intended specifically to test Durkheim's hypothesis that the social suicide rate tends to vary directly as the rate of change of the economic cycle and independently of the direction of that change.

Because the investigation sought to test a specific proposition rather than merely to hunt for factors that would show an acceptable correlation coefficient, it concentrated largely on highly circumscribed categories of data. Since concordantly with Durkheim's hypothesis a state of war would decisively overshadow the effects of economic factors, only data for peacetime years was used. Henry and Short also followed this practice. The data accumulated since *Le Suicide's* publication leave little doubt of an over-riding effect of war conditions in lowering the suicide rate. For this reason, the data used were generally those for the years 1919–40 for the United States. After the Second World War, the outbreak of the Korean War the incessant "cold war", the long sustained policy of "brinkmanship", and finally the outbreak of the war in Viet Nam so badly muddy the problem of defining peace that the data for that period have not been used. Age-standardized race-sex-specific data on suicides for the U.S. were not reported until 1914, and by 1915 Germany had committed belligerent acts against the United States. Moreover, most of the economic series investigated do not commence until 1919. Discontinuous series simply omitting the war years do not lend themselves to lead-lag analysis in which relative shifts in time series are investigated. Everything considered, 1919 seemed the logical starting point and even that may be a little early considering the persistence of war feelings for several years after World War 1.

Age-standardized suicide rates for U.S. white males were used exclusively for the intensive analyses. Hence, there existed excellent control over the factors of age, sex, race, and nationality as well as the war-peace factor. The Durbin-Watson test provided insurance against the acceptance of specious results due to unknown factors.

Most of the effort of the investigation went into the analysis of a variety of economic indices which, when correlated with the suicide rates, would hopefully yield valid results. It was apparent from the outset that any positive test of the hypothesis would have to correlate the absolute values of the first differences of the economic index with the annual suicide rates. The "first differences" are, in fact, the annual slopes and hence the average rates of change between adjacent successive years. The absolute rather than the signed (+ or −) values of these are required by the hypothesis, which postulates, as the significant factor. In all cases, the levels also were tested as a matter of rudimentary precaution. In general, the levels

TABLE 1

Correlation Coefficients and Supplementary Test Statistics for Relationship of Economic Indices to Age-Standardized White Male Suicide Rates: United States, 1919–1940

Independent variable	Type of correlation	Correlation with O lead	Optimum lead	Correlation at optimum lead	Probability under H_o		Best d-value	
					O lead	Optimum lead	Required	Observed
Ayres index	Linear	−0.6710	−3	−0.7261	<0.001	<0.001	1.40	0.84
Relative income*	Linear	0.7724	0	..	<0.001	..	1.43	0.40
Relative income*	Exponential	0.7949	0	..	<0.001	..	1.43	0.69
Relative income*	5° polynomial	0.6697	0	..	NS	..	1.94	0.98
Percent of labour force unemployed	Exponential	0.6747	−3	0.8195	<0.001	<0.001	1.40	1.01
Construction of new dwelling units	Linear	−0.5077	−3	−0.8153	<0.02	<0.001	1.40	0.88
Construction of new dwelling units	Exponential	−0.4711	−3	−0.8208	<0.05	<0.001	1.40	1.00
Five independent variables	Multiple linear	0.8595	−2	0.8656	<0.01	<0.01	1.94	1.11

* With linear trend removed.

NOTE:

The independent variables included in this table are all levels rather than first differences, with one exception to be noted below. The results obtained from first differences were entirely uninteresting. Sources are as follows:

Suicide Rates: Vital Statistics Special Reports, Vol. 43, No. 30, Aug. 22, 1956, *Suicide*. U.S. Dept. of Health, Recreation, and Welfare, Table 1, p. 467.

Ayres Index (of industrial activity): *Economic Almanac, 1964*. National Industrial Conference Board, p. 164.

All other data are from: U.S. Bureau of the Census, *Historical Statistics of the United States; Colonial Times to 1957*. Washington, D.C., 1960: "relative income" (percent shares of total income received by top 5 percent of total population), Series G 134, p. 167; percent of (civilian) labour force unemployed, Series D 47, p. 73; construction of new dwelling units, Series N 106, p. 393.

The "five independent variables" include: relative income (unadjusted), percent of labour force unemployed, and construction of new dwelling units, all as above. The two additional variables are: first differences of percent unemployed (from same source), and deviations from 5th degree polynomial trend calculated from "gallons of motor fuel used on highways," Series Q 319, p. 462.

showed correlations that were far more impressive, but they too succumbed to the relentless onslaught of Messrs. Durbin and Watson. An illustrative sample even of the results that had to be rejected should be instructive. This is presented in Table 1. The d-statistic computed from the observed data must equal or exceed d_u to receive a clear "pass".

The motivation to continue the investigation using various indices and types of correlation came not from failure to confirm the hypothesis but from the indecisiveness of the findings.

After many failures it was finally apparent that meticulous efforts to obtain the most objective possible indices of the economic conditions might be the major impediment to success. This redefinition led to the analysis of data that had previously been consciously bypassed rather than merely overlooked. Would not an index reflecting the public *definition of the situation* be more to the point? Who would be sufficiently apprised of the economic situation at the time it was actually occurring, in any case, for it to have an influence on his behaviour? The facts are reported some time after they occur and even then have meaning only to a handful of experts.

When *the absolute values of the first differences of the index of common stock prices* were correlated by a one-year lead with the suicide rates, the following results were obtained:

$$r = 0.7418$$
$$r^2 = 0.550$$
Probability under $H_o < .001$
$$d_u = 1.42 < 1.774 = d$$

TABLE 2

Regression of Age-Standardized White Male Suicide Rates (Y) on Absolute Value of First Differences of Index of Common Stock Prices (X) with one year lead.

Year (X)	Observed X Values	Year (Y)	Observed Y Values	Computed Y Values[a]	Observed Minus Computed Y Values
1919	124	1920	17.1	22.5	—5.4
1920	80	1921	22.1	22.0	0.1
1921	112	1922	20.9	22.4	—1.5
1922	155	1923	20.1	22.8	—2.7
1923	16	1924	21.2	21.3	—0.1
1924	48	1925	21.1	21.7	—0,6
1925	210	1926	22.0	23.4	—1.4
1926	144	1927	23.2	22.7	0.5
1927	275	1928	24.2	24.1	0.1
1928	461	1929	24.4	26.0	—1.6
1929	607	1930	27.7	27.6	—0.1
1930	499	1931	30.0	26.4	3.6
1931	737	1932	30.9	29.0	1.9
1932	673	1933	28.0	28.3	—0.3
1933	203	1934	25.5	23.3	2.2
1934	88	1935	24.0	22.1	1.9
1935	76	1936	23.7	22.0	1.7
1936	487	1937	24.7	26.3	—1.6
1937	6	1938	25.3	21.2	4.1
1938	392	1939	23.1	25.3	—2.2
1939	57	1940	23.1	21.8	1.3

[a] $Y = 0.01059X + 21.17$.

Note: The "index of common stock prices" from which the first differences were derived is from *Historical Statistics of the United States* (as cited in Table 1), Series X 351, p. 657. The differences were computed from the levels for the years 1918 through 1939. The 1939–40 difference was cut off by the shift in the series to obtain the one year lead of the independent variable.

Not only is this a very acceptable correlation for a single independent variable but the d-statistic is sufficiently large to have sufficed even if three independent variables had been used. More detailed results are presented in Table 2.

It was necessary to establish that the *signed* differences did not yield better results. In fact, the best results obtained from the signed differences occurred with no relative shift in the series, yielding $r = -.4852$ with a probability under the null hypothesis of $.02 < P < .05$ and $d = .40$, placing it squarely in the "unacceptable" range for autocorrelated disturbances.

These findings clearly support Durkheim's hypothesis and in so doing firmly uphold his contention that even a favourable economic prospect tends to elevate the suicide rate—in flat contradiction of Henry and Short's rejection of this. The findings also contradict the optimism-pessimism hypothesis of suicide fluctuations which would appear to be the most logical of the alternatives from the standpoint of compatibility with means-end analysis.

It should not be supposed for a moment that the specific hypothesis is that stock price behaviour somehow causes suicides or even that those who have an awareness of stock market behaviour supply a disproportionate number of suicide victims. It is rather that a general climate of economic uncertainty (anomie, lack of definition) happens to be reflected in both the stock market behaviour and the suicide rates. More specifically, rapid fluctuations of stock market prices in either direction tend to reflect a diffuse lack of definition, a crisis, or anomie, in at least one important dimension of social life. In short, these empirical findings clearly accord with the general hypothesis that the social suicide rate varies directly as anomie.

The one-year lead of the independent variable may be accounted for by the extreme sensitivity of the stock market to prevailing conditions. Its "shakeouts" occur with great rapidity and once accomplished are "discounted" for the future. This happens because those whose actions have the greatest effect on the stock market prices are professionals with a highly developed consciousness of the importance of timing. People who take their lives are not, in general, faced with deadlines for accomplishing it and are not simultaneously counselled by professionals as to the opportune time to act. Perhaps it is even reasonable to suppose that the decision to commit suicide has a gestation period.

The major finding of this investigation may be summarized as follows:

The absolute values of the first differences in the index of common stock prices show a clearly significant correlation with annual suicide rates for the United States in the peacetime years 1919–40. The findings, according to the Durbin-Watson criterion, are free from significant distortion due to autocorrelated errors. These results indicate that suicide rates vary directly as the rate of change in the public definition of the economic situation, independently of the direction of the change. This in turn gives strong support to Durkheim's general hypothesis that the social suicide rate varies directly as anomie.

NOTES

1 Emile Durkheim, *Suicide*, Glencoe, Ill.: The Free Press, 1951. Page references will be to this edition. However, the French edition, *Le Suicide*, Paris: Presses Universitaires de France, 1960, was freely consulted as an extra precaution wherever etymological considerations appeared to be relevant. As it happened, J. A. Spaulding and G. Simpson's English translation proved to be quite acceptable in all cases.

2 "Cohesion" is not Durkheim's term but is used here to denote the combined meanings of *intégration* and *réglementation* in his contextual usage of these. The *règle* appears to relate not to *regula* as a prescriptive rule for conduct but has rather the broader connotation of "regulation" or "control" such as might be suggested by the concepts "exteriority and constraint" to which he gave emphasis elsewhere.

3 The sources of confirmation are many and varied. A representative sample of the sources summarized, together with further confirmations, may be found in Peter Sainsbury, *Suicide in London*, London: Chapman and Hall Ltd., 1955. Census and vital statistics data from a number of countries supply continuous confirmation.

4 Op. cit. The page numbers appear in parentheses after the passages to which they apply.

5 The striking similarity between Durkheim's use of crisis (*la crise*) and that of W. I. Thomas may be noted. This acquires even greater significance in the light of Thomas and Znaniecki's discussion of social disorganization which clearly appears to denote precisely the condition Durkheim identified as *anomie*. See, for instance, E. H. Volkart (ed.), *Social Behaviour and Personality*, New York: Social Science Research Council, 1951, pp. 218–25.

6 Andrew F. Henry and James F. Short, Jr., *Suicide and Homicide*, Free Press paperback edition, 1964 (Reprint of 1954 original in hardback).

7 Ibid., p. 27.

8 'Occupational Mobility and Suicide Among White Males', *American Sociological Review*, 25, April 1963, p. 180. (Reprinted in this volume, pp. 280–297.)

9 J. Durbin and G. S. Watson, 'Testing for Serial Correlation in Least Squares Regression', *Biometrika*, Part I, 1950, pp. 409–28, Part II, 1951, pp. 159–78. In this context, autocorrelation does not refer to the technique of correlating a series with a lagged segment of itself, but rather to autocorrelated errors.

10 The reader with sufficiently strong mathematical preparation is referred to the original articles by Durbin and Watson cited above, and J. Johnston, *Econometric Methods*, New York: McGraw-Hill Book Co., 1963, pp. 177–99. The test statistic is:

$$d = \frac{\sum_{i=2}^{n} (u_i - u_{i-1})^2}{\sum_{i=1}^{n} u_i^2}$$

where the ui are the residuals of the observed values of the dependent variable about the computed values.

At present this test appears to be considerably more widely disseminated among econometricians than among sociologists.

11 Ibid., II, Table 4, p. 173 was used exclusively. This is the table for the 5% significance level which for this statistic is the most stringent of the levels for which the information is supplied. In addition to the ranges of acceptable and unacceptable values, an intermediate range of "doubtful" values is given. To avoid inconclusive results, only values equal to or greater than, d_u, the greatest lower bound of acceptable values, have been regarded as acceptable in the present investigation.

12 Simply to assume that the autocorrelation of the disturbance terms doesn't exist, is to be self-deceptively optimistic. Cochrane and Orcutt's statement that "there is strong evidence in favour of the view that the error terms involved in most current formulations of economic relations are highly positively autocorrelated", applies equally to social data. See D. Cochrane and G. H. Orcutt, "Application of Least Squares Regression to Relationships Containing Autocorrelated Error Terms', *Journal of the American Statistical Association*, 44, March 1949, p. 33.

CHAPTER 22

Suicide and Occupational Mobility*

Warren Breed

Durkhiem maintained that high suicide rates appear with certain broad societal conditions, such as malintegration and lack of "social regulations".[1] His four categories of suicide refer as much to these conditions as to suicide rates. This broad frame of reference, as well as the official data available to him, prevented his dealing with two subjects which are the focus of the present study: the individual process of suicide and social class.

Many *individual* conditions, Durkheim argued, are "not general enough" for sociological analysis.[2] The first four chapters, written partly as an attack on psychological reductionism, were devoted to exorcising individual determinants, as well as other "extra-social" causes of suicide. Yet in various places Durkheim showed uncertainty about his macro-sociological bias. Chapter 6 specified several individual forms of suicide ("Stoic", "Epicurean", etc.), but these turn out to be rather discontinuous versions of his four societal types. He repeatedly spoke of "greed", individual "passions" and "purpose" and "desires", recognizing the relevance of individual aspirations and their relationship to achievement. In his treatment of anomic suicide, he noted briefly that those individuals "less favoured by nature" would require additional amounts of more discipline in accepting their lesser social rewards. And in the crucial passage on anomic suicide (". . . when society is disrupted by some painful crisis . . ."), he moved immediately to the notion that some individuals are faced with "de-classification"—casting them into a lower social position.[3]

Evidence that such a loss occurs, and that particular kinds of individuals show this behaviour, is not produced. Durkheim provided very little information of any kind relating suicide to class. He did not resolve the question of why the lower classes show high rates whereas they possess attributes which elsewhere Durkheim associates with low rates. He was unclear about who was involved in

* Reprinted by permission of the American Sociological Association from 'Occupational Mobility and Suicide Among White Males' in the *American Sociological Review*, Vol. 28, 1963, pp. 179–88.

such categories as "the liberal professions",[4] "public officials",[5] and "industrial occupations".[6] The latter, by his own designation, are not occupations at all but individuals engaged in industry—including labourers. (He acknowledges his regret on this point.)[7] His belief that "anomic" rates rise during prosperity as well as depression has been found incorrect by Henry and Short, who also showed more clearly than Durkheim that economic depression is accompanied by higher rates mostly among the higher income groups.[8] In dealing with this question, Durkheim imputed causation to bankruptcy rates when only correlation with suicide was warranted.[9] One might ask, if high rates accompany depression, what accounts for the still-considerable numbers of "anomic" suicides during prosperity? The closest he came to class *mobility* in the lives of individiuals was brief mention of declassification or disappointment, as with the bankrupt man or the artist whose work is criticized.[10]

To throw light on these questions, which Durkheim either specifically acknowledged he would not study, or was unable to study, research was designed to relate class and class mobility to the lives of individual suicides. Many sociologists would agree that individual role performance, within a normative system and in interaction with other individuals, is a properly "social" as societal states and rates of behaviour. As Inkeles put it, the Durkheimian macro-sociological model is an "S-R proposition" (for "State-Rate"), analogous to the psychological S-R model; questions about intervening variables of normatively oriented role performance, and deviance, are not covered.[11]

Instead of using annual reports, the data to be analysed are detailed materials on selected portions of the life experiences of 103 white males who committed suicide. The major variable intervening between the societal state and the individual suicide, in this section of the report, is taken to be the quality of work-role performance, with special attention to job instability and downward mobility. Because the theory was developed largely after collection of data began, further discussion of the theory will follow presentation of the findings.

PROCEDURE

The data come from interviews with persons who knew men who had committed suicide. Most of the respondents were relatives, but information was also obtained from friends, employers and co-workers, and in some cases neighbours, landlords, physicians, psychiatrists and government records. For purposes of reliability, where the first interview was with a female relative, we attempted to gain a second interview with a male non-relative, and so on. Rapport in most cases was good; respondents seemed to welcome the opportunity to once again go over the "possible causes" of death. The refusal rate was 4.4%. At least one interview was obtained for 103 of the 105 cases in the sample. In twenty-two cases there is one interview, in forty-five cases there are two interviews and in the remaining thirty-six there are three or more. In every case attempts were made to get at least two interviews; for the twenty-two cases, either there was only one respondent available or the details seemed so clear that further information was not sought. In several of the thirty-six cases, the details were so problematic that five and six interviews were made. The data were coded by two coders, who agreed 93% of the time on all categories used in this report.

The sample consisted of 105 consecutive white male suicides in New Orleans for the years 1954–9 inclusive, of men between the ages of twenty and sixty and who had lived in the city for at least six months. No murder-suicides and no attempted suicides were included. Of the 304 deaths called suicides by the authorities during that period, there were also 60 white females; 9 murder-suicides—all white; 40 white Orleans males aged sixty-one or more and 1 under twenty; 26 Negro males and 8 Negro females; and 42 white males and 13 white females not residing in the city for six months—most of whom had entered the city a day or two before death. The decision to restrict the study to men between the ages of twenty and sixty stems from the interest in the male role of work and performance in that role.

To obtain an estimate for comparing the suicides with their peers, a control group was established. Interviewers were sent to each of the 103 blocks where the suicides had lived, with a modification of the schedule used for the suicides. They followed a plan designed to obtain two interviews at random (but keeping five doors away from the suicide's former residence) on that block, or across the street if necessary. Two respondents were asked to give information about one male each, who became members of the control sample of 206 men. This departure from the usual two-person interviewer-respondent relationship was successful in gathering data by the same method standardized for the suicides, but resulted in a much higher refusal rate—18%. People are apparently slow to give information about a still-living third person.

Suicides and controls were matched on the three variables of sex, race, and age. Further, by asking for a relative who lived in that neighbourhood, it was hoped to match for a fourth variable, social class. As it turned out, the two groups differed significantly in class—a substantive matter important for the mobility hypothesis

TABLE 1

Occupational Distribution of Suicides at Time of Death as Compared to Control Group and White Males in the City—per cent

	Suicides	City, Census	Controls
Professional	7	15	13
Managers	16	17	23
Clerical	7	13	11
Sales	6	11	6
Craftsmen-foremen	14	19	22
Operatives	17	14	14
Service	19	7	7
Farm labourers	0	0	0
Labourers	13	5	3
Totals	103	92,320	206

(see Table 1). They were quite similar, however, in the class of their fathers; suicides and controls were raised in similar class surroundings (see Table 2). The control group is also interesting in that, although it was not designed as a random sample, its occupational distribution closely parallels that of the city for white males.

THE VALIDITY OF OFFICIAL DATA

Generally the only question sociologists have asked about suicide data taken from coroners' files is that of representativeness in terms

TABLE 2

Father's Occupations of Suicides and Controls—per cent

	Suicides	Controls
Professional	17	12
Managers	24	27
Clerical	3	8
Sales	8	4
Craftsmen	17	23
Operatives	17	13
Service	4	7
Farm labourers	4	3
Labourers	7	4

of possible under-reporting: Are these all the suicides that took place during this period? Two further questions are also relevant, dealing with possible over-reporting and with the *quality* of the data. This study deals with all three questions.

All studies of suicide, including this one, conclude that some suicides may not have been registered as such, or may have taken place in another jurisdiction. Under-reporting is said to occur because officials favour influential persons by stating relatives' cause of death as natural or accidental, rather than as suicide. In this study, such biases may be present. However, during the six-year period several persons high in influence were declared suicides, including at least ten physicians, lawyers, wealthy businessmen and clubmen, and a relative of one of the two or three most powerful local politicians. A second possible source of under-reporting stems from the fact that New Orleans is a Catholic city (some two-thirds of the whites are Catholics). This potential bias is sharply minimized, in fact, by an institutional mechanism: authorities usually delay stating "cause of death" until final rites are completed. The word "suicide" rarely appears in the local press: cases are said to be "under investigation". A final source of under-reporting is the suicide who leaves town and kills himself in another jurisdiction. During the field work this practice was mentioned by several persons, but closer questioning always ended with the admission that the speaker himself knew of no specific case for the years covered.

Over-reporting is also a possibility. In some eight cases relatives claimed that death was accidental or a consequence of grief. In two or three of these cases, the investigators were left with genuine doubts about mode of death.

Far greater sources of error are inherent, however, in the *quality* of data available from official records. In our investigation and interviewing, we found the following types and frequencies of errors in the 103 cases.

Officially reported occupation higher than actually held   14
Officially reported occupation lower than actually held   8
Officially reported occupation different but of same class
    level   2
Suicide's occupation given and implied as working, actually
    not working full-time (unemployed, part-time, retired)   37
Officially reported as married, actually divorced or separated   8
Officially reported as widowed, actually separated   1
Officially reported as divorced, actually in common-law
    marriage   3

These are sizeable discrepancies, and while some may partly cancel one another out in gross totals, it seems clear that the careful study of such behaviour requires validation checks through data gathered by other than official methods. It is thus not surprising that previous sociological studies of suicide have not embraced the downward mobility hypothesis—their data probably have been over-generous as to class. In sum, while little can be done about the conventional problem of under-reporting, the quality of data can be improved through validation procedures.

OCCUPATION AND WORK STATUS AT DEATH

The question about the social class of suicides has long been open. A recent review of the subject cites the scanty knowledge available, and concludes that in general there is a tendency for higher rates at both extremes of the occupational continuum.[12] Much less attention has been paid to mobility and suicide. A study published after this one was under way dealt with mobility, but concluded—perhaps partly for the methodological reasons just discussed—that downward mobility (intergenerational) was only somewhat more frequent than upward mobility among male suicides.[13]

The New Orleans data show disproportionately high rates in the lower ranks, as compared to controls and census figures (Table 1). All of the five highest work strata show low rates relative to their portion of the population. Whereas only one-fourth of the city's white male labour force works as operatives, service workers and labourers, one-half of the suicides were in those categories at time of death. The meaning of this relationship will be sought below.

One of the single most striking findings is that only fifty-two of the suicides—50% were working full-time just before they committed suicide. The others showed these work situations:

Unemployed	22
Working part-time	11
Sick or disabled	8
Retired before age 60	5
On vacation or leave, killed self within day of return to work	3
Willing and able to work, waiting turn on roster	2

More of the suicides between ages of 20 and 39 were working full-time (63%) than the 40–49 group (43%) and the 50–60 group (49%). Only 40% of those in the lowest occupational group (service and labouring workers) were working full-time. All but one of the five retired men were white-collar men in their fifties. The three on vacation or leave had given signs of disaffection from work before leaving their job—but all three also had difficulties apart from the work sphere.

Why were they not working full-time? Above and beyond those who were sick, retired, on vacation or a work roster, the remainder show this pattern:

Fired (includes three who were laid off with others in a work force)	13
Quit 1–6 days prior to suicide	3
Quit 7 days or more prior to suicide	12

The non-work status in most cases was of considerable duration. Of the fifty-one men not working full-time, only nine had been in this condition less than twenty-one days. The rest had been out of work or working part-time for three weeks or more, and the period stretched out to several years for some.

VERTICAL MOBILITY

As important as class is for the definition of life chances, the longtitudinal direction of movement over time is equally vital. This is seen, for example, in studies of prejudice, political conservatism, and other apparent correlates of "skidding".[14] The working hypothesis in this study singled out downward mobility as an independent variable in male suicide. Here we will be examining behaviour Durkheim saw as "anomic". His discussion of anomic suicide is not static but implies a temporal sequence of events. In stable times, he noted, "society" (internalized in the conscience) sets limits on individual desires. This regulation collapses when society is disturbed by a painful crisis, and society is momentarily unable to exercise this influence. A new scale of controls cannot be quickly institutionalized.[15] The relationship between ends and means is no longer clear to the individual. It was at this point that Durkheim spoke of "declassification" of the individual, coming as close to downward mobility as he ever came. The materials to be presented here provide some insight into the process of declassification, but they also show that this happens in individual cases, and in good times as well as bad.

Intergenerational Mobility. When the occupational level of the suicide and his father are compared, considerable mobility—mostly downward—appears. Using North-Hatt categories for the cases for whom comparative data were available, we find:

	Suicides %	Controls %
Subject's father higher	53	31
Subjects father lower	25	38
Same	22	31
Totals	75	169

A similar pattern is found when the census classification of occupations is used. The effect of intergenerational mobility on suicide is clearly related to age, as shown in Table 3. Almost two-thirds of the younger suicides held a position lower than their father's but this proportion recedes for each age group. Likewise, the proportion of occupational levels shared by father and son is smallest for the young suicides. The "stress and strain" often ascribed to adolescents may continue into the early worklife of many men, if these trends are representative.

Worklife Mobility. Most studies of mobility have used intergenerational data. There is recent evidence, however, that worklife mobility—experienced by the individual during his own career—is likewise relevant.[16] Among the suicides, considerable downward mobility—"skidding"—is found, and relatively little upward mobility. This tendency should not come as a surprise in view of the wide prevalance of non-work in the group, already reported. In this section, however, the status "unemployment" is not taken as a work status to be compared with earlier jobs; all work-life mobility comparisons are made between the last (or present) job held and prior jobs.

TABLE 3

Intergenerational Mobility of Suicides by Age—per cent

	20–39	40–49	50–60
Son higher	22	30	24
Same	13	19	32
Son lower	65	52	44
Totals	23	27	25

One would expect that those suicides not working full-time at death had also experienced more work-like skidding than those who remained at work. This expectation is borne out in the data. Also evident, however, is the finding that more of the terminally employed had experienced downward than upward mobility during the last years of life (see Table 4).

TABLE 4

Worklife Mobility of Working and Non-Working Suicides and Controls, Using Two Occupational Scales—per cent*

Work Status	Suicides Full-time	Suicides Not Full-time	Controls
Using Census categories			
Upward	19	9	12
Same (or only one job)	57	45	83
Downward	24	47	5
Using North-Hatt categories			
Upward	17	9	12
Same (or only one job)	50	41	83
Downward	33	50	5
Totals	52	51	187

* The worklife comparison for the suicides is between last job held and the one preceding. For the controls the comparison was restricted to the past ten-year period; more mobility in both directions would have been shown had a longer work period been studied.

A final index of occupational performance comes from questions about financial income. Incomes were compared for the last year before death and two years before that; for the controls, we used present income as against income received two years earlier. (Some one-fifth of the income figures were estimated, using wage and salary scales prevailing in the city.) Decreasing incomes characterized more than half the suicides, whereas men of the control group were showing gains. The proportions, excluding cases for which data were incomplete, were:

	Suicides %	Controls %
Income increased	8	35
Income decreased	51	11
Income same	41	54
Totals	101	164

Taking all forms of downward mobility as given individually above, and all 103 cases of suicide, it is found that seventy-seven men—75%—suffered at least one of these forms of drop in status. Intergenerational skidding amounts to 53% of the cases and income loss to 51%, while work-life skidding varies in its contribution from 35 to 43% depending upon the base and scale employed. One-half of the intergenerational skidders were also worklife skidders. Evidence is at hand that three-fourths of the suicides showed one or more forms of skidding, with its potential consequences of disappointment, frustration, decreased approval granted by peers, and decreased self-respect. In some of the remaining twenty-six cases, it is still possible that similar disappointments with work were present, such as the failure to receive an expected promotion or raise, but such conditions were not coded.

It must not be forgotten that also among the remaining twenty-six cases, adequate work performance was being carried out, and in some upward worklife mobility was present. Also, skidding was present among the controls. In short, skidding cannot be hypothesized as anything more than one highly significant factor in the complex suicide syndrome. Studies of suicide from the individual point of view which neglect skidding, on the other hand, are overlooking a variable which may be crucial in the etiology of suicide.

Skidding in the Three Classes. Skidding does not occur in random fashion throughout the class hierarchy. Intergenerationally, enormous differences are found between the three occupational strata (see Table 5). The top group (white-collar men) actually contained more upward than downward cases. The ratio is reversed for the middle group, and the lowest stratum shows 88% downward mobility. A similar pattern is found with respect to worklife mobility (see Table 6).

TABLE 5

Intergenerational Mobility of Suicides, by Occupational Class—per cent

	White Collar	Skilled Operative	Service Labour
Son higher	37	38	0
Same	41	8	13
Son lower	22	54	88
Totals	27	24	24

TABLE 6

Worklife Mobility of Suicide, by Occupational Class—per cent

	White Collar	Skilled Operative	Service Labour
Upward	22	13	3
Same (or only one job)	54	50	33
Downward	24	37	64
Totals	33	26	30

The findings about vertical mobility among the white-collar men pose a direct challenge to a central hypothesis of this paper. Further analysis, using the variable of income trend, supplies at least part of the rebuttal. As shown in Table 7, the white-collar men were experiencing the highest rate of income loss of the three work strata. Almost three-fifths of them showed decreasing income over the last two-year period. Thus this stratum too was "downward", although the form it took was more specifically financial than work-level in nature.

Further information on this point about the twenty-four men in the categories "professional, managerial, proprietors and officials" shows a range of strains. Three, for example, were very ill; two others had accidents that impaired regular work and other activities; five or six had alcohol problems; three at most had something of a mental-nervous-emotional problem, although none of these was

TABLE 7

Income Trend of Suicides, by Occupational Class—per cent*

	White Collar	Skilled Operative	Service Labour
Upward	14	6	3
Same	28	50	42
Downward	58	44	55
Totals	36	32	33

* The comparison is between income gained during the last year of life as against income gained two years before that. About one-fifth of the income figures were estimated from rates prevailing in the city.

serious from the evidence obtained; three were former blue-collar men who had entered business and were doing poorly. And about half showed strains from either the mother or the wife relationship; several appeared to have been dominated by their mother, and showed characteristics of dependency[17] (Some individuals displayed more than one of these symptoms.)

None of these factors present so clear a picture for these top-level men, however, as the "work performance" factor. Above and beyond the three former working men with failing businesses, three professional and managerial men failed to receive promotions after many years with a concern; and one manager was demoted after a merger (the respondent's description of the reduced physical dimensions and other status symbols of the man's new office was both vivid and poignant). In only one case, that of an official, was there an outright dismissal. Four had retired; all but one of these had money; one closed his successful business on the death of his wife, with whom he had been inseparable; and one retired to drink a great deal while still talking of business expansion. It is not difficult to form the impression that these men felt acute dissatisfaction with their performance and standing in their respective business and professional circles. They appear to be classic cases of anomic suicide in the world of commerce and industry as depicted by Durkheim.

The work stratum which actually shows the fewest signs of work problems—despite the small amount of technical skidding among the white-collar men—is that of the skilled worker. This is the only working-class stratum which is under-represented among the suicides. Worklife skidding is almost non-existent in this stratum. Perhaps having learned a trade in a day of relatively low supply and high demand for these skills, their work status is secure. Furthermore, most of these men were said to be *good* workers. They showed as many domestic and health problems as the others, but in the work sphere it may be that their very security as artisans turned their aspirations up to entrepreneurial and managerial positions, which all the frustrations and complications of this possible shift in work providing considerable strain. This possibility was suggested by several cases.

In his Tulsa study, Powell found several occupations with much higher suicide rates that others.[18] These included pharmacists, cab drivers, physicians, nurses and lawyers. In New Orleans there were no pharamacist suicides during the six-year period and no nurses were included in the all-male sample. While only one physician appeared in the city sample, two others were among the larger total of 304, but were living in suburbs and thus excluded from study. Two lawyers were among the 103, however, and four cab drivers.

Occupations ranking low in both cities were carpenter, accountant, mechanic, truck driver, engineer, machinist and welder.

Several occupations appeared to be disproportionately represented in New Orleans. These were watchman or guard, 7; police and sheriff employees, 6; sales workers, 8, with an added 3 for route man; bar proprietors, 3, and other small proprietors, 3. Differences with Powell's findings may be due in part to the possible bias stemming from the use of official job titles in the Tulsa study. It seems clear that two jobs (cab driver and watchman-guard) may be dead-ends in the downward path, that sales work is associated with job strains, and that several other men had experienced a chaotic work pattern rather than the smoothly rising gradient typical of successful careers.

While there are differences between the classes in rates of suicide, no such variation appears in the process. Men decide to take their lives in the same way, and for the same kinds of reasons, throughout the class structure.

DOWNWARD MOBILITY AND THE DRIFT HYPOTHESIS

Sociological and ecological data about deviant behaviour, when analysed in terms of class factors, meet the problems of possible "drift": to what extent do data on suicide, mental ill-health, etc., reflect "real" differences in classes and residential areas, or do individuals with morbidity problems "drift" into these classes and neighbourhoods? Studies in Chicago and New Haven have shown that the drift by schizophrenics from higher-class residential areas to slums is not great.[19] The New Haven study revealled also that schizophrenics did not drift downward (intergenerationally) from higher class levels, but were on the same class level as their parents. No data are available from existing studies of suicide; ecological studies agree, however, that the highest rates are found in slum areas.

Our data show that geographical drift, from higher to lower-class neighbourhoods, was infrequent among the 103 suicides. Only three of them clearly moved to the slums within two years before death, and some six or eight others might have—the data are problematic. In any event, well over ninety of the men did not make such a move. When the address-at-death data of the men are plotted on a map, it is seen that they lived in all of the predominantly white areas of the city.

These data suggest an interpretation of the findings in other cities showing high suicide rates in the zones in transition. It will be re-called that our 103 cases had all resided in the city for at least six months, but that during the same six-year period forty-two white males without this residential history had committed suicide within the city limits. Most of these men took their lives in the central areas, in hotels, or rooming house districts—that is, they drifted" in. Had they been included in this study, the ecological distribution would have more closely resembled that found in Chicago, Seattle, etc., where no restriction was placed upon length of residence. From the point of view of this paper, which takes into account reciprocal role performance over time, these in-migrants do not have roots in the community. Other studies of suicide—and of other morbidities—could control for this factor when official data indicate the length of residence in the city.

If the drift hypothesis is recast in terms of vertical mobility, our suicide data show a clear picture of downward drift. Although few suicides drifted to the slums, it might be that the skidders felt they would soon be forced into cheaper housing. This added barb may have strengthened their tendency to end an intolerable situation.

EGOISTIC AND ALTRUISTIC SUICIDE

This report has focused on the relationship between white male suicide, work and class mobility. These factors appear to be more characteristic of Durkheim's "anomic" type of suicide than of his egoistic and altruistic forms. Space limitations prohibit extended discussion of findings under the latter headings, but it should be stated that the 103 suicides also showed marked characteristics of egoistic suicide, as seen in family, group and religious membership and attachment to a set of shared values. Forms of altruistic suicide, quite different from those hypothesized by Powell, were also found. As for related pathologies, mental problems, alcoholism, physical health, and police problems were present, with rates not markedly different from those reported in other studies. Most individual suicides are complex phenomena, involving the individual's role performance in several positions over a period of time; the purpose of this paper was to highlight the relevance of the work role for American males, but not to insist that this is the only major factor involved.

TOWARDS A STRUCTURAL-INTERACTIONAL THEORY OF SUICIDE

Numerous hypotheses have been advanced to account for deviant behaviour. Only those dealing with structured strain and inter-actional process will be considered here. Merton's theory of social structure and anomie posits social and cultural standards, the individual being said to accept or reject goals or institutionally prescribed means when under strain brought on by the malintegration of goals and means.[20] While Merton asks whether or not the individual accepts or rejects (or strives to change) structural conditions, a further notion is being advanced here. Once the individual has decided to accept or reject cultural prescriptions, he acts. Our interest is on the quality of his action, as evaluated by self and others. A focus on the interpersonal consequences of action is contained in the Cooley-Mead tradition, and developed by Lemert to apply to deviance.[21]

The process can be reviewed most simply in terms of Cooley's "looking-glass self". The actor acts, alter assesses, and actor reacts to the other's assessment with a self-feeling, such as pride or shame. A favourable evaluation pleases the actor; a negative one hurts, is damaging to the actor's ego. Now when a man—one of our suicides —is fired, or not re-hired, or when a businessman continually fails to show a profit, these actions may result in encounters with others eventuating in a sense of "shame". On telling his wife the news, or facing colleagues and co-workers in the community, the fact of his inadequate work performance may be reflected in their eyes and lodged in the actor's self-awareness. Even before the news is out, he can anticipate these negative evaluations, having internalized the community's work standards. The norm that American men should be working, and working in adequate fashion, can be taken as axiomatic.

The process sketched here is most clearly informed by the theoretical position of Lemert, which embodies much of the Cooley-Mead tradition. Although he criticized "interaction theory" as insufficient in itself to explain deviance, he has proposed a theory of deviation which emphasizes the social self, the differentiation of the deviant from the group, and progressive sanctions from alter following deviation. Ego's deviations increase, until he accepts for himself the deviant role imputed to him by a growing number of alters.

Several studies suggest the relationship between low achievement and deviation. A psychiatric study of attempted suicides found that many patients mentioned job and work problems as contributing to their feelings of despondency, although none of them reported work as their biggest single problem.[22] Pearlin found that hospital nurses with low job achievement showed high alienation scores, although such feelings were reduced with higher income.[23] Haskell has reported that delinquents who secured and kept jobs did not recidivate, whereas non-working boys did.[24] From a more social-psychological approach, Reckless and his associates found that a group of "good" boys (not considered prone to delinquency) showed more favourable self-conceptions than "bad" boys.[25]

The notion of the quality of role performance is seldom used explicitly by sociologists. Actually it is never far from social-psychological concern. When we use concepts like prestige, esteem, self-conception and the social self, quality of role performance is implied. Parsons, for example, in his treatment of deviance used the notion of "adequacy" in terms of alter's evaluation of ego's performance and ego's awareness of that judgment.[26] Many sociologists make the assumption, usually implicit, that men have certain "needs," such as approval and recognition.

Bredemeier and Toby have recently approached this topic in terms of human standards. "Four kinds of standards, which nearly all human beings acquire, can be distinguished."[27] These are standards of adequacy, worthiness, gratification and security. All of them are relevant to potential deviance, in that they relate the individual to structural forces and requisites, but for present purposes the most crucial is "adequacy". "Measuring up to the standard gives the individual a feeling of achievement and self-satisfaction; falling below it produces a painful sense of failure, or self-devaluation, of shame." Using this criterion, many of our suicides were shown to lack competence on the job. And because in American society the work role is central for the man, work failure is not inadequacy in just one role among many, but spreads through other roles and the self-image to threaten a general collapse of the life organization.

CONCLUSION

New Orleans white male suicides showed substantial problems associated with work, as seen in downward mobility, reduced income, unemployment and other job and business difficulties. This finding can be used to refine Durkheim's treatment of anomic suicide. His data did not permit him to specify the differential consequences of anomie on particular strata of the labour force. Further, Durkheim was committed to focusing on the *increase* in suicide during periods of anomie. This left him in a weak position to account for the existence of substantial amounts of anomic suicide in periods of the kinds of integration he dealt with the *Division of Labour in Society*. Anomic suicide can and does occur under integrated conditions as well as during anomie, and low-achievement performances promote suicide in good times or bad. The questions asked in the two studies differ, but anomie is the focus of both. It was also demonstrated that official data on suicides may be of questionable validity, and that suicides "drift" downward in class but not as much in the ecological sense.

All downwardly mobile men do not, of course, commit suicide

(as shown in the control group), just as all entrepreneurs do not kill themselves during economic crisis. The probabilities of both, however, are higher. It is suggested that certain other aspects of evaluated role performance, as in family relationships, may also yield associations with suicide, and that a structural-interactional approach may be profitably employed in studying the etiology of other individual pathologies such as alcoholism and mental illness.

NOTES

1 Emile Durkheim, *Suicide,* Glencoe: The Free Press, 1951. The book was originally published in 1897.
2 Ibid., p. 51.
3 Ibid, pp. 251–2.
4 Ibid., p. 164.
5 Ibid., p. 166.
6 Ibid., pp. 257–8.
7 Ibid., p. 257.
8 A. F. Henry and J. F. Short, *Suicide and Homicide,* Glencoe: The Free Press, 1954.
9 *Suicide,* p. 242.
10 Ibid., pp. 288–9.
11 Alex Inkeles, 'Personality and Social Structure', in R. K. Merton, Leonard Broom and Leonard S. Cottrell Jr. (eds.), *Sociology Today,* New York: Basic Books, 1959, pp. 249–56. Inkeles recommends the work of Henry and Short, op. cit., as providing an intervening variable in the form of psychodynamics.
12 Jack P. Gibbs, 'Suicide', in R. K. Merton and Robert A Nisbet, *Contemporary Social Problems,* New York: Harcourt, Brace, 1961, pp. 222–61. See also the several studies of Norman L. Farberow and Edwin S. Shneidman; their most recent work is *The Cry for Help,* New York: McGraw-Hill, 1961.
13 Austin L. Porterfield and Jack P. Gibbs, 'Occupational Prestige and Social Mobility of Suicides in New Zealand', *American Journal of Sociology,* 66, September 1960, pp. 147–52.
14 Bruno Bettelheim and Morris Janowitz, *The Dynamics of Prejudice,* New York: Harper, 1950; Melvin M. Tumin, *Desegregation,* Princeton: Princeton University Press, 1958, pp. 127–41; Richard Hofstadter, 'The Pseudo-Conservative Revolt', in Daniel Bell (ed.), *The New American Right,* New York: Criterion Books, 1955; and other works cited in Harold L. Wilensky and Hugh Edwards, 'The Skidder', *American Sociological Review,* 24, April 1959, p. 216.
15 *Suicide,* pp. 248–53.
16 Wilensky and Edwards, op. cit.
17 Farberow and Shneidman, op. cit.
18 Elwin H. Powell, 'Occupation, Status and Suicide', *American Sociological Review,* 23, April 1958, pp. 131–9.
19 See August B. Hollingshead and Fredrick C. Redlich, *Social Class and Mental Illness,* New York: Wiley, 1958, pp. 244–8.
20 Robert K. Merton, *Social Theory and Social Structure,* Glencoe: The Free Press, 1957, pp. 121–94.

21 Edwin M. Lemert, *Social Pathology*, New York: McGraw-Hill, 1951, pp. 3–98.

22 Eli Robins, Edwin H. Schmitt and Patricia O'Neal, 'Some Interrelations of Social Factors and Clinical Diagnosis in Attempted Suicide', *American Journal of Psychiatry*, 114, 1957, pp. 221–31.

23 Leonard Pearlin, 'Alienation from Work', *American Sociological Review*, 27, June 1962, pp. 314–26.

24 Martin R. Haskell, 'Toward a Reference Group Theory of Juvenile Delinquency', *Social Problems*, 8, Winter 1960–1, pp. 220–30.

25 Walter C. Reckless, Simon Dinitz and Ellen Murray, 'Self Concept as an Insulator Against Delinquency', *American Sociological Review*, 21, December 1956, pp. 744–6.

26 Talcott Parsons, *The Social System*, Glencoe: The Free Press, 1951, pp. 259–62.

27 Harry C. Bredemeier and Jackson Toby, *Social Problems in America*, New York: Wiley, 1960, pp. 3–10.

CHAPTER 23

Suicide, Suicide Attempts and Weather*

Alex D. Pokorny, Fred Davis and Wayne Harberson

There is a large body of literature, both technical and popular, which holds that there are causal relationships between weather and affective states, even pathological mood deviations. It is further claimed that weather and physical environment influence suicide rates. Most authorities today appear to view such claims with scepticism, but these statements keep recurring in various contexts. The present study was designed to put such ideas to a definitive test. We felt it should be possible to demonstrate significant relationships if they are there, and to refute them clearly if they are absent. Thus at least one distracting factor could be cleared away in the exploration and clarification of this important aspect of human behaviour.

Review of Literature. *Seasonal variations* in suicide rates are mentioned by many observers. Such variations are usually explained as due to weather changes. There is fairly general agreement that rates are highest in late spring or early summer.[2 4 8 10 13 18]

Farberow and Shneidman,[5] with far better data than any of the previous authors cited, do not find any *significant* variations in suicidal phenomena by month. Stengel and Cook[15] report that all but one of the five subgroups of suicide attempts show a fairly marked peak—in one of the spring months. (However, when we total their five subgroups, the monthly totals even out.)

Durkheim[4] considers that there is a perfect continuity of the curve (increasing from winter to summer), which would tend to eliminate weather fluctuations as the cause; rather, he considers the important factor to be the *length of the day,* increasing the time during which social factors are at work.

The apparent effect of *latitude* is mentioned by Durkheim,[4] quoting Morselli; the area of Central Europe had the highest rates, shading off in both directions; Durkheim does not accept that climate is the cause of this. Curtin[2] also states that suicide is more common in temperate climates than in very hot or very cold regions. Mills[7]

* Reprinted by permission from the *American Journal of Psychiatry,* Vol. 120, 1963, pp. 377–81. Copyright © 1963 The American Psychiatric Association.

says that the higher rates of suicide in the North may be due to "mental exhaustion" in the more rigorous climate.

The effect of *cyclonic storms* and *passage* of fronts in increasing the rates of suicide is discussed by several writers.[2][16] Mills[7] and Petersen[10] are leading American proponents of this view. Smith,[14] in a subjective report, states that he can predict fronts by onset of his own feelings of depression; he considers this to be related to suicide at such periods.

Barometric pressure has been implicated in four different ways. It is alleged that suicide rates are highest during stable high pressure[1] or during falling pressure[7] or during low pressure.[3] Finally, one study[16] finds that there is no significant relationship.

High humidity is linked to high suicide rates by Dexter.[3] Tholuck[16] does not find any significant relationship.

Rain and *precipitation* are mentioned by several authors. Curtin[2] says that suicide rates are low when precipitation is the greatest. Miner[8] finds a small negative correlation between mean precipitation and suicide. Dexter[3] says that suicide rates are lowest on wet, partly cloudy days. Tholuck[16] finds no significant relationship to rain.

Cloudiness or sunny conditions are mentioned by Tholuck[16] as unrelated to suicide, though Dexter[3] states that rates are lower on cloudy days.

Wind velocity is mentioned by Curtin,[2] who considers that suicide and other violence increases with mild winds but decreases if winds are more intense. Dexter[3] says that suicides increase with wind speed.

Hot weather increases suicide rates according to Curtin[2]. Mills[7] also says that suicide rates vary directly with temperature. Miner[8] does not find that temperature is correlated with suicide rate. Many authors advance temperature as an explanation of their observed seasonal variation. Tholuck[16] finds no significant relationship to temperature.

Many of the supposed relationships advanced are complex, involving several variables. For example, Curtin[2] says that in India young females are more suicide prone during highest temperatures! Petersen's[10] theories are of this nature; he holds that when pyknics are alkaline (as during cold fronts) they are irritable, whereas when leptosomes are acid (during warm fronts) they are morose and blue. It should be apparent that some of these complicated ideas are difficult to put to the test.

A rather different theme mentioned by several authors is that good weather is associated with increased suicide. Durkheim[4] says, "Neither in winter nor in autumn does suicide reach its maximum, but during the fine season when nature is most smiling and the temperature mildest." Curtin[2] and Dexter[3] state similar beliefs.

In general, most of the articles on weather, climate, and suicide are speculative and seem to be based on crude data and coarse time intervals. The authors quote each other's statements, findings, and assertions endlessly, with little attempt to control for other factors. These criticisms are less applicable to the recent articles.

METHODS AND RESULTS

Data. All cases of suicide and suicide attempts reported to the Houston Police Department* during 1960 were abstracted. We accepted the decision of the Police Department regarding the ruling of suicide or attempted suicide in all but a very few doubtful cases. Each of the 91 suicides and 400 suicide attempts was then reviewed to establish the time of the act. If this could not be localized within a period of three hours or less the case was excluded. The final list studied consisted of sixty-seven suicides and 373 suicide attempts. In the large majority of cases, the time of the act could be established fairly sharply. The hour which was nearest the midpoint of the probable time of occurrence was then set as the "hour" of the suicide or suicide attempt.

The weather data were obtained from the published hourly US Weather Bureau reports for the Houston Airport Station. These data were also made available on punched cards, one for each hour, or 8,784 cards for the (leap) year.

A. *Detailed (Hourly) Study of Eleven Weather Variables.* From the large number of weather and climatological items reported for each hour, we selected eleven variables for study. This was done on logical grounds and because these variables had been mentioned in the literature. They were 1. Dry bulb temperature; 2. Windspeed; 3. Wind direction; 4. Barometric pressure; 5. Relative humidity; 6. Visibility; 7. Ceiling height; 8. Rain; 9. Fog; 10. Thunderstorms; and 11. Cloudiness. Each of these was reported in steps along a scale (e.g. per cent of humidity, degrees of temperature). We first studied each of these variables for only those hours in which a suicide or, separately, a suicide attempt occurred. This led to some striking and seemingly significant findings. However, it must be recognized that during an entire time interval, such as a year, a particular weather variable will not be evenly distributed over its scale; it will be bunched, skewed, etc. It is likely that the hours

* We are indebted to Inspector Larry W. Fultz, Records Division, Houston Police Department, for his helpfulness and cooperation.

during which suicides or suicide attempts occur would purely by chance, show a similarly bunched or skewed distribution. Therefore one cannot make any valid assertions about relation of suicidal behaviour to a weather variable without taking into consideration the actual yearly distribution of that variable. When this was done with our data the seeming relationships disappeared. For proper evaluation, we had to "partial out" that portion of the correlation that was due to the fact that there were more hours of the year at certain steps or values of the variable.

The first two columns in Table 1 show the high apparent correlations when the suicides or suicide attempts are simply correlated with the weather variable. The last two columns show how all of these become insignificant when the influence of the uneven hourly distribution for the year was "partialled out".

TABLE 1

		Apparent correlation with		True correlation with	
		suicide	suicide attempt	suicide	suicide attempt
1	Temperature	.25	.41	.07	.20
2	Wind speed	—.54	—.63	.22	.20
3	Wind direction	—.93*	—.78*	—.08*	.41*
4	Barometric pressure	.11	.16	—.03	—.05
5	Relative humidity	.51	.63	.10	.06
6	Visibility	.58	.65	—.01	—.13
7	Ceiling height	.25	.18	.01	.18
8	Rain	—.52	—.48	—.12	.02
9	Fog	—.86	—.88	.17	—.15
10	Thunderstorms	—1.00†	—.98	0.00	0.02
11	Cloudiness	—0.39	—0.52	0.33	—0.24

* These values may be spurious, in that the complete circle of wind directions was arbitrarily split and converted to a linear scale. For this variable, our chi square test was more appropriate; it showed no significant relationship.

† This maximally high correlation was due to the complete absence of thunderstorms during the sixty-seven hours of suicides.

The data were also handled graphically, by plotting the total hourly readings for the year on each weather variable, and then superimposing the readings for those hours in which suicides and suicide attempts occurred. In all cases these three gave very similar curves as is illustrated in Figures 1, 2, and 3.

FIGURE 1
Temperature Values for Hours of Suicides, of Suicide Attempts, and of Total Hours of Year

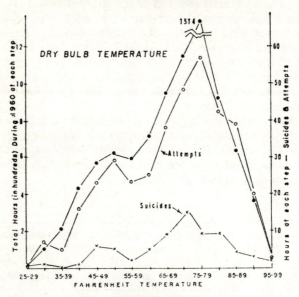

FIGURE 2
Barometric Pressure Values for Hours of Suicides, of Suicide Attempts, and of Total Hours of Year

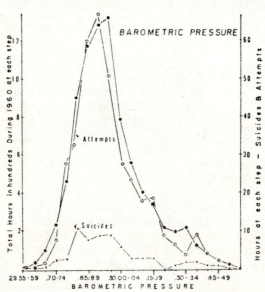

FIGURE 3
Relative Humidity Values for Hours of Suicides, of Suicide Attempts, and of Total Hours of Year

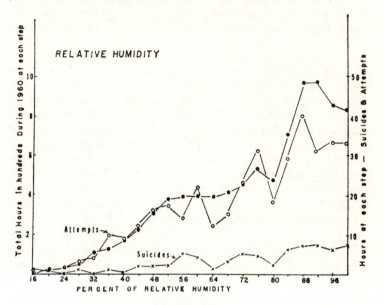

FIGURE 4
Suicide Rates by States

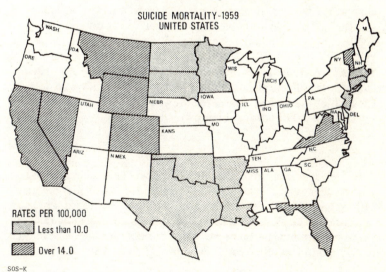

SOS-K

In each figure the scale along the baseline represents the steps or intervals of the weather variable. The dot line, with its appropriate scale on the left, represents the distribution of all the hours of the year. The X and O lines, with their scale on the right, represent the suicide and suicide attempt hours' distribution on this weather variable.

In addition to the method of partial correlations, a chi square value was calculated for each weather variable. None of these twenty-two values showed any significant deviation from chance.

B. *Month and Season.* For this evaluation we used the entire group of four hundred suicide attempts and ninety-one suicides. There was no significant relation of month of year or of season with either suicide or suicide attempts. To check this more fully, we obtained data on the entire State of Texas for the years 1956 through 1961. Each year considered separately would show some month-by-month variation. However, when the five years were plotted on the same graph, the ups and downs did not coincide and there was no clean, repetitive seasonal distribution.

C. *Fronts.* The weather data for 1960 were next studied for passage of fronts. Twenty-eight recognizable northerly cool fronts were identified. The twenty-eight days on which these fronts passed were then compared with the twenty-eight preceding days and the twenty-eight following days, in terms of how many suicides and suicide attempts occurred. The numbers were almost exactly the same (4, 4, 4 suicides; 27, 27, 25 suicide attempts). These days were then lumped together into eighty-four days of presumably turbulent or changeable weather related to passage of fronts. The incidence of suicides and suicide attempts was not significantly different on these eight-four days from the incidence during the remainder of the year.

D. *Distribution of Suicide Rates in the United States.* In an attempt to check the effects of latitude, we looked at the crude suicide rates for each of the United States, for the year 1959. There is no visible relationship to latitude (see Figure 4).

DISCUSSION

It is evident that no relationship of suicide or suicide attempts to any weather variable was found. It seems likely to us that the many claims and alleged findings in the literature are based on poor, inaccurate data. We have demonstrated that many seeming relationships evaporate when one takes into consideration the very uneven distribution of weather conditions throughout a year; the hours of suicides and suicide attempts turn out to be fairly typical samples of the hours of the year.

It might be claimed that we failed to demonstrate seasonal or monthly changes because of mild weather in Houston. The same might be said of the similar negative findings of Farberow and Shneidman in Los Angeles County. However, any resident of Texas will acknowledge that we have a highly changeable and strenuous climate.

A question might also be raised concerning the possible influence of widespread air conditioning, in lessening the formerly-noted effects of weather. The data for Texas for the years 1949 through 1961 do not show any decrease in adjusted suicide rates (range of 7.5 to 9.4/100,000/yr.)[9] Yet during these twenty years there was a rapid spread in use of air conditioning in the state.

Of course it is a commonplace observation that weather affects how we feel, in the sense of "exhilarating", "gloomy", "oppressive", "bright", "dismal", etc. days. Such mild, "normal" mood responses to weather conditions are a far cry quantitatively from the degree of mental upheaval that is associated with suicide; there may also be a qualitative difference.

SUMMARY

The sixty-seven suicides and 373 suicide attempts occurring in Houston in 1960, in which the time of occurrence could be established, were studied in terms of weather conditions at time of their occurrence. Eleven weather variables (temperature, wind speed, wind direction, barometric pressure, relative humidity, visibility, ceiling height, rain, fog, thunderstorms, and cloudiness) were studied. The distribution of each for all hours of the year was obtained, and this was compared with the distribution during those hours in which a suicide or suicide attempt occurred. No single significant relationship was found. The twenty-eight northerly fronts of 1960 were not found to be associated with any change in rate of suicide or suicide attempts. Month and season likewise showed no significant relationship. It is concluded that suicide and suicide attempts are not significantly related to weather phenomena.

NOTES

1 S. Blumer, *Gesundht. Wohlft.*, 25 : 89, 1945.
2 R. G. Curtin, *Trans. Am. Clin. Climat. Ass.*, 25 : 141, 1909.
3 E. G. Dexter, *Pop. Sci. Mon.*, 58 : 604, 1900.
4 Emile Durkheim, *Suicide*, Glencoe, Ill. : Free Press, 1951.

5 N. L. Farberow, and E. S. Shneidman, *The Cry for Help,* New York: McGraw-Hill, 1961.

6 C. H. Hughes, *Alien Neurol.,* 30: 634, 1909.

7 C. A. Mills, *Am. J. Psychiat.,* 91: 669, 1934.

8 J. R. Miner, *Am. J. Hyg.,* Monogr. Ser., No. 2: 1, 1922.

9 Personal Communication: Records and Statistics Section, Texas State Dept. of Health, Austin, Texas, 1963.

10 W. F. Peterson, *The Patient and the Weather,* Vol. III, Ann Arbor, Mich.: Edwards Bros., 1934.

11 ——, *Man, Weather, Sun,* Springfield, Ill.: C. C. Thomas, 1947.

12 W. F. R. Phillips, *Trans. Am. Clin. Climat. Ass.,* 25: 156, 1909.

13 P. Sainsbury, *Suicide in London,* London: Chapman & Hall, 1955.

14 F. H. Smith, *Lancet,* 2: 837, 1908.

15 E. Stengel and N. G. Cook, *Attempted Suicide,* London: Chapman & Hall, 1958.

16 H. J. Tholuck, *Beitr. Gerichtl. Med.,* 16: 121, 1942.

17 U.S. Department of Commerce, Weather Bureau, Hourly and Monthly Climatological Data, Houston, Texas, International Airport, 1960.

18 G. Vidoni, *Manicomio,* 38: 107, 1925.

CHAPTER 24

Suicide and Suggestibility—the Role of the Press*

Jerome A. Motto

> That suicides are alarmingly frequent in this country is evident
> to all—and as a means of prevention, we respectfully suggest
> the propriety of not publishing the details of such occurrences.
> "No fact", says a late writer, "is better established in science
> than that suicide is often committed from imitation. A single
> paragraph may suggest suicide to twenty persons. Some particu-
> lars of the act, or expressions, seize the imagination, and the
> disposition to repeat it, in a moment of morbid excitement,
> proves irresistible." In the justness of these remarks we concur,
> and commend them to the consideration of the conductors of
> the periodical press.[1]

This statement made in 1845 by Amariah Brigham, the founder
and first editor of the *American Journal of Insanity* gives only a
hint of the heated battle that later was to ensue around the role
of newspaper reporting as a factor in suicidal deaths. In 1894 the
New York Times charged that the *New York World* had precipitated an unprecedented number of suicides by publishing an article
on the relationship of suicide to sin.

An effort to validate this charge statistically revealed no basis for
it, but the *Times* nevertheless maintained that many suicides in subsequent months or years would doubtless be due to the *World's*
dissemination of this article.[10] The effect was compared to a lingering infection which newspapers thrust upon the reading public, to
appear at some later time in suicidal or criminal acts.[10,13]

The controversy seemed to reach a peak in the first decade of the
1900s, culminating in a rash of suicides in Cleveland, Ohio, in 1910.[3]
The American Academy of Medicine devoted a section of its annual
meeting in 1911 to this matter, and the medical, legal, and religious
opinions expressed were unanimous in characterizing the public
press in such terms as "incendiary literature", "vile and pernicious",
and "an accomplice in crimes against the person".[10,14]

* Reprinted by permission from the *American Journal of Psychiatry*,
Vol. 124, 1967, pp. 252–6. Copyright © 1967 The American Psychiatric
Association.

In the same year, the National Association of Retail Druggists protested newspaper accounts giving names and dosages of poisons used in suicide attempts as "inducing morbid people and criminals to use these poison".[7] Two years later a wave of suicides by ingestion of bichloride of mercury was noted to subside after newspaper accounts deleted mention of the drug.[8]

In England, a district health officer asserted in the London *Times* in 1931 that the ultimate cause of suicide is "the repeated reading of the unrestricted reports in the press of cases of suicide and the method whereby life has been taken",[2] and the British Medical Association moved in 1948 to prohibit press reports of inquests in cases of suicide, observing that the publicity might lead to imitative suicides.[12] Louis Dublin, an experienced investigator of suicide, commented in 1963, "if the press would refrain from exploiting suicide by disclosing all the gruesome details and would publish only a casual death notice, a very definite reform would be achieved".[4]

Although imitation has long been recognized as an important factor influencing human behaviour, its significance as regards suicide has remained in the realm of speculation. Newspapers have been seen as a stimulus for imitation through their wide circulation and tendency to print "news" or suicide in detail. Unfortunately the lack of systematic inquiry has precluded all but theoretical controversy. A search for reports of such an inquiry has produced only Wadsworth's investigation, which led him to the conclusion in 1911 that "physicians and other experts . . . rarely keep records of the influence of reading matter (on suicide and crime), but have a quite general conviction of the power of suggestion in this as in other directions".[13]

This report attempts to establish a firmer base for understanding this facet of the highly complex problem of suicide.

METHOD

The hypothesis tested is that the suppression of newspaper accounts of suicidal behaviour will significantly reduce such behaviour in the population concerned. Time periods were identified during which large metropolitan areas in the U.S. were completely without local newspaper coverage, i.e. no newspaper was being published in the city during the period in question. These were periods during which strikes led to complete cessation of publishing activities.

Importation of some newspapers from neighbouring cities occurred, but this is regarded as negligible when compared to normal circulation. Further contamination is recognized from the increased radio and television usage that presumably would occur when newspapers are not available.

The incidence of suicide in these areas during the period of newspaper blackout was determined, as was the incidence during the same months of each of the five years prior to the newspaper blackout. The number of suicides during these periods was converted to rates per 100,000 population per year for purposes of comparison. The resulting figures were plotted to determine whether a trend existed prior to the blackout period which might influence the comparison.

The suicide rate during the period of newspaper blackout was then compared to the mean rate for the prior five years, accounting for population increase (use of rate rather than incidence), seasonal variation (same months), population characteristics (same city), and previously existing trends (visual inspection of plotted rates).

Seven cities were found to meet the requirement for "complete" cessation of newspaper publication. The many strikes in this country and in Europe which allowed even one paper to publish or saw an abbreviated publication by management personnel were not included. The seven cities included in this report represent two from the east coast (New York, Baltimore), two north central (Cleveland, Detroit), two west coast (Portland, Seattle), and one of atypical population for an American city (Honolulu).

RESULTS

The data obtained are summarized in Table 1. Visual inspection reveals, that in five cities the suicide rate during the newspaper blackout was lower than the mean of the control years (Baltimore,

TABLE 1

Suicide Rates During Periods of Newspaper Blackout and Control Periods

City	Blackout Duration (Days)	Year	Suicide Rate per 100,000 per Year*								
				Years Surrounding Blackout Period						Five-Year Mean, No Blackout	Black-out Period
			−5	−4	−3	−2	−1	+1	+2		
Baltimore	48	1965	13.4	9.70	14.2	11.1	13.6	—	—	12.4	11.1
New York	109	1963	10.3	8.94	10.5	10.0	9.33	—	—	9.81	9.78
Cleveland[a]	130	1963	—	—	12.1	10.2	12.6	7.60	10.1	10.5	9.90
Detroit	135	1964	8.49	10.0	9.90	8.40	9.30	—	—	9.22	9.30
Portland[b]	25	1949	12.7	28.0	25.9	22.0	13.3	—	—	22.3	22.1
Seattle[c]	56	1945	55.2	41.4	34.0	27.1	17.3	33.7	46.5	36.5	31.5
Honolulu	63	1963	10.0	9.72	6.76	17.0	11.3	—	—	11.0	13.3
(Oahu)	(63)	(1963)	(9.55)	(14.4)	(11.3)	(19.3)	(12.7)	—	—	(13.4)	(22.2)[d]

* Rates are for the months of newspaper blackout and the comparable control periods only, expanded to a yearly rate per 100,000.
[a] Includes two years following blackout because figures are available for only three years.
[b] 1944 omitted in calculations to minimize contamination of World War II.
[c] Includes two subsequent years to clarify trend.
[d] Significant at 0.01 level.

New York, Cleveland, Portland, and Seattle). In none of these is the degree of variation from the expected figure significant (chi square). In the two cities with a higher suicide rate during the newspaper black out than during the control period (Detroit and Honolulu) the variation is similarly within the chance fluctuation of the control years. It is of interest that if the entire island of Oahu is considered rather than the city of Honolulu alone, the increase in suicide during the newspaper blackout is significantly higher than the expected figure (chi square, $p = < .01$). No significant trends were observed with the exception of Seattle, in which the blackout period initiated a rising rate following a marked dip in the plotted pattern of the prior five years.

The Wilcoxon matched-pairs signed-ranks test, which considers the magnitude as well as the direction of differences in the suicide rates of the control and experimental populations, likewise indicates that the observed differences in the rates of these populations are not significant at the .05 level.

DISCUSSION

Increasing interest in preventive programmes in community psychiatry adds urgency to the need for a sound body of data on which action can be based. The contention that unrestricted newspaper reporting of suicidal behaviour precipitates such behaviour on the part of susceptible readers is not supported by the data presented here. In at least one population (Oahu) the reverse is seen, in that cessation of newspaper coverage was attended by an increase in suicidal behaviour rather than the hypothesized decrease. This may reflect a significant difference in the characteristics of the Hawaiian population.

In any case it forces us to ask whether the sense of contact afforded by the newspaper may serve an integrating function for many persons that outweighs the negative influence of lurid reporting. An ideal experimental situation would permit newspaper publishing as usual, but with reports of suicide omitted or limited to a single statement that the event occurred.

Two issues demand special consideration in interpreting these data. Firstly, other pertinent social variables must be taken into account—economic forces, changing ratios of subcultures and age groups in the population studied, states of war or national emergency, coroners' attitudes about identification and reporting of suicide, and the effect on suicide attempts as well as on completed suicides.

Secondly, there is a chicken/egg controversy as to whether we focus on the suggestive potential of the reported "news" or on the pathological suggestibility of the person exposed to it. Meerloo emphasizes the former in terms of a universal "mystic yearning for self-destruction" that can be stirred through example to "drag ... people into hidden masochism".[9]

Durkheim takes the opposite view, insisting on the "very slight" role of imitation on suicidal behaviour, yet recognizing the frequency with which publicized details of such behaviour expose "a state which is the true cause of the act and which probably would have produced its natural effect even had imitation not intervened".[5] Granting that it might possibly reduce the annual incidence of suicide, Durkheim correctly predicted that legislators would hesitate to suppress publicity for such doubtful advantages.

Meerloo provides an example of how news media may trigger the suicide of a predisposed person by citing the death of a 38-year-old woman who killed herself after seeing a TV programme about cancer. She had previously feared cancer, "worried about her eyes", and had previously threatened suicide.[11]

Durkheim emphasized that although some individuals may respond to suicidal suggestion, this has no sociological implications, i.e. the suicide rate of the society would not be affected. This intuitive view appears to gain support from the 40% increase in suicides in Los Angeles during the month of the suicide of Marilyn Monroe in August 1962 without significant change in the yearly suicide rate. It is of interest that this immediate increase was attributable largely to a jump in male suicides for that month only, suggesting a "reaction to loss" element.

On the other hand, the subsequent year saw a 42% increase in female suicides, which raises the issue of identification with the person whose suicide is publicized. Though each case would require study to clarify this, clinical experience suggests that such identification prior to the reported suicide can be an important factor, compounded in this instance by the "acting out" element in the personality structure of those likely to identify with this particular person.

No such flurry of suicides was noted after the self-inflicted death of Ernest Hemingway, whose unusual sensitivity was tempered by a rugged and confident pattern of living. It is likely that when identification is limited to the act of suicide alone rather than with the person who has suicided, it can provide some reduction of suicidal drive through the vicarious experience of the destructive acts detailed in the press.

An effort to determine in one city (Detroit) the effect of a newspaper blackout on suicide attempts as distinct from completed suicide provided the information that a rising trend has been interrupted (Table 2). The significance of this change and the role of

TABLE 2

Suicide Attempts in Detroit per 100,000 Population

Year	Rate per 100,000 per year
1959	43.2
1960	53.7
1961	60.7
1962	80.0
1963	83.0
1964	79.0*

* Period (131 days) of newspaper blackout.

the newspaper in it could not be determined here, but this aspect of suicide attempts appears to deserve further consideration as a dimension of the degree to which persons who make suicide attempts and those who complete that act comprize different populations.

An example of an apparent change which is clearly attributable to a trend is seen in the data for Seattle. This reflects the full impact of World War II during the years preceding the newspaper blackout, with the experimental period fitting smoothly into the postwar increase in suicide. Hence this large observed increase cannot be considered statistically significant.

The data reported here would seem to remove any onus from the newspaper practice of publishing details of suicides. This writer joins in the subjective view of Durkheim[5], Fenton[6], and Dublin[4] that the value system inherent in the manner news is usually reported has a deleterious influence on the emotional growth of immature readers, which in turn can later be conducive to increased suicide potential. The contention, however, that newspaper reporting of suicidal behaviour increases by suggestion the incidence of such behaviour in the reading public is yet to be systematically verified.

SUMMARY

The assertion that newspaper reporting of suicidal behaviour precipitates suicide among suggestible readers was examined. The rates of suicide during periods of complete cessation of newspaper publishing in seven major cities were compared with the mean rates for the same calendar periods of the prior five years in each city. The sign test and signed-rank test revealed no significant change during the experimental periods. In one area (the island of Oahu) a significant change was noted in the direction contrary to the hypothesis tested.

The author agrees with others who have considered this question that whatever deleterious effect newspapers may exert on their readers stems more from the implied and expressed attitudes and values system than from news content.

NOTES

1 A. Brigham, 'Statistics of Suicides in the United States'. *Amer. J. Insanity*, 12:253–63, **1911.**

2 'Causes of Suicide; A Mentally Infectious Disease', London *Times*, 28 March 1931, p. 8.

3 *Cleveland Plain-Dealer*, 29 September 1910.

4 L. Dublin, *Suicide*, New York: Ronald Press, 1953.

5 E. Durkheim, *Suicide*, Glencoe, Ill.: The Free Press, 1951, p. 141.

6 F. Fenton, 'The Press and Crimes Against the Person', *Bull. Amer. Acad. Med.*, 12:307–15, 1911.

7 H. Hemenway, 'To What Extent Are Suicide and Crimes Against the Person Due to Suggestion from the Press?', *Bull. Amer. Acad. Med.*, 12:253–63, 1911.

8 R. Kern, 'The Growing Problem of Suicide', *Calif. Med.*, 79:6–10, 1953.

9 J. Meerloo, *Suicide and Mass Suicide*, New York: Grune & Stratton, 1962, p. 136.

10 E. Phelps, 'Neurotic Books and Newspapers as Factors in the Mortality of Suicide and Crime', *Bull Amer. Acad. Med.*, 12:264–306, 1911.

11 'Suicide After Watching Television' (Letter to the Editor), *J.A.M.A.*, 29 497, 1958.

12 'Suicide Inquest Reports; 'Press Ban Proposed by Doctors', London *Times*, 29 June 1948, p. 6.

13 W. Wadsworth, 'The Newspapers and Crime', *Bull. Amer. Acad. Med.*, 12:316–25, 1911.

14 A. Woodbury, quoted by E. Phelps, 'Neurotic Books and Newspapers as Factors in the Mortality of Suicide and Crime', *Bull. Amer. Acad. Med.*, 12:264–306, 1911.

PART V

CHAPTER 25

The Social Context of the Suicidal Act

A vast body of research on suicide, particularly that of a more psychological nature, has been based upon material gathered about people who have attempted suicide "unsuccessfully". The reasons for this are obvious: very often the only information which is available about people who "successfully" kill themselves is *ex post facto*. In one sense it would be wrong to draw a clear-cut division between "attempted suicide" on the one hand, and "completed suicide" on the other, since whether or not a given suicidal act "fails" is dependent upon various different circumstances. From this aspect it is clear that "suicidal actions" should be studied as a whole. From another aspect, however, it is necessary to differentiate degrees of "seriousness of intent" in suicidal actions: because, in a broad range of suicidal or self-punitive actions death is not the sole objective, but nor is the act one of pure dissimulation.

The *mélange* of motives and ideas which usually seems to be present in suicidal actions probably in most cases involves both conscious and unconscious elements. Unconscious motives are probably especially important with regard to the notion of death held by an individual, which in turn is of some significance in influencing suicide.[1] Hendin's paper is relevant here.[2] He bases his approach upon the theory of depression set out in Freud's short paper "Mourning and melancholia", and developed by Rado. Hendin points to the shortcomings of these ideas as a theory of suicide: not all suicidal individuals by any means show the typical depressive melancholic pattern, and not all depressed people manifest any recognizable suicidal tendencies. It is necessary, therefore, both to modify and add to the classical theory of depression. Hendin attempts to do so, in relation to a cross-cultural comparison which includes cases from Scandinavia as well as from the United States. He separates the cases he discussess into three categories: those who attempted suicide (but survived) with "maximal suicidal intent"; those who did so with "moderate intent"; and those who had only "minimal intent" in carrying out a suicidal act. On the basis of these, Hendin sets out a number of "psychodynamic constellations" related to death, which he considers most significant in influencing the character and the degree of "seriousness" of the suicide attempt.

Some of the earliest studies of suicide in the nineteenth century used suicide notes as a means of information; but since only a minority of those who kill themselves leave notes, many students have regarded them as a dubious form of evidence. Such notes are, however, often the only source of information which we have, apart from what a suicide may have said to others, of a man's conscious intentions prior to killing himself. Jacobs uses suicide notes to attempt to construct a picture of how a suicidal individual conceives his proposed action, stressing what the author sees as distinctively rational elements in most of these statements of intention.

Rational deliberation is an obvious quality of many suicide pacts, as Cohen makes clear. As he points out, agreement to commit suicide jointly usually involves a certain amount of conscious preparation and deliberate intent. When two people plan to die together by their own hand, their resolve is apparently in most instances hardened well before the act itself takes place. "Their grim secret is carefully guarded", Cohen says, "if necessary for weeks or months before the appointed day ... mostly the preparations for death are so meticulous that both parties perish". Cohen shows that the popular notion that suicide pacts are mostly made by illicit lovers is, in England at least, false. About 80% of the cases he examined involved husband and wife partnerships. A common circumstance leading to a suicide pact between man and wife is where one partner is seriously ill, and where the other has no wish to survive him. The cases which Cohen describes are notably lacking in any aggressive connotations expressed towards others, and it is a problem of some interest how far suicide pacts can be interpreted in terms of existing theories of suicide.

The following paper, by Robins and others, examines the very important question of the type of "warnings of intent" given by suicides prior to the act. They attempt to circumvent some of the methodological problems involved in studying this type of problem by interviewing relatives and friends soon after the occurrence of a suicide. Their most significant conclusion is that nearly 70% of the suicides in the group studied gave some prior warning to others of their intention to kill themselves. While this prior communication of intent took a number of forms, in over 40% of cases the individuals had made a verbal statement of intention to commit suicide. The authors find no significant differences in the proportion of suicides giving prior warning of intent between men and women, nor any differences in age, marital status, religion, education or occupation.

The concluding three papers each grapple directly with the problem of the relationship between attempted and completed suicide. Both Weiss and Stengel discuss evidence that implies that, as the former expresses it, "successful suicides and unsuccessful suicidal attempts represent two different kinds of acts performed in different ways by different people". Both authors consider suicides and attempted suicides to be separate, although overlapping, populations. Weiss quotes an estimate that true rates of attempted suicide are up to seven times as great as completed suicide; Stengel believes the ratio is probably as high as ten to one. Both indicate some of the well-known differentials in rates of attempted and completed suicide: that, for example, rates of completed suicide are higher for men, and increase with age, while rates of attempted suicide are higher for women and reach a peak in the younger age-groups. Wilkins' article offers a heavily annotated survey of the recent literature on attempted suicide. Summarizing the results of a large number of studies, he shows that, according to their findings, between 7% to 16% of people who kill themselves had made at least one prior attempt, although in one study the proportion was as high as a third. Approaching the same issue from the other side, studies of the percentage of people attempting suicide who subsequently actually kill themselves indicate that the proportion is usually between 2% to 10%. Research upon the frequency with which people who have attempted suicide later attempt again ("unsuccessfully") indicates that as many as 25% do so. Finally, analysing research upon the degree to which suicidal actions are preceded by some form of verbal warning of intention given by the actor, Wilkins points out that prior warnings seem to be given in a higher percentage of cases of completed suicide than in cases of attempted suicide, a fact which has a number of potentially important implications.

NOTES

1 Cf. in relation to this point the interesting discussion by Shneidman and Farberow in 'The logic of suicide', in Edwin S. Shneidman and Norman L. Farberow, *Clues to Suicide,* New York, 1957; and Herman Feifel, *The Meanings of Death,* New York, 1959.
2 See also his *Suicide and Scandinavia,* New York, 1964.

CHAPTER 26

The Psychodynamics of Suicide*

Herbert Hendin

What the suicidal patient wishes to get away from in life is only part of his story. His observed attitudes towards death, dying and afterlife are equally revealing about him and his motivation for suicide. This paper will indicate some psychodynamic patterns of suicide based on differing attitudes towards death on the part of suicidal patients. The case illustrations are taken from patients seen by the writer in New York City at Bellevue Hospital, the New York State Psychiatric Institute and St Luke's Hospital, as well as from patients observed in three Scandinavian countries.[4-8]

BACKGROUND OF THE PROBLEM

The first important psychological insight in the literature about suicide came from Freud. He was not working directly with the problem of suicide and in his work described only one patient who actually made a suicide attempt.[3] What he did see, however, and in good number, were depressed patients. Freud observed in "Mourning and Melancholia" (1916) that the self-hatred seen in depression originated in anger toward a love object turned back by the individual on himself.[1] Freud reasoned that suicide was the ultimate form of the phenomenon and that there would be no suicide without the earlier repressed desire to kill someone else. The concept that suicide can be a kind of inverted murder was extremely important, although unfortunately it became overworked by some in an effort to explain all suicide.

Freud made his observations on depression years before he had concluded that anger or aggression could be non-erotic in origin. At the time he wrote "Mourning and Melancholia", all aggression had to have, in Freud's view, a sexual origin, so that the paper is filled with complicated and undemonstrable discussion of what amounts to retroflexed anger. Ten years later Freud expressed

* Reprinted from the *Journal of Nervous and Mental Disease*, Vol. 136, 1963, pp. 236–44. Copyright © 1963 The Williams & Wilkins Company, Baltimore, Md., 21202, U.S.A.

surprise at his having overlooked the "universality of non-erotic aggression".[3] He never rewrote his earlier work so the extraneous libidinal explanations for the existence of anger remain unaltered. This, however, should not lead one to overlook the basic psychological truth contained in the 1916 paper, namely, that anger can become self-directed, can lead to depression and can be a motivating force in suicide.

The current view of depression has also been revised over the years. The significance of both dependency and expiation in depression was made clear by Sandor Rado.[10] The idea that retroflexed anger and self-punishment can have atonement or expiation as goals, the individual hoping thus to win back love and affection, does not appear in Mourning and Melancholia, and was primarily Rado's contribution. And just as retroflexed anger can at times be the motivating force in suicidal patients, so too, can suicide be an act of expiation.

Despite the help that a knowledge of the psychology of depression gives to the understanding of suicide, it is far from the whole picture. A great number of suicidal patients do not manifest the clinical features or classical psychodynamics associated with depression. Most important to keep in mind, however, is the fact that many depressed patients are just not suicidal. This alone would emphasize that the psychodynamics of depression are not sufficient to explain suicide, and thus the study of depressed patients cannot be used as a substitute for directly studying suicidal patients. In investigating suicidal patients one often sees patients who appear to view their death as internalized murder, while others' suicide attempts are acts of expiation, but there is, in addition, a broad range of other attitudes towards death and meanings of the act of suicide.

HOW TO STUDY THE PROBLEM

In first working with the problem of suicide at Bellevue, 100 consecutive admissions of attempted suicides to the hospital were interviewed. They were seen as often as was felt necessary to get a full psychodynamic picture of each case. Patients who had made suicide attempts were later taken into therapy, criteria for selection being as varied a sampling of suicidal motivations and situations as possible. As many as fifteen patients who had made suicide attempts were in therapy at one period during this investigation. Currently at St Luke's Hospital, in addition to the intensive interviewing of the suicidal patients, the writer has also been working with hypnosis, in an attempt to get at the psychodynamics of individual patients and what their motivations for suicide are. In all these approaches, however, as well as in cross-cultural work that the writer has been doing with suicidal patients in Scandinavia, all patients seen have attempted suicide and, obviously, survived. The question often raised—are those who attempted suicide and survived a comparable group in terms of personality and motivation to those who actually died?—bears on any evaluation of the psychodynamics of suicide.

Long ago it proved helpful to rate or evaluate suicidal patients on a scale of one to three with regard to their suicidal intent (1—the patients with minimal intent; 2—with moderate intent; and 3— with maximal suicidal intent [4]). The following two cases illustrate types of patients in the maximal intent group. One was a girl who jumped under a subway train, had two cars pass over her and still lived. This was possible in the particular subway, since there was sufficient room between the wheels and under the train, but this was not known by the girl at the time. A second patient had made a suicide pact with his homosexual partner. They made their attempt in their hotel room on a Saturday night, knowing they would probably not be discovered by the chambermaid until Monday morning. They each took fifty barbiturates of 1/10th gramme strength. When found and admitted to the hospital on Monday, they were both comatose and remained so for several days. The initial hospital opinion was that neither would survive. As it turned out, one died and the other lived. The one who lived, however, was placed in the group of those with maximal intent.

It seems reasonable to include the girl under the train and the homosexual man in this group and to assume that in working with them one is working with a situation as close to that resulting in actual suicide as one needs to get. When suicidal patients are divided into intent groups, the group with maximal intent has an age and sex distribution statistically comparable to that of actual suicides, and is quite different from that found when one takes all attempted suicides together.[4]

A great deal about suicide can also be learned from the study of patients in the lower intent groups. When, for example, suicide is an act of self-punishment, for one patient only death will be sufficient atonement, while for another the self-damage done in a suicide attempt may suffice. The study of both types, however, throws light on the psychology of self-punishment and its relation to suicide.

While distinguishing between a patient who is very serious about suicide and one who is not serious at all is not very difficult, the situation is a little more complicated with patients who are in the intermediate group. Patients who have survived taking as many as twenty-five sleeping pills may say they only wished to sleep and yet admit that they did have the thought that it might be nice never to wake up. They can appear themselves to be unsure whether they wanted to die. One is impressed that there are mixed feelings about the wish to die in most suicidal patients. Menninger, in particular, has stressed and illustrated some of the variations seen in patients' conscious and unconscious wishes with regard to dying.[9] Tolstoy describes in *Anna Karenina* the heroine's last feelings and sensations after jumping in front of a train: she feels that she has perhaps made a mistake and struggles unsuccessfully to get up before the train hits her. Tolstoy's sensitive intuition in this regard seems very much borne out by what is learned from actual suicidal patients. One suspects that if a man jumping from a tall building could be interviewed while still in the air three floors down from the top, his feelings about dying would often be already different from what they had been a few seconds before. A recently interviewed patient said she had wished to change her mind right before jumping from a building, but that since she had committed herself in a letter to this action, she was unable to back out.

Hypnosis can be useful in evaluating a patient's suicidal intent as well as his motivation. It is of most obvious use in reconstructing and recovering amnesias connected with suicide attempts. Patients who were under the influence of alcohol at the time and are vague as to the details of the attempt can often recall under hypnosis far more than otherwise. Similarly, one patient who had shot himself with a shotgun and survived was amnestic for all that happened in the minutes prior to pulling the trigger. Under hypnosis his thoughts and feelings during that period as well as the details of his attempt could be recovered.

The most important use of hypnosis as a research tool in studying suicide, however, comes from another direction. As will be more evident in the section below on the psychodynamics of suicide, the dreams of these patients immediately before or after their suicide attempts often deal directly with their death or suicide and are of very great value in getting a psychodynamic picture of the patient. This seems natural enough, for when patients are interviewed soon after their attempts, the dynamics are close to consciousness and apt to be revealed in their dreams. When months have elapsed, these dynamics may be so repressed that a patient may have to be seen in therapy for a long time before the material becomes similarly accessible. Thus, generally it is advisable to see patients within the first days after their attempted suicide. When patients have not been obliging enough to remember dreams during the period of their suicide attempts, hypnosis can be of value. The writer has hypnotized such patients and had them go back in their thoughts to the time of their attempt and to the mood of that time. It was then suggested to them that they would have a dream while under hypnosis, such as they might have had the night they made their suicide attempt, and which would throw some light on their reasons for wanting to kill themselves. While such a technique is productive with only about a third of suicidal patients, from the research standpoint invaluable material can be so learned. In discussing the psychodynamics of suicide some of this material will be considered.

THE PSYCHODYNAMICS OF SUICIDE

The details, method and circumstances of the suicide attempt often give the first important clue as to the psychodynamics of the particular patient, and they must be carefully established. Often the suicide attempt is a kind of psychological drama and the very way in which it is made is extremely revealing. One woman jumped from a window with a picture of her son in her brassiere and a message on the back of the picture saying, "Timmy knows I love him". Years before, at the time of her divorce, this woman actually had given away her young son to be raised by his paternal grandparents. While she still saw him up to the time of the attempt, she appeared to be tortured by her difficulties in love relationships and her inability to love her son. The picture and message were an attempt to deny the true state of affairs and yet gave the first clue that put one on the right track.

Another older man who made an attempt with barbiturates arranged his attempt so he might be found by his son before succumbing. The man had been separated from his wife for a year, after twenty-five years of marriage, and despite the details of the attempt the relationship with his wife appeared to be the crucial factor. Only when, after three days in the hospital, he reported a dream in which his son fed him poison was it possible for me to reverse my thinking: it became obvious it was the patient's relationship with his son which was the major determinant in this case.

The choice of method involved may very often reveal a good deal about the organization and integration of the personality. Disorganized or multiple suicidal methods, or those carried out in a chaotic manner and lasting over several days, are generally chosen by disorganized, schizoid patients.

It may seem surprising that, in many studies of suicide in the literature, the attitudes of suicidal patients towards death, dying and afterlife have been neglected. In a large measure, this can be attributed to anxiety and inhibition of psychiatrists in relation to suicidal patients. It is reflected right down to the resident on the ward who will ask a patient after ten minutes' acquaintance if he has had homosexual experiences or what he does with regard to masturbation, but will not ask a suicidal patient about his attitude towards death, about what he thinks happens after death, about what he thought of after he turned on the gas and what he might have dreamt of while he was unconscious. These last four questions can elicit invaluable material bearing on the understanding of suicidal patients and their motivation.

The following are some of the varying psychodynamic constellations with regard to death and suicide that have been observed in suicidal patients:

Death as retaliatory abandonment: A homosexual college boy of eighteen who was failing in school was seen following a serious suicide attempt with sixty barbituate pills which he barely survived. During a hypnotic interview it was suggested to the patient that he would have a dream such as he might have had the night of his suicidal attempt. His dream was a simple one. He was working for the United Nations and had an office that occupied the entire first floor of the UN building in New York. A friend of his was applying for a position and the patient was interviewing him and reviewing his qualifications. He told his friend that he did not qualify and could not have the job. During his waking associations to the dream he revealed his preoccupation with this friend. It appeared that he "had a crush on", but had never tried to become involved sexually with the friend although the friend may have become alarmed at the intensity of the patient's feelings. The friend had been quite obviously backing out of the relationship and several months prior to the attempt had more or less broken off with the patient.

What does the patient accomplish in the dream and by the suicide attempt? He gains an illusory control over the situation that involves rejection. In the dream, if there is any rejecting to be done, he is going to do it; by committing suicide, he is the one who leaves or does the rejecting. The conception that death involves an act of leaving, i.e. an abandonment, is known to derive from childhood. Children's reactions to death most frequently centre around its being a violent act inflicted on the dead person or as his having "left" voluntarily. Children who lose or are separated from their mothers invariably react as though the mothers had chosen to leave them. The continuation of this psychological equation is seen in adult life among patients with extreme fears of dying which are usually emotionally linked with the most primitive abandonment fears from childhood.

That this patient also experienced a *feeling of omnipotent mastery through death* is strongly suggested by the important UN position

and large office in his dream. Suicide attempts and the idea of suicide seem to give an illusory feeling of mastery over a situation
through the control one has over whether one lives or dies. Another
patient who had been a chemistry major in college had struggled
through school with a cyanide capsule in his desk, consoling himself
with the thought that if he could not manage his work he could
always take the cyanide. On graduation he threw it out and never
made a suicide attempt. A female patient who eventually did make
a very serious suicide attempt, had in the years prior to her attempt,
kept a toy pistol in her drawer and had comforted herself through an
unhappy love affair with the fantasy that if things got too bad she
could always kill herself.

Death as retroflexed murder: A woman of forty-four had made
a serious suicide attempt with sleeping pills about a year after the
break-up of her marriage. Her husband had been unfaithful during
their twenty years' marriage and she had alternately managed to
deny this to herself or to reassure herself by saying that these
affairs were unimportant to him. The last such relationship, however,
had gone on for almost two years and, while her husband evidently
still did not want to leave her, she precipitated a crisis by barging in
on him in the other woman's apartment. He had then begun to live
with this woman. About six months later she herself became involved
rather unsatisfactorily with a younger man. Her stated attitude immediately following her suicide attempt was that both of her children
and her husband would be better off with her dead. The children
were a boy of nineteen and a girl of fifteen and she said that they
would be better off in a new home. There had been an earlier attempt
ten days before: she had gone out to a lake with the intention of
drowning herself, "changed her mind" and came home and took
fifteen sleeping pills instead. She woke up by herself a day and a
half later and the next time took twice that dose. While under the
influence of the first pills she had the following dream: she saw a
cap belonging to her husband's father floating on the sea and realized
that he had drowned. Her husband's father had been a sea captain
whom she saw as very much like her husband—extremely domineer-
ing, critical and difficult to get along with. At first she saw the dream
in terms of her own martyred role, but eventually she related it to
her desire to strike back at her husband. She spoke vindictively of
the problems with the children that her death would cause him. It
soon became evident that her suicide attempt came out of her anger
at her husband and was an ineffective attempt at revenge. She was
the kind of woman who could do little that was effective with her
anger or self-assertion and could not even fight for her children. Her

situation illustrates the classical one described by Freud in which the suicide is basically an inverted homicide.

Death as a reunion: One patient made three suicide attempts, scattered over a period of some twenty to twenty-five years. When seen for the first time, following her third suicide attempt, she was forty-seven years old. Each attempt had been more serious than the one before; she had been extremely fortunate to survive the last one, with gas. An unfortunate or unhappy love affair was time-related to all three attempts. After two months of treatment following the last attempt, during which the same love affair as had preceded it was continuing unsuccessfully, the patient became acutely suicidal and required admission to the hospital. That night she had the following dream: "I was living in an apartment in Baltimore that I lived in twenty-five years ago. There were a lot of people around telling me to put on a beautiful wedding dress that was hanging on the wall, and I would not put it on."

Her association was to the apartment in Baltimore where her first romantic liaison had lasted for two years, until one night her lover told her he was going to marry another girl. She thereupon made a suicide attempt. Everything in the dream was the same as it had been in her room at the time of that first attempt. In the wedding ceremonies of her two unhappy marriages she had never worn a wedding dress although she had always wanted to. She felt she had lost the really great love of her life with the end of this first relationship. What impressed her most in the dream was that the wedding dress "looked more like a shroud than like a wedding dress". Union with this first love was to be achieved, apparently, only through her death. This patient recalled that she had had this same dream recurrently before each suicide attempt, an interesting detail.

She was, in her dream, refusing to put on the dress, while struggling, in reality, against suicide. Death was the unpleasant price she must pay for the gratification of her desires for love and affection. For other patients with similar but more masochistic psychodynamics, the act of dying itself can be conceived as pleasurably incorporated into the reunion fantasy. Most frequently the emphasis is not put on the dying but on the gratification to follow; the feeling tone in the reunion dreams of such patients is pleasant. In the overwhelming majority the gratification is of an extremely dependent variety, either directly with parental figures or with wives, husbands or siblings operating as substitute parental figures.

While usually such fantasies are unconscious and have to be elicited from dreams, they can also be conscious. One patient, who was seen following a suicide attempt which eventually proved to be fatal, spent the entire year after his wife's death preoccupied with fantasies about her and with mental pictures of being reunited with her in death.

Death as rebirth: A young woman in her twenties had jumped under a train and lost a leg; this suicide attempt was precipitated by one of the unhappy and impossible love relationships with which her life had been filled. Several years earlier she had been intensely involved with a married Negro man. A few years before that she had been involved with a Communist under investigation by the FBI, who was at that time trying to use his relationship with her to get into the United States. This patient was both extremely bright and well-educated. When she was thirteen years old, her father had deserted the family and she had never seen or heard from him again. She had some fascination with death and dying all through adolescence and always remembered by heart death scenes in novels. Under hypnosis and with the suggestion to have a dream about her suicide attempt, she produced the following: She was in a long, narrow tunnel and could see a light at the end of it. She walked towards the light and when she got there, saw a man and woman standing over a manger. In her associations to the dream, the tunnel suggested to her the subway from which she jumped and the way in which the train came out of the tunnel and into the lighted platform area. Coming out of the darkness of the tunnel into light brought to her mind the process of birth. The man and woman she saw as her mother and father. The child in the manger was both the Christ-child and herself. One can see how much she accomplishes in her death fantasy. She is reborn, is a boy, is reunited with her father and is, in addition, omnipotent. It is not hard to imagine that for a patient with such fantasies, dying has a very strong appeal.

Death as a self-punishment: A lawyer in his thirties had made a moderately serious suicide attempt stemming from his lack of success in a legal career. It was impossible to hypnotize him during his stay in the hospital following his suicide attempt; he exemplifies one of the difficulties involved if one were tempted to use hypnosis as a routine matter for the evaluation of all psychiatric patients. He was later quite easy to hypnotize when he returned for a second try after hospital discharge, and it became evident that he feared being hypnotized while in the hospital when he was still actively preoccupied with suicide because he felt that if he revealed material related to the suicide attempt, he would not be discharged. His dreams under hypnosis were of the most elemental kind, involving his running to catch a boat and just missing it. His associations revealed that "missing the boat" symbolized the view he took of his entire career. His legal ambitions were very great and he could make no compromise with his grandiose success fantasies. The aggression connected with this grandiosity interfered with his actual performance. This constellation is frequently observed in male patients with extremely high and rigid standards for themselves. What they see as failure causes an enormous degree of self-hatred, and their suicide can be a self-inflicted punishment for having failed. A high percentage of the male patients in this group have demonstrated a paranoid personality structure in the years prior to their becoming depressed or suicidal.[7] A typical example is one stock-broker of fifty-five who had been depressed to the extent that he was unable to work for several years prior to the suicide attempt which occasioned his being seen by the writer. Before that he had a career spanning thirty years, but changed positions every two or three years. In each he had been the victim, he said, of mistreatment, personal favouritism or corruption. Eventually a combination of these factors and the emotional breakdown of his daughter proved too great for his paranoid defences, and what was probably always a latent depression made itself evident. He then began blaming himself and his unworthiness for his work failures and bemoaning his misfortune with his daughter. In the course of several months' therapy he became paranoid towards the writer; at the same time, his depression lifted sufficiently so that he could resume work. When his paranoid defences were activated in relation to his psychiatrist, his depressive symptomatology lessened and he became able to function.

These sorts of suicidal self-punishment reactions with women over failure to work have not been observed, however. A suicidal self-punishment reaction that is often seen in women was illustrated by the case mentioned earlier of the woman who felt herself unable to love her child. When a woman is unable to love her child and this is accompanied by the expectation that she should feel what she is not feeling—strong self-hatred with a consequent need for self-punishment can be the result.

A variation of the view of suicide as a self-punishment seen in patients of both sexes may be illustrated by the following patient. He was a thirty-year-old man from a relatively stable rural family. He was the sixth of eight children and stated that he had felt "superfluous" since childhood. All the other siblings were married and he felt that they were leading responsible lives, and that he was the black sheep of the family. Since the age of eighteen he had been a moderately severe alcoholic. He had made an impossible marriage in which he also had felt "superfluous" and which quickly led to divorce. His employment had been mainly as a seaman, but his explosive temper and frequent fights aboard ship had made it impossible for him to continue in this capacity and he was depressed over this. He reported the following dream immediately prior to an impulsive suicide attempt in which he jumped in front of a moving car. "An atom bomb was falling." ... "I was in hell and about to be burned. My brother was above, saying that I should be burned." The patient said he would end up in hell if he did not lead "a more Christian life". Eight months earlier he had begun attending church in an effort to force himself to live differently, but without success. His mother was extremely religious and opposed to drinking, smoking or any amusement for its own sake. He had never been close to her, but had taken over her religious beliefs, although he felt unable to live up to them. The brother in the dream was the family member the patient had felt most close to although the relationship has been characterized by fights and reconciliations until the time of his brother's death three years earlier.

The patient had made several impulsive suicide attempts during the previous eight years, including one where he jumped in front of a moving jeep and had been severely injured. Suicide was for him an act of atonement, and death a punishment he felt he deserved for his explosiveness, his anger towards his siblings and the world and for the asocial existence he was leading.

Among the most disturbed male and female suicidal patients seen in the mental hospital, feelings of being worthless and no good predominate, and self-punishment is a prominent feature. The original motivation may be centred around failure, guilt over aggression or attempted expiation, but the self-punishment can become dissociated from these goals and become almost an end in itself. Such patients can then become preoccupied with delusional feelings of guilt, sin and unworthiness.

The patient who sees himself as already dead: One man who jumped in front of a train had lost one leg almost to the hip, and an arm. Some months after the attempt he related a dream in which he was shopping for a coffin, and the coffin-maker told him that his coffin was a little over half-finished. Considering that he had lost two limbs in his suicide attempt, the dream seemed a fairly obvious current picture of himself. His associations and elaborations to the dream indicated that he felt that only his physical death was half completed. He considered that he had died emotionally or affectively several years before making any suicide attempt.

One very withdrawn suicidal girl of eighteen seen by the writer had a recurrent nightmare in which she saw dry ice coming closer and closer to her and threatening to envelop her, until she woke in panic. She was tormented by her inability to feel for people and she not only felt dead but her physical and motor appearance suggested a kind of walking death. Her dry ice image was a self-image that was seen as permanently frozen, dangerous to others and self-destructive.

These patients were representative of an entire group who are preoccupied with feeling already dead, generally not in a delusional sense but in the sense of being emotionally dead. Strong feelings of detachment, repressed aggression and dampened affectivity are often perceived by the patients as a kind of emotional dying or death. Clinically, they will often appear apathetic rather than depressed, and their suicide attempts do not usually change this mood. Despite the overt apathy, such deadness is experienced by the suicidal patients as extremely torturous and they seem to see suicide both as a release from suffering and as merely carrying out an event which has already happened.

SUMMARY

This article attempts to demonstrate some of the psychodynamic patterns seen in suicidal patients based on different fantasies and attitudes towards death. Seven such patterns are outlined and illustrated: death as abandonment, death as omnipotent mastery, death as retroflexed murder, death as a reunion, death as rebirth, death as self-punishment or atonement, death as a process that in an emotional sense has already taken place.

NOTES

1 S. Freud, 'Mourning and melancholia' (1917), Collected Papers, Vol. 4, pp. 152–70, Hogarth Press, London, 1949.
2 S. Freud, 'Psychogenesis of a case of homosexuality in a woman' (1920), Collected Papers, Vol. 11, pp. 202–31, Hogarth Press, London, 1949.
3 S. Freud, Civilization and Its Discontents (1930), Hogarth Press, London, 1949.
4 H. Hendin, 'Attempted suicide: A psychiatric and statistical study', Psychiat. Quart., 24:39–46, 1950.
5 H. Hendin, 'Suicide', Psychiat. Quart., 30:267–82, 1956.
6 H. Hendin, 'Suicide in Denmark', Psychiat. Quart., 34: 443–60, 1960.
7 H. Hendin, 'Suicide: Psychoanalytic point of view'. In N. L. Farberow, and E. S. Shneidman (eds.), The Cry for Help, pp. 181–92, McGraw-Hill, New York, 1961.
8 H. Hendin, 'Suicide in Sweden', Psychiat. Quart., 35:1–28, 1962.
9 K. Menninger, Man Against Himself, pp. 71–6, Harcourt, Brace. New York, 1938.
10 S. Rado, 'Psychodynamics of depression from the etiological point of view', Psychosom. Med., 13:51–5, 1951.

CHAPTER 27

A Phenomenological Study of Suicide Notes*

Jerry Jacobs

According to Durkheim, the prospect of finding a common denominator in the personal situations of suicides is minimal.

> ... the circumstances are almost infinite in number which are supposed to cause suicide because they rather frequently accompany it.

In defining the range and effect of personal circumstances on the individual, Durkheim tells us:

> ... some men resist horrible misfortune, while others kill themselves after slight troubles. Moreover, we have shown that those who suffer most are not those who kill themselves most.... At least, if it really sometimes occurs that the victim's personal situation is the effective cause of his resolve, such cases are very rare indeed....

Given the above assumptions, it is not surprising to find that,

> Accordingly, even those who have ascribed most influence to individual conditions have sought these conditions less in such external incidents than in the intrinsic nature of the person, that is, his biological constitution and the physical concomitants on which it depends.[1]

What is most interesting, of course, is that Durkheim abandoned the search for a common denominator to suicide before beginning it. Never having studied a specific case of suicide in detail, indeed at all, so far as I know, how could he know that "some resist horrible misfortune, while others kill themselves after slight troubles," or that "those who suffer most are not those who kill themselves most," or that the victim's personal situation is very rarely the cause of suicide? The author feels that such common-sense assumptions are unwarranted.

There is no need to intuit, as Durkheim has done above, the effects

* Reprinted by permission of the Society for the Study of Social Problems, from *Social Problems,* Vol. 15, 1967, pp. 60–72.

of one's personal situation on suicide. We have available, after all, the best possible authority on the subject—the suicide himself.

> I claim that any man who commits suicide of necessity suffers more than any who continues to live. I don't want to die. I cannot make any outsider realize by anything I can write how I have tried to avoid this step. I have tried every subterfuge to fool myself, to kid myself along that life wasn't so bad after all.[2]

The above statement is much more consistent with the position of suicidal persons as related in suicide notes, letters, and diaries than the contentions of Durkheim given above. It is, of course, opposed to what Durkheim believed, since persons do not appear to be killing themselves over arbitrary "personal problems" or "impulsively" as in the case of insane suicides. Everyone is forced to kill themselves for the same reason, i.e. they suffer more "than any who continues to live" and are unable, notwithstanding their every effort, to resolve the suffering. In brief, those who suffer most are those who kill themselves most.

The last sentence of Durkheim's concluding statement warrants particular attention as it relates to those who "ascribe most influence to individual conditions" in seeking an explanation of suicide. Such persons rely primarily upon case history accounts, suicide persons as sources of data. However, even they ". . . sought these conditions less in such external incidents than in the intrinsic nature of the person. . . ."

This has been the general approach of psychiatrists, psychologists, and of some less positivistic sociologists. The reason for this has been that even among those dealing with the individual's personal situation through the study of case histories or suicide notes, they found no common denominator for suicide.

The inability of previous investigators to explain suicide as resulting from a conscious rational process has led them to conclude the necessity of in some way inferring the "real" meaning of the suicide's story, either by superimposing upon the data an unconscious irrational explanation or some other such synthetic system.

> They (suicide notes) strongly suggest the possibility of viewing them as projective devices (in much the same way as MAPS tests or TAT protocols are projective products) from which information may be *inferred* about the subject (emphasis added).[3]

Psychiatrists also tend to interpret the accounts of their patients from this general perspective. Here the emphasis is one the unconscious, irrational elements, the apparent rational aspects notwithstanding.

> ... suicide is not preeminently a rational act pursued to achieve rational ends, even when it is effected by persons who appear to be eminently rational. Rather, it is a magical act, actuated to achieve irrational, delusional, and illusory ends.[4]

The dilemma confronting those proceeding on the above assumption is well put by C. Wright Mills.

> The quest for "real motives" set over against "more rationalization" is often informed by a metaphysical view that the "real" motives are in some way biological. Accompanying such quests for something more real and back of rationalization is the view held by many sociologists that language is an external manifestation or concomitant of something prior, more genuine, and "deep" in the individual, "Real attitudes" versus "mere verbalization" or "opinion" implies that at best we only infer from his language what "really" is the individual's attitude or motive.
>
> Now what *could we possible* so infer? Of precisely *what is* verbalization symptomatic? We cannot infer physiological processes from lingual phenomena. All we can infer and empirically check is another verbalization of the agent's which we believe was orienting and controlling behaviour at the time the act was performed. The only social items that can "lie deeper" are other lingual forms. The "Real Attitude or Motive" is not something different in kind from the verbalization of the "opinion". They turn out to be only relatively and temporally different.[5]

The author feels that in order to overcome this telling criticism it is necessary to offer an explanation of suicide which is both derived from and validated by some empirical referent. I feel the life situations of suicides as related by them in suicide notes offer such a potential. I will seek to establish the common denominator of suicide in the formal aspects of a process, rather than in some independent event such as a childhood trauma or a later "precipitating cause."

Suicide notes offer an invaluable source of data for gaining some insight into what it was that brought the individual to adopt this form of behaviour. Their importance is based upon the assumption made by this and other authors that they contain an unsolicited account of the victim's thoughts and emotions regarding his intended act and, often, what he felt was responsible for it.[6] A study of suicide in Philadelphia by Tuckman, Kleiner, and Lavell reveals that of the 742 suicides which occurred between 1951 and 1955, 24% left suicide notes.[7] Shneidman and Farberow note that in each year of a ten year period between 1945 and 1954, from 12 to 15% of those committing suicide in Los Angeles County left suicide notes.[8]

There seems to be no significant difference in the social, mental, or physical condition of persons leaving notes and those who do not.[9] With few exceptions, suicide notes are coherent.[10]

Tuckman *et al.* further acknowledge: "In this study, the writers were impressed with the possibility that in a number of cases, the suicide could have resulted from a conscious 'rational' decision . . . although, to a lesser extent, unconscious factors may have been operating."[11] Having analysed 112 notes of persons successful in suicide in the Los Angeles area, I was also taken with their rational and coherent character. The conscious rational factors were after all obvious in the notes themselves, whereas the unconscious factors to a lesser extent "may have been operating".

Most theories of suicide make some provision for both psychic and environmental factors. Whereas environmental factors are often cited and categorized by those analysing suicide notes, none has offered an explanation of psychic factors which can be verified by the notes themselves. The psychic formulations of psychiatrists and psychologists are always of an inferred nature.

The author believes that an explanation of suicide can be empirically derived from the notes themselves without the necessity of referring to a synthetic outside system. There is no need to proceed in the traditional fashion of either imputing meaning to the notes or, since there are essentially an infinite number of categorical distinctions to be made, categorizing them on whatever common sense grounds strike the analyst as being either potentially "fruitful" or expedient, e.g. demographic, environmental, physical, or psychological categories. A description of suicidal motivation and the experiences and thoughts processes involved in acquiring it are not likely to be arrived at without some broader theoretical perspective which in turn is given to some empirical validation by the notes themselves. The author intends to offer such a formulation after first briefly considering some existing sociological theories of suicide.

FORMER SOCIOLOGICAL THEORIES OF SUICIDE

I do not wish to get involved in a critique of previous sociological theories of suicide within the limits of this paper. However, by way of giving some general indication of how this formulation differs from others, it may be noted that Durkheim,[12] Gibbs and Martin,[13] Henry and Short,[14] and Powell[15] all have in common the fact that their theories rest basically on an analysis of official suicide rates. The theories consist essentially of an explanation of these official rates by imputing meaning to the correlations which are found to exist between the rates and certain social conditions. They are not based on actual cases of suicidal persons, their beliefs or writings.

Some of the above, while using the common base of statistical analysis of official suicide rates, incorporate psychological and psychoanalytical notions as well. Durkheim was also aware that, ultimately, if social norms were to act as a constraint, they must be internalized. Having acknowledged this, he did not involve himself in how this was to be accomplished. The author's formulation not only recognizes that norms must be internalized if they are to constrain the individual (or inversely, that the constraints of internalized norms must be overcome if one is to act contrary to them), but undertakes to set forth the process whereby this is accomplished. It also views suicide as a social fact which has its antecedents in previous social facts. It differs from Durkheim's formulation, however, in that it undertakes to establish these previous social facts through analysis of suicide notes.

BASIS OF THE FORMULATION

The data and insights upon which this formulation is based come from two main sources: 112 suicide notes of adults and adolescents who succeeded in suicide in the Los Angeles area, and insights gained by the author through his participation in a study of adolescent suicide attempters for two-and-a-half years.[16]

Whereas participation in this study has provided me with many valuable insights used in the formulation, the data on which it is based are taken from the 112 suicide notes previously mentioned. The paper will offer a sampling of notes from the various categories identified by the author. These will be analysed and discussed within the framework of a theoretical perspective which is designed to account for the conscious deliberations that take place before the individual is able to consider and execute the act of suicide. This is seen within the broader context of what the individual must experience in order to become capable of these verbalizations. The notes provide the basis for the formulation and, at the same time, offer the reader a means of verifying it. It is the author's belief that such verification is not contingent upon these notes in particular, but that any set of notes collected from within the same cultural environment would do as well.

The key to this formulation, i.e., the concept of trust violation, and how the individual accomplishes it while remaining convinced that he is a trusted person, is taken from Donald Cressey's work on embezzlement, *Other People's Money*.[17] The final form of the evolved hypothesis reads:

> Trusted persons become trust violators when they conceive of themselves as having a financial problem which is non-share-able, are aware that this problem can be secretly resolved by violation of the position of financial trust, and are able to apply to their own conduct in that situation verbalizations which enable them to adjust their conceptions of themselves as users of the entrusted funds or property.[18]

This conception of trust violation is extended to the act of suicide, i.e. the individual's violation of the sacred trust of life, and to the verbalizations he must entertain in order to reconcile the image of himself as a trusted person with his act of trust violation—suicide. It followed from these considerations that an excellent source of data for this undertaking would be the transcribed accounts of these verbalizations found in suicide notes. Here the similarity with Cressey's work ends, since the method of the author in studying the above is not one of analytic induction.

Both suicides and suicide attempters are considered in this paper. The events and processes leading them to these acts are held to be equatable within the following definitions of these terms, i.e. the suicide attempt is considered as a suicide attempt only if death was intended but did not result. Persons "attempting suicide" with the intent of not dying but only of using the "attempt" as an "attention-getting device", a "manipulative technique", etc., were not considered by the author as suicide attempters within the limits of this paper. The intentions of persons "attempting suicide" as an attention-getting device may miscarry and result in death. Persons actually attempting suicide may, through some misinformation or fortuitous circumstances, continue to live. This in no way alters their intent or the experiences which led them to entertain the verbalizations necessary for establishing this intent. It is in this sense that suicide and suicide attempts are considered by the author to be synonymous.

These three categories of persons were distinguished from one another in the following way. The authors of the 112 notes to be discussed in this paper were all considered to be suicides based upon a designation assigned to them by the Los Angeles County Coroner's Office upon investigating the circumstances of their death. The distinction between suicide attempters and attention-getters" was based upon the adolescent's account of his intentions at the time of his act. All adolescent suicide attempters in the above-mentioned study were seen within forty-eight hours of the attempt. Their intentions were related to three separate persons during their voluntary commitment at the hospital—to the attending physician who treated them in the emergency room, to the psychiatrist during a psychiatric interview, and to the author or his assistant in an interview which lasted about two hours. The designation by the author of suicide attempter was based upon a comparison and assessment of these three accounts. The three adolescent suicide attempters referred to later in this paper in a section dealing with the "next world" all intended at the same time of the attempt to take their own lives.

INTRODUCTION TO THE FORMULATION

Nearly all of the suicide notes studied were found to fall within one of six general categories, i.e. "first form notes", "sorry illness notes", "not sorry illness notes", "direct accusation notes", "will and testament notes" and "notes of instruction". The sum total of all six categories of suicide notes and the explanations given for the notes taking the form they do, constitute "The Formulation"— a systematic explanation for all but ten notes, i.e. 102 out of 112 notes studied by the author. The exceptions are noted later. The ten point process to be discussed is characteristic of "first form notes". Thirty-five of the 112 notes took this form. In addition, "sorry illness notes" also contained all or most of the characteristics found in "first form notes," depending upon their length. The reader is cautioned not to view the other four forms of notes as exceptions which tend to negate the process associated with "first form" and "sorry illness notes". These four forms and the explanations accompanying them are not exceptions but qualified additions that supplement the scope of the original ten points.

By way of analogy, consider the statement "light travels in a straight line", except when it encounters an opaque object, except in the case of refraction; except in the case of diffraction, etc. One does not say of these "exceptions" that they tend to negate the Principle of the Rectilinear Propagation of Light. They simply work to narrow its scope and set its limits. (The recognition and discussion of the four categories of notes cited above serve the same purpose.) To the extent that one is able to explain the "exceptions" in such a way that the explanations are consistent with the evidence, the sum of these explanations constitutes a more detailed and inclusive understanding of light, or, in the case of the author's formulation, of suicide. The author also believes that the formulation will provide an explanation of suicide, within this culture, that is both empirically derived and more consistent with the evidence than any he has thus far encountered.

THE FORMULATION

Trusted persons appear to become trust violators when they conceive of themselves as having a problem, the nature of which is a view of the past plagued by troubles, a troubled present, and the expectation of future troubles erupting unpredictably in the course of their lives. Paradoxically, these unpredictable troubles occur with absolute predictability in that it is held that they are sure to come—as sure as they are here now, unexpectedly, as sure as they arose unexpectedly in the past, and as sure as one's future existence to arise unexpectedly in the future. The problem is thus seen to be as absolute as life and must be resolved by something no less absolute than death. Since it is impossible to dispose of the problem of change, where change is viewed as unanticipated, inevitable, and inevitably for the worse, and since one sees it necessary to resolve this problem in order to live, i.e. to fulfil one's trust, and since the absolute nature of the problem makes it amenable only to absolute solutions, and since there is only one absolute solution, one finds it necessary to resolve the problem of living by dying, or—to put it another way—one appears to betray one's most sacred public trust by the private act of suicide.

Implicit or explicit in most of the suicide notes is the notion that "they didn't want it this way . . . but. . . ." From this perspective, they are now in a position to view themselves as blameless, i.e. trusted persons, while at the same time knowing that you will view them as trust violators because you have not experienced what they have and therefore cannot see the moral and reasonable nature of the act. With this in mind, they beg your indulgence and ask your forgiveness, for, in short, they know what they're doing, but they also know that you cannot know.

Life's problems, which one is morally obligated to resolve by way of not violating the sacred trust of life, can only be resolved by death, a not-too-pretty paradox, but from the perspective of the potential suicde, a necessary and consequently reasonable and moral view. From the absence of choice, i.e. no freedom, emerges the greatest freedom—"the recognition of necessity"—stemming from the apparent lack of choice. Thus it is that the suicidal person sees in the act of suicide at long last the potential for the freedom he has sought in life. This can be seen in the notes themselves. The note writers are rarely "depressed" or "hostile". The notes are by and large very even, as though at the time of writing the suffering no longer existed and a resolution to the problem had been reached. Tuckman states that 51% of the notes he studied expressed "positive affect without hostility" and another 25% expressed "neutral affect".[19] This is further supported by the finding of Farberow *et al.* that the period of the highest risk was not during the depression or "illness" but just after it when the patient seemed much improved.[20]

FIRST FROM NOTES

The outline presented below describes the formal aspects of a process that the individual must first experience in order to be able to seriously entertain suicide and then actually attempt it. The extent to which this process is operative will be illustrated through an analysis of "first form" notes. The extent to which the other five forms of notes deviate from the characteristics found in "first form notes" will be discussed in the explanation accompanying each of the five remaining forms. The sum total of all six forms of notes and their accompanying explanations constitute "The Formulation", i.e. a systematic rational explanation of suicide based upon the suicide's own accounts at the time of the act.

Durkheim went to great lengths to show that private acts contrary to the public trust are irrational and/or immoral and constrained by public sanctions from ever occurring. In order to overcome these constraints and appear to others as a trust violator, the private individual must (1) be faced with an unexpected, intolerable, and unsolvable problem; (2) view this not as an isolated unpleasant incident, but within the context of a long biography of such troubled situations, and the expectation of future ones; (3) believe that death is the only absolute answer to this apparent absolute dilemma of life; (4) come to this point of view (*a*) by way of an increasing social isolation whereby he is unable to share his problem with the person or persons who must share it if it is to be resolved, or (*b*) being isolated from the cure of some incurable illness which in turn isolates him from health and the community, thereby doubly insuring the insolubility of the problem; (5) overcome the social constraints, i.e. the social norms he had internalized whereby he views suicide as irrational and/or immoral; (6) succeed in this because he feels himself less an integral part of the society than the others and therefore is held less firmly by its bonds; (7) succeed in accomplishing step 6 by applying to his intended suicide a verbalization which enables him to adjust his conception of himself as a trusted person with his conception of himself as a trust violator; (8) succeed in doing this by defining the situation such that the problem is (*a*) not of his own making (*b*) unresolved, but not from any lack of personal effort, and (*c*) not given to any resolution known to him except death (he doesn't want it this way, but... it's "the only way out"); (9) in short, define death as necessary by the above process and in so doing remove all choice and with it sin and immorality; and finally, (10) make some provision for insuring against the recurrence of these problems in the afterlife.

Thirty-five out of 112 notes were "first form notes" and expressed all or most of the above aspects, depending on their length. All "first form" notes are characterized by the author's begging of forgiveness or request for indulgence. The following will serve to illustrate the general tenor.

> It is hard to say why you don't want to live. I have only one real reason. The three people I have in the world which I love don't want me.
>
> Tom, I love you so dearly but you have told me you don't want me and don't love me. I never thought you would let me go this far, but I am now at the end which is the best thing for you. You have so many problems and I am sorry I added to them.
>
> Daddy, I hurt you so much and I guess I really hurt myself. You only wanted the very best for me and you must believe this is it.
>
> Mommy, you tried so hard to make me happy and to make things right for all of us. I love you too so very much. You did not fail, I did.
>
> I had no place to go so I am back where I always seem to find peace. I have failed in everything I have done and I hope I do not fail in this.
>
> I love you all dearly and am sorry this is the way I have to say goodbye.
>
> Please forgive me and be happy.
>
> Your wife and your daughter.

First, the problem is not of their own making. At first glance the suicide seems to be saying just the opposite. "You did not fail, I did", "I have failed in everything." However, having acknowledged this, she states: "Tom, I love you so dearly but you have told me you don't want me and don't love me. *I never thought you would let me go this far.*" Then, of course, she loves them. It is they who do not love here, and this is "the problem".

Second, a long-standing history of problems. "Mommy, you tried so hard to make me happy and to make things right for all of us. I love you too so very much. You did not fail, I did," or "Tom . . . you have so many problems and I am sorry I added to them," etc. It seems from this that she has created a long-standing history of problems. She was, nevertheless, subject to them as well. "Daddy, I hurt you so much and I guess I *really hurt myself.*"

Third, the escalation of problems of late beyond human endurance. "It is hard to say why you don't want to live. I have only one real reason. The three people I have in the world which I love don't want me", or "Tom, I love you so dearly but you have told me you don't want me and don't love me."

These particular problems are clearly of recent origin and of greater magnitude than any she had previously experienced. By her own account, had she experienced problems of this order before, she would have taken her life before, since they led to her losing what had previously constituted sufficient reason for her to go on living.

Fourth, death must be seen as necessary. "It is hard to say why you don't want to live. I have only one real reason. The three people I have in the world which I love don't want me", or "... but now I'm at the end ...", and finally, "I love you all dearly and am sorry this is the way *I have to* say goodbye."

Fifth, beg your indulgence. "I love you all dearly and am *sorry* this is the way I have to say goodbye."

Sixth, thy know what they're doing but know you cannot know. "Daddy ... You only wanted the very best for me and *you must believe this is it.*"

It is the author's opinion that the suicide's message in point (3) is the same as that given by nearly all the others who attempt or succeed in suicide, insofar as this is a particular of "a progressive social isolation". Ellen West, whose case history is perhaps the most famous, wrote in her diary less than a year before taking her life:

> ... by this fearful illness I am withdrawing more and more from people. I feel myself excluded from all real life. I am quite isolated. I sit in a glass ball. I see people through a glass wall, their voices come to me muffled. I have an unutterable longing to get to them, I scream, but they do not hear me. I stretch out my arms towards them; but my hands merely beat against the walls of my glass ball.[21]

All of the remaining "first form" notes have all or most of the above characteristics in common. *All of the notes in this class, without exception, beg forgiveness or indulgence on the part of the survivors.*

Illness Notes

Requests for forgiveness or indulgence may be omitted when the writer feels that the public *may have* made exceptions to its general indignation at suicide, exceptions which should be known to all, e.g. in the case of persons suffering from an incurable disease, suffering great pain etc. In such cases the suicide may feel that no apologies are necessary, and request, for forgiveness may be included or excluded, due to the ambiguity surrounding the degree of public acceptance of the above view.

Thirty-four notes were included in the "illness" category. Twenty-two of these omitted requests for forgiveness; twelve included them. This category of notes has most of the same general characteristics as those of the "first form". How many conditions of the "first form" notes are met by those of the "illness' category depends primarily on their length. The two formal distinguishing features of these two sets of notes are that the "illness" set may or may not beg forgiveness for the reasons stated above, and, secondly, the source of the problem is generally better defined and restricted to the area of illness, pain, etc. and its social and personal implications to the individual. Some examples of illness notes follow.

Sorry Illness Notes:

> Dearly Beloved Children: For the last three weeks I have lost my blood circulation in my feet and in my hands. I can hardly hold a spoon in my hand. Before I get a stroke on top of my other troubles of my legs I decided that this would be the easier for me. I have always loved you all dearly. Think of me kindly sometimes. Please forgive me. I cannot endure any more pains. Lovingly, mother.

Not Sorry Illness Notes:

> If you receive this letter you will know that I have emptied my bottle of sleeping pills.

And a second note by the same author addressed to the same person included the line: *"Surely there must be a justifiable mercy death."*
Another reads:

> Dear Jane: You are ruining your health and your life just for me, and I cannot let you do it. The pains in my face seem worse every day and there is a limit to what a man can take. I love you dear.
>
> Bill

Notes of Direct Accusation

None of the notes in this class beg forgiveness or offer an apology. The suicide feels that not only is the problem not of his making, but he knows who is responsible for his having to commit suicide. As a result, he feels righteously indignant and omits requests for indulgence, especially when the note is directed to the guilty party. "Direct accusation notes" are generally very brief, rarely more than a few lines long. Ten of the 112 notes studied were of the "direct accusation" type. For example:

> You Bob and Jane caused this—this all.

> Goodbye Jane. I couldn't take no more from you. Bob.
>
> Mary, I hope you're satisfied. Bill.
>
> If you had read page 150 of Red Ribbons this wouldn't have happened.

Last Will and Testaments and Notes of Instructions

None of these notes contained requests for forgiveness or indulgence either. This ommision, as in the above case, results from the form of the notes themselves. These notes usually concern themselves exclusively with the manner in which the suicide's property is to be apportioned. They give no mention of the circumstances of the suicide and, as a result, there is no need for the notewriter to admit of guilt or request forgiveness. None of them do so.

Last Will and Testaments:

> I hereby bequeath all my worldly goods and holdings to Bill Smith. $1 to Chris Baker, $1 to Ann Barnes. Signed in sober consideration.
>
> Mary Smith

Notes of Instructions

The following are some examples of notes of instructions. They are almost notes of instruction. They are almost always very brief and the above comments regarding "last will and testaments" apply here as well.

> Call Jane. S. Street, Apt. 2. Thank Officer No. 10.

> I have gone down to the ocean. Pick out the cheapest coffin Jones Bros. has. I don't remember the cost. I'll put my purse in the trunk of the car.

Precautions Taken to Exclude This World's Problems from the Next World

To guard against the eventuality of a similar set of troubles erupting in the afterlife, the very thing one is dying to overcome, one of six possible courses of action are formulated and internalized. These forms first came to the attention of the author while studying suicidal adolescents; the suicide notes tend to bear them out.

(1) The potential suicide who was in the past quite religious and a diligent church-goer rather abruptly stops attending church and starts considering himself a non-religious person. He thereby disposes of heaven and hell, makes death absolute, and secures for himself all the benefits of the non-believer with respect to the act of suicide.

(2) The person who attended church irregularly but had enough re-

ligious training to make him ambivalent about an afterlife, suddenly begins to make inquiries of very religious persons as to whether "God forgives suicides" or "Will God forgive anything?" And those to whom the question is put, believing that He does, or pleased that it was asked, or anxious for the convert, or for whatever reason, say "Yes, of course, if you really believe, God will forgive anything", at which point the suicidal person suddenly "gets religion" and tries very hard to "believe", thus securing a place in heaven free from future troubles.

The following is an abstract of a note written by a sixteen-year-old female suicide attempter. Both the adolescent and her mother reported that the girl's preoccupation with religion began unexpectedly within the last few months. The note is illustrative of the adolescent's attempt to resolve the anticipated problems of the hereafter through the process described in (2) above.

> Please forgive me, God. . . . In my heart I know there is a Christ everywhere in the world that is being with everyone. Every second of every day and he represents God in every way. I know that in my brain (mind) I think evil things about different situations and sometimes I think that Christ never existed. But my heart always is strong and that when I think that Christ never lived I know that in my heart He did. . . . *Mother thinks that there is no hell and no heaven (I guess) and I know there is a hell and heaven. I don't want to go to the devil, God, so please forgive me to what I have just done. John L. said that if I believe in and accept Jesus that I would go to heaven. Some people say that if you ask forgiveness to God for things you do to yourself or others, that he would forgive you (if you believe in Jesus and love him)* . . .
>
> *. . . Heaven is so peaceful and the earth is very troublesome and terrifying.*

(3) The religious person, believing that suicide is an absolute, irreversible, and damnable sin, will make an attempt to resolve this by asking a mother or some other authority, "Will God forgive anything?", knowing full well that suicide is the exception, and will be answered, "If you believe." The Pope's pronouncement to the contrary notwithstanding, the suicidal person will accept this and act as though it were true.

(4) The religious person, believing that he is unable to secure a place in heaven or insure an absolute death, or any other resolution to his present problem, will fly in the face of God, e.g. "Even if I go to hell, at least I won't have those headaches and worry about the baby and that will be one thing anyway." At least you don't have to violate a trust in hell, for no one on earth has ever told you

how to act in hell, and you are left to your resources without the problem of becoming a trust violater. Its very ambiguity allows for a happy ending, or beginning.

Parts of a lengthy note written by a man to his wife and family serve to illustrate the uncertainty of the hereafter.

> My Dearest Ones:
>   When you get this it will all be over for me on earth *but just the beginning of my punishment for what I have done to you all* ... I have given what I am about to do lots of thought and each time I have thought about it there seems no other way...*I don't know what's on the other side perhaps it will be worse than here.*

It is interesting to see that the author of the note begins by stating that his punishment in the hereafter is just beginning. It is a very positive statement; the punishment seems a certainty. However, the letter ends on this note: "I don't know what's on the other side *perhaps* it will be worse than here". The "perhaps" nature of this statement provides for the possibility that "perhaps" it will be better In the hope of tipping the scales in the right direction, the suicide concludes his note with ...

> I love you all *May God help me and forgive for what I am about to do.*
>   Again good-bye.
>   Jack and Daddy

(5) Another group concerned with the prospect of hell will request in a suicide note that others "pray for my soul" or "God forgive me" and—having taken this precaution—hope for the best.

(6) Reincarnation is the last form of possible salvation: "Maybe it will be better the next time around; it couldn't be worse." This resolution to life's problems and the hope of preventing future ones was discovered through interviews with adolescent suicide attempters. One fifteen-year-old Jewish boy, who until a year ago when the family moved from New York had been attending the synagogue regularly, suddenly stopped attending services and recently be came preoccupied with the prospect of reincarnation. A fourteen-year-old Negro Baptist girl, who until about a year ago had been a steady church-goer, also stopped attending church and became interested in reincarnation. It is perhaps unnecessary to point out how peculiar it is for a Jew and a Baptist to undergo a conversion to the expectations of reincarnation, especially since there seem to be no external indoctrinating influence. Both adolescents also recognized its peculiarity to the outsider and although they mentioned its existence, refused to discuss it in detail.

In brief, religious convictions do not appear to be ultimately binding upon the individual as a constraint against suicide, since one tends to interpret religious dogma as one has a need to interpret it.

It is true that Durkheim dealt at length with this notion by establishing the degree of social integration within various religions as the constraining factor against suicide, rather than the religious dogma *per se*. However, what has not been discussed is the way in which religious dogma, specifically intended to prevent suicide, can, with the proper "rationalization", serve to encourage suicide. The preceding discussion dealt with why and how this is actually accomplished by the potential suicide.

The author acknowledges that some exceptions occurred within the above categories. But among the 112 suicide notes studied, the paucity of cases falling into a "residual category" is heartening. There were ten of these in all, four of which contained the only elements of humour found in all the notes. For example:

> Please do not disturb. Someone sleeping. (Hung on the dashboard of his car.)

CONCLUSIONS

If it is true as Hume believed that ". . . such is our natural horror of death, that small motives will never be able to reconcile us to it . . ."[22] it is also true that the horror of life is no small motive. I believe that most people prefer the uncertainties of life to the uncertainties of death, because in life they have defined for themselves the possibility of certain sets of events occurring and live in the expectation that "anything can happen", i.e. "life is full of ups and downs". If one's view of life excludes uncertainty, i.e. life is not full of ups and downs—only downs, and anything can't happen—things can only get worse, then one might better try the uncertainties of death for its very ambiguity allows for either. By accepting death one provides the possibility of resolving life's problems, while at the same time insuring against future problems (or at least providing the possibility of resolving future problems when they arise).

I believe it is necessary to take seriously what the suicide writes in attempting to explain to the survivors, as a reasonable person, why he is committing suicide, and suggest that the reader will be aided in this task by applying the formulation presented by the author. I am further convinced that a fuller understanding of suicide will emerge only if one's procedures for "transcending the data" do not end by ignoring it, and that the "data" transcended ought to have some direct relation to the real life phenomenon under study, i.e. suicide.

NOTES

1 Emile Durkheim, *Suicide*, New York: The Free Press, 1951, pp. 297–8.
2 'A Youth Who Was Prematurely Tired', in Ruth Cavan, *Suicide*, Chicago: University of Chicago Press, 1928, p. 242.
3 Edwin S. Shneidman and Norman L. Farberow, 'Appendix: Genuine and Simulated Suicide Notes', in *Clues to Suicide*, New York: McGraw-Hill, 1957, p. 197.
4 Charles William Wahl, 'Suicide as a Magical Act', in Edwin S. Shneidman and Norman L. Farberow, editors, *Clues to Suicide*, New York: McGraw-Hill, 1957, p. 23.
5 C. Wright Mills, 'Situated Actions and Vocabularies of Motives', *American Sociological Review*, 5, December 1940, p. 909.
6 Jacob Tuckman, Robert J. Kleiner and Martha Lavell, 'Emotional Content of Suicide Notes', *American Journal of Psychiatry*, July 1959, p. 59.
7 Ibid.
8 Shneidman and Farberow, op. cit., p. 198.
9 Tuckman, et. al., op. cit., p. 59; and Shneidman and Farberow, op. cit., p. 48.
10 Tuckman, et al., op. cit., p. 60.
11 Ibid., p. 62.
12 Emile Durkheim, op. cit.
13 Jack P. Gibbs and Walter T. Martin, *Status Integration and Suicide*, Eugene, Ore.: University of Oregon Press, 1964.
14 Andrew F. Henry and James F. Short, *Suicide and Homicide*, Glencoe, Ill.: The Free Press, 1954.
15 Elwin H. Powell, 'Occupational Status and Suicide: Toward a Redefinition of *Anomie*', *American Sociological Review*, 23, April 1950, pp. 131–9.
16 Adolescent Attempted Suicide Study, supported by the National Institute of Mental Health and conducted at the Los Angeles County General Hospital under the direction of Joseph D. Teicher, M.D., Professor of Southern California School of Medicine, and Jerry Jacobs, Ph.D., Research Associate, University of South California School of Medicine.
17 Donald R. Cressey, *Other People's Money*, Glencoe, Ill.: The Free Press, 1951.
18 Ibid., p. 30.
19 Tuckman, et al., op. cit., p. 61.
20 Norman L. Farberow, Edwin S. Shneidman and Robert E. Litman, 'The Suicidal Patient and the Physician', *Mind*, 1:69, March 1963.
21 Ludwig Brinswanger, 'The Case of Ellen West', in Rollo May et al., editors, *Existence*, New York: Basic Books, 1958, p. 256.
22 David Hume, 'Of Suicide', in Alasdair MacIntyre, editor, *Hume's Ethical Writings*, New York: Collier Books, 1965, p. 305.

CHAPTER 28

A Study of Suicide Pacts*

John Cohen

During recent decades the factual literature on suicide has certainly grown apace. So far as I am aware, however, the systematic study of suicide pacts seems to have escaped attention. The present paper therefore represents an attempt to indicate their frequency, the age of those involved and their relationship to each other, the circumstances in which the pacts are made, and, if possible, the motives which lead to them.

The enquiry was made possible by advice from the Home Office and help from the General Register Office. The latter Office provided the dates of inquests in England and Wales, in the period 1955–8, which resulted in the registration of two deaths from suicide and which, from the place and date of death, appeared to be connected. The names and districts of the Coroners concerned were also provided. Without exception, all Coroners courteously and helpfully supplied the original documents (or copies) relating to the inquests, including letters (or copies) left by the deceased. In one instance alone the documents were not to be found.

NUMBER OF PACTS AND CHARACTERISTICS OF THE DECEASED

A suicide pact is a mutual arrangement between two people who resolve to die at the same time and, nearly always, in the same place. The fateful decision is usually reached by both together from the start; they decide independently at first, and then jointly. Their grim secret is carefully guarded, if necessary for weeks or months before the appointed day. Very rarely the plan miscarries and one partner to the pact survives, but mostly the preparations for death are so meticulous that both partners perish.

The total number of "double suicides" in England and Wales in the four years 1955–8 was sixty-five, of which fifty-eight were due to suicide pacts in the proper sense. In two of the remaining seven instances, the death of one person was precipitated by the death

* Reprinted by permission from the *Medico-Legal Journal*, Vol. 29, 1961, Part 3, pp. 144–51.

of the other, and in five instances the two deaths were coincidental.

The number of pacts, year by year, was as follows: 1955, eleven; 1956, twelve; 1957, twenty; and 1958, fifteen. The "peak" month was January, with February a close second. A third of the total number of pacts occurred in these two months.

Suicide pacts are commonly believed to be made by lovers who encounter insurmountable obstacles to marriage. In fact, only a small proportion of the pacts were of this sort. Of the fifty-eight pacts, forty-two were made by husband and wife, and five by lovers. The remaining pacts included other relationships: mother-son (two), mother-daughter (one), father-son (one), brother-sister (two), sister-sister (two), male homosexuals (one) and friends (two).

The ages of the deceased are shown in Table 1. The distribution resembles that of all suicides (20,788) in the same period.

TABLE 1

Age of those who Died by Suicide Pact, 1955–8*

Age	Husbands*	Wives*	Others Males	Others Females	Total No.	%
Under 30	1	1	2	3	7	6.1
30–9	1	2	2	3	8	7.0
40–9	2	7	6	3	18	15.8
50–9	18	15	1	2	36	31.6
60–9	11	10	3	3	27	23.7
70–9	6	5	—	4	15	13.2
80 and over	2	1	—	—	3	2.6
	41	41	14	18	114	100.0

* Excluding one married couple about whom information is not available.

The average age at death of the group as a whole was 55.2 years, and of the four sub-groups:

Husbands	60.2 years
Wives	56.2 „
Males	44.1 „
Females	50.1 „

Twenty of the married couples were childless. Twelve couples had one child (in one instance a still birth), five had two children, and one couple had eleven children. The number of children is unknown in the case of four couples. In the four parent-child pacts, the son or daughter that died with the parent was an only child.

Taking the married couples only, we note that at least sixteen of the husbands were out of work, unoccupied or retired. This is a large proportion (40%) of the group as compared with the corresponding proportion (14%) in the industrial male population as a whole. The excess is of course related to differences in age distribulation. The suicides consisted mostly of skilled or unskilled workers or clerks, a small number of business owners or employers, a few doctors, some minor civil servants, and one company director who could not survive a love tangle which, in the end, cost four lives.

In seventeen of the pacts both partners were seriously ill, and in the entire group about seventy were victims of some disability, physical or mental.

The foregoing data exclude suicide pacts made abroad by persons normally resident in England and Wales. One such pact has come to my notice, that of a fifty-six-year-old Englishman and his forty-five-year old wife. Once wealthy, they had been overtaken by financial disaster, and they tried to recoup their losses in the gambling casinos in France. When their money ran out, they took their car up a mountain track where they died from carbon monoxide poisoning due to the exhaust fumes of their car.

SITUATIONS LEADING TO PACTS

The documents relating to married couples yield a general impression of an ageing man and woman, one or both suffering from grave illness, which constantly occupies their thoughts. A deeply devoted pair, childless, with few friends or interests, they are absorbed in their own small world. Religious considerations hardly seem to enter their minds, though very occasionally one of them asks for God's forgiveness. In modest or humble circumstances, they are mostly untroubled by financial difficulties. Prolonged insomnia seems to facilitate the decisive act. "We are at the end of our tether" is a phrase which is often met in the letters left behind.

Here is a typical situation in which both husband and wife longed to die. A fifty-six-year-old ex-miner, with impaired vision and an injured leg, underwent an operation for cancer of the bowel. The operation was not successful and he was confined to his bed with frequent and violent attacks of pain. For twenty-five years his wife had been disabled by Parkinson's disease, and for fifteen years she had been partially paralysed.

In some instances, the wife refused to survive her husband (or, it may be, the husband cannot live on without his wife). A sixty-six-year-old retired chauffeur, victim of a degenerative disease, was rapidly deteriorating, and in great pain. His wife chose to die with him. "He was such a wonderful man," she wrote, "I can't live without him. Please don't say I am insane. With my dear husband in such agony, I prefer to die with him. Please bury us in one grave. I am sorry to take my little Blackie with us."

There are other situations in which an unforeseen event or situation brings ruin in its train. An elderly couple had devoted their entire resources to caring for a spastic son until he died at the age of twenty-five. His death brought disillusionment and a blank that nothing could fill. "The craving we had to provide for him", wrote the father, "has resulted in disaster for us. The sad thing in our life was to see him powerless to enjoy the pleasures that his friends could have. He missed so much in his twenty-five years"; and the mother wrote: "For twenty-five years we have lived a life of sadness, stress and strain, and for most of these years we have been obsessed with the need to provide for our son's future.: I think now we must have been mad and only became sane when he lay dead and we realized how empty our lives were and that we had worked so hard for no real effect."

Another middle-aged couple, compelled to move their home, were unable to take roots in their new dwelling. "Moving to this house was a dreadful mistake" wrote a forty-five-year-old wife, "something has gone out of our lives which we can never replace. These last five weeks have been horrible. We have been reduced to such a state of unhappiness and exhaustion that we are both too tired to carry on.... I know he (the husband) would not have been able to carry on with anything much longer. Look after mother. tell her my cat is alright."

Ageing, ill-health and low "vitality" are also prominent factors in the pacts between brother and sister, between sister and sister, and between friends.

Inhalation of coal gas was the favoured method of dying, often with the aid of alcohol or barbiturates "to dull the mind." The bodies were usually found in bed in night attire, with bed clothes pulled over the heads, or, blanketed and equipped with a hot water bottle, sitting in armchairs or lying with the face towards the gas oven. Two couples chose to die from the exhaust fumes of their cars. In four pacts, death was due to barbiturate poisoning, in one pact to cyanide poisoning, and in one to drowning.

LOVERS' PACTS

The five lovers' pacts will doubtless be of special interest. In three instances, both lovers were married, in one pact only the man was married, and in one pact both partners were unmarried. A sketch of the circumstances in each of these five pacts follows.

(i) A man aged thirty-one, father of four children, became deeply enamoured of a woman of thirty-three, a mother of two. In a letter left by the man he wrote: "... I can only say I am torn in two and I feel as though I can't think any more ... I can't concentrate on a job any more ... I keep seeing the children in my mind and hate myself more and more ... I've broken two homes and I feel like going out and ending everything for good. I'm no good to anyone any more. Anyway I couldn't face anyone I know again...."

And this is the message the woman sent to her husband: "By the time you receive this I shall have used the shilling (gas) slot in our room. It is all for the best, as you must see. Look after the 'nips' (children). Don't tell them, if possible. I was in love for the first time in my life, but we both find this love of ours is too big even for us. So goodbye. Don't feel sorry for me. I'm not. It was well worth it." They died from coal gas poisoning.

(ii) A man aged forty-one fell in love with a divorced woman aged thirty-six. He had one daughter from his marriage and she had one son from hers. "Realizing how much we had wronged," he wrote, "we knew that there was only one possible answer to it all. I knew that I had failed as a father and a husband.... Both she and I are perfectly aware of what we are doing, and are fully prepared to pay the price for our love."

The woman wrote to her mother: "I think you may have realized that I was deeply in love with him and he with me—love I have never, never known. We tried to fight against it but the more we did the greater our love became. We made up our minds some time ago that this had to be, otherwise we would cause everyone much more suffering. I am extremely happy and we have spent a most wonderful week with each other ... I'm not afraid, our love for each other is too deep for that to be so." Their dead bodies were found in a car.

(iii) A miner aged thirty-two, father of two children, fell in love with a young married woman aged twenty-four, who was living apart from her husband. They were found dead in bed, the woman's left arm embracing the man's neck. A note from the man to his mother stated that he did not want to end his life in this way but that his wife wanted him to die. The young woman wrote to her mother saying "they want me to stop seeing him and I love him with all my heart".

⌈(iv) A married man aged twenty-one fell in love with a single girl aged twenty-six, but he was unable to obtain a divorce from his wife. They died together by gas poisoning in a guest house. The man left the following note: "All my love is for . . . (the girl he died with). My wife will not let us be together. This way we can be."⌋

(v) In the case of the engaged couple, the young man's affections had weakened while those of the girl had remained unchanged. He was a struggling student, a complex and highly introverted individual, and he saw no material future for himself which could satisfy his aspirations. No one, he felt, understood him, not even his fiancée, who now seemed to him a naive and simple girl to whom he would be tied for life in a meaningless marriage. He began to entertain agonizing doubts about his love for his betrothed, as well as about his career, but he had neither the heart to break away from her nor the courage to die alone. For her part, the girl remained bound to him heart and soul. They had been separated for some time by force of circumstances. Then he rejoined her, ostensibly to explain his decision to break off the engagement. The meeting resulted in death for both. Evidently unprepared to die alone, he was ready to go with her together. They were found dead from gas poisoning in her room.

SURVIVORS OF PACTS

Not included among the fifty-eight pacts are those rare instances in which one partner dies and the other survives. In one case a young man of twenty-one was accused of murder after surviving a suicide pact with his nineteen-year-old wife. It emerged that they were deeply in debt and that they also owed a sum of money for rent. In order to meet these debts the wife played the part of a prostitute for a few nights, until they decided to put an end to their lives.

In another instance a girl, aged seventeen, survived an attempted pact with her lover aged twenty-one. This was precipitated by parental opposition to their marriage. The girl had written a letter saying: "We were not allowed to have our only wish which was to get married so I think that explains things. . . . We both wish to be cremated together, so I hope you will do that thing for us. . . . He and I have always done everything together and this is the last thing we will ever do. . . . He and I were different from anybody else, we handled life in our own way and now we just want to be forgotten . . . we done it because of love." She then went on to say that after the gas jets had been turned on she sat in an armchair by the fire "with my eyes open for a while and then closed them. After a little while

I felt very dizzy and faint. I remember saying: 'I've got a headache' and (he) said: 'It's nearly over now.' "

LOVERS' BELIEFS ABOUT SURVIVAL

In death pacts between lovers we touch an age old belief, found in folklore, myth and literature, that two people who die together are for ever united beyond the tomb, a belief which prompted Hero to join her beloved Leander by throwing herself from a tower into the Hellespont, and which induced many a Roman wife to share her husband's suicide or even to instigate it. German romantic literature is pervaded by this belief. It is embodied in the Japanese practice of *shinju* or *aitaishi* ("dying between two parties"), a death pact between unhappy lovers who seek to escape their earthly tribulations by seeking a happier life in the hereafter. The most common method used to be drowning, the lovers binding themselves together with a rope. Such pacts became so frequent in eighteenth-century Japan that in 1723 special laws forbidding it were promulgated. The bodies were refused burial and any survivors were condemned to public shame or exile. In recent years, other methods of dying have become more common; the frequency of lovers' pacts is said to be still very high (Sato and Sonahara, 1957), though statistics are not available.

In literature the lovers' wish to sleep together in the grave may be represented as symbolic of the bed. The idea of the erotic insatiability of the dead is given sinister expression as a form of vampirism in Goethe's famous ballad *The Bride of Corinth*; and Heine, in a poem, writes "Thou hast called me from the grave, By thy bewitching will.... The dead can never be sated." A more innocent impulse inspires Sophocles' Antigone when she says: "I shall be content to lie beside a brother whom I love. We have only a little time to please the living but all eternity to love the dead."

We recall too the celebrated suicide pact between the famous dramatist Heinrich von Kleist and Henrietta Vogel. He yearned for death as the only way to achieve a deathless love, and in the end it was Henrietta's willingness to die with him that drew him irresistibly to her. "Her grave", he wrote, "is dearer to me than the beds of all the Empresses in the world." On his death-bed Modigliani begged Jeane Héburterne to follow him to the grave so that he could possess his favourite model in Paradise and enjoy with her eternal bliss.

The lively existence of this belief today, however vaguely and innocently it may be held, is attested by the large numbers of young girls and women who attach themselves even more to a popular idol after he is dead than while he remains alive. When

James Dean died, each of his admirers cherished the fantasy that he was hers alone and could never desert her for another.

This belief is echoed by one of our lovers whose words "This way we can be" express the romantic idea that two people who die together are not parted but travel together to a destination beyond the grave where they will remain eternally united. "We have sworn eternal love, and death, terrible death, shall find us united", was the message sketched on the wall of a room where two lovers perished together. The following note was found on the bodies of a young woman and a man, tied together and recovered from the Seine: "O you, whoever you are. . . . You shall find these two bodies united, know that we loved each other with the most ardent affection, and that we have perished together that we may be eternally united." Another young couple who died by pact left a note saying: "We have no alternative but separation or death; and believing death to be one eternal dream of bliss, we have determined to kill each other" (Winslow, 1840).

DISCUSSION

A number of reflections, some specific and some of a more general character, are prompted by this enquiry.

(i) One is struck by the care taken by the deceased to cope with the detailed domestic and other problems that would be created by their death: a warning about leaking gas, a note on the doorstep: "No more milk until I let you know"; and a message "Please bury little Pippin in the garden with all our other pets."

(ii) In nearly every one of the pacts the deaths took by surprise relatives, acquaintances and neighbours alike. There was no sign of previous attempts to die by pact, although some 10% of the *individuals* had previously attempted to kill themselves or threatened to do so. This is the proportion we should expect from the study of individual suicide (Stengel, 1958; Cohen, 1960).

(iii) A death pact appears to have little in common with an individual suicide which appears typically to be an act of aggression, a hostile blow obliquely directed at some *particular* other person. The man who takes his life alone is not troubled if others are grievously hurt or are even dragged to the grave with him (Forbes and Bradley, 1959). The death pact characteristically lacks the homicidal quality which is present in individual suicide.

(iv) This difference may account for the fact that an attempted suicide pact, in which both partners survive, rarely if ever occurs, although for each *individual* suicide, there may well be ten unsuccessful attempts. The attempted suicide has an element of moral blackmail to coerce affection. The motive in some types of threatened suicide is illustrated by the characteristic reaction of one of Esquirol's patients who had frequently threatened to take her life and one day informed him that she was about to take the final step. "Very well," he replied, "it is nothing to me, and your husband will be delivered of great torment." The lady forthwith changed her plans (Esquirol, 1838). Such situations are doubtless not uncommon today. Moral blackmail would be pointless in a death pact, except possibly in a pact between two young lovers.

(v) When the love is "illicit," the reactions of a man and woman contrast sharply. He is stricken by a fatal remorse while she meets death in exultation and ecstasy. In general, and this is also true of "innocent" love, the man is destroyed by the situation whereas the woman yields her life for the man. Byron expressed this difference in his line "For all of theirs (i.e. of women) upon that die (love) is thrown."

(vi) In past ages, when religious belief was vigorous, suicide, whether denounced as a crime or imposed as a punishment, carried for the individual some germ of hope for his future. In this respect, a Petronius Arbiter stands apart from the vast majority of suicides. In the Indian suttee, a widow immolated herself on the funeral pile of her husband, fortified by a mirage of thirty-five million years of connubial bliss in the hereafter. No such mirage transfigures our aged couples who take their lives. They die without hope.

(vii) If we ourselves reflect on the pacts, we may be led to confront our own relationship to death, which, together with old age, we strive to suppress from our thoughts. We come to terms with life and death alike by the exercise of that vital organ for encountering the future which we call "hope". When that again fails, our surrender is unconditional.

(viii) So far as individual suicides are concerned, we must distinguish those attempts which are almost certain to succeed from those that are almost certain to fail. Among those who succeed—and this applies to pacts as well—we must differentiate those whose chief aim is to safeguard their ultimate ftuure from the majority who have no future, those in whom all hope is extinguished and irrecoverably lost.

(ix) It would appear, finally, that we are unequally affected by deaths from different causes. What seems to matter to us is *how* people die. Death by violence disturbs us more than death by accident, and an individual suicide perhaps moves us less profoundly than a suicide pact.

NOTES

John Cohen, *Chance, Skill and Luck,* Harmondsworth: Pelican Books. 1960, 40–1.

E. Esquirol, *Des Maladies Mentales,* Paris, 1838, 2 vols.

G. Forbes and A. Bradley, *The Police Journal,* July–September 1959, 197–202.

Koji Sato and Taro Sonahara, *Psychologia,* 1957, 1, 71–3.

E. Stengel, *Attempted Suicide: its social significance and effects,* London: Chapman & Hall, 1958.

Forbes Winslow, *Anatomy of Suicide,* London: Renshaw, 1840.

CHAPTER 29

The Communication of Suicidal Intent*

Eli Robins, Seymour Gassner, Jack Kayes,
Robert H. Wilkinson and George E. Murphy

There are many phenomena related to successful (completed) suicide that cannot be studied adequately by statistical methods from coroners' records, by individual case reports, or by obtaining only hospital records of suicides who may have been hospitalized sometime prior to their deaths. The communication of suicidal intent is one such phenomenon. One method of investigating such phenomena is the study of a consecutive series of successful suicides a short time after their suicidal acts, through systematic interviews with relatives, inlaws, friends, job associates, physicians and others.[1] By means of such interviews we have obtained information concerning the expression of suicidal intent by persons who recently committed suicide. In the present report certain findings concerning suicidal communication will be described: 1. The ways in which these persons communicated their suicidal intentions, whether by a direct statement or by indirect allusions to their imminent deaths. 2. The frequency and chronology, as related to the time of suicide, of such communications. 3. To whom the communications were made. 4. The relationships between communication or failure to communicate, and sex, age, clinical diagnosis, marital state, occupation, education, whether a suicide note was written, and whether the person was living alone or not. The relationships of these findings to certain other aspects of successful suicide will be also discussed.

METHOD

In the one-year period between 15 May, 1956, and 15 May, 1957, the coroners of the City of St Louis and of St Louis County[2] returned a verdict of suicide in the deaths of 134 persons. In 119 of these cases we have held a primary interview with close relatives or friends within a few weeks to a few months after the suicide. The relatives refused an interview in thirteen cases and two suicides were transients in St Louis. In addition to the primary interview,

* Reprinted from the *American Journal of Psychiatry*, Vol. 115, 1959, pp. 724–33. Copyright © 1959 The American Psychiatric Association.

interviews were obtained with other relatives, friends, job associates, clergymen, landladies, bartenders, nurses, attorneys, policemen, and physicians. A total of 305 interviews of the fifteen persons for whom no primary interview was obtained. General and mental hospital records, Social Service Exchange and police records were also examined.

The primary interview was a systematic open-ended interview which lasted an average of over two hours. This interview covered past and present medical and psychiatric history, personal and social history, and details of the successful suicide and the events which led up to it. The following items were particularly noted: 1. The ways of communicating suicidal intent. 2. The frequency of such communication. 3. To whom communicated. 4. Interval between the communication and the suicide. 5. Frequency of repeated expression of suicidal ideas. 6. Content of suicide notes and to whom addressed. 7. Prior suicide attempts, number of circumstances. 8. Medical and psychiatric care given these patients. These items were systematically asked for, and additional information was also obtained in the "free" portion of the interview where the respondent gave a description of the person, his illness, and the circumstances of the suicidal act. The interview also contained items designed to elicit the history and symptoms, if present, of the psychoses, psychoneuroses, sociopathic personality disturbances (psychopathic personality, chronic alcoholism, drug addiction), and homosexuality. The clinical diagnostic criteria used will be described in another publication. Statistical methods used have been described.[3]

RESULTS

Kinds of Communication of Suicidal Ideas.—The most striking finding was that over two-thirds (69%) of the entire group communicated their suicidal ideas (Table 1). The ways of communicating these ideas were highly varied, requiring 26 categories[3] to group the responses of the 134 persons (Table 1). The most frequent manner was a direct and specific statement of the intent to commit suicide (41% of the entire group). There were, however, many other ways of communicating suicidal ideas. Examples presented below suggest the variety of communications of individual persons.

Manic-depressive depression group.—(a) sixty-four-year-old man. Frequently said that he wanted to die, that his family would be better off when he was dead, and that he was going to commit suicide. He threatened to drink a solution of Drano. He began to fear that he would hurt himself and was taken to the hospital by his wife. (b) fifty-eight-year-old man. He said he would be better off dead. He put his affairs in his wife's name. On being told he was going to the hospital, he said, "I know I'm not coming back."[4] He spoke frequently of doing the "Dutch" act and often went through a pantomime of shooting himself in the head, saying, "If I had a gun I'd do it myself." He made two suicide attempts in the eight weeks preceding his successful suicide. (c) Fifty-nine-year-old woman. She spoke frequently of wanting to die, of fearing that she would kill herself, and of wanting to jump in the river. Shortly before her suicide she frequently said, "If I don't get better, I'm going to stick my head in the oven." She did indeed finally commit suicide by putting her head in an oven in a closed room. (d) Forty-two-year-old woman. The night before her suicide, while combing her sixteen-year-old daughter's hair, she suddenly (and quite uncharacteristically) asked, "What would you do without me?" Her husband stated that on the morning of the day of her suicide she was sweeter and more attentive than ever before, "She kissed me better than she ever had before."

Chronic alcoholic group.—(a) Thirty-year-old man. The night before his suicide he told his friends in a tavern that they would see his death notice in the newspapers on Thursday. This actually happened, since he borrowed a gun from his brother-in-law on Wednesday and shot himself that evening. (b) Thirty-seven-year-old man. This man spoke repeatedly of wanting to die, of being better off if he were dead, and of his family being better off if he were dead. He told his six-year-old child that he was going to kill himself. His anguished and pathetic communications to his current wife ("Mommy, I'm going to have to go away." "Mommy, where are you going to bury me?" "Mommy, I won't be here in the morning. I'm going to die tonight." "Oh, Mommy, come and sleep with me this one night more, and hold me tight, I'm so afraid.") contrasted with his bitter telephone statement to his ex-wife ("Come out and see my grave sometime"). On the day of his suicide he took a religious medallion with him (which he had never done before). Just before his suicide, he called the mother of his ex-wife and told her to burn a candle for him. (c) Fifty-six-year-old woman. She wondered, to her son and relatives, how quick death by hanging would be. A week before her death she said, "If things don't change in a week, I am going to hang myself by November 25." However, she did not wait until the 25th, but hanged herself on 23 November. (d) Thirty-four-year-old woman. She spoke of killing herself on many occasions. On the day of her suicide, she said to her husband, "This is the last time I will see you." She committed suicide two hours later.

Miscellaneous group: (a) Forty-five-year-old man, dying from

TABLE 1

Twenty-six kinds of Communication of Suicidal Ideas in Persons who have Committed Suicide

Manner of Communication	Men N = 103 %	Women N = 31 %	Total Group N = 134 %*
Statement of intent to commit suicide	41	42	41
Better off dead ; tired of living	26	16	24
Desire to die	23	19	22
Suicide attempts	19	32	22
References to methods of committing suicide	20	10	18
Dire predictions†	17	13	16
Statement that his family would be better off if he were dead	15	6	12
References to dying before or with spouse	7	3	6
Putting affairs in order, or planning to	6	3	5
Can't take it any longer ; no other way out	3	3	3
References to burial or to grave	4	0	3
Statement of not being afraid, or being afraid, to die	3	0	3
Talk about suicides of other people	3	3	3
The game is over ; this is the end	2	3	2
Insistent that spouse not buy new things for him	2	0	1
Called old friends whom not spoken to in ten years	1	3	1
Miscellaneous‡	7	13	8
Total communicating at least one suicidal idea	68	74	69
No communication of suicidal ideas	32	26	31

* The percentages total more than 100% because some persons used more than one kind of communication.

† These included such statements as, "I won't be here tomorrow"; "You'll find a dead man in the street"; "I am going to get off the face of the earth"; "Don't be surprised if you find I walked into the water"; "I know I'm not coming back (from the hospital)"; "Some day you'll find me dead"; "Buddy, goodbye now, you don't know how you're going to find me"; "This is your last kiss"; "I'll never leave alive"; "This is the last time I will see you"; "By that time it will be too late (when physician referred her to a psychiatrist)"; "You won't see me again except in a hearse"; "I won't be here Thursday"; "If something happens to me, don't be surprised".

carcinoma of the lung. On the day before his suicide he spoke aloud to a friend who had died in 1950. "Wait, George, don't get too far ahead, I'll be coming soon." On the night before his suicide he pleaded with his wife, "I saw your (deceased) father, and I could take you to him if you want to go." The wife refused. (*b*) Sixty-two-year-old man with an undiagnosed psychiatric illness. A year prior to his suicide he suggested that he and his wife commit suicide together. On the afternoon of his suicide, he turned as he was leaving his place of business and, with a flamboyant gesture, said to his employees, "Goodbye, everybody!" (One of these employees who had been with him twenty years said that he had never before said goodbye when leaving in the afternoon.) (*c*) Thirty-one-year-old man with an undiagnosed psychiatric illness. During the nine months preceding his suicide he spoke repeatedly of wanting to die and of committing suicide. On one occasion he pointed a gun at his wife and threatened to kill her and himself. On another occasion he held a knife to his bare chest and taunted his wife saying, "I wonder how it would feel." On a third occasion he took his wife down to the basement, put a rope around a beam, made a hangman's noose, put his head in it and said to his wife, "I wonder how it would feel." (*d*) Sixty-two-year-old woman, dying of lymphosarcoma. During the three weeks prior to her suicide she had repeatedly said, "I'm through. I'm whipped. This is the end. I can't take it any longer." During the final week she added, "I will not die a lingering death." On the morning of her suicide, she kissed her husband goodbye as he was leaving for work and said to him, "Darling, this is your last kiss." She committed suicide later that morning.

As these examples and the data in Table 1 show, the communicated suicidal ideas covered a wide range of explicit statements and of (inferred) emotional states. Most of the statements showed preoccupation with suicide, with methods of committing suicide, and with death. It was striking that in the vast majority of instances the relatives and friends did not regard these communications as efforts to manipulate the environment by playing on the emotions of the hearers. Instances of taunts (subject (*b*) in the miscellaneous group

---

‡ These included such statements and actions as, "I'm going to throw everything in your lap (to son)"; "I will not die a lingering death"; "I'm ready to go"; "You'd better watch me, I'm not responsible for what I do"; "Wait, George (to dead friend) don't get too far ahead; I'll be coming soon"; asked daughter night before suicide, "What would you do without me?"; phoned ex-wife's mother and asked her to burn a candle for him; repeatedly went through a pantomime of shooting himself (without a gun in his hand).

TABLE 2

Some Features of the Communication of Suicidal Ideas

	Men N = 70	Women N = 23	Total Group N = 93
Kinds of suicidal ideas			
Mean number per person	3.4	2.6	3.2
Proportion of persons with > 1 way			
of communication (%)	68	57	65
Maximum number in any one person	12	7	12
To whom expressed			
Spouse (%)	65	43	60
Relatives, including in-laws (%)	50	57	51
Friends (%)	34	39	35
Job associates (%)	5	4	5
Physicians (%)	13	35	18
Others: ministers, police, landlady (%)	5	4	5
Mean number per person*	1.8	1.9	1.8
Repeated vs. infrequent expression			
Repeatedly (%)	68	70	67
Once or at most a few times (%)	34	30	33
Time of first expression of suicidal ideas			
Within one year of suicide† (%)	74	70	73
More than one year, with an increase			
within one year (%)	10	22	13
More than one year, without an increase within one year (%)	16	8	14
Considered a genuine warning by respondents			
Genuine (%)	69	87	73
Not genuine‡ (%)	31	13	27

* This number is *not* the mean number of individuals to whom the *suicidal* person communicated his intent, but is the number of different *groups* of individuals to whom a suicidal communication was made. (Only the category spouse necessarily refers to a single individual.)

† It is striking that 39% of the men and 52% of the women (43% of the total group) first expressed suicidal ideas within three months of the time of their suicides.

‡ Scored as "not genuine" if there were occasional instances when the person communicated his intent, but is the number of different *groups* of it did not signify a real intent to commit suicide. It was scored this way even if there were other times when the statement of suicidal intent was considered genuine.

above), were rare. A small minority (5% of the total number of communications) appeared to be bitter and hostile. The majority were considered as expressions of anguish, hopelessness, and defeat, and the wish to disappear ("I am going to get off the face of the earth." "You'll never see me again").

Men and women did not differ significantly in the frequency of suicidal communication (Table 1).

Other Features of the Communication of Suicidal Ideas: In addition to analyzing the content of the suicidal ideas and the proportion of persons expressing them, other features, including frequency, time of expression, and to whom expressed, were studied (Table 2). Almost two-thirds (65%) of the persons used more than one type of expression. The mean number of ways per person of expressing suicidal ideas was 3.2. In the majority of instances, expressions of suicidal ideas were diverse even for individual persons. The ideas were communicated, on the average, to two different groups (footnote, Table 2); and in two-thirds (67%) of instances the communications were repeated. Thus, not only did the communications occur in a high proportion of cases but they tended to be multiple, repeated, and expressed to a number of different persons.

A question arises whether these communications were of long standing or reflected only a current preoccupation with suicide and death. In almost three-quarters of the persons (73%) these ideas had been expressed for less than one year and in 43% for less than three months. Of the remaining 27%, 13% of those who had expressed these ideas prior to one year ago had shown an increase in the frequency of the communications within one year. Therefore, 86% of the persons who were reported to have expressed suicidal ideas had recently expressed them for the first time or had shown a recent intensification of these ideas.

Since all these persons had in fact committed suicide, one might expect respondents retrospectively to change their opinion as to whether the threat of suicide had been genuine. It was of interest, however, that one-quarter of the respondents still reported that they thought that at times the suicidal ruminations had not been genuine (Table 2). There were others who felt that the communications were genuine but were nevertheless irritated and angered by them.

In Table 2 the only difference between men and women which was statistically significant (significance ratio, 2.27) was the greater proportion of women who communicated suicidal ideas to their physicians. This may be a reflection of the fact that a greater proportion of the women than of the men were seen by physicians for their psychiatric symptoms within a year prior to their suicides.

TABLE 3

Communication of Suicidal Ideas: Diagnostic Groups

| Diagnostic Group | Number and Proportion Communicating by Any Means (see Table 1) | | | | | |
| | Men | | Women | | Total | |
	No.	%	No.	%	No.	%
Manic-depressive depression*	29	69	12	67	41	68
Chronic alcoholism†	20	74	4	+	24	77
Miscellaneous illnesses‡	21	62	7	+	28	67
Total	70	68	23	74	93	69

* 42 men and 18 women.

† 27 men and 4 women.

‡ 34 men and 9 women, including, among the men, 4 chronic brain syndromes, 3 schizophrenics, 1 drug addict, 17 undiagnosed psychiatric illnesses, 3 insufficient information for diagnosis, 3 with terminal medical illness, and 3 who apparently were clinically well; and, among the women, 1 chronic brain syndrome, 2 terminal medical illnesses, 1 conversion reaction associated with drug addiction, 3 undiagnosed psychiatric illnesses, and 2 insufficient information for diagnosis.

+ Percentages not calculated, less than ten women in each group.

Relation of Communication of Suicidal Ideas to Clinical Diagnosis—For purposes of the present report, the suicides have been divided into three groups by clinical diagnosis: Manic-depressive depression,[5] chronic alcoholism, and a miscellaneous group. (See Table 3). No significant differences were found between the groups as to the number who communicated suicidal ideas. A comparison of the three groups with respect to the variables in Table 2 shows that the chronic alcoholics significantly more frequently expressed a greater variety of suicidal ideas than the other two groups (means: alcoholics 4.2, manic-depressive depressions 3.1, and miscellaneous group 2.5). There were no differences among the diagnostic groups with regard to whom the ideas were expressed, to whether the expression was repeated, and to the time of first expressing these ideas. The suicidal communications of the chronic alcoholics were considered to be not genuine (see footnote to Table 2 for definition) in 46%, of the miscellaneous group in 25% and of the manic-depressive group in 17%. The difference between the alcoholic and manic-depressive groups was statistically significant (significance ratio, 2.52).

More of the chronic alcoholics made the specific statement of in-

TABLE 4

Specific Statement of Intent to Commit Suicide: Diagnostic Groups

| | *Men* | | *Women* | | *Total Group* | |
	No.	%*	No.	%*	No.	%*
Manic-depressive depression	18	43	5	28	23	38
Chronic alcoholism	15	56	4	+	19	59
Miscellaneous illnesses	9	26	4	+	13	31
	42	41	13	42	55	41

* Percentages based on total diagnostic groups, not just those persons communicating suicidal ideas.
+ Percentages not calculated, less than ten women in each group.

tent to commit suicide than did the manic-depressives (significance ratio, 1.92) or the miscellaneous group (significance ratio, 2.41) (Table 4). Since in Table 3, the chronic alcoholic group also had the highest proportion who communicated suicidal ideas (although not statistically significant), there may be a real but slight tendency for the chronic alcoholics to be more communicative in this respect.

Relations of Communication of Suicidal Ideas to Selected Social Variables (Table 5)—Sex, age, marital state, socio-economic status, religion and whether living alone or not did not significantly affect the proportion of suicides who communicated their suicidal ideas.

Relation of the Communication of Suicide Ideas to the Leaving of a Suicide Note—Of the ninety-three persons who had communicated their suicidal ideas, 37% left a suicide note; of the forty-one persons who did not communicate their suicidal ideas, 27% left a note. Therefore, there was no significant relationship between prior communication of suicidal ideas and leaving a suicide note.

Psychiatric and Medical Care—The direct communication of suicidal ideas and of preoccupation with death has been discussed. The question arises whether these were isolated statements and actions in persons who gave no clear evidence of being clinically ill. From the diagnoses presented in Table 3 it is evident that only three persons, all men, could be considered clinically well. In the remainder of the suicides (131 persons), there was little or no question of the presence of either a terminal medical illness or a psychiatric illness, even though a clear-cut diagnosis could not always be made in the latter group. People in whom a clear-cut diagnosis could not be made were considered psychiatrically ill if they had a multiplicity of psychiatric symptoms or disturbances in behaviour. In the manic-depressive

TABLE 5

The Relation of the Communication of Suicidal Ideas to Selected
Social Variables

Social Variables	Proportion Who Communicated Suicidal Ideas %
Sex	
Men (N = 103)	68
Women (N = 31)	74
Age	
> 44 (N = 36)	75
44–59 (N = 45)	67
> 59 (N = 53)	70
Marital State	
Married (N = 83)	69
Not Married (N = 51)*	74
Religion	
Protestant (N = 60)	67
Catholic (N = 30)	73
Jewish (N = 6)	†
None (N = 20)	75
Other Members of Household	
Immediate Family (N =90)	70
Other Relatives (N = 13)‡	69
None (Living alone) (N = 30)	73
Income (Annual)	
< $3,000 (N = 28)	71
$3,000–$5,000 (N = 43)	70
> $5,000 (N =24)	50
Education	
8 grades or less (N = 59)	76
> 8 grades (N = 45)	64
Occupation	
Lower status (N = 52)§	66
Higher status (N= 72)§	69

* Not married includes never married, divorced, separated, and widowed.
†Percentages not calculated; N is less than 10.
‡ Includes 2 persons living with friends.
§ Lower status—lower than skilled workers; higher status—skilled workers or higher. Housewives' occupational statuses were classified according to their husbands' occupations.

group, the symptoms and behaviour disturbances were usually of only a few months' duration, whereas, in the chronic alcoholics, the disturbances were of at least five years' and more frequently of over ten years' duration. In the vast majority of instances, therefore, the suicidal ideas and the eventual suicide were the accompaniments and culmination of an obvious and severe psychiatric disturbance. The respondents knew the suicides were clinically ill not only because they directly communicated suicidal ideas but also because they had other symptoms—for example, depression, loss of interest, joylessness, anorexia, weight loss, insomnia, job disability, delusions, and excessive alcoholic intake with its consequences. These perceptions of the respondents are supported by the findings that within the year preceding the suicide, over 50% of the group had had medical or psychiatric care for psychiatric disease, including approximately one-fifth who had seen a psychiatrist and some of whom had been in a psychiatric hospital. It is noteworthy that an uncomplicated "neurosis" (anxiety reaction, conversion reaction, or obsessive-compulsive reaction) did not occur in any person in the study. Communication of the possibility of suicide, therefore, involves not only the direct allusions to suicidal ideas by the suicidal person but also the awareness on the part of the respondent that this is not an "ordinary kind of nervousness" (a quote from a respondent) even in a severe form, but that there has been a recent *change* in the person or that his uncontrolled alcoholism has got him into serious difficulties.

DISCUSSION

Methodological Considerations—This is probably the first study of an unselected series of suicides in which relatives and other relevant persons were systematically interviewed shortly after the suicide. As to the validity of these respondents' reports, we can only point out that the descriptions of the illnesses from which the suicides suffered were detailed and coherent enough to allow a specific diagnosis to be made in 82% of the cases, although the diagnostic features of these illnesses were unknown to the respondents. This suggests that the respondents were reasonably accurate observers of these phenomena. The whole problem of the validity of psychiatric histories taken from relatives or even from patients themselves is a largely neglected area in psychiatric investigation.

There are certain hiatuses in our knowledge of the suicides which are inevitable when the ill person himself is not examined. These, however, do not seem especially important for the purposes of the present paper. With regard to communication, the recipient of the communication is as integral a part of the communication process as is the communicator, and it may be as valuable to interview the recipient as it is to interview the communicators. In fact, it is our impression that we received a more extensive, lucid, and verbatim report from the respondents about the communication of suicidal ideas than it is possible to obtain from suicidal patients themselves.

It should be emphasized that the reports of suicidal communications, although strikingly frequent in these persons, probably represents only a minimal figure. It is likely that at least some of the 31% of the suicides whom we report as having not made a suicidal communication actually had made such communication to someone who was not interviewed or had made one to the respondent interviewed which he subsequently forgot or did not tell us.

Communication of Suicidal Ideas—Our most striking finding was that two-thirds of the persons who commit suicide communicate their suicidal ideas and preoccupation with imminent death prior to the suicidal act. Persons who talk about suicide may, therefore, very well commit it. In the majority of instances these communications are repeatedly verbalized, diverse in content, and expressed to many different persons. In three-quarters of the suicides who communicated their suicidal ideas, their expression is of recent onset and is *not* found in the persons' usual behaviour. The vast majority of these persons were clinically ill prior to their suicides, and half of them had received medical or psychiatric care for their psychiatric illness. There were, therefore, two factors involved in communication of suicidal ideas: the direct expression of such ideas, and the perception by the relatives, physicians, and often by the suicidal person himself that he was ill, or at least very different from his usual self.

Analysis of the Results as a System of Communication—We were greatly aided in this analysis by the formal description of the process of communication by Hovland and his colleagues [4, 5]. The study of communication requires the investigation and analysis of four factors [5]: (a) The one who makes the communication, that is, the suicidal person. (b) The content of the communication. (c) The audience responding to the communication (relatives, friends, job associates, physicians, and others). (d) The responses made by the audience.

(a) The communicator. Since these persons committed suicide, it must be accepted that they wanted to die. Perhaps the most easily understood behaviour would have been for the person to decide to kill himself and to do so without any communication. Since this did not happen in the majority of instances, what are some of the possible explanations? There are at least four. The first three possibilities imply a specific purpose in making the suicidal communication. First, the person is ambivalent about dying, both wanting and not wanting to, or being afraid of dying. His communications may be considered as a means of bringing his plight to the attention of others so that they can help him. Second, the communications may reflect the desire to warn the audience of what the communicator is about to do and, therefore, in some way prepare them for his death so that it will be less of a shock. Third, even though he wished to die, the communications are also meant as taunts or threats. A possible subcategory would consist of this hostile use of the communications without a genuine desire to die. This subcategory probably occurred only once in this series, since only one of these deaths appeared to be accidental resulting from a spurious suicide attempt. The fourth possibility contrasts with the first three in that it does *not* imply a specific purpose. The nature and consequences of the illnesses from which these persons suffer might be such that the person becomes so preoccupied with ideas of suicide and death that he is merely expressing the content of his thoughts, rather than trying to achieve any particular goals through his suicidal communications. In analyzing our data (see especially Table 1) we have the impression that all four explanations are relevant in some cases, but that the fourth possibility is the most common reason for the expression of suicidal ideas.

(*b*) The content of the communication. The contents have been described in detail. The outstanding characteristic is that they probably tended to produce anxiety and arouse fear in the respondents.

(*c*) The audience. The chief characteristics of the audience relevant to the present analysis are: whether those who received the suicidal communications desired the death of the communicator, were indifferent to it, or were distressed by it. As far as could be ascertained from our interviews, only a very small minority of the respondents appeared to desire or welcome the death of the suicidal person, or to be indifferent. The indifference did not appear to be complete; the suicide was at least unwelcome and unpleasant to this group. By far the largest number of respondents were genuinely distressed and upset by the suicidal death.

(*d*) Responses of the audience. The majority of the respondents expressed a feeling of marked tension. They were being repeatedly warned of the possible or even probable occurrence of a dire event about which they could do nothing definitive. They did not feel able either to prevent the suicidal act or to ameliorate the psychiatric illnesses. Nor had they been able to turn total responsibility for the person over to anyone else. Although half of the suicidal persons had been seen by a physician, only 6% were in a hospital at the time of their suicides. In the majority of the remaining cases, therefore, the respondent felt some degree of responsibility for the suicidal person prior to and at the time of the suicide.

What then are the ways in which the respondents attempted to deal with this dilemma? Their attempts will be analysed in accordance with the discussion of Hovland, Janis, and Kelley [5] concerning audience response to what they term fear-arousing appeals. The work of these authors is based on an experimental situation in which the communicator was, for the most part, directly threatening the audience with pain, cancer, etc., if they did not take care of their teeth properly. In spite of the marked differences between this experimental situation and the present study, many aspects of their analysis are nevertheless applicable. Like their respondents, our respondents tended to deal with the dilemma in three ways: [6] 1. By changing their original attitudes towards the communication itself; 2. By changing their attitudes to the communicator; 3. By changing their perceptions of their own roles in this situation.

Changes towards the communication itself included the following: The outright rejection of a fear-arousing communication, when after the first rush of dismay and alarm, the respondents began to regard the possibility of suicide as improbable ("I thought he didn't really mean it." "I didn't think it would happen.") or, if possible, then perhaps at some remote time ("He might do it but not now. Maybe if he gets worse"). Since it was usual for the suicidal person to communicate his suicidal ideas repeatedly and over a period of time, the respondents began to discount their seriousness because of their frequent repetition with no suicidal action having been taken ("She had been saying it for so long I became more used to it". "He'd said it so many times, I just began to hope it would never happen."). Finally, we have the impression that a very high level of anxiety in the respondent acted directly in some fashion to reduce his panicky and severely distressful reactions to the suicidal communication ("I just got worn out with the constant worry").

Changes in attitudes towards the suicidal person included the following: After the initial shock and belief that the suicidal person might commit suicide, the respondent would cease to believe that the suicide would happen because, "He had never talked or acted this way before. It just wasn't like him. He couldn't do something like that." Related to the preceding response was the belief initially that the person was ill and as a result he might commit suicide. This would then change to the idea that he was ill but not sick enough to commit suicide ("He's sick but he's not that much 'off'; he won't do it. He's just not himself") In other instances the respondents became so angry and irritated at the suicidal person's repeatedly making them anxious and distressed ("I got so mad at her constantly talking about it (suicide and death) that I just didn't listen.") that they rejected the significance of the communication. Finally, a mixture of anger and outright disbelief occurred when the suicidal person taunted the respondent with his suicidal communications.

Changes in the respondents' perceptions of their own roles: It was our impression that initially the critical considerations here were whether the respondent had little or no idea of what to do for the suicidal persons or whether he believed he should see a psychiatrist or other physician had examined the suicidal person and had not hospitalized him or had hospitalized him only briefly, the respondents were left with the problem of a communicator who was in part their responsibility and for whom they knew nothing definitive to do. As a result, the original picture of themselves as being helpful and effective in getting the suicidal person to a physician was changed and they were left with an insoluble problem. It should be pointed out that there is a lack of realistic information concerning what a respondent should do when confronted with this kind of situation. This is due to a lack of knowledge of the medical profession and not only of the respondents. No clear-cut information is available to physicians or to the public as to what should be done in this situation. A very real dilemma, therefore, confronts the respondent.

SUMMARY

1. A study of the communication of suicidal ideas by 134 consecutive suicides has been done by means of systematic interviews with family, in-laws, friends, job associates, physicians, ministers, and others a short time after the suicide.

2. Two striking findings were that over two-thirds (69%) of the suicides had communicated suicidal ideas and that 41% had specifically stated they intended to commit suicide. In the majority of instances, the suicidal communications were of recent onset (months), repeatedly verbalized, and expressed to many persons.

3. Another striking finding was that 98% of these persons were probably clinically ill prior to their suicides.

4. The frequency of expression of suicidal ideas was not significantly related to age, sex, marital state, religion, whether living alone or not, clinical diagnosis, occupational status, income, or education. Chronic alcoholics had a somewhat greater tendency than the other diagnostic groups to make the specific statement that they intended to commit suicide.

5. The communication of suicidal ideas was analyzed as a general system of communication with reference to experimental psychological studies.

NOTES

1 This method of studying suicide is not a new one. Over thirty years ago Serin [1, 2] studied suicides and attempted suicides in Paris by interviews with relatives and others. Since her reports did not separate attempted from successful suicide, it is difficult to interpret her results. It is also not clear whether a consecutive series was studied (she obtained the names from newspapers) or whether a systematic interview was used. So far as the authors are aware, this is probably the first study in which a consecutive series was systematically interviewed.

2 We wish to thank the coroners for the City of St Louis (Patrick J. Taylor) and for St Louis County (Arnold J. Willmann and Raymond I. Harris) and their staffs (Mary Alice Quinn, Mildred B. Saemann and Rose Marie Algarda) without whose co-operation this study would not have been possible.

3 These twenty-six ways include twenty-five which were direct verbal references to suicide and death or to the possibility of imminent death, and one which was non-verbal, a suicide attempt. The occurrence, for example, of feelings and expressions of depression, of hopelessness, of illness, and of being a burden will be considered later in the paper.

4 The quoted statements throughout the paper are verbatim quotes from interviews.

5 This diagnostic term is used to include also psychotic depressive reaction and involutional melancholia. The relations between the diagnoses of manic-depressive depression and neurotic depressive reaction will be discussed in another paper. Here it should be pointed out that there was no patient who had *only* a phobic, anxiety, obsessive, or conversion reaction. It is the belief of the authors that what is ordinarily called neurotic depressive reaction, *in the absence of a pre-existing clinically evident neurotic disorder,* is a manic-depressive (or psychotic) depression without delusions or grossly apparent psychomotor retardation.

6 It must be emphasized that we do not have systematic data concerning the respondents' ways of dealing with this dilemma. Not only were these sorts of questions not asked systematically in the questionnaire but also too close questioning of the respondents concerning their own feelings or actions tended to break up the interview. The ways to be described in which respondents dealt with this dilemma, therefore, will represent examples where we have clear evidence that at least a few of the respondents used this technique. This area of audience responses appears to be a fruitful one for further research on the nature of suicide.

BIBLIOGRAPHY

[1] S. Serin, *Presse Med.,* 2 : 1404, 1926.

[2] S. Serin, *Ann. Medico-psychol.,* 84 : 356, 1926.

[3] J. J. Purtell, E. Robins and M. E. Cohen, *J.A.M.A..,* 146 : 902, 1951.

[4] C. I. Hovland, *Proc. Am. Philos. Soc.,* 92 : 371, 1948.

[5] C. I. Hovland, I. L. Janis and H. H. Kelley, *Communication and Persuasion: Psychological Studies of Opinion Change, New* Haven : Yale University Press, 1953.

CHAPTER 30

The Social Effects of Attempted Suicide*

E. Stengel

It is a measure of the relative neglect of research into attempted suicide that only very recently the important problem of the incidence of suicide among those who had attempted suicide before has received attention. Dahlgren (1945) of Malmo followed up a series of cases, and similar studies have been carried out in London by myself (Stengel, 1952) in association with Cook and Kreeger, by Pierre-B. Schneider (1954) in Lausanne, by Schmidt and his associates in St Louis (1954), and by Batchelor (1954) in Edinburgh. The periods covered by these follow-ups are still too short for definite conclusions to be drawn, but it can be said already that only a small or very small minority of those who are known to have attempted suicide finally kill themselves.

It is too often taken for granted that, by and large, people who commit and those who attempt suicide can be viewed as one population. There are considerable differences between the two groups. Women have been found to be in the majority among attempted suicides but in the minority among suicides. Attempted suicide appears to be comparatively more frequent among the younger age groups than suicide. As to the size of the two groups, in spite of what has sometimes been said about suicide rates, it can be assumed that the cases on which they are based constitute the majority of suicides and that the available samples are representative. The same cannot be said of the suicidal attempts which come to our knowledge. Some workers believe that the total of admissions for attempted suicide to hospitals for all types does not fall very short of the incidence of attempts in the area concerned, and most workers are confident that at least they are representative samples. Both these assumptions are doubtful. The estimate that attempted suicide is at least six times as frequent as suicide (1941), based on observations made in two American cities, sounds more realistic though it probably is still too conservative. A number of surveys in urban communities indicate that the ratio of suicides to

* Reprinted by permission from the *Canadian Medical Association Journal*, Vol. 74, No. 2, January 1956, pp. 116–20.

suicidal attempts is about 1 : 10. If this is the case, the representative character of the admissions to hospital becomes very uncertain. But there are other reasons for doubting it. I want to mention only one. Among suicides, higher socio-economic groups are more heavily represented than the lower classes (Weiss, 1954; Sainsbury, 1955). This has not been the case among our patients admitted to public psychiatric and general hospitals because of suicidal attempts, and I do not expect the material of other workers to differ from ours in this respect. Unless the representation of the various socio-economic classes among attempted suicides is the opposite of that among suicides, which is improbable, we have to assume that a proportion of suicidal attempts eludes us. We cannot, therefore, be sure of the representative character of the groups available. The factors which lead to admission to hospital after a suicidal attempt are very complex and variable, even in one and the same case on different occasions. The degree of damage inflicted is only one of them. All these considerations should be a warning against too confident generalizations from statistical data obtained from material on suicidal attempts to which we have access.

We can safely assume, then, that attempted suicides are much more numerous than suicides, that the groups differ in several aspects from each other, and that only a small proportion of the former enters into the latter group. There is much to be said for treating them as two populations epidemiologically, in spite of the absence of a clear demarcation and in spite of what they have in common from the psycho-pathological point of view. This formulation has frequently been misunderstood. It does not mean that they are two groups consisting of two different types of people. It is, for instance, quite legitimate to say that those suffering from tuberculosis consist of two populations, those who recover and those who die. Both of them suffer, of course, from the same disease.

There are still other reasons why the suicidal attempt merits special consideration. We want to look at it as a behaviour pattern and not view it as an act whose only purpose is self-destruction, and which in the large majority of cases fails in this purpose because the person is either too well or too ill or not sincere or determined enough to kill himself. I believe that by having made death the hallmark of success and the only legitimate outcome of a common and varied behaviour pattern such as a suicidal act, we have deprived ourselves of full understanding of its significance. There are many features which, though regular parts of the behaviour pattern do not serve the purpose of self-destruction. There is a social element in most suicidal acts. Once we look for it we find it without difficulty. There is a tendency to give warning of the impending act and to give others a chance to intervene. Those who attempt suicide tend, in the suicidal act, to remain within or to move towards a social group. In most suicidal attempts, irrespective of the mental state in which they are made, we can discern an appeal to other human beings. This appeal also acts as a powerful threat. We regard the appeal character of the suicidal attempt, which is usually unconscious, as one of its essential features. This particular quality has been generally recognized as a feature of the suicidal attempts of hysterics and certain psychopaths, and it is often very obvious in these cases. But it is inherent in the suicidal acts of others also. Every one of us has seen many suicidal acts among schizophrenic and depressive patients when the threat to life was so small that, had the patients been neurotics or psychopaths, they could have served as typical examples of insincere or even faked attempts. In these cases the facile explanation has been advanced that they were too ill to make a success of their suicidal acts. I have, on the contrary, often marvelled at the circumspection with which those very sick people appear to balance the danger and the safety devices in their very genuine suicidal acts. This takes us to another feature of the suicidal act which may be called its ordeal character, the term ordeal being used in its original sense, i.e. of a trial in which a person submitted himself, or was subjected, before the community, to a dangerous test the outcome of which was taken as divine judgement. The so-called failure of a suicidal act is usually accepted without demur, at least for a time. To prevent misunderstandings, I should like to make it clear that I fully agree with those who have emphasized the aggressive nature of suicidal acts. The emphasis on the appeal character of suicidal acts has sometimes been understood to refer only to those cases where the manipulative intention was manifest and conscious. It was argued, therefore, that only a minority of suicidal acts had an appeal character. If, however, one considers the effect of suicidal acts on other people, irrespective of conscious intention, every such act has an appeal effect. If the outcome is fatal that effect is posthumous. It is perfectly justified to state that every suicidal act has a potential appeal effect.

Once we have dropped the idea that most suicidal attempts are nothing but unsuccessful suicides, many interesting questions arise. What are the effects of the suicidal attempt on the person concerned and his group? If it had been the result of inner conflict, what happens to that conflict? If it was motivated by a crisis of human relations, are they modified by it, and if so, how? Sociologists have told us that suicide is due to social disintegration and isolation. Is this true for suicidal attempts also, and if so, are those social conditions modified by it? If self-destruction is not the only purpose of attempted suicide, what is the function of this behaviour pattern in our society? We have been studying these questions at the Institute of Psychiatry in London since 1951, and a monograph reporting our findings to date has been completed (E. Stengel and N. J. Cook: *Attempted Suicide*, London, 1958). I can on this occasion refer only to some of our results.

We found that among the 138 patients admitted to a mental observation ward in the course of twelve months, thirty-one, i.e. 22% had been living in isolation, which came near to the proportion found by Sainsbury among suicides in London, and was about three times the rate found among the general population. A follow-up carried out five years later revealed that five of those thirty-one had died within two months after admission, and that six had remained in a mental hospital. The mode of life had changed in five cases, the change resulting in an end of their isolation. In eleven cases the mode of life had remained unchanged but there had been improvements in contacts in two of them. Four patients could not be traced.

The social constellation in the situation of the suicidal attempt was studied in several groups, of which I want to mention only one. Of 147 unselected patients admitted to a mental observation ward after attempted suicide in 1953 only forty-four were alone during the attempt. The rest were together with or near people. Forty of the total moved towards people during the attempt. In a comparable group of suicides the percentage of those who were alone and not near people at the time of the act was almost double.

The psychological and social sequelæ of the suicidal attempt for the individual and his group had never been studied when we started our investigations in London in 1951. There is one exception only, i.e. the occasional immediate therapeutic effect of the attempt on the mental state, especially on depressions, which has been known to psychiatrists for a long time. We have studied two series of cases so far. We interviewed the patients and their relatives and endeavoured to gain insight into the development of their human relations since the suicidal attempts, with special consideration of the influence the latter might have had on modifying them. It was often difficult to arrive at conclusions, for various reasons. We had to be on our guard against associating changes in a person's human relations to the suicidal attempt indiscriminately. Secondly, in many cases it was impossible to say whether some of the changes had been due to the suicidal attempt or to the underlying mental disorder. In the large majority of cases studied by us the suicidal attempt resulted in temporary hospitalization and treatment, while in some it meant removal from the scene of conflict only. These surely are highly significant changes in a person's relationship to his environment, however temporary. In more than half of those hospitalized, the condition requiring hospital treatment had existed for some time untreated. In these cases the suicidal attempt had caused the patient to be admitted to hospital and to be given appropriate treatment. This often happens in depressives and schizophrenics, but occasionally also in other conditions. The following case is an example of this important function of the suicidal attempt. A man of 33 had married a girl who was pregnant by him, although his attitude to her had been ambivalent. He had been anxious for some time, and four days after the wedding he developed a state of panic and confusion in which he cut his wrists. He lost a considerable amount of blood and waited for death to come. When nothing happened he went to the police and was taken to the observation ward, where he was found to have general paresis. Six months later he was discharged from hospital recovered. He had in the meantime become reconciled with his marriage, and his relationship to his wife has remained satisfactory. Why should we not call this a successful suicidal attempt? It is true, it failed in its purpose of self-destruction, but it fulfilled its function as a signal of alarm and as an appeal for help admirably. Not all attempts have such unexpected and gratifying results, but many of them achieve temporary or permanent changes in the person's life situation which fail to impress us greatly, either because they are so common or because they are so subtle.

There was a group of patients whose attempts had been the last endeavour at controlling their fate before finally surrendering to the symptoms of their mental illness. Those were the ones whose admission had resulted in permanent hospitalization. There were others who aimed at forestalling death from physical illness.

Where it was possible to relate changes in human relations directly to the suicidal attempt the following sequelæ were found: changes vis-à-vis a special person, usually resulting in mutual concessions and in an improvement of crumbling relationships, the final breaking up of threatened human relations; a greater dependence, emotionally and materially; a change in the patient's mode of life or in the mode of life by a member of his group. The following tables give an example of the frequency with which some of those effects were found in one of the series of cases studied.

Of 138 patients admitted to a mental observation ward in London from the suicidal attempt which had caused their admission, ninety-seven cases resulted in temporary hospitalization and treatment (Table 1). In twenty-one cases hospitalization was permanent, while in twelve cases admission was followed by death not attributable to self injury within two to three months. In eight cases the suicidal

Table 1

Sequelae of Suicidal Attempts in 138 Cases

Temporary hospitalization and treatment	97
Permanent hospitalization	21
Death within two months after admission	12
Removal from the scene of conflict	8
(Suicidal attempt secured treatment	58)

Table 2

Changes in Human Relations
Attributable to the Suicidal Attempt

Changes *vis-à-vis* a special person	27
Break	5
Finalizing of separation, loss or break	9
Greater dependence	4
Change of mode of life by patient	10
by others	3
Community aid roused	11

attempt had achieved a temporary removal from the scene of conflict only. These were patients who were discharged from the observation ward within two weeks. Table 2 illustrates the various types of changes in human relations observed where it was possible to relate them to the suicidal attempt. It also shows the proportion of cases in which the suicidal attempt had failed to prevent separation, the threat of which had played a part in the causation of the suicidal act. In these cases the attempt had the effect of finalizing an unwanted development. There was a group in which community aid of a material and moral kind had been roused as a result of the attempt. In some the attempt had resulted in no change in social relations. One would expect this group to be bigger in a series of cases with a smaller proportion of mentally ill. There were two cases in which the attempt caused invalidism and thus permanently transformed the patient's life. There was a sizeable group of patients whose mode of life had changed as the result of the suicidal attempt. They gave up living in isolation, or changed their work. In a number of cases the suicidal attempt had caused members of the family to change their mode of life. An example would be the wife who stopped going out to work to look after her physically sick husband, or the husband who changed his employment in order to be nearer or more often with his wife.

There were many more cases in which the patient's relationship to his environment had changed after discharge from hospital, but in these it was impossible to decide how much was due to the suicidal attempt and how much to the change in the patient's mental state after treatment and to the mobilization of social aid called forth by the illness.

Among the whole group of 138 cases, subsequent attempts were known to have occurred in twenty-two. Only one patient killed himself. This happened ten months after his first and only suicidal attempt. There were sixteen cases in which attempted suicide had been a regular behaviour pattern in circumstances of stress. Of these, eleven had continued to react in this way. In four cases this behaviour pattern had ceased and there was reason to believe that this was due to hospitalization and treatment following their last suicidal attempt.

I have given an illustration of various effects the suicidal attempt had in a special group of patients. Naturally, these effects will be differently represented in a series of patients admitted to a general hospital, or not admitted to hospital at all, and there may be still other effects not observed in this particular series.

The effects of the suicidal attempt are often short-lived, and sometimes it fails to alter anything. In such cases it is apt to be repeated. All this is highly relevant for the treatment of people who have made suicidal attempts. It is not enough to treat the underlying condition. We must also try to understand in every individual case the hidden message of the act of self-injury.

The emphasis on the death instinct as the main and only driving force has tended to obscure the complex psychodynamics of suicidal acts. The study of attempted suicide as a social behaviour pattern should go some way to remedying the stagnation in psychopathological research into suicidal acts. There is need for a re-examination of the various ways in which aggressive tendencies manifest themselves in suicidal acts and interact with those which make for preservation and consolidation of human ties. It is not only the relative strength of those mental forces which decides the outcome of suicidal acts. It depends also on the way the environment intervenes. The variables are so numerous and so difficult to measure that prediction will always remain hazardous, all the more so as an element of unpredictability is one of the inherent qualities of the suicidal attempt, the one that I called its ordeal character.

There is another aspect of attempted suicide worthy of attention, i.e. its incidence in societies which differ from ours in their reactions to the individual's appeal for help. If our thesis of the appeal function of the suicidal attempt is correct, one would expect to have fewer suicidal attempts in a society unsympathetic or hostile to the individual. And this appears to be true. We know from Dr Kral and other observers that in German concentration camps suicidal attempts were extremely rare, though suicide by giving up the struggle or by self-exposure to certain death were frequent. This is only one, and an extreme example, of the various ways in which the individual's relation to society affects the incidence of suicidal attempts as well as the forms of suicide.

The observation presented here should contribute to an understanding of attempted suicide and thus to its prevention. A better understanding of attempted suicide is likely to benefit not only the knowledge and treatment of that costly and dangerous behaviour pattern, but also the study of suicide and the reduction of its incidence. Small as the number of suicides may be, among those who have previously attempted suicide, it is still much larger than among the general population.

In this short presentation I have dealt mainly with the effects of attempted suicide on human relations which can be discerned without exploration of the more subtle and deeper psychological changes in those concerned, i.e. the person who has inflicted the self-injury on himself, and his group or groups. These are problems in need of careful study. At this stage it can only be said that often the experience of the suicidal attempt signifies to the patient death, survival and a new beginning. To those close to him it often stands for bereavement and therefore gives rise to mental reactions identical with mourning. It is apt to create the peculiar situation in which somebody who has died and yet survived is being mourned. All these complex reactions tend to make for revision and renewal of human relations. The outward effects of these reactions have been the subject of our investigations. But they spring from intra-psychic events. Here, as in other fields, changes in social behaviour cannot be understood without the knowledge of what is happening in the minds of individuals.

NOTES

1 I. R. C. Batchelor and M. B. Napier, *J. Neurol., Neurosurg. and Psychiat.*, 17: 261, 1954.
2 K. G. Dahlgren, *On Suicide and Attempted Suicide*, Lindstedts, Lund, 1945.
3 V. A. Kral, *Am. J. Psychiat.*, 108: 185, 1951.
4 P. Sainsbury, *Suicide in London: An Ecological Study*, London: Chapman & Hall Ltd., 1955.

5 E. H. Schmidt, P. O'Neal and E. Robins, *J. Amer. Med. Ass.*, 155: 549, 1954.
6 P.-B. Schneider, *La tentative de suicide,* Paris, 1954.
7 *Statis. Bull. Metrop. Life Insur. Co.*, 22(5): 13, 1941.
8 E. Stengel, *Proc. Roy. Soc. Med.*, 45: 613, 1952.
9 J. M. Weiss, *Psychiat. Quart.*, 28: 225, 1954.

CHAPTER 31

The Gamble with Death in Attempted Suicide*

James M. A. Weiss

Inextricably involved with the attitudes, folkways, mores, and laws of culture and subculture, with tragedy for the person and the group, with emotions and values, suicide is a sociopsychiatric phenomenon about which much confusion exists. The nature of this phenomenon is complex, and its scientific study is difficult. It seems evident that there are three chief etiological factors in suicide: the group attitudes in each particular society; the adverse extraneous situations which the person must meet; and the interaction of these with his character and personality. This last single variable appears to be the most important one. But very little is known about the actual psychodynamic factors operative in successful suicides, for the obvious reason that persons who have committed successful suicide are no longer available for psychological or psychiatric study. Thus dynamic theories about suicides have been formulated to a large extent by extrapolation from what has been learned in clinical studies of patients who have *attempted* suicide—as if there were an implicit understanding that successful suicide is simply an exaggerated or completed form of attempted suicide. Current data indicate, however, that such extrapolation is justified only in limited areas and that the psychodynamic patterns in many suicidal attempts are quite different from the patterns in successful suicidal acts.

Most psychiatrists and psychoanalysts have related suicide to aggressive impulses. Fenichel states that the most frequent causes of suicide are "an ambivalent dependence on a sadistic superego and the necessity to get rid of an unbearable guilt tension at any cost". The person submits to punishment and to the superego's cruelty, and may express the passive thought of giving up any active fighting; more actively, and at the same time, there is a turning of sadism against the person himself, a rebellion against the punishing superego.[1] Freud emphasizes that suicide is often the result of aggression directed towards an introjected love object—that is, a love object with whom the subject had previously identified himself.[2] Alexander considers suicide an extreme example of the disintegration of iso-

* Reprinted by permission from *Psychiatry*, Vol. 20, 1957, pp. 17–25.

lated aggressive impulses which are normally subordinated.[3] Schilder believes that suicide can serve as a form of self-aggression, or as self-punishment for aggressive behaviour previously directed towards another (loved) person, or as a form of punishment for a person who may have earlier denied love to the subject, or as a form of peace (or reunion with a love object), or certainly as an escape from insupportable difficulties.[4]

These and similar psychodynamic theories of suicide may be valid, but they contain inherent methodological errors. They are based on data derived either from persons who, during or after a period of psychoanalytic scrutiny, successfully committed suicide or from persons who unsuccessfully attempted suicide. Generalizing from the few cases of the former type may not be correct, for it is certainly possible that new dynamic forces—occurring between the last interview and the time of the actual suicide, and therefore not available for analysis—played a part. The relevance of pre-mortem analytic data to an understanding of the actual crisis which resulted in any particular successful suicide is then open to question. Therefore, most investigations, trying to learn more about the dynamics of suicide, have turned to the person who attempts suicide unsuccessfully.

However, attempted suicide apparently does not represent a simple dynamic or even diagnostic pattern. On the basis of interviews with 109 patients who attempted suicide in St Louis, Missouri, during a five-month period in 1952 and 1953, Schmidt, O'Neal, and Robins found the psychiatric disorders represented to be classifiable—using careful criteria—into nine different diagnostic categories. (No attempter was found who was thought to be normal prior to the attempt.) Diagnostic differentiation was not even very helpful in separating the "serious" from the "not serious" attempts.[5] Thus attempted suicide is probably a symptom which can be associated with a variety of clinical psychiatric disorders.

From the epidemiologic point of view, the relationship of attempted suicide to successful suicide becomes more complicated. Successful suicide is considered to be one outcome—the fatal end—of an ecologic process representing the reaction between a host and his environment. Gordon has pointed out that each illness in a living organism varies clinically in frequency and character, and can end in uneventful recovery, complication, or death.[6] In successful suicide, one can know only about those cases that terminate fatally; by definition, suicide is a deliberate, violent, self-inflicted, destructive action resulting in death. Thus suicide rates represent mortality rates for a type of mental disorder which, prior to its termination in death, is in itself marginal and poorly described. Lindemann suggests that this mental disorder which *may* end in suicide be termed *hypereridism* (from *Eris,* the Greek goddess of wrath and anger).[7] Then hypereridism—or whatever the specific disorder which ends in successful suicide is called—may or may not be one of the variety of emotional disorders of which attempted suicide is a symptom.

Increasing evidence indicates that successful suicides and unsuccessful suicidal attempts represent two different kinds of acts performed in different ways by different people. For example, successful suicides are more common in the older age groups, and among the single, divorced, or widowed; reported unsuccessful suicidal attempts are more likely to occur in the younger age groups, and among females, and in the married population. In the United States during the past forty years, about two-thirds of the persons who successfully committed suicide used methods of shooting or hanging; most persons reported to have unsuccessfully attempted suicide used methods of ingestion of poison, cutting or slashing or inhalation of gas—all less efficient than shooting and hanging, which only rarely fail to cause death.[8]

A continuum between attempted and successful suicide which might be postulated logically is that of "lethal probability". If attempted suicide is defined as a deliberate, violent, self-inflicted, destructive action which the person concerned or others interpret as likely to result in death—therefore not including verbal threats short of action—such a continuum of lethal probability could be arranged graphically. At the left end of the abscissa would be placed those attempts in which the probability of death actually resulting is minimum. Attempts with increasing probability of death would be arranged along the abscissa towards the right end, where those attempts with a maximum probability of death resulting would be placed. Thus, at the left end (minimum lethal probability) would be placed such cases as that of a young woman who ingested five sedative tablets in the presence of her husband and with a telephone near by. At the right end (maximum lethal probability) would be placed such cases as that of a man who shot himself through the roof of the mouth. Along the ordinate would be the number of persons who make such attempts in any given unit of time.

It is currently impossible to obtain complete data for such a graph. However, from data already available, it appears likely that if such a graph could be made, there would be two separate population curves. Towards the left end of the graph would be grouped a very large number of cases of unsuccessful attempted suicide; this curve would be skewed towards the right. At the right end of the graph would be grouped a much smaller number of cases of successfully committed suicide; this curve would be skewed towards the left. The two populations would be distinct but overlapping.

One reason for the overlap is that some persons who attempt suicide without any firm intention of succeeding make some fatal mistake. Such a case in my series is that of a thirty-one-year-old white housewife who was having various marital difficulties. One day there had been an especially violent quarrel before the husband left for work in the morning. At approximately 5.10 p.m. that evening the wife turned on all the jets of her gas stove, knowing that during six years of marriage her husband had returned from work regularly at 5.15 p.m. Unfortunately, on this particular day the husband stopped at a tavern for a few beers—something he had never done before. He arrived home at about 5.30 p.m. to find his wife comatose. At the hospital she was rendered conscious long enough to state that she had not expected to die; she had thought that her husband would come home "in plenty of time" to save her life. However, she relapsed into coma and, despite medical care, later died—so that her attempt was reported as a successful suicide.

At the other end, there are a certain number of persons who have every intention of ending life, who truly believe that the action they take will result in death, but who through ignorance or chance or medical intervention are saved. Such cases are occasionally noted in the newspapers: for example, the case of the man who jumped from a tenth-storey window and landed on a store awning, which saved his life.

Despite such overlapping of two apparently different populations, inaccuracies in suicide statistics appear to be comparatively small and constant. Reports of the rates and patterns of successful suicides are thus probably valid and reliable. But reports of the rates of suicidal *attempts,* on the other hand, obviously represent only a fraction of the real incidence of *all* suicidal attempts among the general population.[9] To be included in any statistical study, a suicidal attempt must be of such nature that the person making the attempt is brought to the attention of a physician, a policeman, or some similar authority; and that authority must take action to report the attempt as such. For a variety of reasons, including the fact that in most areas of this country attempted suicide is a legally punishable offence, most suicidal attempts are not so registered. In many reports the number of suicidal attempts is listed as *less* than the number of successful suicides.[10] Yet the excellent biostatisticians of the Metropolitan Life Insurance Company of New York have ventured the educated but conservative guess that the real rates of suicidal attempts are at least six or seven times as great as those of successful suicides.[11]

Assuming that those who attempt suicide and those who successfully commit suicide represent two different populations, it would be expected that the number of persons who, after earlier unsuccessful attempts, later commit suicide successfully would be proportionately small. Although difficult to collect, there are some limited data on this point. Sainsbury found a previous suicidal attempt reported in the records of 9% of all persons who committed suicide in North London from 1936 to 1938.[12] Stengel and Cook found a previous suicidal attempt reported in the records of slightly more than 13% of 119 cases of successful suicide registered in the same area in 1953.[13]

As the attempted suicides which are reported probably represent only a small sample of *all* attempted suicides (reported and unreported), information gathered to indicate how many of those who attempt suicide finally kill themselves is again of only approximate validity. But several such studies have been made and show surprisingly consistent results, despite reference to different countries and different times. In St Louis, the Schmidt group followed up their previously mentioned 109 patients who had attempted suicide in 1952 and 1953; eight months after the attempt only two of these patients had subsequently killed themselves.[14] In London, Stengel and Cook followed up seventy-two patients—all admitted to Bethlem Royal and Maudsley Hospitals in 1949 because of suicidal attempts. Three years later two patients of this group had killed themselves.[15] In Sweden, Dahlgren found that of 230 people who had attempted suicide in a certain period, 6% had killed themselves within four years.[16] In another study, Stengel followed up 138 patients—all admitted to a London mental observation ward in 1946 and 1947. Five years later only one of these patients had killed himself.[17] Although the total number of persons who finally commit suicide after a previous suicidal attempt obviously increases as the period lapsing after the attempt becomes longer, it can be seen that only small proportions of those reported as having made a suicidal attempt finally kill themselves, and that the proportion of *all* persons attempting suicide who finally kill themselves is probably very small.

PATTERNS OF EXPECTATION IN ATTEMPTED SUICIDE

It has become more and more obvious, then, that attempted suicide is not simply a less severe form of successful suicide, but often a different kind of act, involving considerably different psychological mechanisms. Menninger has pointed out that the truly suicidal person must expect to kill, be killed, and die; in contrast, many attempted suicides are not intended to end life but only to serve as a gesture to bring another person to terms.[18] Considerable other evidence has been published to support the view that such a gesture or secondary gain motivation exists in attempted suicide. In a study of all reported suicides and suicidal attempts in Detroit during 1942 and 1943, it was found that the success of the attempt varied markedly with the reported conscious "motive" and that, where there was little chance that a person could gain by using suicide solely as a gesture, the attempt was more likely to be successful—that is, to end in death. Thus, among males, 50% of the attempts in which the motive was judged to be "ill health" were successful, as compared with only 14% and 10% respectively of the attempts in which the motive was judged to be "domestic or family worries" or "love affairs". Among females, 25% of the attempts in which the judged motive was "ill health" were successful, against only 2% and 1% respectively of the attempts in which the judged motive was "domestic difficulties" or "love affairs".[19]

The knowledge of this secondary gain motivation has been wrongfully utilized as justification for a growing tendency to dismiss the person who has made a suicidal attempt as someone acting out in an hysterical manipulatory manner and not deserving of serious psychiatric attention. Such an attitude is superficial: the suicidal attempt is usually overdetermined behaviour involving both the person himself and the social environment in which he functions. Many suicidal attempts have at least in part the character of a gamble with death, a sort of Russian roulette, the outcome of which depends to some extent on chance. The attempts are consciously or unconsciously arranged in such a manner that the lethal probability may vary from almost certain survival to almost certain death; and "fate"—or at least some force external to the conscious choice of the person—is compelled in some perhaps magical way to make the final decision.[20]

Such a conception can be substantiated by clinical evidence. During the period July 1951, through April 1954, I interviewed, as part of my regular duties, 156 patients who had made suicidal attempts. Of these patients, forty-three were seen in the Admitting Room or Neuropsychiatric Service of the Veterans Administration Hospital, Newington, Connecticut (July 1951 to July 1952); fifty-nine were seen in the Receiving Room or the Psychiatric Dispensary of the Grace-New Haven Community Hospital, New Haven, Connecticut (July 1952 to April 1953); and fifty-four were seen at the Central Dispensary or the Mental Hygiene Consultation Service, Fort Bliss, Texas (April 1953 to July 1954). Because of selective factors in patient reception at these institutions, 104 patients of the total group were male, and most were in the younger age groups (eighteen to forty-five years old). As part of the psychiatric interview, each patient was asked questions along the following lines: "Were you certain that you would die as a result of your action? Are you surprised to be still living? Were you uncertain as to whether or not you would die as a result of your action? Did you think there was a good chance (some chance, any chance) that you would die? Were you certain that you would *not* die as a result of your action?"

Of the total 156 patients interviewed, twenty-three indicated that they would die as a result of their action—that they were surprised to be still living. A larger number, 113 patients, had been uncertain as to whether or not they would die; their estimates of the probability of death resulting from the attempt varied considerably, but every patient in this group thought that there was *some* possibility that he would die. Finally, twenty patients had been certain that they would *not* die as a result of their action.

It would be misleading to attempt further statistical analysis of this data. The important fact indicated is that persons who attempt suicide can be divided into three groups: (1) comparatively small numbers who are certain that they will die as a result of their action, whose attempt is really intended to end life; (2) substantial numbers who are uncertain as to whether or not they will die as a result of their action but who believe, at the time of the attempt, that there is some chance of death; and (3) other persons, whose number is small among *reported* attempted suicides but is probably much larger among unreported attempted suicides, who are certain at the time of the attempt that they will not die as a result of their action.[21]

Attempts in the first group might well be termed *aborted successful suicides*, for persons in this group are quite sincere in their intention to end life, expect to die, and except for chance, fortunate medical intervention, or the person's ignorance or inaptitude, *would die* as a result of the suicidal action. Probably most persons who attempt such aborted successful suicides are brought to the attention of police, physicians, or hospitals, and are included in the statistical reporting of suicidal attempts.

Attempts in the second group might be termed *true suicidal attempts*, for persons in this group are acting in such a way that, at least according to their own stated belief, death might result from their action; they believe that there is at least some possibility that the attempt will be successful; their action, in fact, has the nature of a gamble with death—whether or not the gamble results in a medically serious condition. Of course, in some of these true suicidal attempts the gamble with death is undoubtedly lost—the attempter dies and the attempt is counted as a completed successful suicide. Many of these true suicidal attempts may not be brought to the attention of the authorities, but the large numbers that are made known to them appear to make up the major segment of all reported cases of suicidal attempts.

Attempts in the third group might be termed *suicidal gestures*, for persons in this group do *not* intend to end life and are certain that they will *not* die as a result of their action, although the action is performed in a manner that other persons might interpret as suicidal in purpose. Such attempts seem to be made in many or most cases to gain attention or to influence other persons, and the attempter often takes considerable precaution to make sure of remaining alive by making the attempt with other persons present, informing someone of the attempt, or initiating his own rescue. Some such suicidal gestures are included among the reported cases of suicidal attempts, but probably most persons who make this type of suicidal gesture are not brought to the attention of reporting agencies.

Examples of these various types of suicidal attempts follow.

Case 1 (aborted successful suicide).—A twenty-eight-year-old divorced white male, a meat cutter by trade, was admitted to the hospital after being found lying unconscious on a busy highway under a high overpass bridge. He had suffered multiple fractures and some internal injuries, and during the course of hospitalization also developed a subdural abscess and pulmonary effusion. Extensive medical care over a two-months' period was required to save his life.

The patient had an eight-year history of periodic episodes of severe alcoholic intoxication. A year after his divorce he met another woman, fell in love, and formed a common-law marital relationship which lasted for several years. However, the last few months were marked by disputes about his drinking, and the woman finally left him. During the next two weeks this man became more and more depressed, drinking off and on, and finally one day while hitch-hiking along the highway he decided to jump off the bridge and "do away with myself".

The patient stated that at the time of the attempt he had felt anxious, restless, and depressed. "I was completely disgusted with myself. It seemed to me I had nothing to offer this girl, or anyone else, for that matter." He later stated that he had seriously intended to end his life and expected certain death as a result of his jump from the bridge—that he was surprised when he found himself in the hospital still alive.

Case 2 (true suicidal attempt with high lethal probability).— A nineteen-year-old single white male soldier was referred to the Mental Hygiene Consultation Service in his fifth week of basic training because of symptoms of anxiety and depression.

Psychological examination revealed considerable evidence that this man's anxiety was related to latent unconscious homosexual conflicts aggravated by the stress of being in an all-male environment. While still in the process of evaluation at the Consultation Service—which takes several days—he remained alone in his army hutment one day when the other trainees were leaving on a hike. Another soldier, returning for some forgotten article, found him hanging by a rope from the rafters. He was cut down and quickly recovered.

Later the patient stated that he could not tolerate life in the army and that he felt Consultation Service personnel would not be able to get him separated from military service: "I would be better off dead than in the army." He had realized prior to the attempt, he admitted, that someone might enter the hutment and discover him before strangulation was complete ; but he thought there was a fairly good chance that he would be dead before he was found. The patient expected that if he did not die he would either be hospitalized for a long period or dishonourably discharged from the army—and he stated that any alternative was preferable to remaining on duty as a soldier.

Case 3 (true suicidal attempt with low lethal probability).— A twenty-seven-year-old white housewife was discovered in the act of sexual intercourse with the man who lived next door, by her husband who that afternoon had returned home from work unexpectedly. The wife became very agitated, pleading that this was "the first time" and that she loved her husband dearly. (The neighbour dressed hurriedly and left.) The husband, shocked, finally told his wife that he was going to divorce her. The wife began to cry and scream, and then ran into the kitchen, seized a bread knife, and slashed herself three times across the abdomen.

At the hospital the woman stated that she had thought there was some chance she might bleed to death as a result of her action—that although she had made the attempt in front of her husband, who was likely to rush her to a hospital, "it might not be in time." She said she would rather be dead than divorced. "Anyway, it showed my husband how much I love him."

*Case 4 (suicidal gesture).—*A forty-one-year-old white male, a steamfitter, presented himself at the hospital accompanied by a woman whom he termed his "girl friend". In front of this woman, the patient said that he had just tried to commit suicide by drinking the contents of a bottle of iodine because "she doesn't love me any more". The woman was on the verge of crying and said several times, "It's all my fault."

Immediate gastric lavage revealed only a trace of iodine in the stomach contents. When the patient was questioned alone, he admitted that he had been separated from his legal wife for several years, that the "girl friend" with him had been his mistress for about a year, and that for the last week she had been berating him because he wished to send anniversary greetings to his wife. This day the patient had told his mistress that her "constant nagging" was driving him to suicide. She laughed and said that he was "too yellow" to kill himself. He went into the bathroom, poured out most of the contents of a bottle of iodine, and filled up the bottle with water. Returning to the woman, he dramatically drank the mixture. To me, he stated that this was a gesture: "I figured after this the girl friend would stop nagging me.... Of course I was sure I wouldn't die. I knew that little bit of iodine couldn't kill me. I wouldn't even have come to the hospital, but she insisted and, besides, I wanted to make her think I meant business."

THE DYNAMIC MEANING OF ATTEMPTED SUICIDE—SOCIAL AND PSYCHOLOGICAL CONSEQUENCES

The case histories cited suggest other aspects of the character of the true suicidal attempt. One, which has been noted in a number of psychoanalytic studies, is that the true suicidal attempt serves to discharge aggressive tendencies directed against the self or against introjected parental figures—that is, the superego; self-mutilation may play a part in this.[22] Frequently patients in this series who had made true suicidal attempts, whether or not they were then treated in any psychotherapeutic manner, demonstrated considerable subsequent improvement in affective state and general outlook. In some cases improvement following the attempt appeared to be related to a guilt-relieving mechanism: the patients felt that in the attempt itself, and in the associated gamble with death, they were punished for whatever acts committed or fantasies entertained had contributed to the feeling of guilt. Stengel and Cook have noted that the outcome of the attempt "is almost invariably accepted for the time being and further attempts are rarely made immediately, even if there is no lack of opportunity. The outcome of the attempt is accepted like that of a trial by ordeal in mediaeval times."[23]

It might be said that the patient listens to the demands of a severe superego, atones for his sins by attempting suicide in such a manner that he gambles with death, and accepts the outcome—life—as the answer (or perhaps reward), in a general sense, of fate, and, more specifically, of the superego. In the same way a child, after committing some forbidden act, will sometimes present himself to a parent for punishment, gambling that by his own action in presenting himself he might escape *severe* punishment, and assuming that by the gamble whatever punishment he does receive, he has "made up" for his sins and once again may obtain parental favour.

In most of the true suicidal attempts examined, there was discernible in addition an aspect of hidden or overt appeal to society, a call for help. The attempts were causally related to difficulties with interpersonal relationships and the social environment, but most attempters managed to maintain some contact with other persons, so that the call for help might be recognized. Stengel and Cook demonstrated that such an appeal is inherent in most suicidal attempts, irrespective of the mental state and the personality of the attempter.[24] Evoking some change in the social situation, through the responses of individuals or groups to this conscious or unconscious appeal for help, is then one of the primary functions of the true suicidal attempt. The simplest and commonest consequence of the reported suicidal attempt—hospitalization—occurs because the call for help is recognized by other persons and by society. Many people, whether responding as friends, policemen, or physicians, do not *consciously* recognize this appeal; nevertheless they are shocked and interested by the fact that some human being was so disturbed that he would attempt to take his own life. The suicidal act, though taboo in Jewish-Christian culture, arouses sufficient sympathy so that some change in the circumstances surrounding the person who makes the attempt is likely to take place. In those cases which are not reported, it is likely that the person's difficulties are so modified as a consequence of the suicidal attempt that no relevant further action is required.

This concept, that most suicidal attempts serve an accessory function in manipulation of the extrapsychic environment, can also be substantiated by clinical evidence. The 156 patients described previously were each asked, "What did you expect to gain by this attempt? What did you think might happen as a result of the attempt? Did you expect that, if you survived, your circumstances might change? If so, in what way?"

Answers varied from patient to patient, a few expecting simply to die, one stating, "I thought this [taking an overdose of barbiturates] would prove to my parents that they were wrong to accuse me of doing bad things with my boy friend." Most patients could not specifically verbalize *what* they thought might happen as a result of their attempt, but almost all were perfectly certain that "something" would happen. What that "something" might be was to many vague and variable, but in every case the attempt brought the plight of the person to the attention of friends, family, police, or physicians— any of whom, in the mind of the patient, might have the power somehow to satisfy at least some of the patient's needs. For some persons these needs were as simple and as real as the need for food, shelter, or clothes. For more persons they were needs for some kind of social or psychological support. In many such cases the relationship of the patient to other persons, or to groups, was found to undergo marked changes as a consequence of the suicidal attempt. Some relationships were strengthened, some terminated, but in almost all cases the suicidal attempt resulted in some immediate change in the constellation of relationships of the person to other persons or to the social group as a whole. The fact that as a consequence of the suicidal attempt many persons were admitted to a hospital, there to remain for varying lengths of time, in itself often effected far-reaching changes.

In summary, evidence has been presented in this paper that successful suicides and unsuccessful suicidal attempts probably represent different kinds of acts performed in different ways by different groups of people, although there is some overlapping. Interviews with 156 persons who made unsuccessful suicidal attempts indicated that such attempts can be categorized in three classes: (1) aborted successful suicides, in which the attempter truly intended to end life and was certain that he would die as a result of his action, (2) true suicidal attempts, in which the attempter thought that he might die as a result of his action but was not certain, and (3) suicidal gestures in which the attempter was certain that he would *not* die as a result of his action. From the data now available, the psychodynamics of the aborted successful suicide appear to be similar to or identical with the dynamics of the completed successful suicide. The dynamics of the suicidal gestures are related primarily to the need to influence someone to do something, and not to the intention to end life. The dynamics of the true suicidal attempt are complicated, and involve in all cases a discharge of self-directed aggressive tendencies through a gamble with death (of varying lethal probability), in most cases an appeal for help, and in some cases a need for punishment and a trial by ordeal. Persons who make such attempts are so emotionally disordered that they are willing to risk their lives in this gamble, and it is the responsibility of physicians and other representatives of society who come in contact with such persons to consider the meaning of each suicidal attempt in terms of how best to respond to the implied need for help.

NOTES

1 Otto Fenichel, *The Psychoanalytic Theory of Neurosis*, New York: Norton, 1945; p. 294.
2 Sigmund Freud, *The Basic Writings of Sigmund Freud,* edited by A. A.

Brill; New York, Random House, 1938. Freud, 'Mourning and Melancholia', in *Collected Papers*, 4:152–70, London: Hogarth Press, 1925.

3 Franz Alexander, *Fundamentals of Psychoanalysis*, New York: Norton, 1948.

4 Paul Schilder, *Psychotherapy*, New York: Norton, 1951.

5 E. H. Schmidt, P. O'Neal, and E. Robins, 'Evaluation of Suicide Attempts as Guide to Therapy', *J. Amer. Med. Assn.*, 1954, 155:549–57.

6 J. E. Gordon, E. Lindemann, J. Ipsen and W. T. Vaughan, 'An Epidemiologic Analysis of Suicide', pp. 136–75, in *Epidemiology of Mental Disorders*, New York: Milbank Memorial Fund, 1950; see especially pp. 138–40.

7 Reference footnote 6; see especially p. 140.

8 In England, those persons who successfully committed suicide used most frequently the method of asphyxiation by gas; those persons who were reported to have unsuccessfully attempted suicide used most frequently the method of ingestion of drugs. See Herbert Hendin, 'Attempted Suicide', *Psychiatric Quart.*, 1950, 24:39–46. See also: Metropolitan Life Insurance Company, 'Suicides That Fail', *Statistical Bull.*, May 1941. M. Moore, 'Cases of Attempted Suicide in a General Hospital', *New England J. Med.*, 1937, 217:291–303. P. Piker, '1817 Cases of Suicidal Attempt', *Amer. J. Psychiatry*, 1938, 95:97–115. A. B. Siewers and E. Davidoff, 'Attempted Suicide', *J. N. and M. Disease*, 1942, 95:427–41. E. Stengel and N. G. Cook, 'Recent Research into Suicide and Attempted Suicide', *J. Forensic Med.*, 1954, 1:252–9. J. M. A. Weiss, 'Suicide: An Epidemiologic Analysis', *Psychiatric Quart.*, 1954, 28:225–52.

9 See, for instance, Weiss, reference footnote 8.

10 See Stengel and Cook, reference footnote 8.

11 Many examples of what happens to produce this situation are available. On a recent television programme, a popular American singer, frankly admitted that several years ago she had "taken a bottle of sleeping pills" with the avowed intention of ending her life. Changing her mind, she did not call a physician because she was afraid that her parents would find out. She phoned a friend instead, who successfully treated her with coffee, walking, fresh air, and "talk". This case, like many similar ones, was of course never reported to any authority.

12 Peter Sainsbury, *Suicide in London: An Ecological Study*; New York, Basic Books, 1956.

13 Stengel and Cook, reference footnote 8.

14 Reference footnote 5.

15 Stengel and Cook, reference footnote 8.

16 K. G. Dahlgren, *On Suicide and Attempted Suicide*, Lund (Sweden): Lindstedts, 1945.

17 E. Stengel, 'Enquiries Into Attempted Suicide', *Proc. Royal Soc. Med.*, 1952, 45:613–20.

18 Karl A. Menninger, *Man Against Himself*, New York: Harcourt, Brace, 1938. Menninger, 'Psychoanalytic Aspects of Suicide', *Internat. J. Psycho-Anal.* 1933, 14:376–90.

19 Metropolitan Life Insurance Company, 'Why Do People Kill Themselves?' *Statistical Bull.*, February 1945.

20 The psychodynamic factors involved in attempted suicide are not unlike those involved in gambling *per se*. In both acts the person may be responding to the demands of a severe superego; the character of gambling, playful in the beginning, may under the pressure of inner tensions become

a matter of life and death. As Fenichel has pointed out, "Gambling in its essence, is a provocation of fate, which is forced to make its decision for or against the individual.... The gambler ... is ready ... to run the risk of being killed." The excitement of gambling corresponds to the excitement related both to sexual activity and to death: "that of winning to orgasm (and to killing); that of losing to punishment by castration (and by being killed)". Reference footnote 1; p. 372.

21 The 109 patients interviewed by Schmidt, O'Neal and Robins were asked, "Do you believe that this attempt was (a) a serious one, (b) a gesture, or (c) can you not tell which it was?" Forty-seven patients stated that their attempt was a serious one; almost half of these attempts were evaluated by the examiners as "psychiatrically" and/or "medically" serious. Forty patients were uncertain; one-fourth of these attempts were evaluated as "serious". Twenty-two patients stated that their attempt was a gesture; only two of these attempts were evaluated as "serious". Reference footnote 5.

22 See the following: Fenichel, reference footnote 1. N. D. C. Lewis, 'Studies in Suicide', *Psychoanalytic Rev.*, 1933, 20:241–73. Menninger, reference footnote 18.

23 Stengel and Cook, reference 8; p. 257.

24 Stengel and Cook, reference footnote 8.

CHAPTER 32

Suicidal Behaviour*

James Wilkins

Medical and psychiatric personnel and researchers who make direct observations of persons who attempt suicide often comment on how frequently hairbreadth differences permit these people to survive. For example, Arieff, McCulloch and Rotman conclude that of attempters in Chicago, "60% could have met with death".[1] Trautman comments regarding his sample of New York Puerto Ricans who survived attempts that "how many might have died in the absence of the well-organized and alert rescue service of the hospital cannot be estimated"[2] Or, as Jensen and Petty put it, "equivocation (on the part of anyone who might intervene or interrupt) will change his function from rescuer to pallbearer".[3] Similarly, the work of Raines and Thompson shows that "what appears to be a suicidal gesture can, in a considerable percentage of cases, miscarry and end in actual death."[4] Considering persons who threaten or attempt suicide, Oliven noted that "fatal accidents are apt to happen . . . leaning too far out of a window, overdosing with "harmless" drugs, or miscalculating the arrival of someone to shut off the gas jets. Especially under the influence of alcohol, their judgement may fail them, with lethal results."[5] More broadly, Raymond Firth, in his analysis of suicide and attempts among the Tikopia, saw "risk taking" to be the theme, as have others who write of the "gamble" or "trial by ordeal" with death, meaning that suicidal behaviours generally carry a risk of death rather than a guarantee of either death or survival.[6]

These observations are in sharp contrast to the habitual sociological position, which characteristically assumes a sharp difference between attempted and completed suicides. The major statements of Durkheim,[7] Gibbs and Martin,[8] Henry and Short,[9] and many others[10] have no place for those who have not died. Because these authors provide no reason in support of this restriction, the curious reader is left to surmise. The restriction might be due solely to the convenience of obtaining data on completed suicides. On the other hand, some attempted suicides are distinguished by a difference of "intent".

* Reprinted by permission of the American Sociological Association from the *American Sociological Review*, Vol. 32, 1967, pp. 286–98.

This proposition is treacherous for several reasons, among the difficulty of obtaining an independent measure of intent (or, in Durkheim's view, *any* measure of it)[11] the lack of support for this contention from such data as have been collected among attempted suicides,[12] and the absence of "comparable" and supportive data concerning intent among completed suicides.[13] A very pointed comment on the distinction between suicidal ideation and action has been made by Kubie:

> The layman tries to dispose of this subtle problem by reducing it to assumptions about simply quantitative differences: "If he wants to die hard enough he will succeed." This is convenient. It puts the blame squarely where we feel most comfortable with it—on the shoulders of the patient. It also serves the self-inflating purpose of making us feel superior by nurturing the illusion that we have understood and explained something when in fact we have only redescribed it in circular terms ... students of suicide have been unduly influenced by the uniformity and finality of the end result. They have assumed tacitly that suicide is invariably the expression of an impulse to put an end to living.[14]

Acquiescence to folklore about suicidal intent may bring peace of mind but it also brings obstruction of inquiry.

A large body of data has been accumulated by persons unaccredited in sociology but to whom sociological matters appear to be important. Evidently this literature is in the main unknown to sociologists; a secondary purpose of this paper is to make it more available for further analyses of those data not presented here.[15] Our primary purpose is to encourage further investigations into the social patterns which inhibit and facilitate suicidal behaviours and their outcomes.

ESTIMATING THE CONNECTION BETWEEN ATTEMPTED AND COMPLETED SUICIDE

Some studies of completed suicide have included inquiry about prior attempts. In Table 1, the samples of Beisser and Blanchette, Farberow and Shneidman, Wheat and Jameison were restricted to formerly hospitalized mental patients who suicided, while the other studies used unselected series of suicides from public records. Probably for this reason the findings of those four tend to stand apart from the others. Despite other dissimilarities among the samples studied, the data show some agreement. Eight of the ten general samples indicate that between 7% and 16% of completed suicides

TABLE 1

Percentages of Completed Suicides
Who Had a Prior Attempt

Reference	Percentage
General Samples	
Gibbs[1]	7
Coe[2]	9
Tuckman and Lapell[3]	9
Sainsbury[4]	9
Parnell and Skottowe[5]	11
Yessler, et al.[6]	12
Stengel and Cook[7]	14
Jones[8]	16
Robbins, et al.[9]	23–29
Dorpat, et al.[10]	33
Formerly Hospitalized Mental Patient Samples	
Wheat[11]	30
Beisser and Blanchette[12]	50
Farberow and Shneidman[13]	62
Jamieson[14]	77

1 Jack P. Gibbs, 'Suicide', in R. K. Merton and R. A. Nisbet, editors, *Contemporary Social Problems*, New York: Harcourt Brace and Company, 1961, p. 260.

2 John I. Coe, 'Suicides: A Statistical and Pathological Report', *Minnesota Medicine*, 46, 1962, p. 26.

3 Jacob Tuckman and Martha Lavell, 'Study of Suicide in Philadelphia', *Public Health Reports*, 73, 1958, p. 5.

4 Peter Sainsbury, *Suicide in London*, New York: Basic Books, Inc., 1956, p. 64.

5 R. W. Parnell and Ian Skottowe, 'Towards Preventing Suicide', *The Lancet*, 272, 1957, pp. 206–8.

6 Paul G. Yessler, James J. Gibbs and Herman Becker, 'On the Communication of Suicidal Ideas, I and II', *Archives of General Psychiatry*, 3 and 5, 1960 and 1961.

7 Erwin Stengel and Nancy Cook, *Attempted Suicide*, Oxford: Oxford University Press, 1958, p. 103.

8 Kingsley Jones, 'Suicide in the Hospital Service', *British Journal of Psychiatry*, 111, 1956, p. 629.

9 In the several reports by Robbins and colleagues using apparently the same data, we find these to be the limits of the percentage. They appear in the following sources: Eli Ribbins, *et al.*, 'The Communication of Suicidal Intent Prior to Psychiatric Hospitalization', *American Journal of Psychiatry*, 117, 1961, pp. 605–705.

10 Theodore L. Dorpat and John W. Boswell, 'Evaluation of Suicidal Intent in Suicidal Attempts', *Comprehensive Psychiatry*, 4, 1963, pp. 120–1.

11 William D. Wheat, 'Motivational Aspects of Suicide in Patients During and After Psychiatric Treatment', *Southern Medical Journal*, 53, March, 1960, p. 274.

12 Arnold R. Beisser and James E. Blanchette, 'A study of Suicides in a Mental Hospital', *Diseases of the Nervous System*, 22, July, 1961, p. 367.

13 Norman L. Farberow and Edwin Shneidman, 'Attempted, Threatened and Completed Suicide', *Journal of Abnormal and Social Psychology*, 50, 1955, p. 230.

14 Gerald R. Jamieson, 'Suicide and Mental Disease', *Archives of Neurology and Psychiatry*, 36, 1936, pp. 1–11.

had prior attempts. In some of these researches witnesses were regularly questioned on the point of prior attempts and in others not.[16] From the published accounts of Robbins, Dorpat and their respective colleagues, it appears that their procedures of conducting private and intensive interviews managed to unearth or coax what may be an upper bound to the proportion of previous attempters.[17]

Another basis for estimating the connection between completions and attempts is the relative size of the two populations. A temporally consistent disproportion would seem to be a measure of the number of persons who do not participate in both. The greatest variability in estimates of the ratio of attempted to completed suicides is due to the sources the researchers consulted. Police and public officials have relatively least contact with cases of attempts, and a progressively greater proportion of them come to the attention of poison control centres, hospitals, and private physicians. This may be discerned from the patterns in the following data and on the basis that samples of Woodside and Stengel showed only 24% to 31% of attempters admitted to London hospitals were known to the police as such, and no others were subsequently reported to them.[18] Accordingly, in Seattle, Schmid and Van Arsdol reported a ratio of two attempts to each completion by using only records of the Seattle Police Department to determine the number of attempts,[19] while Dorpat and Ripley reported 4:1, using hospital data for the same territory.[20] Tuckman, Youngman and Bleiberg supplemented police records with information from the poison control centre in Philadelphia for a ratio of 3.1:1[21] In other studies using hospital data, Klintworth found 3.2:1 in Johannesburg,[22] Middleton 3.5:1 in Gateshead,[23] and Kessel and Lee 4:1 in Edinburgh.[24] In Sheffield, Parkin and Stengel surveyed physicians for attempts not admitted to a hospital, and found a ratio of 9.7:1, as contrasted to 8.5:1 exclusive of these cases.[25] In Los Angeles county, data from many physicians and most hospitals produced a ratio of 8:1.[26] Shaw and Shelkin concluded from their review of research that "the ratios most often

TABLE 2

Percentages of Attempters Who Subsequently Suicide

Reference	Percentage	Follow-Up Period
Farberow and Shneidman[1]	69	1 year
Moss and Hamilton[2]	22	Up to 20 years
O'Neal and Robbins[3]	10.5	2 years
Schneider[4]	12	18 years
	9	10 years
	4	1 year
Ettlinger[5]	9	10 years
Ekblom and Frisk[6]	8.7	6 to 8 years
Moto[7]	8	5 years
Dahlgren[8]	6	12 years
Hove[9]	5	2 to 3 years
Pokorny[10]	4	1 month to 14 years
Ettlinger and Flordh[11]	3.6	8 to 24 months
Forssman[12]	3	1 year
Stengel II[13]	3	5 years
McCarthy[14]	3	2 to 3 years
Batchelor and Napier[15]	2	1 year
Gardner, Bahn and Mack[16]	2	1 year
Tuckman and Youngman[17]	2	1 year
Schmidt, et al.[18]	2	8 months
Jansson[19]	1.3	1 year
Forssman and Jansson[20]	1.1	1 year
Stengel I[21]	1	5 years
Ringel[22]	0.3	Up to 3.5 years
Kiorbo[23]	0.2	9 years

1 Norman Farberow and Edwin Shneidman, 'Attempted, Threatened and Completed Suicide', *Journal of Abnormal and Social Psychology*, 50, 1955, p. 230.

2 Leonard Moss and Donald Hamilton, 'The Psychotherapy of the Suicidal Patient', *American Journal of Psychiatry*, 112, 1956, pp. 814–820.

3 Patricia O'Neal, Eli Robbins and Edwin H. Schmidt, 'A Psychiatric Study of Attempted Suicide in Persons Over Sixty Years of Age', *Archives of Neurology and Psychiatry*, 75, 1956, pp. 275–284.

4 Cited in Bengt Jansson, 'A Catamnestic Study of 476 Attempted Suicides', *Acta Psychiatrica Scandinavica*, 38, 1962, p. 192; Erwin Stengel and Nancy Cook, *Attempted Suicide*, Oxford University Press, 1958, p. 24.

5 Ruth W. Ettlinger, 'Suicides in a Group of Patients Who Had Previously Attempted Suicide', *Acta Psychiatrica Scandinavica*, 40, 1964, p. 365.

6 Ibid., p. 363; Jansson, op. cit., p. 184.

7 Jerome A. Moto, 'Suicide Attempts', *Archives of General Psychiatry*, 13, 1965, p. 518.

8 Cited in Jesse Carr, 'Suicide', *International Record of Medicine*, 170,

1957, p. 618; Ettlinger, Ibid.; Jansson, op. cit., p. 192; Stengel and Cook, op. cit., p. 20.

9 Gordon K. Klintworth, 'Suicide and Attempted Suicide', *South African Medical Journal*, 34, 1960, p. 363; Ettlinger, op. cit., p. 363; Jansson, op. cit., pp. 191–2; Stengel and Cook, op. cit., p. 23.

10 Alex D. Pokorny, 'A Follow-Up Study of 618 Suicidal Patients', *Scientific Proceedings of the Annual Meetings of the American Psychiatric Association of 1965*, pp. 133–4.

11 Ruth W. Ettlinger and Per Flordh, 'Attempted Suicide: Experience of 500 Cases at a General Hospital', *Acta Psychiatrica Scandinavica,* Supplement 103, 1955, p. 8.

12 Jansson, op. cit., p. 192.

13 Stengel and Cook, op. cit., p. 69.

14 P. D. McCarthy and Dermot Walsh, 'Attempted Suicide in Dublin', *Journal of the Irish Medical Association*, 57, 1965, p. 12.

15 I. R. C. Batchelor, 'Psychopathic States and Attempted Suicide', *British Medical Journal*, 4875, 1954, p. 1346; I. R. C. Batchelor and Margaret B. Napier, 'The Sequelae and Short-Term Prognosis of Attempted Suicide', *Journal of Neurology and Psychiatry*, 17, 1954, pp. 261–6.

16 Elmer A. Gardner, Anita K. Bahn and Marjorie Mack, 'Suicide and Psychiatric Care in the Aging', *Archives of General Psychiatry*, 10, 1964, p. 550.

17 Jacob Tuckman and William F. Youngman, 'Identifying Suicide Risk Groups among Attempted Suicides', *Public Health Reports*, 78, 1963, p. 586.

18 Edwin Schmidt, Patricia O'Neal and Eli Robbins, 'Evaluation of Suicide Attempts as a Guide to Therapy', *Journal of the American Medical Association*, 155, 1954, p. 21.

19 Jansson, op. cit.

20 Ibid., p. 192.

21 Stengel and Cook, op. cit., pp. 49–52.

22 Ibid., p. 23; Ettlinger, op. cit.; Moto, op. cit., p. 520.

23 Ettlinger and Flordh, op. cit, p. 8.

---

reported range from ten to one to five to one".[27] It seems safe to regard lower estimates as due to underreporting.

The low estimate of a constant ratio of five attempters to one consummated suicide might be interpreted to mean that at most only 20% of attempters would eventually complete. However, this figure would require the assumption that all persons completing suicide had previously attempted, which we know to be false. We might try to patch together these estimates and the data concerning the proportion of suicides who are found to have had prior attempts: (1) If we use an estimate of seven attempters to one completer in the population, and (2) the reports showing a range between 7% and 33% of suicides who have had prior attempts, then (3) we would conclude that between 1 and 5% of attempters subsequently filter into the population of completed suicides.[28] If the ratio of attempters to completers were higher, the percentage, of course, would decrease.[29]

Another set of data useful to evaluate the connection between attempts and completions comes from several follow-up studies of attempters (Table 2). There is much agreement among these results, although the samples and the length of the follow-up periods vary considerably. Those reports which depart from the common findings are distinguished in other respects as well: (1) Farberow and Shniedman, as noted earlier, followed formerly hospitalized mental patients; (2) Moss and Hamilton stressed that they selected a sample in which "only by chance were the attempts unsuccessful" and in which there was a "characteristic reactivation of the suicidal drive in over 90% of the cases";[30] and (3) O'Neal and Robbins used a sample of persons sixty-five years of age and older.

Concerning the follow-up period, Jansson and Forssman found that repetition of suicidal behaviour after one year was not connected with the earlier episode and ought not to be confounded with it.[31] On this basis, long follow-up periods would represent an artificial inflation of the risk of repetition deriving from the attempt.[32]

It is reasonable to be sceptical of these approaches to the topic individually by pointing to the methodological deficiencies in each which are the advantages of the others.[33] Taken together, the results of these different approaches do not seem to contradict one another, but to cohere more than one might expect—at least to the extent that it may no longer be necessary to entertain many of the arguments about these connections, which altogether span the entire range of possible relationships. Perhaps they cohere sufficiently that the criterion of precision within an established range may become a meaningful objective of future research. They also seem to reveal a definite linkage between attempted and completed suicide. Certainly, it must not be forgotten that while the percentage of attempters who filter into the suicide rate is small, the number of persons is very large and their contribution to that rate is substantial. The data recommend the inference that the social behaviours surrounding attempted suicide are quite important to know more about, and they suggest pushing forward to explore how this linkage comes to be.

Finally, information is also available on repetition of attempts. This is presented in Table 3, in which the datings refer to the time when the attempter happened to fall into a sample. The variation among reports certainly is wide, but it may not have been appreciated that the extent of repetition is as great as most of these studies show it to be. Among the reports of lower percentages of repeaters, it is clear that at least for Lendrum and Schmid and Van Arsdol, the collection of the information we are citing on this point was quite incidental to their research and many cases may have escaped their view.[34]

TABLE 3

Percentage of Attempters Who Are Repeaters

Reference	Prior Attempts		Later Attempts
Farberow[1]	40		—
Bruhn[2]	38		—
Stengel III[3]	37		—
Finn[4]	35		—
Fairbank[5]	33		—
Moto[6]	33		—
Stengel II[7]	33		—
Dorpat and Boswell[8]	28		—
Ellis, et al.[9]	28		—
Woodside[10]	28		—
Goss-Moffit[11]	27		—
Schmidt, et al.[12]	26		—
Yessler, et al.[13]	24		—
Batchelor[14]	23		—
Stengel I[15]	22		—
Stengel V[16]	22		—
Oltman[17]	21		—
Harrington and Cross[18]	20		—
Klintworth[19]	20		—
Sclare[20]	20		—
Arieff, et al.[21]	18		—
Wallinga[22]	18		—
Hopkins[23]	13		—
Middleton[24]	13		—
McCarthy[25]	12		—
Fischer[26]	11		—
Ettlinger and Flordh[27]	9		—
McGeorge[28]	7		—
Linnane, et al.[29]	6		—
Lendrum[30]	2		—
Kiorbo[31]	1		—
Schmid and Van Arsdol[32]	4	(or)	4
Batchelor and Napier[33]	—		3.5
Schmidt, et al.[34]	—		8
Jansson[35]	—		9
Taylor[36]	—		12
Hove[37]	—		14
Stengel II[38]	—		15
Farberow[39]	—		16
Moto[40]	—		18
Stengel I[41]	—		19
Ekblom and Frisk[42]	—		23
Moss and Hamilton[43]	—		28

1 Norman L. Farberow, 'Personality Patterns of Suicidal Mental Hospital Patients', *Genetic Psychology Monographs*, 42, 1950, pp. 32–33.

2 J. G. Bruhn, 'Comparative Study of Attempted Suicides and Psychiatric Out-Patients', *British Journal of Preventive and Social Medicine*, 17, 1963, p. 200.

3 Erwin Stengel and Nancy Cook, *Attempted Suicide*, Oxford: Oxford University Press, 1958, p. 84.

4 Murray E. Finn, 'Study in Suicidal Attempts', *Journal of Nervous and Mental Diseases*, 121, 1955, p. 174.

5 E. Fairbank, 'Suicide', *Journal of the American Medical Association*, 98, 1932, pp. 1710–4.

6 Jerome A. Moto, 'Suicide Attempts', *Archives of General Psychiatry*, 13, 1965, p. 516.

7 Stengel and Cook, op. cit., p. 69.

8 Theodore Dorpat and John Boswell, 'An Evaluation of Suicide Intent in Suicidal Attempts', *Comprehensive Psychiatry*, 4, 1963, pp. 120–1.

9 G. G. Ellis, K. A. Comish and R. L. Hewer, 'Attempted Suicides in Leicester', *The Practitioner*, 196, 1966, p. 560.

10 Moya Woodside, 'Attempted Suicides Arriving at a General Hospital', *British Medical Journal*, 5093, 1958, pp. 411–3.

11 Nina Goss Moffitt, 'Attempted Suicide', *The Journal of the Kentucky State Medical Association*, 61, 1963, p. 586.

12 Edwin Schmidt, Patricia O'Neal and Eli Robbins, 'Evaluation of Suicide Attempts', *Journal of the American Medical Association*, 155, 1954, p. 21.

13 Paul Yessler, James G. Gibbs and Herman Becker, 'On Communication of Suicidal Ideas, I and II', *Archives of General Psychiatry*, 3 and 5, 1960 and 1961.

14 I. R. C. Batchelor, 'Repeated Suicidal Attempts', *The British Journal of Medical Psychology*, 27, 1954, pp. 158–63.

15 Stengel and Cook, op. cit., pp. 49–51.

16 Ibid., p. 97.

17 Jane E. Oltman and Samuel Friedman, 'Study of Suicidal Attempts in Patients Admitted to a state Psychiatric Hospital', *Diseases of the Nervous System*, 23, 1962, pp. 433–9.

18 J. A. Harrington and K. W. Cross, 'Cases of Attempted Suicide Admitted to a General Hospital', *British Medical Journal*, 5150, 1959, p. 20.

19 Gordon K. Klintworth, 'Suicide and Attempted Suicide', *South African Medical Journal*, 34, 1960, p. 359.

20 A. Balfour Sclare and C. M. Hamilton, 'Attempted Suicide in Glasgow', *British Journal of Psychiatry*, 109, 1963, pp. 609–15.

21 Alex J. Arieff, Rook McCulloch and D. B. Rotman, 'Unsuccessful Suicide Attempts', *Diseases of the Nervous System*, 9, 1948. p. 175.

22 Jack V. Wallinga, 'Attempted Suicide: A Ten Year Survey', *Diseases of the Nervous System*, 10, 1949, p. 18.

23 F. Hopkins, 'Attempted Suicide: An Investigation', *Journal of Mental Science*, 83, 1937, p. 82.

24 G. D. Middleton, Desmond W. Ashby and F. Clark, 'An Analysis of Attempted Suicide in an Urban Industrial District', *The Practitioner*, 187, 1961, p. 777.

25 P. D. McCarthy and Dermot Walsh, 'Attempted Suicide in Dublin', *Journal of the Irish Medical Association*, 57, 1965, pp. 11–12.

26 Cited in E. Cunningham Dax, 'The Prevention of Suicide', *The Medical Journal of Australia*, I, 1961, p. 47.

27 Ruth W. Ettlinger and Per Flordh, 'Attempted Suicide', *Acta Psychiatrica Scandinavica*, Supplement, 103, 1955, p. 39.

28 John McGeorge, 'Attempted Suicide', *The Medical Journal of Australia*, I, 1942, p. 70.

29 J. Linnane, R. C. Buckle and N. McConaghy, 'A Comparison of Patients Seen at the Alfred Hospital After Suicidal Attempts', *The Medical Journal of Australia*, I, 1966, p. 667.

30 F. C. Lendrum, 'A Thousand Cases of Attempted Suicide', *American Journal of Psychiatry*, 13, 1933, pp. 479–500.

31 Ettlinger and Flordh, op. cit., p. 8.

32 Calvin F. Schmid and Maurice Van Arsdol, 'Completed and Attempted Suicides', *American Sociological Review*, 20, 1959, p. 3.

33 I. R. C. Batchelor and Margaret B. Napier, 'The Sequelae and Short-Term Prognosis of Attempted Suicide', *Journal of Neurology, Neurosurgery and Psychiatry*, 17, 1954, p. 263.

34 Schmidt, op. cit.

35 Bengt Jansson, 'A Catamnestic Study of 476 Attempted Suicides', *Acta Psychiatrica Scandinavica*, 38, 1962, pp. 183–98.

36 D. J. E. Taylor, F. Dudley Hart and Dennis Burley, 'Suicide in South London', *The Practitioner*, 192, 1964, pp. 251–6.

37 Jansson, op cit.; Ettlinger and Flordh, op. cit.

38 Stengel and Cook, op. cit., p. 69.

39 Farberow, op. cit., pp. 32–3.

40 Moto, op. cit., p. 519.

41 Stengel and Cook, op. cit., pp. 49–51.

42 Jansson, op. cit., p. 184.

43 Leonard Moss and Donald Hamilton, 'The Psychotherapy of the Suicidal Patient', *American Journal of Psychiatry*, 112, 1956, pp. 814–20.

Additional data are available concerning multiple attempts:

1 In the Dorpat and Boswell series, 11% had attempted two or more times previously;

2 In Stengel I, 75% of the 12% who had attempted more than once later attempted again;

3 Fifteen per cent of those persons in Stengel II were recurrent attempters prior to admission;

4 Of the twenty-three instances of prior attempts reported to Lendrum, seven had made two attempts and three had made three attempts previously;

5 In Klintworth's Johannesburg sample, 11% had only one previous attempt, 3% had two, and 6.3% had more than two;

6 Among Goss-Moffitt's Louisville sample, this was the second attempt for 21%, and 5% had attempted more often than that previously.

These data may suggest that there is a population in which attempted suicide is a way of life.[35] Although the data do not tell us how

TABLE 4

Percentages of Completed and Attempted Suicides Who Forewarned

Reference	Percentage Who Forewarned
Among Attempters	
Fisch[1]	14
Robbins, et al.[2]	16
Yessler, et al.[3]	28
Fairbank[4]	33
Schmidt[5]	35
Dorpat and Boswell[6]	53
Among Suicides	
Gibbs[7]	26
Yessler, et al.[8]	30
Stengel and Cook[9]	34
Beisser and Blanchette[10]	51
Vail[11]	53
Pollack[12]	59
Wheat[13]	66
Robbins, et al.[14]	67
Englehardt[15]	69
Farberow[16]	75
Pokorny[17]	75
Dorpat and Boswell[18]	83

1 M. Fisch, 'The Suicidal Gesture: A Study of 114 Military Patients Because of Abortive Suicide Attempts', *American Journal of Psychiatry*, 111, 1954, p. 35.

2 Eli Robbins, *et al.*, 'Some Clinical Considerations in the Prevention of Suicide Based on a Study of 134 Successful Suicides', *American Journal of Public Health*, 49, 1959, pp. 888–99.

3 Paul G. Yessler, James J. Gibbs and Herman Becker, 'On the Communication of Suicidal Ideas, I and III', *Archives of General Psychiatry*, 3 and 5, 1960 and 1961.

4 Ruth E. Fairbank, 'Suicide', *Journal of the American Medical Association*, 98, 1932, p. 1712.

5 Edwin H. Schmidt, Patricia O'Neal and Eli Robbins, 'Evaluation of Suicide Attempts as a Guide to Therapy', *Journal of the American Medical Association*, 155, 1954, pp. 549–57.

6 Theodore L. Dorpat and John W. Boswell, 'An Evaluation of Suicide Intent in Suicidal Attempts', *Comprehensive Psychiatry*, 4, 1963, pp. 120–1.

7 Jack P. Gibbs, 'Suicide', in R. K. Merton and R. A. Nisbet, editors, *Contemporary Social Problems*, New York: Harcourt, Brace and Company, 1961, p. 260.

8 Yessler, Ibid.

9 Erwin Stengel and Nancy Cook, *Attempted Suicide*, Oxford: Oxford University Press, 1958, p. 103.

10 Arnold R. Beisser and James E. Blanchette, 'A Study of Suicides in a Mental Hospital', *Diseases of the Nervous System*, 22, 1961, p. 367.

11 D. G. Vail, 'Suicide and Medical Responsibility', *American Journal of Psychiatry*, 115, 1959, p. 1007.

12 Benjamin Pollack, 'A Study of the Problem of Suicide', *The Psychiatric Quarterly*, 12, 1938, pp. 322–5.

13 William D. Wheat, 'Motivational Aspects of Suicide in Patients During and After Psychiatric Treatment', *Southern Medical Journal*, 53, 1960, p. 274.

14 Eli Robbins, *et al.*, 'The Communication of Suicidal Intent', *American Journal of Psychiatry*, 115, 1959, pp. 724–733.

15 Cited in Kingsley Jones, 'Suicide and the Hospital Service: A Study of Hospital Records of Patients Who Subsequently Committed Suicide', *British Journal of Psychiatry*, 111, 1965, p. 625.

16 Norman Farberow, 'Personality Patterns of Suicidal Mental Hospital Patients', *Genetic Psychology Monographs*, 42, 1950.

17 Alex D. Pokorny, 'Characteristics of Forty-Four Patients Who Subsequently Committed Suicide', *Archives of General Psychiatry*, 2, 1960, p. 315.

18 Theodore L. Dorpat and John W. Boswell, 'Evaluation of Suicide Intent in Suicide Attempts', *Comprehensive Psychiatry*, 4, 1963, pp. 120–1; Theodore L. Dorpat and Herbert S. Ripley, 'Study of Suicide in King County, Washington', *Northwest Medicine*, 61, August 1962.

---

many of these eventually die of their efforts, they do suggest special attention for the category of repeated attempters.[36]

The foregoing indicates that an "unsuccessful suicide attempt is an absorbing or terminal state for at least 95% of those who enter it. While perhaps as many as one-third return to attempt again, few die of it. However, those who do die of it comprise between one out of ten and one out of three completed and recorded suicides. Owing to the disparity in size of the two populations, the circumstances and sequelae of nonfatal suicidal behaviour appear to be crucial for the magnitude of the final rate and theories of its production.

ESTIMATING THE CONNECTION BETWEEN SUICIDAL BEHAVIOUR
AND FOREWARNINGS

Other than attempts, under the heading of forewarnings come a set of communicative behaviours, including threats, hints, announcements and implications.[37] In some cases under review, there are both these communications and attempt, and in others it is unclear which is the appropriate designation for the action. Further, it seems apparent that the rules for inclusion as forewarning vary from sample to sample, and in some cases no hint is given of what they may be. These features militate against detailed analysis. Despite this, I find the data in Table 4 instructive.

One of the most striking suggestions from these studies is that there is remarkably little overlap in the percentages between attempters and completers. This conclusion is strengthened by the observation that the same authors consistently report a higher percentage of completers than attempters to have communicated. Thus, while Dorpat and Boswell found an unusually high proportion of attempters who forewarned, they also found a much higher proportion of persons forewarning among completers.

Forewarnings may not predict well to what people will do after they have forewarned. Sometimes forewarnings may be asymmetric: they may be invested with much significance by the potential suicide and with relatively little by his audience. Suicidal communications are not commonly seen as calling for the attention of anyone not already directly involved, in contrast to a death or injury requiring medical assistance. Thus, they tend to remain private unless they are accompanied by manifestations that are interpreted to require additional help.

This does not imply that threats are customarily ignored. In the view of Siegal and Friedman,

> Suicidal threats ... whether carried out successfully or unsuccessfully, pervade our entire social structure. ... Our study has disclosed that the threat of suicide forces persons to marry, prevents marriage dissolutions, coerces companionship between persons despite their mutual infidelity, prevents marriages, forces parents to acquiesce in their offspring's vicious habits, precludes institutionalization, is rewarded by escape from further military duty, is used to obtain favoured treatment over siblings, is employed as a device to avoid military induction. It should be significantly stated that these, by no means, represent an inventory of all factual situations embracing suicidal threats.[38]

If suicide threats are endemic and powerful stimuli to produce reciprocity and compliance, this means that these behaviours ought not continue to be either ignored in research or treated separately from the topic of suicide. Litman[39] and Farberow[40] each found 40% of their samples of threateners to have a history of a prior attempt, and Pokorny found the suicide rate among those who previously threatened or communicated suicidal ideas to be sixty to seventy times that of the US population.[41] Because suicide threats may become the basis for many apparently ordinary social arrangements and at the same time may themselves offer that stimulus to suicide (e.g. creating a situation in which one's "bluff may be called") found to have been present in a very high proportion of those who complete, they should receive further attention in research.

CONCLUSIONS

Johnson recently pointed out to the audience of the *American Sociological Review* that "although Durkheim's *Suicide* is among the most widely read classics in our field, sociologists rarely seek to clarify the theory it contains".[42] I suggest that this is an understatement, and might well read, "... rarely seek to clarify their knowledge of the phenomena it addresses or to develop the theories appropriate to them".

MacIver succinctly stated a point concerning suicide which needs to be heard again: "That act is the end of a process, and the significant object of study is the process that terminates thus."[43] Directly to the point of process—a series of options which develop a course of behaviour to its outcome—is Stengel's observation, in reviewing his and others' researches and experiences: "The behaviour of the majority of persons who commit suicidal acts suggests that the human environment is given a chance to intervene. . . . Only in a minority of suicidal acts is nothing left to chance. . . . We cannot fully understand suicidal acts unless we take these reactions of individuals and groups into account."[44]

The sociological *post mortem*—cross-sectional, retrospective, sampling only the deceased—is distinctly limited in its prospects for disclosing much about such processes, and need not be permitted to dominate research on the topic. It is more than conceivable that the differentials in the suicide rate, which are the basis for current theories, are the hazy outlines of a series of superimpositions of several selection processes which lead into or away from suicide in different ways for differently situated persons.

The magnitude and appearance of suicide rates are importantly affected by the social context and response to suicidal attempts and communications of suicidal predispositions. Since some persons who attempt and/or forewarn die of suicide while others do not, the sociologist probably would have something to contribute to the task of explaining how persons are sorted into these outcomes. The data show that for many persons (several hundred thousand in the US each year), communication or attempt will terminate their suicidal behaviour. But for many, and perhaps most, completed suicides, at least one of these options were exercised. Further, it appears that the less likely is an option to mobilize others,[45] the less likely that its use will provide a conclusion to suicidal behaviour. That only a minority of communicators and attempters eventually complete is testimony to the strength of the social response to awareness of their dispositions.[46] To understand the effect of social response does not demand any particular perspective given the present level of information, as illustrated in the following interpretations:

  1 There is, of course, only one effect of suicidal behaviour in case of survival which can be generally predicted, namely that somebody will somehow make the attempter feel, if only for a fleeting moment, that he cares whether he lives or dies. This is an assurance which it is difficult for many people to obtain otherwise.[47]

  2 The study of the immediate and long term effects of suicidal attempts showed a great variety of ways in which the attempters' life situations had been changed temporarily or permanently as the result of suicidal acts.[48]

This suggests that relatively little more can be learned about suicide by adhering to the traditional methods and assumptions for its study—especially those which prohibit or discourage analysis of attempted suicide and suicidal communication.

Those characteristics of completed suicides that have served as the bases for developing theories to explain the suicidal act are not the same, and often are the reverse of, those of attempted suicides.[49] Consequently, it does not seem likely that present theories of suicide would be adequate to explain the data for both completions and attempts. These theories are therefore misleading to the extent that (1) they wrongly dissociate completion, attempt and forewarning of suicide, and that (2) although these theories generally seek to describe conditions which generate suicidal predispositions, it seems closer to the truth to think that they would be properly addressed instead to these conditions which permit the effective execution of those predispositions.

An improved theory of suicide would (1) deal with conditions that predispose to suicide—as the theoretical portions of current works would have us believe that they do—but with due recognition that these predispositions may be halted in their course; and (2) deal with those conditions under which a distinct and particular minority of such persons are permitted to complete their intentions.

It may be tenable that exposure to anomie, role conflict or similar conditions precede suicide more often than not, but it is evident that suicide follows such exposure for an exceedingly small proportion of those exposed *in the general population*. Considered with regard to the base population of all those who have been led to suicidal behaviour, however, the connection between these conditions and *completion* is far more impressive. A reinterpretation of these explanatory systems may be desirable, so as to focus them more precisely upon what they are capable of explaining, viz., not the genesis of suicidal behaviour, but the conditions under which persons once begun on a suicidal course are permitted to complete it by suicidal death. Least encouraging for the prospect that a single theme would be sufficient to explain the suicidal process is the improbability that a meaningful concept would be flexible enough to fit the complex patterns of the data. Traditionally, there is often some variable such as social isolation used as a theme in understanding suicide, but it is a complex relationship between isolation, or the situations in which it is manifested, and the performance of suicide. If isolation from the interference of others is important to completing suicide, one would expect a higher relationship between attempting and dying of suicide than the literature shows. Unless "isolation" is specified in two different ways, the present data suggest that while it might be important in stimulating suicidal behaviour or in facilitating its completion by death, only for a very small proportion of the cases could it exercise both these influences. On the face of it, the finding that forewarnings are more characteristic of completed suicides than of unsuccessful attempters does not promote the idea that those who will complete are more isolated, although it might indicate that a "final straw" for a large number of these persons is to be unable to elicit a helpful response from others.

These observations seem to apply equally to all sociological work that uses data which are comparisons of social characteristics of (1) a general population and (2) persons who die of suicide (e.g. Durkheim, Gibbs and Martin, Henry and Short, and others cited earlier). Such data blanket the process of suiciding. One consequence of this is that the data are demonstrably unsuited to the problem customarily addressed: the sources of suicidal predispositions. To use those data for that purpose is to omit the greatest number of persons who show evidence of suicidal predisposition and to use instead a subsample which is, on the evidence, unrepresentative. If it is clear that these theories do not emerge from observable differences in the production of suicidal predispositions, it is much less clear what the observed differences used in these theories do reflect.

Attempted suicide and suicidal communication are sociologically important in themselves. But, if only in order to better explain completed suicide, the evidence suggests further research to discover how persons are deterred from, or permitted, encouraged, and—according to a number of case reports—even pushed to suicide.[50] Such research would be crucial for the interpretation and growth of current theories to the extent that differentials in these responses produce the differentials observed in the rates of completions.[51]

NOTES

1 Alex Arieff, Rook McCulloch and D. B. Rotman, 'Unsuccessful Suicidal Attempts', *Diseases of the Nervous System*, 9, 1948, p. 179. See also John McGeorge, 'Attempted Suicide', *The Medical Journal of Australia*, I, 3, 1942, p. 69.

2 Edgar C. Trautman, 'Suicide Attempts of Puerto Rican Immigrants', *Psychiatric Quarterly*, 35, 1961, p. 3. Also, Nina Goss-Moffit, 'Attempted Suicide', *The Journal of the Kentucky State Medical Association*, 61, 7, 1963, p. 585.

3 Viggo Jensen and Thomas Petty, 'The Fantasy of Being Rescued in Suicide', *Psychoanalytic Quarterly*, 27, 1959, p. 337. Also, Robert D. Dripps, Maurice E. Linden, Harold H. Phillips, 'Medical, Social and Legal Aspects of Suicide', *Journal of the American Medical Association*, 171, 1959, p. 525; Irving S. Kreeger, 'Initial Assessment of Suicidal Risk', *Proceedings of the Royal Society of Medicine*, 59, 1966, p. 93.

4 George Raines and Samuel Thomson, 'Suicide: Some Basic Considerations', *Digest of Neurology and Psychiatry*, 18, 1950, pp. 101–2. Also, Harry Pozner, 'Suicidal Incidents in Military Personnel', *The British Journal of Medical Psychology*, 26, 1953, pp. 93–109; A. E. Moll, 'Suicide', *The Canadian Medical Association Journal*, 74, 1956, pp. 110–11; Milton H. Miller, Carl H. Fellner and Norman S. Greenfield, 'Depression, Suicide and Suicidal Gesture in Medical Practice', *Annals of Internal Medicine*, 51, 1959, p. 84.

5 John F. Oliven, 'The Suicidal Risk', *The New England Journal of Medicine*, 245, 1951, p. 488. Also, Marcel I. Assael, 'Thanatophilia', *Diseases of the Nervous System*, 26, 1965, p. 778; R. D. Nashold, 'Attempted Suicide by Chemical Agents', *The Wisconsin Medical Journal*, 64, 1965, p. 328; Kreeger, op. cit., p. 93; J. Krupinski, P. Polke and A. Stoller, 'Psychiatric Disturbance in Attempted and Completed Suicides in Victoria During 1963', *The Medical Journal of Australia*, II, 1965, p. 778; American Medical Association Committee on Alcoholism and Addiction and Council on Mental Health, 'Dependence on Barbiturates and Other Sedative Drugs', *Journal of the American Medical Association*, 193, 1965, p. 675.

6 Raymond Firth, 'Suicide and Risk-Taking in Tikopia Society', *Psychiatry*, 24, 1961, pp. 1–17; also, James Weiss (both reprinted in this volume, pp. 197; 384); 'The Gamble with Death in Attempted Suicide', *Psychiatry*, 20, 1957, pp. 17–25; Erwin Stengel, Nancy Cook and Irving S. Kreeger, *Attempted Suicide*, London: Chapman and Hall, Ltd., 1958, pp. 115; 118. Further analyses of the social factors contributing to life or death from suicide efforts are in preparation by this writer.

7 Emile Durkheim, *Suicide*, Glencoe, Illinois: Free Press, 1951, Translated by John A. Spaulding and George Simpson.

8 Jack P. Gibbs and Walter T. Martin, *Status Integration and Suicide*, Eugene: University of Oregon Press, 1964.

9 Andrew F. Henry and James F. Short, *Suicide and Homicide*, Glencoe, Illinois: Free Press, 1954.

10 For example, Warren Breed, 'Occupational Mobility and Suicide Among White Males', *American Sociological Review*, 28, 1963, pp. 179–88 (reprinted in this volume, pp. 280–297); Austin L. Porterfield and Jack Gibbs, 'Occupational Prestige and Social Mobility of Suicides in New

Zealand', *American Journal of Sociology*, 66, 1960, pp. 147–52; Peter Sainsbury, *Suicide in London*, New York; Basic Books, Inc., 1956; Elwin H. Powell, 'Occupation, Status and Suicide: Toward a Redefinition of Anomie', *American Sociological Review*, 23, 1958, pp. 131–9; Barclay D. Johnson, 'Durkheim's One Cause of Suicide', *American Sociological Review*, 30, 1965, pp. 875–86; Austin L. Porterfield, 'Suicide and Crime in the Social Structure of an Urban Setting: Fort Worth, 1930–50', *American Sociological Review*, 17, 1952, pp. 341–9; Martin Gold, 'Suicide, Homicide and the Socialization of Aggression', *American Journal of Sociology*, 63, 1958, pp. 651–61.

11 Op. cit., p. 43.

12 Erwin Stengel, 'Attempted Suicide', *Lancet*, 7275, 1963, p. 233; Norman Tabachnick and Norman Farberow, 'The Assessment of Self-Destructive Personality' in Norman Farberow and Edwin Shneidman, editors, *The Cry for Help*, New York: McGraw-Hill, 1961, pp. 60–61; J. A. Harrington and K. W. Cross, 'Cases of Attempted Suicide Admitted to a General Hospital', *British Medical Journal*, 5150, 1959, p. 465; I. R. C. Batchelor, 'Psychopathic States and Attempted Suicide', *British Medical Journal*, 4875, 1954, p. 1345; Jerome A. Moto, 'Suicide Attempts', *Archives of General Psychiatry*, 13, 1965, p. 518; George C. Sisler, 'The Treatment of Suicidal Attempts', *The Canadian Medical Association Journal*, 74, 1956, p. 113; Firth, op. cit., p. 12; Norman Farberow, 'Personality Patterns of Suicidal Mental Hospital Patients', *Genetic Psychology Monographs*, 42, 1950, p. 65; Alex D. Pokorny, 'A Follow-Up Study of 618 Suicidal Patients', *American Journal of Psychiatry*, 122, 1956, p. 1113; Earl Cohen, Jerome A. Moto and Richard H. Seiden, 'An Instrument for Evaluating Suicide Potential', *American Journal of Psychiatry*, 122, 1966, pp. 889–90, Rosalie A. Harris, 'Factors Related to Continued Suicidal Behavior in Dyadic Relationships', *Nursing Research*, 15, 1966, p. 74. On some particulars of this matter, see Ruth W. Ettlinger and Per Flordh, 'Attempted Suicide: Experience of 500 Cases at a General Hospital', *Acta Psychiatrica et Neurologica Scandinavia, Supplement* 103, 1955, p. 19; Merrill Moore, 'Cases of Attempted Suicide in a General Hospital: A Problem in Social and Psychologic Medicine', *The New England Journal of Medicine*, 217, 1937, p. 296; F. Hopkins, 'Attempted Suicide: An Investigation', *The Journal of Mental Science*, 83, 1937, p. 82; Merrill Moore, 'Alcoholism and Attempted Suicide', *The New England Journal of Medicine*, 221, 1939, p. 693. Cf. Theodore L. Dorpat and John W. Boswell, 'An Evaluation of Suicidal Intent in Suicidal Attempts', *Comprehensive Psychiatry*, 4, 1963, p. 124, which illustrates the use of "intent" to mean "degree of risk taken".

13 Jesse L. Carr, 'Suicide', *The International Record of Medicine*, 170, 1957, p. 616; Harrington and Cross, op. cit., p. 464; Robert E. Litman, Edwin S. Shneidman and Norman L. Farberow, 'A Suicide Prevention Center', mimeo, n.d., p. 8. Additional problems are cited by Bengt Jansson, 'Drug Automatism as a Cause of Pseudo Suicide', *Post-Graduate Medicine*, 30, 1961, A–34—A–40; Oliven, op. cit., pp. 488; 494; Neil Kessel, Wallace McCulloch and Esme Simpson, 'Psychiatric Service in a Centre for the Treatment of Poisoning', *British Medical Journal*, 5363, 1963, p. 987.

14 Lawrence S. Kubie, 'Multiple Determinants of Suicidal Efforts,' *The Journal of Nervous and Mental Disease*, 138, 1964, pp. 4; 7. Also, Erwin Stengel, 'The Social Effects of Attempted Suicide,' *Canadian Medical Association Journal*, 74, 1956, p. 117.

15 Some limitations to this report are: (1) the nearly exclusive use of American and British data, in order to reduce the number of relevant variables; (2) elimination of a large number of studies which collectively might have added to the evidence but individually offered little (e.g. case reports); (3) compression of a variety of behaviours into the categories of "completions," "attempts," and "communication"; (4) the neglect to explore the contributions of differences among the samples (e.g., location, composition, procedures of data collection and analysis) as these might bear upon differences in their results, in order to assess whatever measure of agreement exists notwithstanding sampling variations.

16 Jacob Tuckman and Martha Lavell, 'Study of Suicide in Philadelphia', *Public Health Reports*, 73, 1958, p. 5, felt that three-quarters of the records they examined lacked information, while Erwin Stengel and Nancy Cook noted that relatives "almost invariably hope for a verdict of unsound mind", *Attempted Suicide*, Oxford: Oxford University Press, 1958, p. 103.

17 It has been suggested that "witnesses are probably reluctant to report that the victim's behaviour suggested suicide and that they did not prevent it," (e.g. Jack Gibbs, 'Suicide,' in Robert K. Merton and Robert A. Nisbet, editors, *Contemporary Social Problems*, New York: Harcourt, Brace and World, 1961, p. 260). This objection loses some force for the present investigation when it is to the benefit of the witnesses to report prior attempts, as Stengel and Cook pointed out (ibid.) and since the British data (Stengel and Sainsbury) show the same results as the others.

18 Moya Woodside, 'Attempted Suicides Arriving at a General Hospital', *British Medical Journal*, 5093, 1958, p. 413; Stengel and Cook, op. cit., pp. 31; 68; 96. Attempted suicide was a criminal offence in both London and Seattle at the times of these studies.

19 Calvin F. Schmid and Maurice D. Van Arsdol, 'Completed and Attempted Suicides', *American Sociological Review*, 20, 1959, p. 273.

20 T. L. Dorpat, J. K. Jackson and H. S. Ripley, 'Broken Homes and Attempted and Completed Suicide', *Archives of General Psychiatry*, 12, 1965, p. 355.

21 J. Tuckman, W. Youngman and B. Bleiberg, 'Attempted Suicide by Adults', *Public Health Reports*, 77, 1962, p. 614.

22 Gordon K. Klintworth, 'Suicide and Attempted Suicide', *South African Medical Journal*, 34, 1960, p. 361.

23 G. D. Middleton, Desmond W. Ashby and F. Clark, 'An Analysis of Attempted Suicide in an Urban Industrial District', *The Practitioner*, 187, 1961, p. 776.

24 Neil Kessel and Elizabeth Lee, 'Attempted Suicide in Edinburgh', *Scottish Medical Journal*, 7, 1962, p. 133.

25 D. Parkin and Erwin Stengel, 'Incidence of Suicidal Attempts in an Urban Community', *British Medical Journal*, 5454, 1965, p. 136.

26 Norman L. Farberow and Edwin Shneidman, *The Cry for Help*, New York: McGraw-Hill, 1961, p. 24.

27 Charles Shaw and Ruth Schelkin, 'Suicidal Behavior in Children', *Psychiatry*, 28, 1965, p. 164.

28 Five per cent is based upon the highest report, that 33% of completers have formerly attempted. To the extent that the ratio is higher, the percentage decreases, of course.

29 Some suicide attempts do not come to the attention of either hospitals, physicians or the police, and these are not included here. "Lesser" mani-

festations of suicidal interest are considered in the following section. A degree of self-damage is needed which would require the attention of someone in a special capacity.

30 Leonard M. Moss and Donald M. Hamilton, 'The Psychotherapy of the Suicidal Patient', *American Journal of Psychiatry*, 112, 1956, p. 814.

31 Bengt Jansson, 'A Catamnestic Study of 476 Attempted Suicides', *Acta Psychiatrica Scandinavica*, 38, 1962, pp. 184–185.

32 See also, I. R. C. Batchelor and Margaret B. Napier, 'The Sequelae and Short-Term Prognosis of Attempted Suicide', *Journal of Neurology, Neurosurgery and Psychiatry*, 17, 1954, p. 261. This does not imply that the objective probabilities of suicidal behaviour are unaffected by previous suicidal behaviour even though several years may have elapsed since an attempt. The point is that the reasons for the connection are different in a short term and a long term. Gardner, Bahn and Mack came to a similar conclusion, evidently independently of other writers, in a study of suicide among persons using the psychiatric facilities of Monroe County, New York, stating it perhaps more clearly: 'The suicide drive is episodic rather than continuous'. [Elmer A. Gardner, Anita K. Bahn and Marjorie Mack, 'Suicide and Psychiatric Care in the Aging', *Archives of General Psychiatry*, 10, 1964, p. 522.] To the extent that data from shorter follow-up periods are preferred here, it is (1) because re-activation of suicidal interest after a long term is less probable and seems to occur for quite different reasons, and (2) for comparability to the other data considered in this paper, since it is much more likely that previous attempts or forewarnings by either completed or attempted suicides will be recalled and reported if they are part of the same "episode" rather than one which is past and on the face of it unconnected with the present behaviour.

33 For some time, some reasonable men have rejected the use of "public," or even any form of statistical, data for the study of suicide. For example, Douglas recently referred to the former as "meaningless" (review of Kobler and Stotland, The End of Hope, *American Journal of Sociology*, 71, 1966, p. 574). Nonetheless, sociologists have preferred to use such data, at least until some other approach is shown to be more productive. This paper follows that tradition.

34 This analysis was incidental in the reports of Lendrum and Schmid and Van Arsdol. In fact, Schmid presented these data only to indicate that in his sample of attempters each was counted only once. This may account for the low proportions in the table.

35 However, as Parkin and Stengel noted of their sample of hospital admissions for attempted suicide, "if there was a history of a previous attempt, the patient was almost invariably sent to hospital", op. cit., p. 136.

36 I. R. C. Batchelor, 'Repeated Suicidal Attempts', *The British Journal of Medical Psychology*, 27, 1954, pp. 158–63.

37 This excludes communications which require psychiatric or psychoanalytic training to be perceived.

38 Lewis Siegal and Jacob Friedman, 'The Threat of Suicide', *Diseases of the Nervous System*, 16, 1955, p. 45.

39 Robert E. Litman, Norman L. Farberow, Edwin S. Shneidman, Sam M. Heilig and Jan A. Kramer, 'Suicide-Prevention Telephone Service', *Journal of the American Medical Association*, 192, 1965, p. 23.

40 Farberow, op. cit., pp. 2–3.

41 Alex D. Pokorny, 'A Follow-Up Study of 618 Suicidal Patients', *Scientific*

Proceedings of the Annual Meetings of the American Psychiatric Association of 1965, pp. 133–4.

42 Johnson, op. cit., p. 875.

43 R. M. MacIver, *Social Causation*, Boston: Ginn, 1942, p. 139.

44 Erwin Stengel, 'Recent Research into Suicide and Attempted Suicide', *American Journal of Psychiatry*, 118, 1962, p. 726.

45 For example: "Why did the important people not respond to the patient's other pleas, and yet respond positively to the patient after a suicide attempt? A suicidal threat is a drastic and powerful weapon, even more effective when it is acted upon." Robert Rubenstein, Rafael Moses and Theodore Lidz, 'On Attempted Suicide', *Archives of Neurology and Psychiatry*, 79, 1958, p. 111.

46 In some cases, the physical effects of the wound or injury itself alter the victim's perspective, e.g. Eric Guttman, 'Suicidal Head Injuries', *The Journal of Mental Science*, 89, 1943, pp. 85–91; Lawson G. Lowrary, 'An Analysis of Suicidal Attempts', *The Journal of Nervous and Mental Disease*, 52, 1920, pp. 478–9.

47 Erwin Stengel, 'Recent Research into Suicide and Attempted Suicide', *American Journal of Psychiatry*, 118, 1962, p. 727.

48 Ibid. Also, Carr, op. cit., p. 618; Angelo Vitanza, Edwin Church, and William Offenkrantz, 'Suicide: A Review of the Literature', *International Record of Medicine*, 170, 1957, p. 681.

49 For example, Schmid and Van Arsdol, op. cit.; P. M. Yap, *Suicide in Hong King*, Hong Kong: Oxford University Press-Hong Kong University Press, 1958, Chapter 2; Shneidman and Farberow, op. cit., esp. pp. 25–7; Louis L. Dublin, *Suicide*, New York: Ronald Press, 1963, pp. 11–12; Stengel and Cook, op. cit., pp. 27–8; S. J. Minogue, 'Attempted Suicide', *The Medical Journal of Australia*, 7, 1942, pp. 209–10; Guido M. Crocetti, 'Suicide and Public Health—An Attempt at Reconceptualization,' *American Journal of Public Health*, 49, 1959, p. 884; Goss-Moffitt, op. cit., pp. 585–6.

50 For example, Carl H. Fellner, 'Provocation of Suicidal Attempts', *Journal of Nervous and Mental Disease*, 133, 1961; Norman Tabachnick, 'Interpersonal Relations in Suicidal Attempts', *Archives of General Psychiatry*, 4, 1961; Arthur Kobler and Ezra Stotland, *The End of Hope*, London: The Free Press, 1964.

51 For some suggestive data on this possibility, one source to consult is Rubenstein, *et al.*, op. cit.

The Statistics of Suicide

Since the beginnings of research into suicide in modern times, a sharp division of opinion has existed among students of the subject concerning the validity of using official statistics. Many have considered that the methods whereby "suicides" are identified and catalogued officially as such, probably vary a great deal between different countries and even between different regions within the same country, and have concluded that official statistics are useless as a basis for generalization about suicide. But, however inadequate they may be, these statistics form the only indication we have of the general distribution of suicide, and there is no doubt that students of suicide will continue to make extensive use of them.

In terms of its statistical importance, suicide ranks fairly highly among the main causes of death in industrial societies, as shown in Table 1 below.

TABLE 1

Rank of suicide among the fifty major causes of death in selected countries

Country	Suicide Rate (per 100,000 pop.)	Rank of suicide among causes of death
Hungary (1966)	29.6	6th
England and Wales (1966)	10.4	12th
United States (1966)	10.9	13th
Italy (1965)	5.4	26th

Moreover, the distribution of suicide is much more evenly spread over the younger and middle age-groups (i.e. from twenty years of age to sixty) than are the diseases which claim the highest percentage of lives. The heart diseases, for example, which are the most important cause of death in industrial societies, are primarily concentrated in the higher age ranges (fifty years of age and over). As compared with the various forms of fatal disease, therefore, suicide tends to claim a higher relative proportion of individuals who are physically in the prime of life. Suicide rates are almost everywhere much higher than rates of homicide; but the proportion of people who die in road accidents in the more developed societies is in turn normally higher than the proportion of deaths as a result of suicide (Table 2, below).

TABLE 2

Suicide rates compared to rates of death from motor accidents, and to rates of homicide, in selected countries (per 100,000 pop.)

Country (1960)	Suicide Rate	Homicide Rate	Rates of death from motor accidents
England and Wales	11.2	0.6	14.5
France	15.8	1.7	17.9
Greece	3.8	1.5	4.7
Italy	6.3	1.5	17.7
Poland	8.0	1.4	4.5
United States	10.6	4.7	21.2

Comparison between the rates of suicide and homicide of different countries indicates that there is, in general, an inverse correlation between the two: those states which have high rates of suicide tend to have low rates of homicide, and vice versa. The existence of this relationship has often been adduced as corroborative of the thesis that suicide and homicide are both manifestations of aggression, which in the one case comes to be directed against the self, and in the second case is expressed externally against others. However, there are a considerable number of countries for which the relationship does not hold: the United States, for example, has a very high homicide rate but also has a fairly high rate of suicide.

Rates of suicide for selected countries are shown in Table 3 below. There are consistent differences between countries in their rates of suicide, with the more industrialized societies generally showing much higher rates than the less developed ones.

That there is no completely precise correlation between level of industrialization and suicide rates is shown by the fact that certain of the most advanced societies—such as the United States or Australia—have lower rates of suicide than some less developed countries—such as Hungary.

Gross national suicide rates may conceal wide variations inside different regions within the same country. In most countries it is the

TABLE 3

Suicides rates for selected countries, 1960–65 (per 100,000 pop.)

			Suicide rate			
Country	1960	1961	1962	1963	1964	1965
Australia	10.6	11.9	13.7	15.7	14.5	14.8
Austria	23.1	21.8	22.4	21.7	22.8	22.8
Bulgaria	7.6	8.7	8.0	8.4	8.7	9.2
Chile	7.4	7.8	6.6	—	3.0	—
Cuba*	14.7	14.9	12.9	10.8	11.3	—
Denmark	20.3	16.9	19.0	19.1	21.0	—
England and Wales	11.2	11.3	12.0	12.2	11.7	10.8
France	15.8	15.8	15.1	15.5	14.9	15.0
Germany (West)	18.8	18.7	17.6	18.5	19.2	—
Greece	3.8	4.3	3.4	3.8	3.2	3.2
Hungary	25.0	25.4	24.9	26.8	28.6	29.8
India*	0.3	0.5	—	—	—	—
Italy	6.3	5.6	5.5	5.3	5.5	—
Japan	21.6	19.6	17.6	16.2	15.2	14.5
Mexico	1.9	1.7	2.0	1.8	1.8	1.7
Spain	5.5	5.2	4.9	4.9	—	—
Sweden	17.4	16.9	18.5	18.5	19.8	18.9
United Arab Republic*	0.1	0.1	0.1	0.1	—	—

* The data in these cases are of "unknown reliability".

case that urban areas have markedly higher rates of suicide than rural areas. But, this is by no means universally true. In the United States, urban rates exceeded rural rates at the turn of this century. But the difference between the two has gradually diminished, so that today urban and rural areas have almost identical rates of suicide. No such diminution of the differential between urban and rural areas in respect of frequency of suicide has occurred, however, in the United Kingdom, where urban rates are still considerably higher than rural rates.

In virtually all the societies for which officially published statistics are available, men have higher rates of suicide than women. (See Table 4, below). The ratio of male to female suicides varies from something like 4 : 1 to about 1.3 : 1 in different countries. In several of the more highly industrialized societies, the disparity between male and female suicide rates has diminished over the past few decades. Thus in England and Wales, for example, the rate for males has declined since 1930, while the female rate has climbed quite steeply.[4]

Statistics show fairly consistent patterns of variation according to

TABLE 4[5]

Suicide rates by sex in selected countries (per 100,000 pop.)

Country	Male	Female
Austria (1966)	32.9	14.5
Bulgaria (1966)	13.7	6.1
England and Wales (1966)	12.1	8.8
Finland (1966)	30.1	9.1
Hong Kong (1966)	10.2	8.8
Japan (1965)	17.3	12.2
United States (1966)	16.1	5.9

age. In all countries, suicide is very uncommon prior to adolescence. From adolescence onwards, in most countries, rates tend to rise fairly evenly. In the majority of instances, the male rate continues to rise with age throughout the life-span; but the female rate very often declines after the age of sixty or so. Japan forms a notable exception to this general pattern. In Japan, rates of suicides for both males and females rise to a sharp peak in young adulthood; suicide is relatively much less frequent in the middle age groups, between twenty-five and fifty.

There are a considerable number of further statistical generalizations about the distribution of suicide which have been accepted for many years, but where the relevant statistical documentation is more partial and less unequivocal than in those discussed above. One of these links suicide to social class: those in higher socio-economic

TABLE 5[6]

Deaths from suicide and deaths from all causes: Standardized Mortality Ratios for occupied and retired males aged 20–64, according to social class, in England and Wales

Cause	Period	Social Class				
		1	2	3	4	5
Suicide	1921–3	116	128	91	89	98
	1930–2	120	137	95	87	87
	1950	134	110	89	99	119
All causes	1921–3	82	94	95	101	125
	1930–2	90	94	97	102	111
	1950	97	86	102	94	118

positions tend to have higher rates of suicide than individuals in lower class groups. Thus in England and Wales, as is shown in Table 5, there is a fairly close relationship between suicide rates and the census classes.

This table shows that, during the three periods covered, suicide is most frequent in the two highest classes. Moreover, since the proportion of deaths from other causes in these two classes is well below that of the rest of the population, the concentration of suicides in the highest classes is even greater than would appear from the suicide figures alone. The fact that the rate of suicide tends to go up again in the lowest social class bears out observations made in other societies that rates of suicide tend to be highest at both ends of the class hierarchy, with rates among those in the very lowest strata matching or even superseding those of men in the highest class groups.[7]

Suicide rates also tend to vary according to religious affiliation. The difference in suicide rates between Catholic and Protestant communities was given much prominence by some of the early students of suicide in Europe in the nineteenth century. This difference still persists: countries such as Ireland and Italy have much lower rates than societies which are predominantly Protestant, such as Denmark or Sweden. There are, however, obvious exceptions; Austria, a Catholic country, has one of the highest suicide rates in the world. France has a higher suicide rate than England and Wales (See Table 3).

A variety of relationships have at times been claimed to exist between suicide rates and geographical or climatic factors. Most of these, however, are of dubious validity. The most reliably established generalization of this type is that frequency of suicide varies in regular fashion according to the seasons of the year. England and Wales is fairly typical in this respect: here suicide rates reach a peak during the summer months of April, May and June, and are lowest during the winter months of October, November and December.[8]

Many of the countries which publish official suicide statistics also collect and publish statistics upon attempted suicide. For obvious reasons, these have to be treated with great caution. The most reliable statistical data upon attempted suicide come from studies of local communities carried out by independent researchers. A comprehensive study in Los Angeles in 1957 showed the existence of marked variation in the relative distribution of completed and attempted suicide.[9] The most notable difference—and one which is borne out in other studies—is that the normal sex ratio for suicide is reversed in the case of attempted suicide. While male rates of completed suicide outranked female rates by 7:3, female rates of attempted suicide outstripped male rates by an almost identical ratio. A further important difference was found in the age-distribution of suicide and attempted suicide. For both sexes, rates of attempted suicide were, compared to completed suicide, high in the younger age groups (reaching a peak for those in their late twenties and early thirties). Attempted suicide is certainly almost everywhere several times more frequent than completed suicide; in Los Angeles, the ratio of attempted to completed suicides was found to be of the order of 8:1.

NOTES

1 From the *United Nations Demographic Yearbook*, 1967, Table 24.
2 Ibid., 1966, Table 20.
3 Ibid., Table 20.
4 The most comprehensive recent statistical discussion of suicide in England and Wales is in *The Registrar General's Statistical Review of England and Wales*, 1961, Part 3, pp. 240–66.
5 *From the United Nations Demographic Yearbook*, 1967, Table 24.
6 *Statistical Review*, 1961, Part 3, p. 254. The Standardized Mortality Ratio here is the number of deaths occurring among occupied and retired men aged 20–64 in a given social class, expressed as a percentage of the deaths which would have occurred (within each age-group) if the death rate of that class were the same as that of the total population of occupied and retired men.
7 cf. J. P. Gibbs: 'Suicide', in Robert K. Merton and Robert A. Nisbet: *Contemporary Social Problems*, New York, 1966, p. 303.
8 *Statistical Review*, 1961, Part 3, p. 251.
9 E. S. Shneidman and N. L. Farberow, 'Statistical comparisons between attempted and committed suicides', in N. L. Farberow and E. S. Shneidman, *The Cry for Help*, New York, 1961, pp. 19–47.